POLITICAL ASYLUM

POLITICAL ASYLUM

CARTOONS AND CARICATURES

MALCOLM MAYES

NeWest

First Edition

Canadian Cataloguing in Publication Data

Mayes, Malcolm, 1962-
Political asylum

ISBN 0-920897-91-6

1. Canada--Politics and government--1984-1993--Caricatures and cartoons.* 2. Canada--Politics and government--1993- --Caricatures and cartoons.* 3. Canadian wit and humor, Pictorial. I. Title.
NC 1449.M39A4 1995   741.5'971   C95-910729-0

Editor for the Press: Satya Das
Cover and book design: John Luckhurst/GDL

NeWest Press gratefully acknowledges the financial assistance of The Canada Council; The Alberta Foundation for the Arts, a beneficiary of the Lottery Fund of the Government of Alberta; and The NeWest Institute for Western Canadian Studies.

Printed and bound in Canada

NeWest Publishers Limited
Suite 310, 10359 - 82 Avenue
Edmonton, Alberta T6E 1Z9

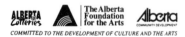

Alberta Lotteries The Alberta Foundation for the Arts Alberta Community Development
COMMITTED TO THE DEVELOPMENT OF CULTURE AND THE ARTS

TO MICHELLE AND KELSEY.

ALWAYS.

Special thanks to these artists for inspiring me to draw better and think clearer: Yardley Jones, Roy Peterson, Jeff MacNelly, Mike Peters, Jim Borgman, Bill Watterson, Berke Breathed, Walt Kelly, and Walt Disney.

Thanks also to Satya Das and the gang at NeWest Press for helping me compile this beast.

FOREWORD BY

GREG KENNEDY

How would one describe working in a busy metro newsroom with Malcolm Mayes?

First of all, if you spot him at all, it is to watch him float by, often wraithlike – or pass softly on athletic shoes with padding as silent as panther paws. It's not that he's antisocial. No sir. Not at all.

It's just that his mind is elsewhere. He is scheming up a sketch. Or digesting so much political hot air that his feet, buoyed by the gusts from Ottawa, and other political hot spots, barely graze the carpet.

Once in a while, Malcolm actually stops at your desk to ask a favour. (It's impossible to refuse this impossibly polite, boyish-grinned colleague.) He holds up two drawings – one in each hand – to ask: "Which one works for you?" More often than not, both do, and the task becomes to pick the greater of the two comic, cartoony evils. Nasty sells.

The real fun, of course, is watching Malcolm watching you as you size up his art. This is the crack in his veneer, that glimpse into every artist's insecurity. His mouth smiles, as if to say, "This is funny. You're going to love it. *PLEASE* love it. Or I just worked all day for diddly-squat."

And he worries for nothing. His cartoons display an instantly recognizable style, biting wit, and that greatest of all gifts – the ability to find a fresh take, to see the conundrum of the day from a new vantage point. To boldly joke where no man has joked before.

~

Two personal favourites? Four dour, black-suited "pollbearers" in stovepipe hats – Reid, Gallup, Crop, and Decima – bear "the chin" (unpopular ex-Prime Minister Brian Mulroney) to his rest. In another, Trial of the Century star O. J. Simpson peers from behind the bars of a DNA spiral, his fate cast to the gods of forensic science.

After art college, Malcolm went pro in 1986 for the *Edmonton Journal*, where he continues to practice his black arts today. Although *Political Asylum* is his first solo book, selected cartoons have appeared in books, newspapers, and magazines across North America and abroad.

So what is my connection to this 2H-mechanical-penciled pundit? As destiny would have it, I'm married to a childhood friend of his, Wendy Kennedy.

Wendy, his classroom chum from grades one to six in northeast Edmonton, recalls his desk. "He'd open his book, but he'd have draw-ings underneath. He'd draw while the teacher was talking. Everyone knew that.

"We had a teacher in grade six. His name was Mr. Campbell. Malcolm drew a can of Campbell's Soup, with a head and legs and arms. Mr. Campbell hung it up in the window of the door to his classroom. It was neat." (Andy Warhol, eat your heart.)

She remembers Malcolm as "an all-round good guy. He was a perfect student. A perfect nice guy. He was always considerate of others. Easy to get along with. Across from the principal's office there was a glass showcase. Malcolm's stuff was always in this showcase. And he always got picked to paint the backgrounds in plays."

Malcolm reminisces, "One of my father's hobbies was cartooning, so very early in life I started emulating him, and have drawn ever since. By my late teens I was a serious news junkie and read newspapers voraciously. This, combined with my love of drawing and my desire to do something different, steered me towards editorial cartoons."

Today, he ruefully jokes, "I thought it would be an easy way to make a living. Later on I found out there was a little more to it than I ever imagined."

Rue or no rue, what sets this book apart from the crowd is Malcolm's strong western slant on Canadian issues. He is part of a new wave of cartoonists now making an impact. This generation relies more on humour and less on satire than the previous generation.

When all is sketched, said, and done, the last word here belongs to Malcolm:

"I always try to keep my feet planted in the real world. Occasionally, I feel some writers lose sight of where they came from or how the issues in the newspaper affect the guy down the street. I try to stay plugged in to what's happening on the ground. Often I'll value what I hear in a neighbourhood bar over what I hear in the newsroom.

"There's an expression that goes like this: An opinion is the cheapest commodity in the world, because you can get one from any-one at any time for nothing. I kind of approach my cartoons that way. They're my opinion. Somebody else's opinion could be just as valid."

Greg Kennedy, a perennial Malcolm Mayes groupie, is also a journalist and screenwriter with credits in film, television, animation, and radio.

FACES

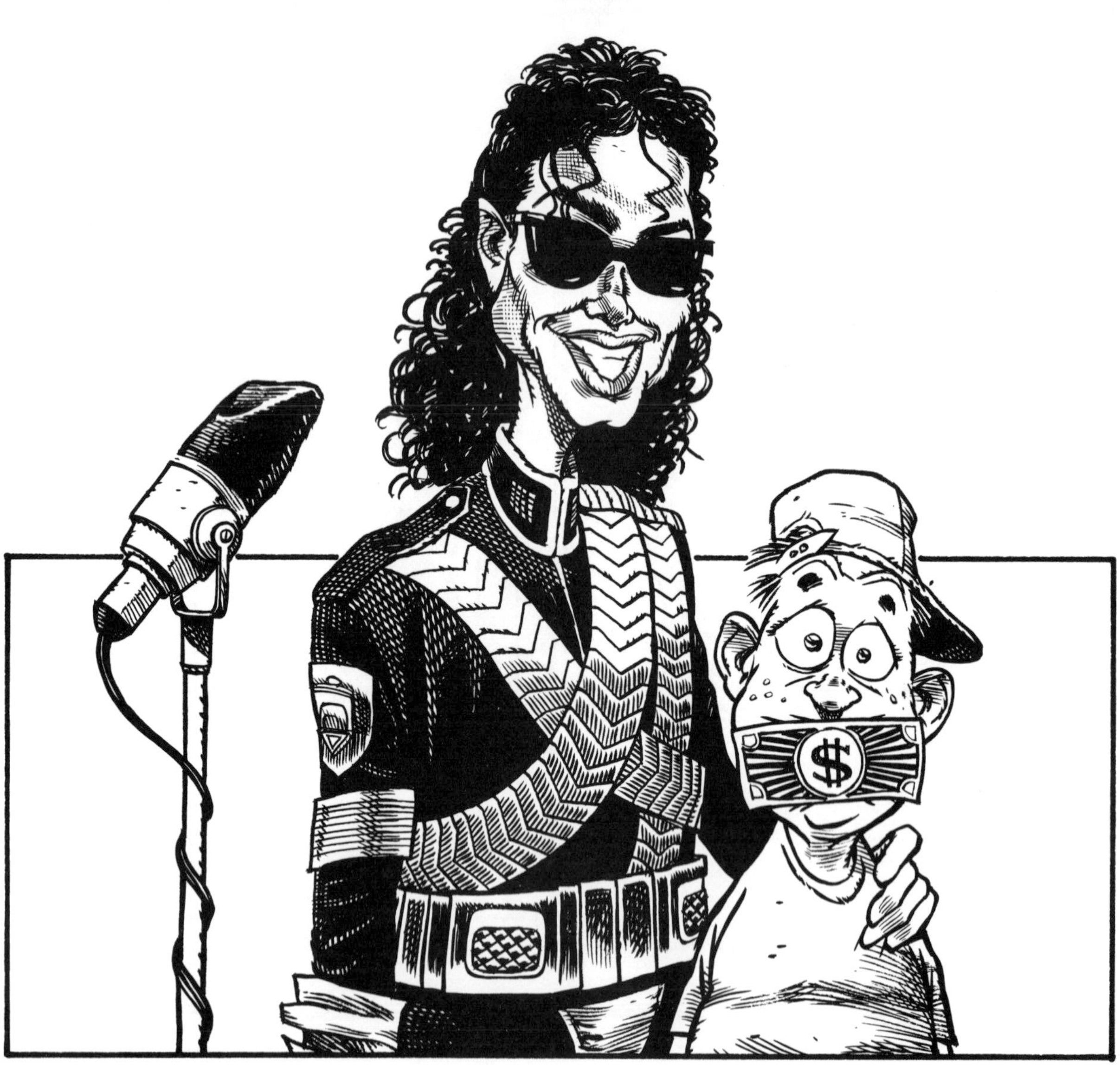
$

Michael Jackson and friend

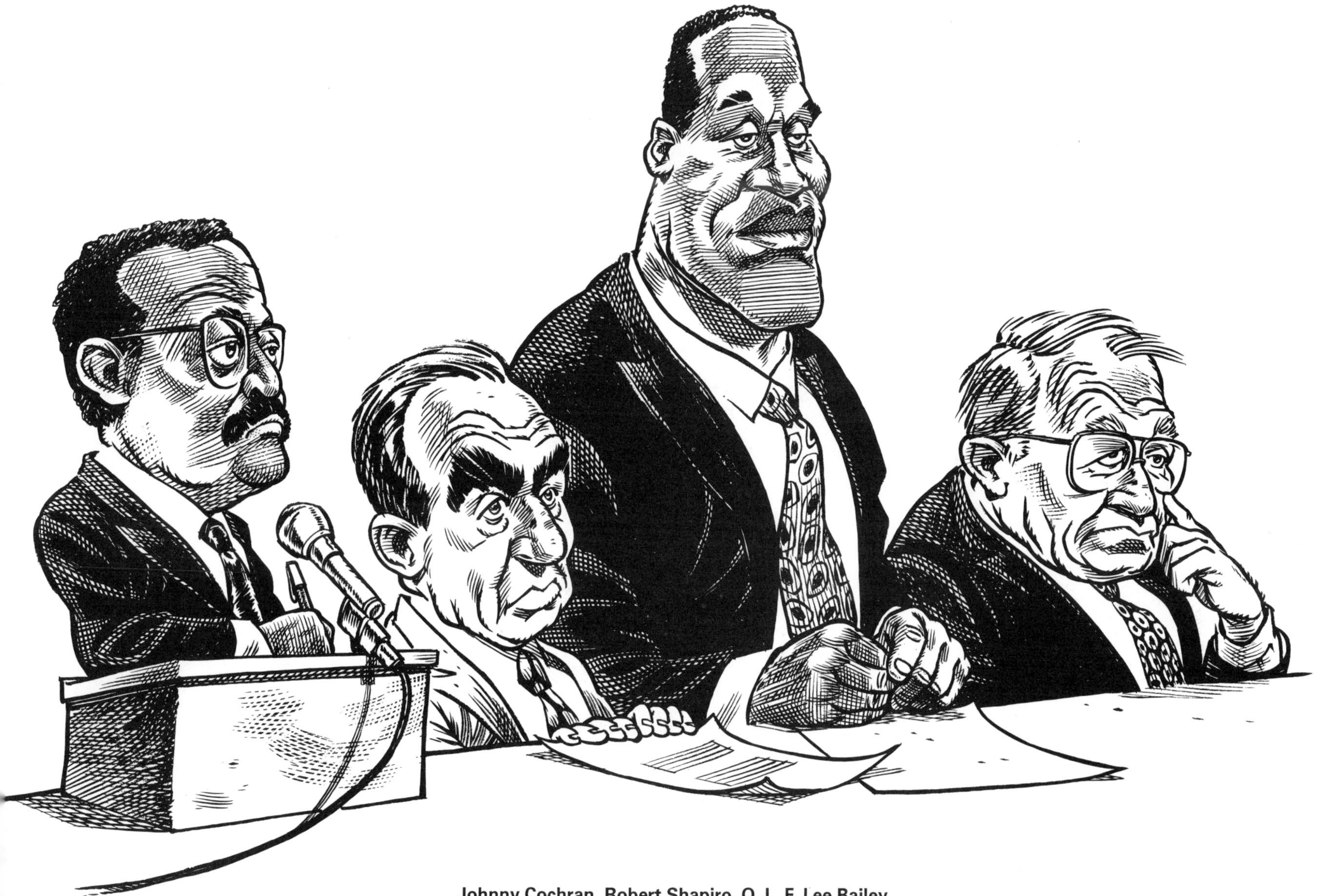

Johnny Cochran, Robert Shapiro, O.J., F. Lee Bailey

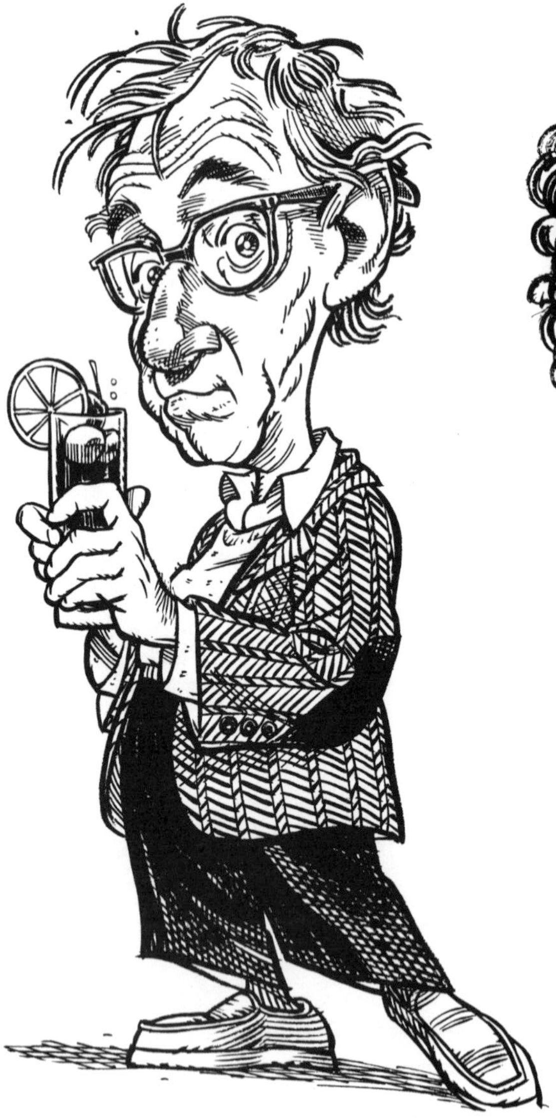

Woody Allen

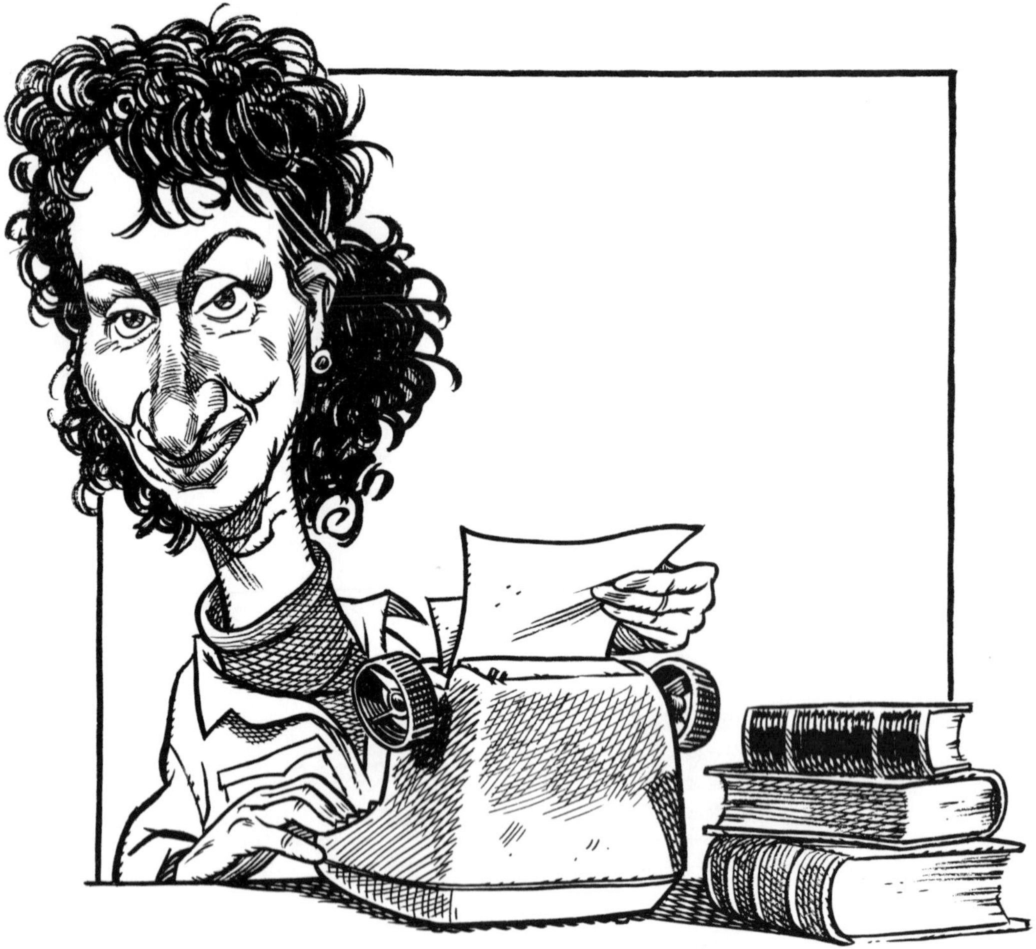

Margaret Atwood

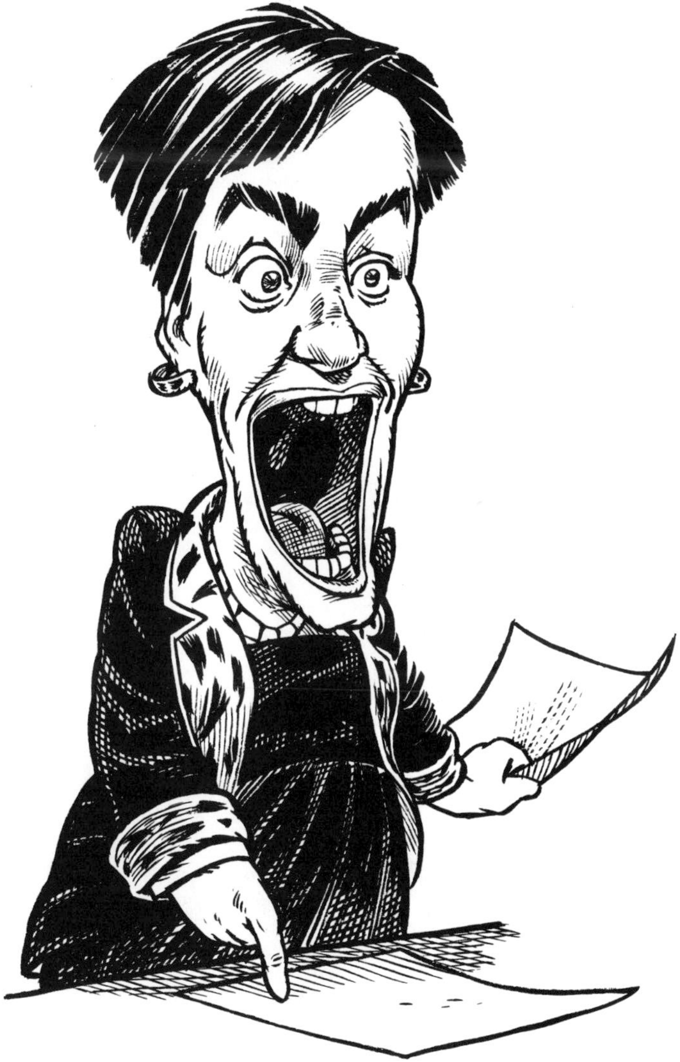

Sheila Copps

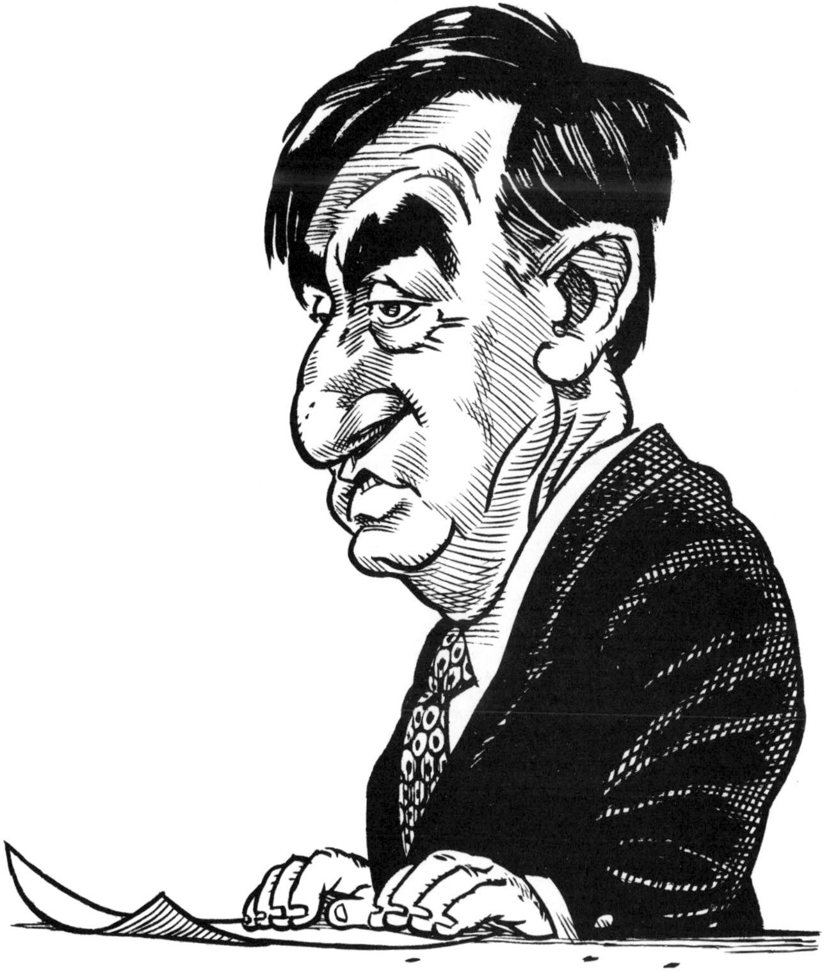

Lucien Bouchard

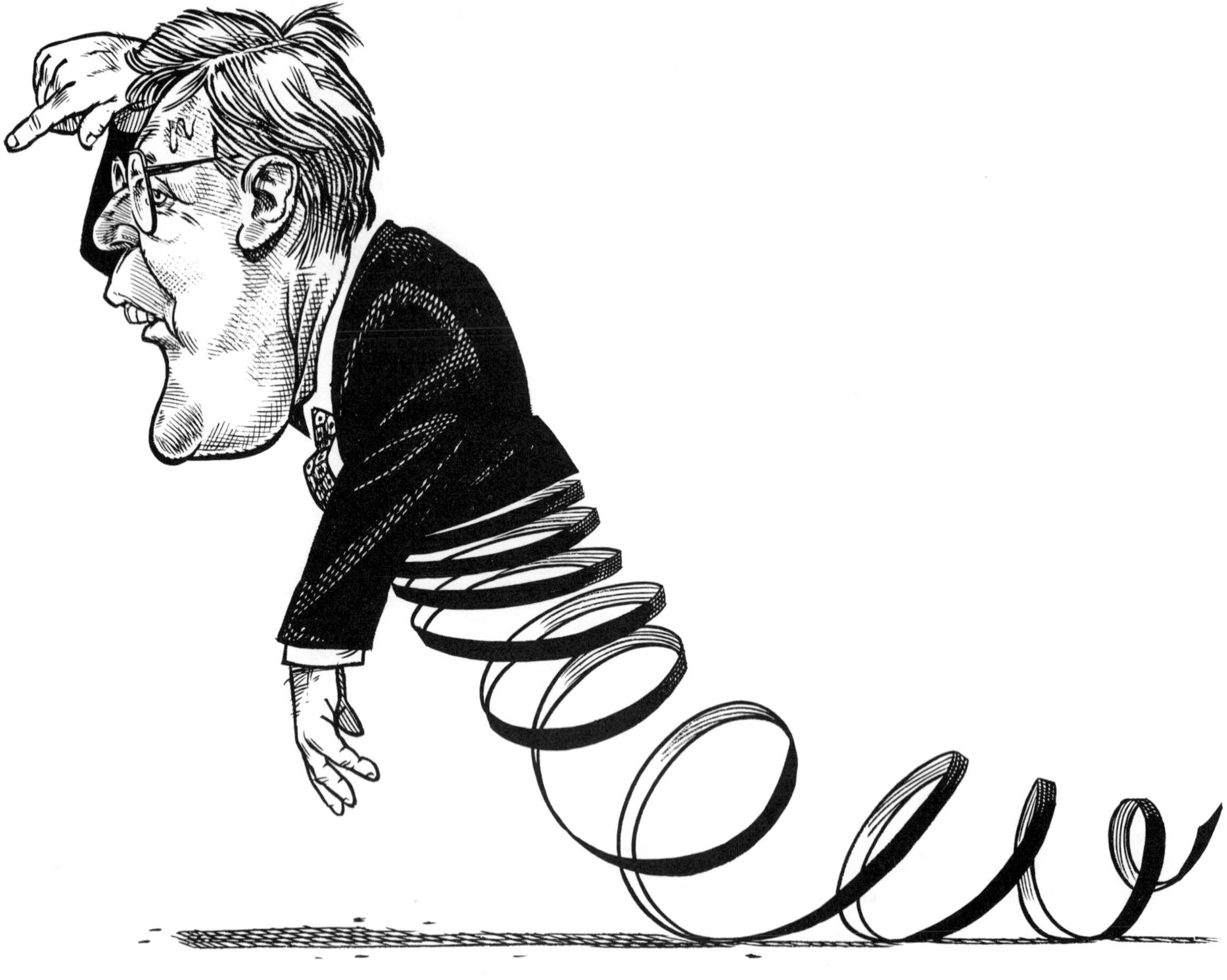

Bob Rae

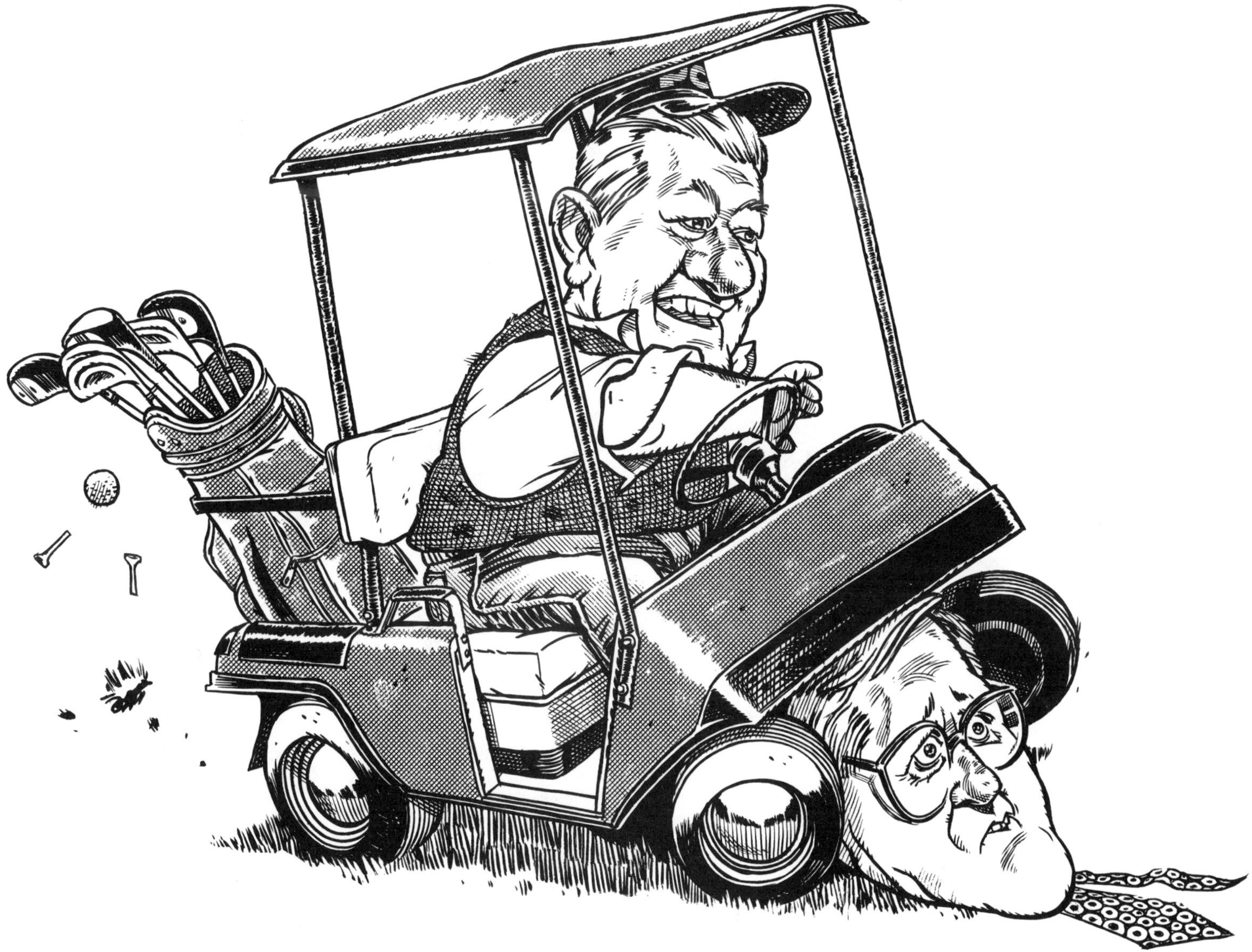
PC

Mike Harris and Bob Rae

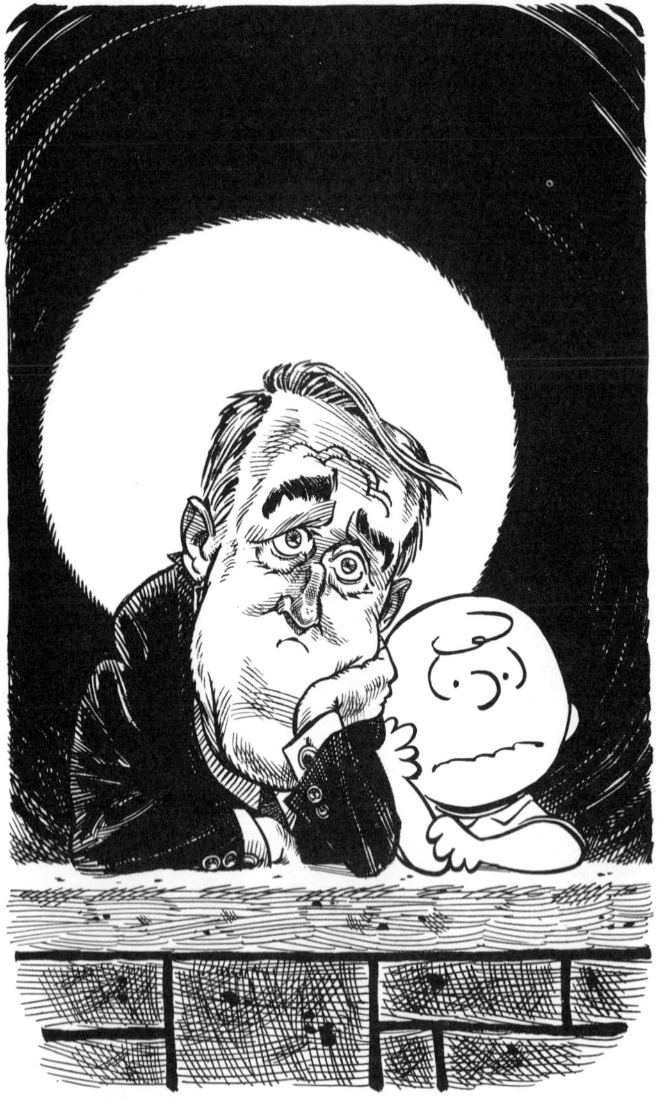

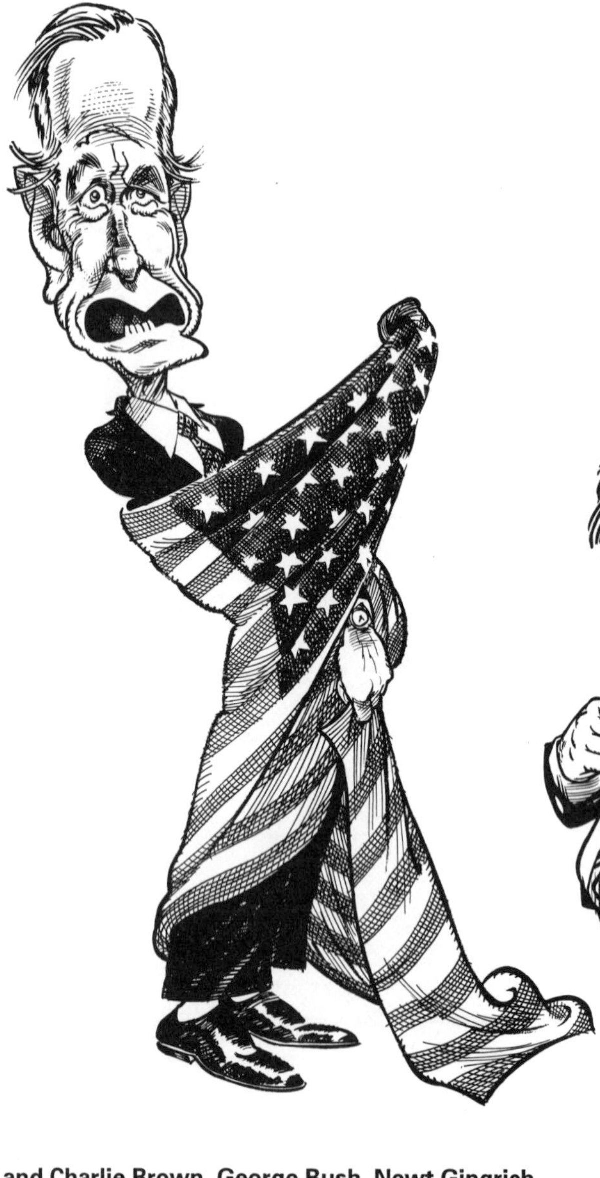

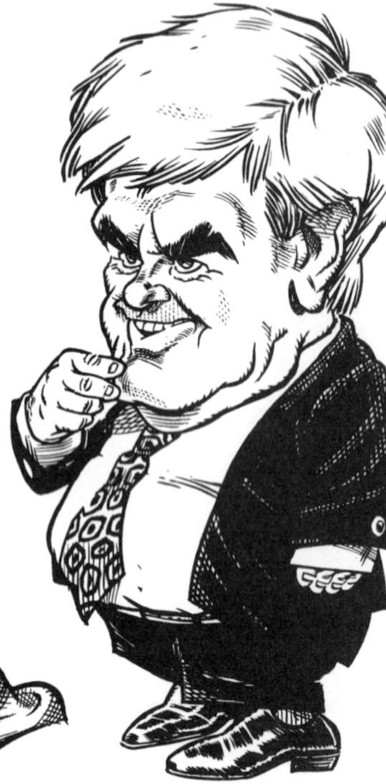

Left to right: Brian Mulroney and Charlie Brown, George Bush, Newt Gingrich

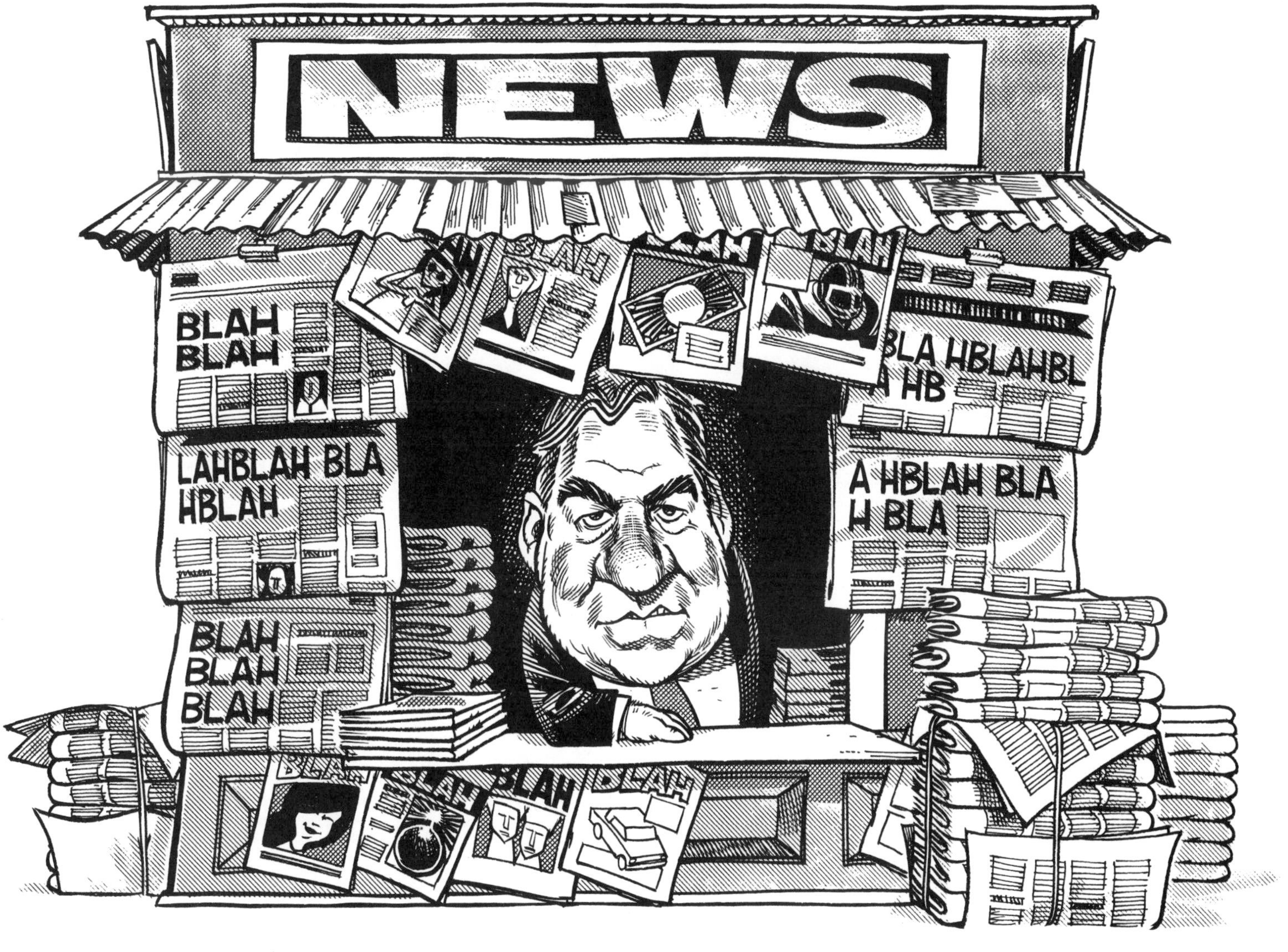
NEWS
BLAH
BLAH
LAHBLAH BLA
HBLAH
BLAH
BLAH
BLAH
BLA HBLAHBL
A HB
A HBLAH BLA
H BLA
BLAH
BLAH
BLAH
BLAH
BLAH
BLAH
BLAH

Conrad Black

THE WILD WEST

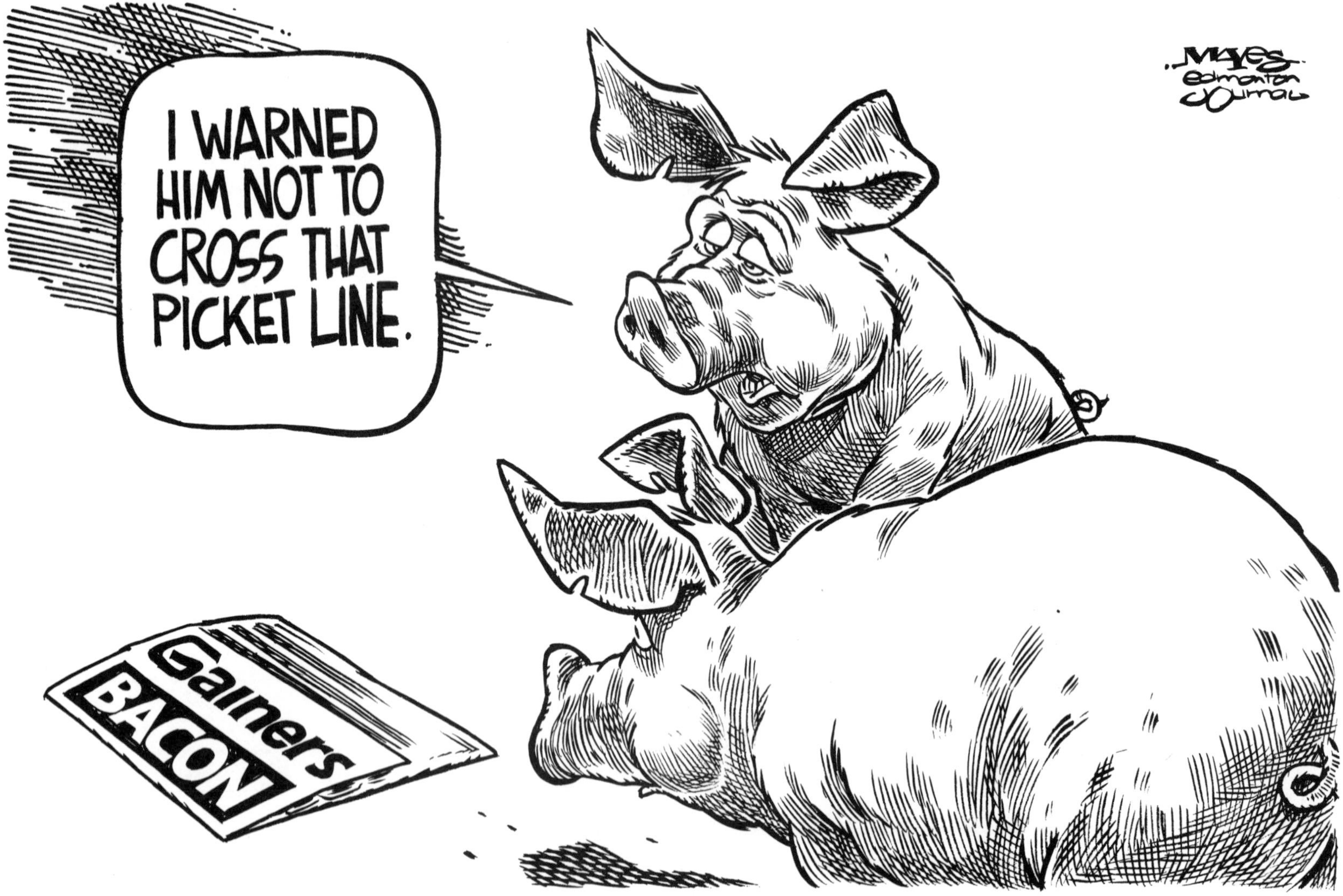
I WARNED HIM NOT TO CROSS THAT PICKET LINE.
Gainers BACON
MAYES Edmonton Journal

A strike at an Edmonton meat-packing plant turns ugly.

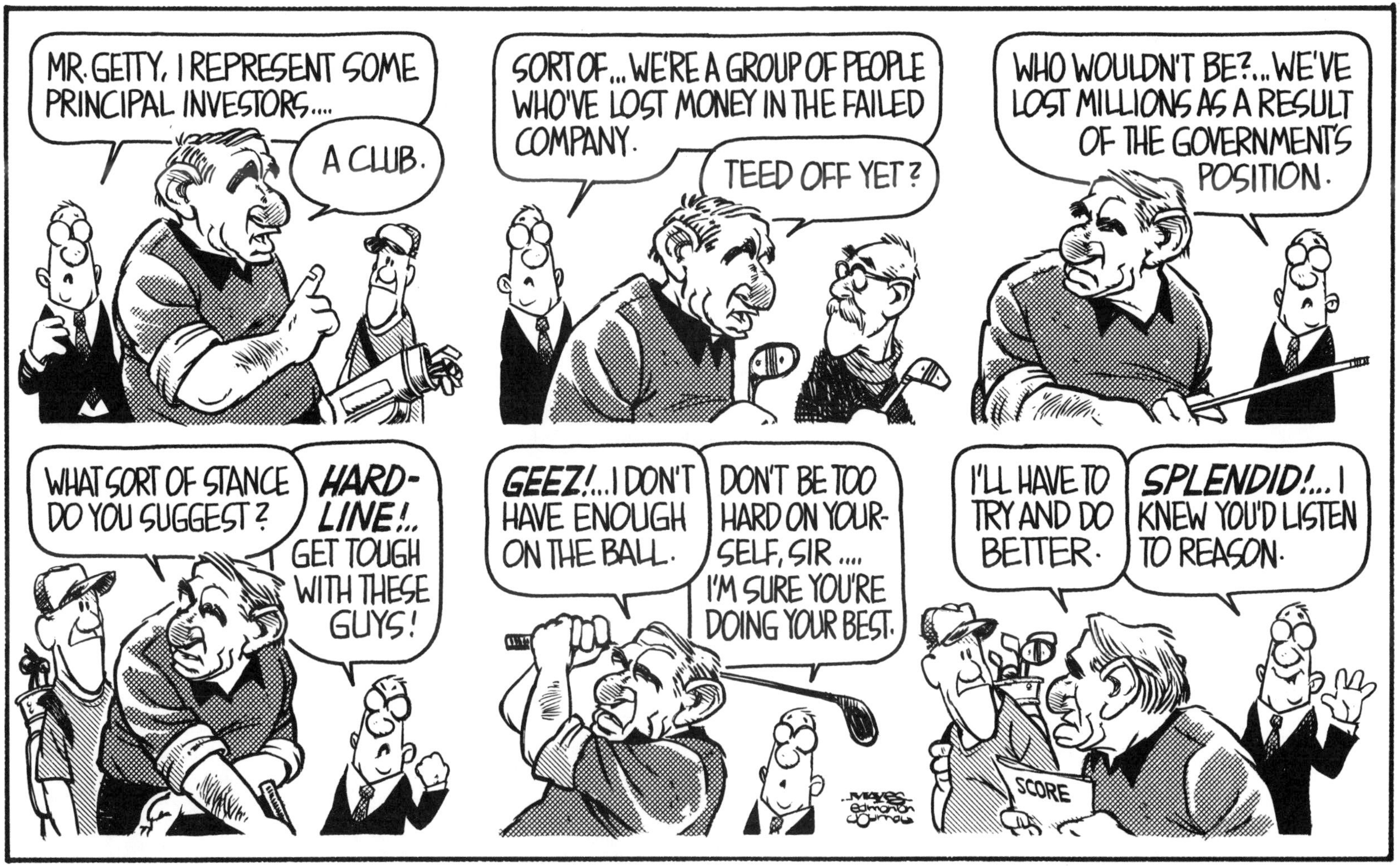
MR. GETTY, I REPRESENT SOME PRINCIPAL INVESTORS....
A CLUB.
SORT OF... WE'RE A GROUP OF PEOPLE WHO'VE LOST MONEY IN THE FAILED COMPANY.
TEED OFF YET?
WHO WOULDN'T BE?... WE'VE LOST MILLIONS AS A RESULT OF THE GOVERNMENT'S POSITION.
WHAT SORT OF STANCE DO YOU SUGGEST?
HARD-LINE!.. GET TOUGH WITH THESE GUYS!
GEEZ!... I DON'T HAVE ENOUGH ON THE BALL.
DON'T BE TOO HARD ON YOURSELF, SIR.... I'M SURE YOU'RE DOING YOUR BEST.
I'LL HAVE TO TRY AND DO BETTER.
SPLENDID!... I KNEW YOU'D LISTEN TO REASON.
SCORE

A ROUND OF TALKS WITH THE PREMIER.

Don Getty was always "on the ball" when big problems came to the FORE.

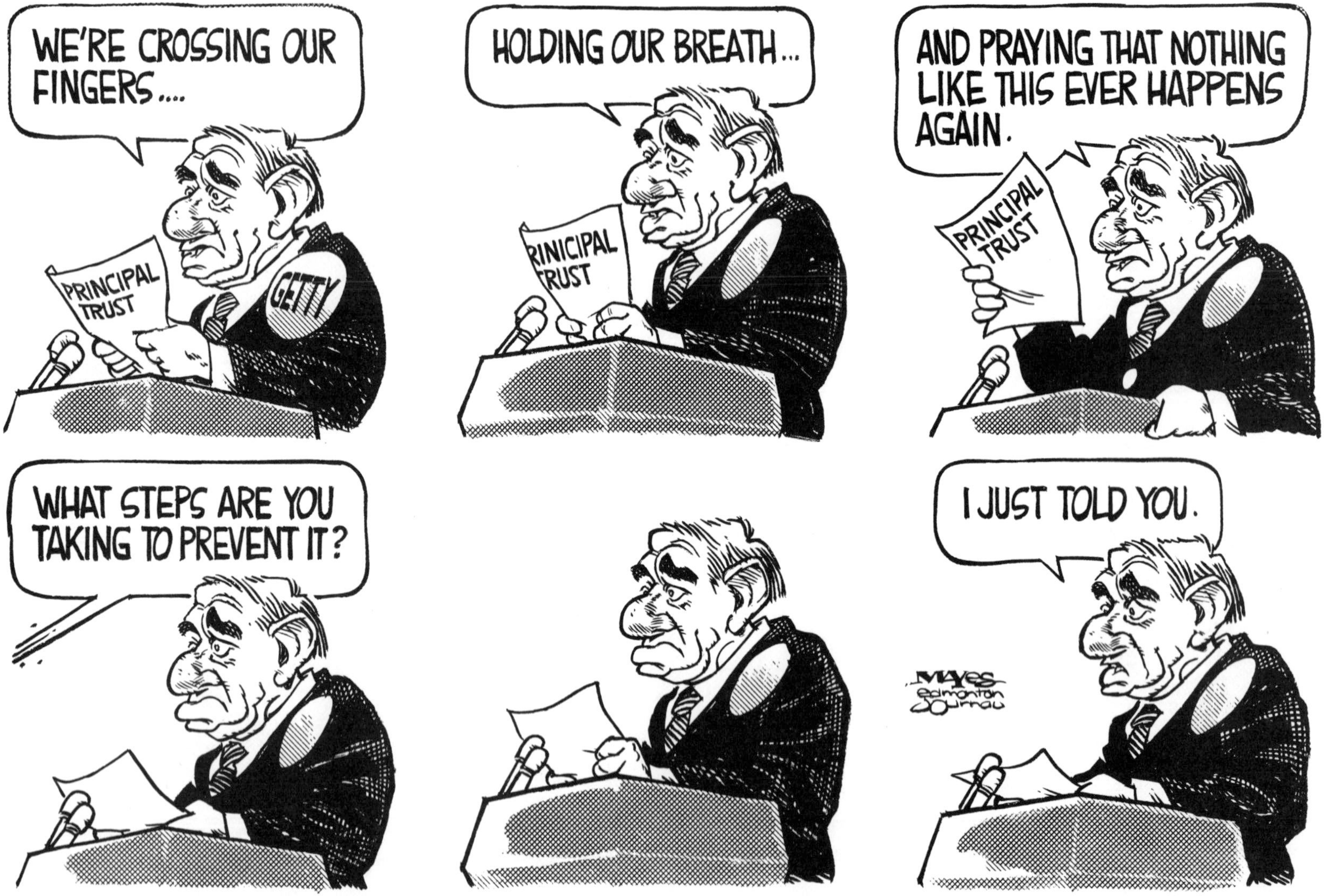
WE'RE CROSSING OUR FINGERS....
PRINCIPAL TRUST
GETTY
HOLDING OUR BREATH...
RINICIPAL TRUST
AND PRAYING THAT NOTHING LIKE THIS EVER HAPPENS AGAIN.
PRINCIPAL TRUST
WHAT STEPS ARE YOU TAKING TO PREVENT IT?
I JUST TOLD YOU.
MAYES
Edmonton Journal

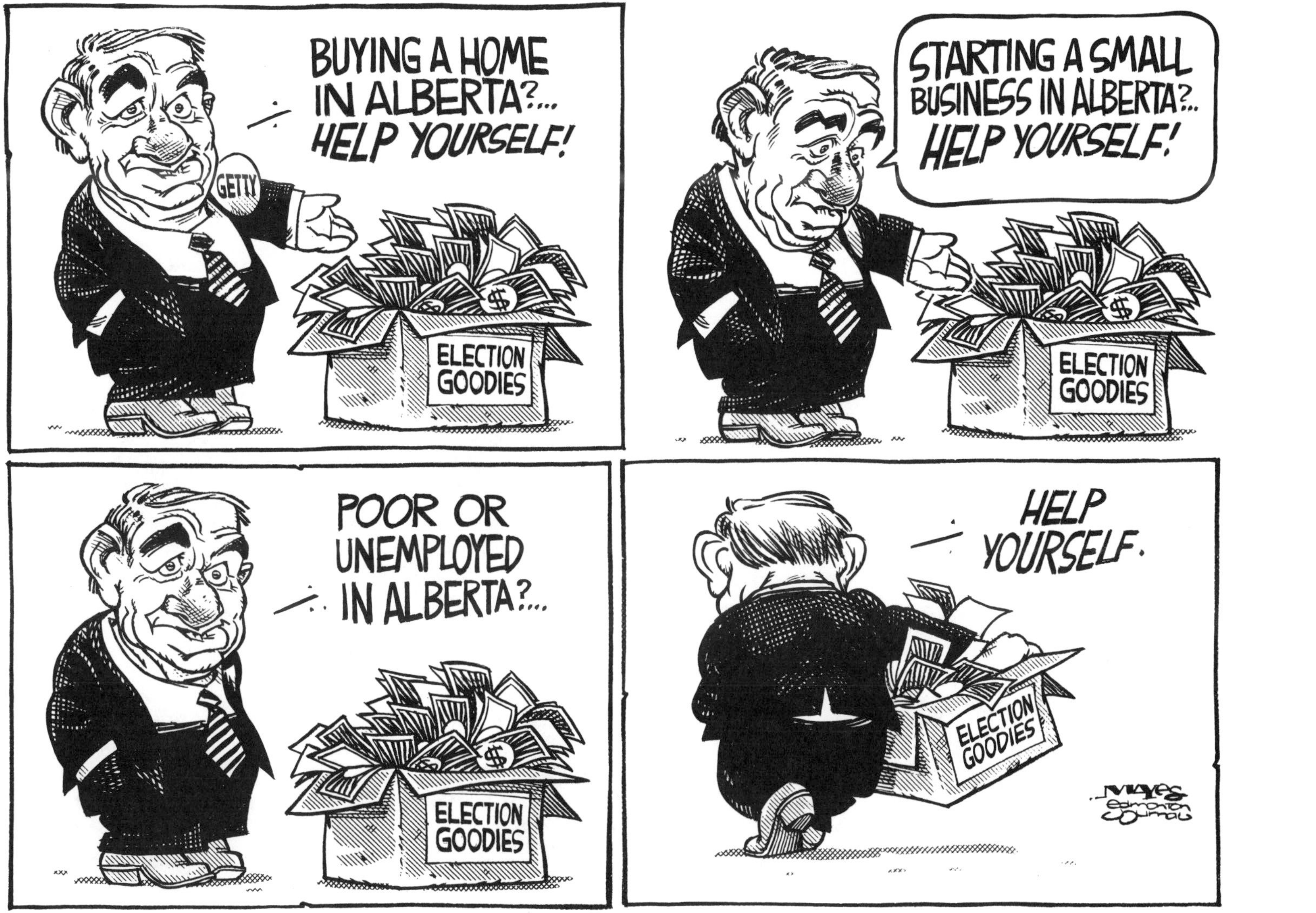
BUYING A HOME IN ALBERTA?... HELP YOURSELF!
GETTY
ELECTION GOODIES
STARTING A SMALL BUSINESS IN ALBERTA?.. HELP YOURSELF!
ELECTION GOODIES
POOR OR UNEMPLOYED IN ALBERTA?...
ELECTION GOODIES
HELP YOURSELF.
ELECTION GOODIES
MAYES
Edmonton Journal

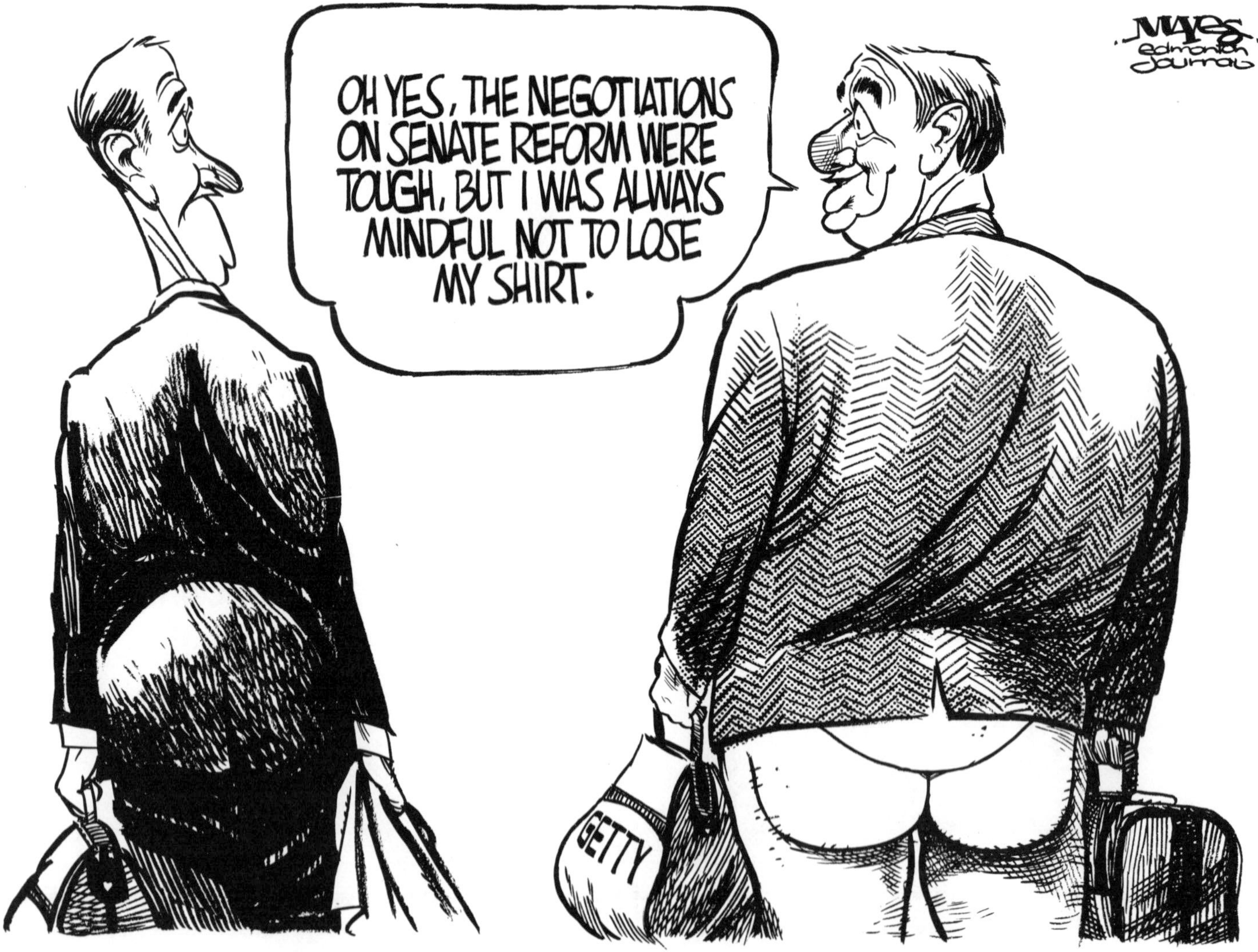
OH YES, THE NEGOTIATIONS ON SENATE REFORM WERE TOUGH, BUT I WAS ALWAYS MINDFUL NOT TO LOSE MY SHIRT.
GETTY
MAYES edmonton journal

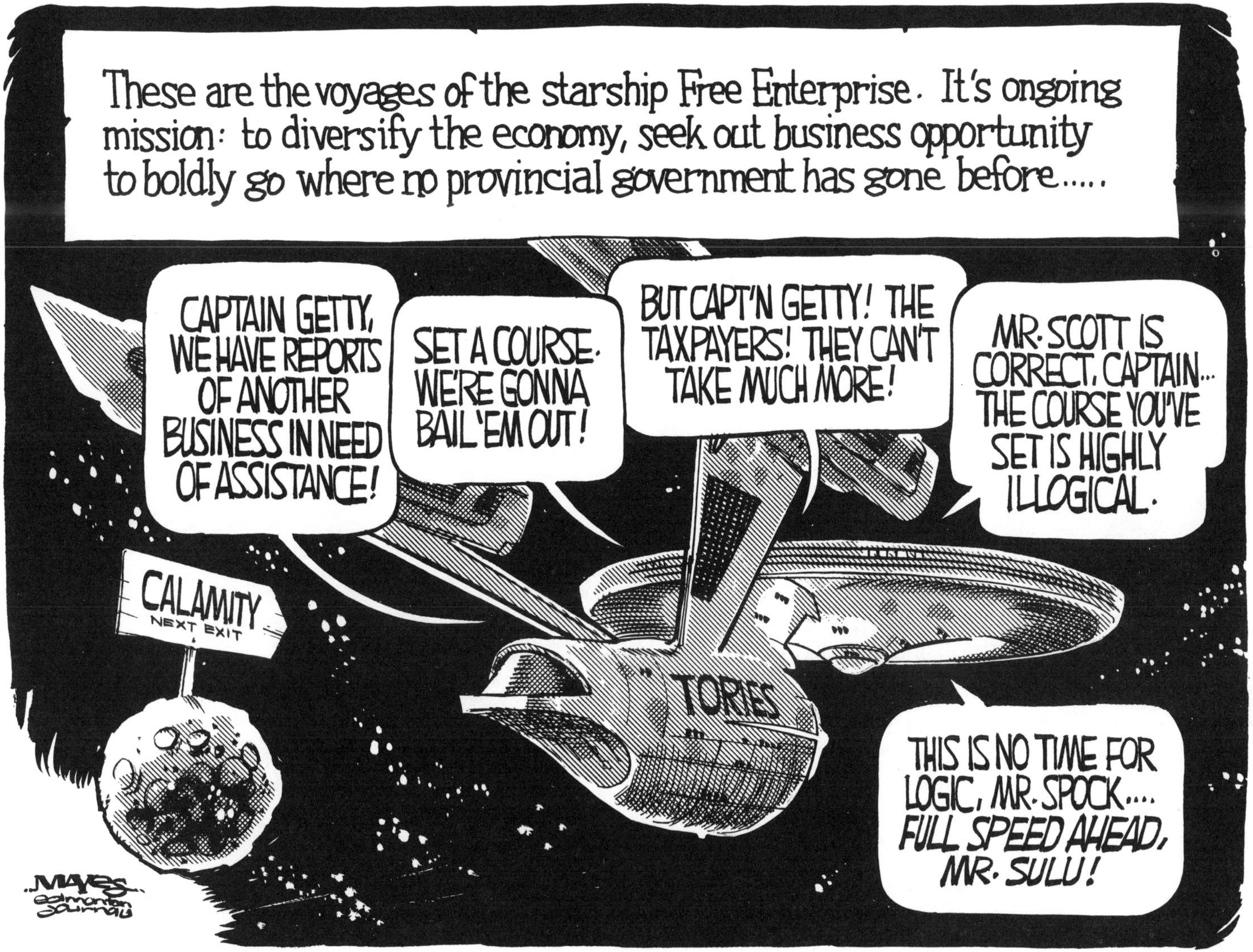
These are the voyages of the starship Free Enterprise. It's ongoing mission: to diversify the economy, seek out business opportunity to boldly go where no provincial government has gone before.....
CAPTAIN GETTY, WE HAVE REPORTS OF ANOTHER BUSINESS IN NEED OF ASSISTANCE!
SET A COURSE. WE'RE GONNA BAIL 'EM OUT!
BUT CAPT'N GETTY! THE TAXPAYERS! THEY CAN'T TAKE MUCH MORE!
MR. SCOTT IS CORRECT, CAPTAIN... THE COURSE YOU'VE SET IS HIGHLY ILLOGICAL.
THIS IS NO TIME FOR LOGIC, MR. SPOCK.... FULL SPEED AHEAD, MR. SULU!
CALAMITY
NEXT EXIT
TORIES
MAYES
edmonton journal

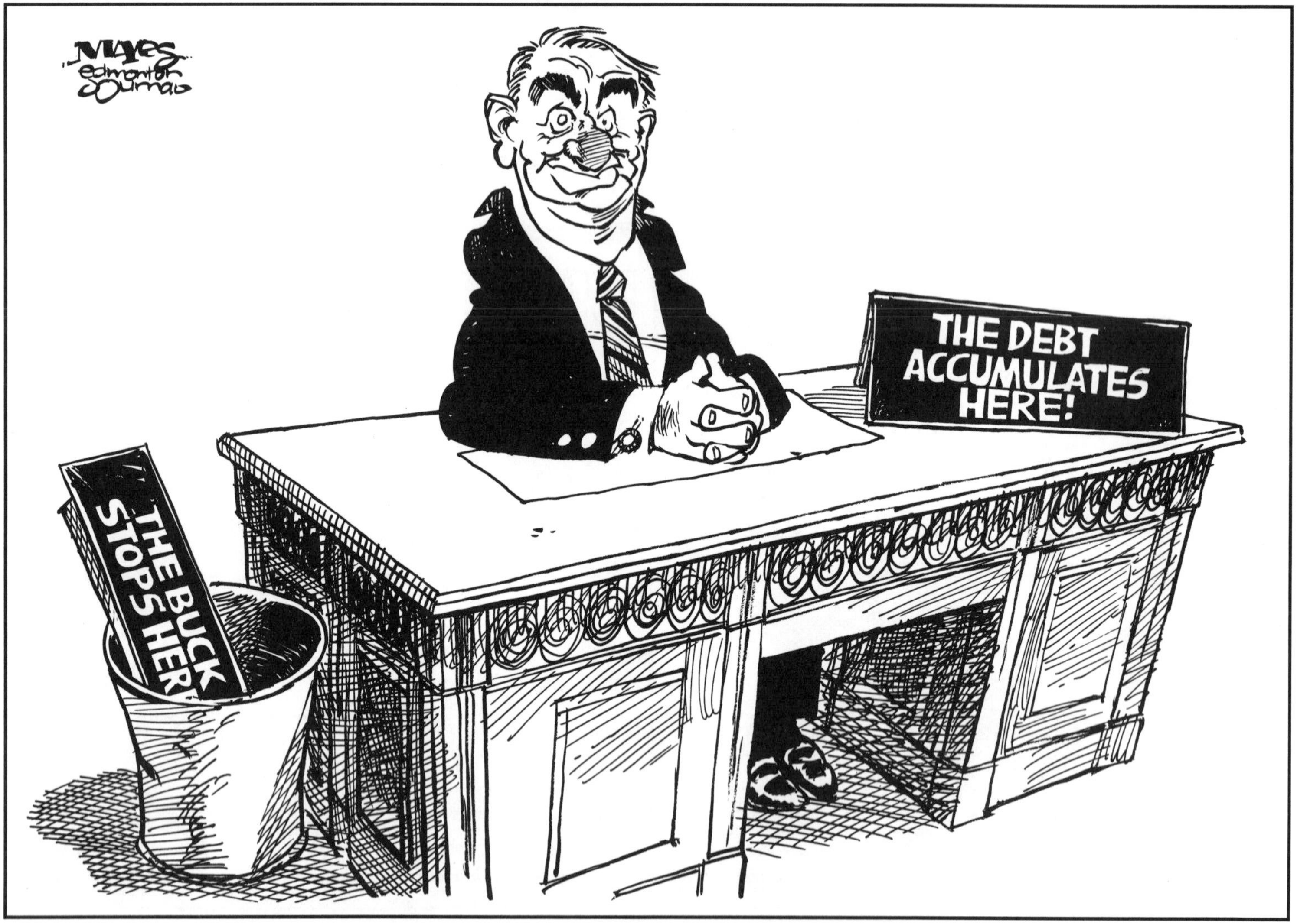
MAYES
edmonton journal
THE DEBT ACCUMULATES HERE!
THE BUCK STOPS HER

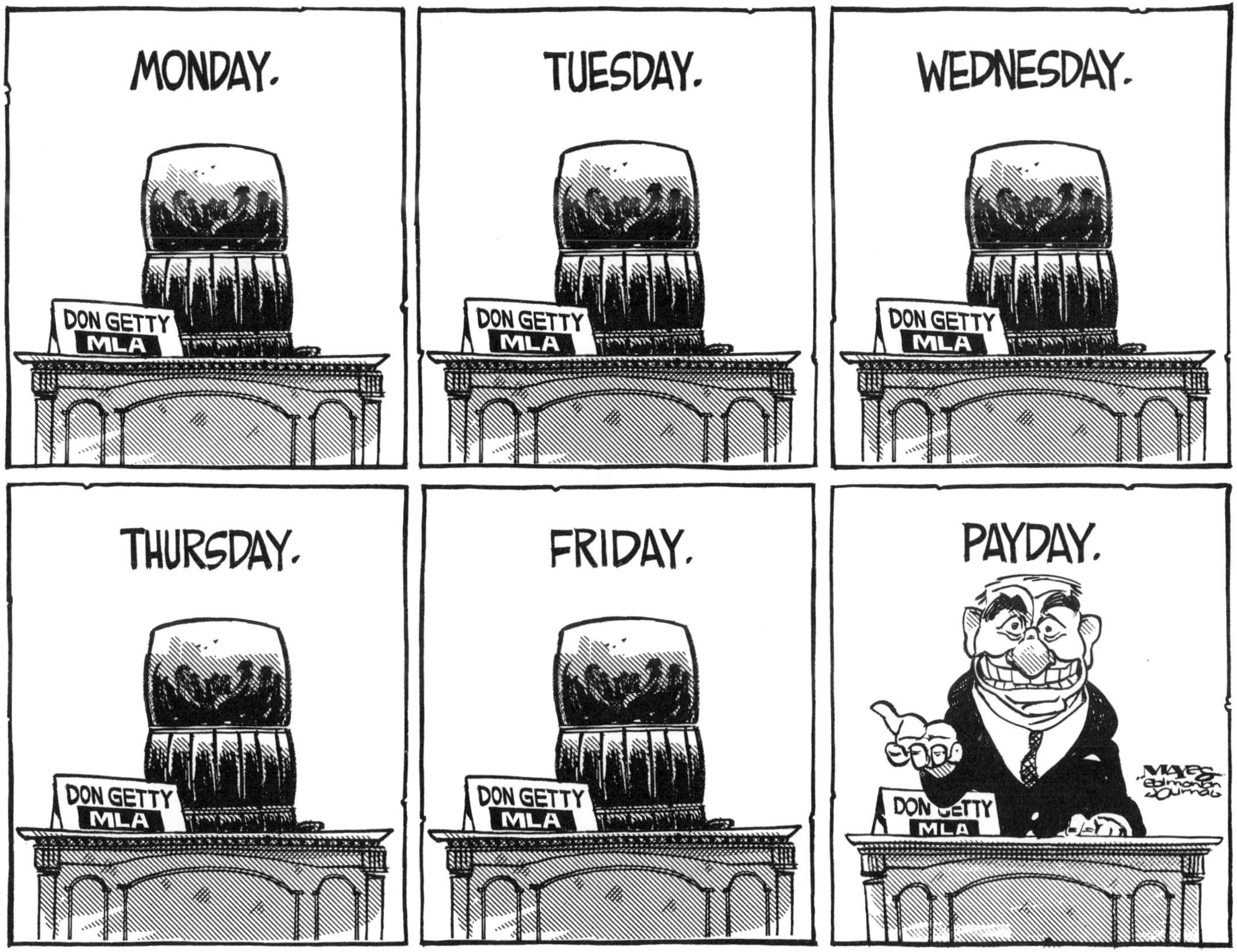
MONDAY.
DON GETTY
MLA
TUESDAY.
DON GETTY
MLA
WEDNESDAY.
DON GETTY
MLA
THURSDAY.
DON GETTY
MLA
FRIDAY.
DON GETTY
MLA
PAYDAY.
MLA
MAYES

Premier Getty is criticized for rarely attending legislative sessions.

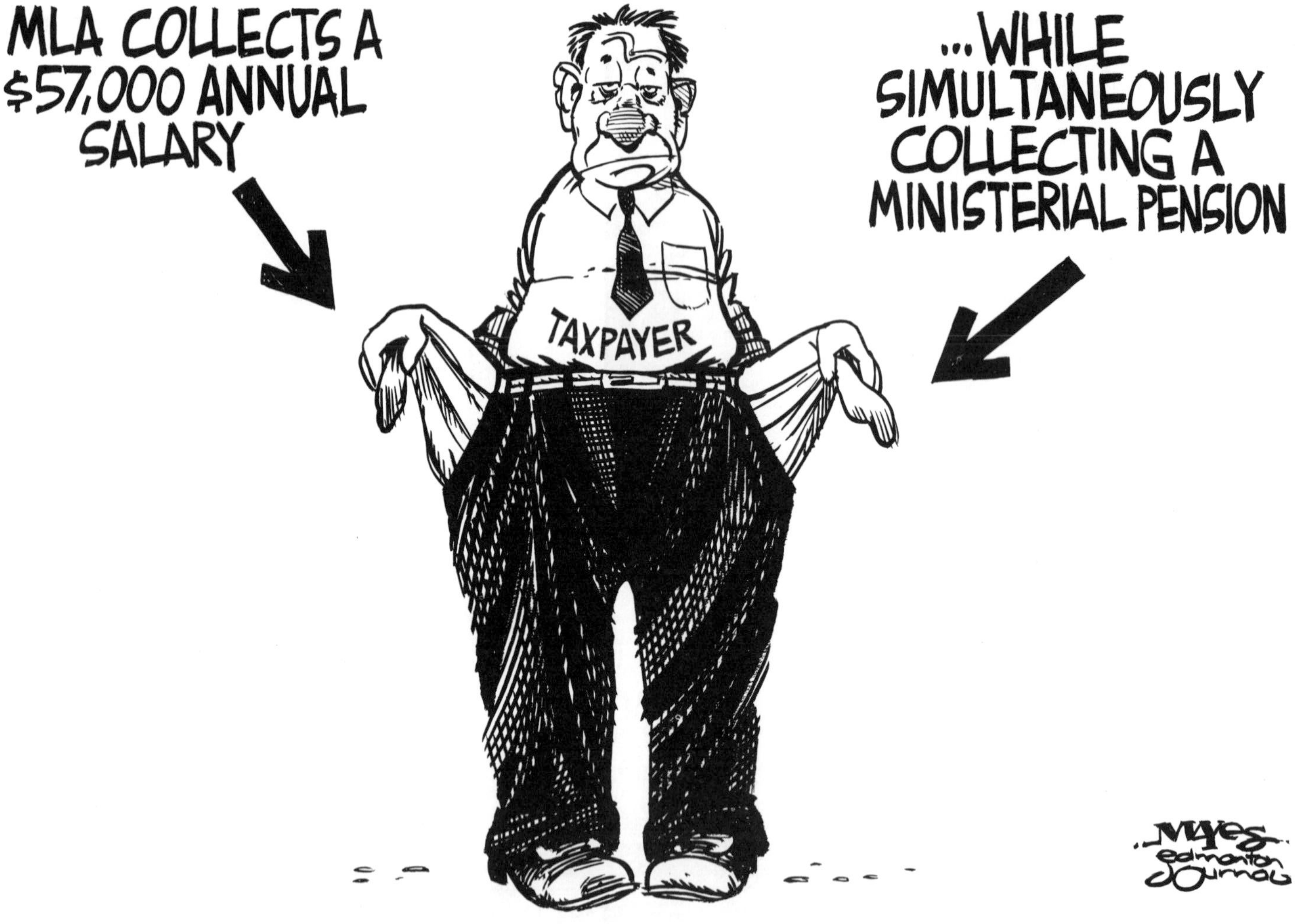
MLA COLLECTS A $57,000 ANNUAL SALARY
...WHILE SIMULTANEOUSLY COLLECTING A MINISTERIAL PENSION
TAXPAYER
MAYES
edmonton journal

Double-dipping explained.

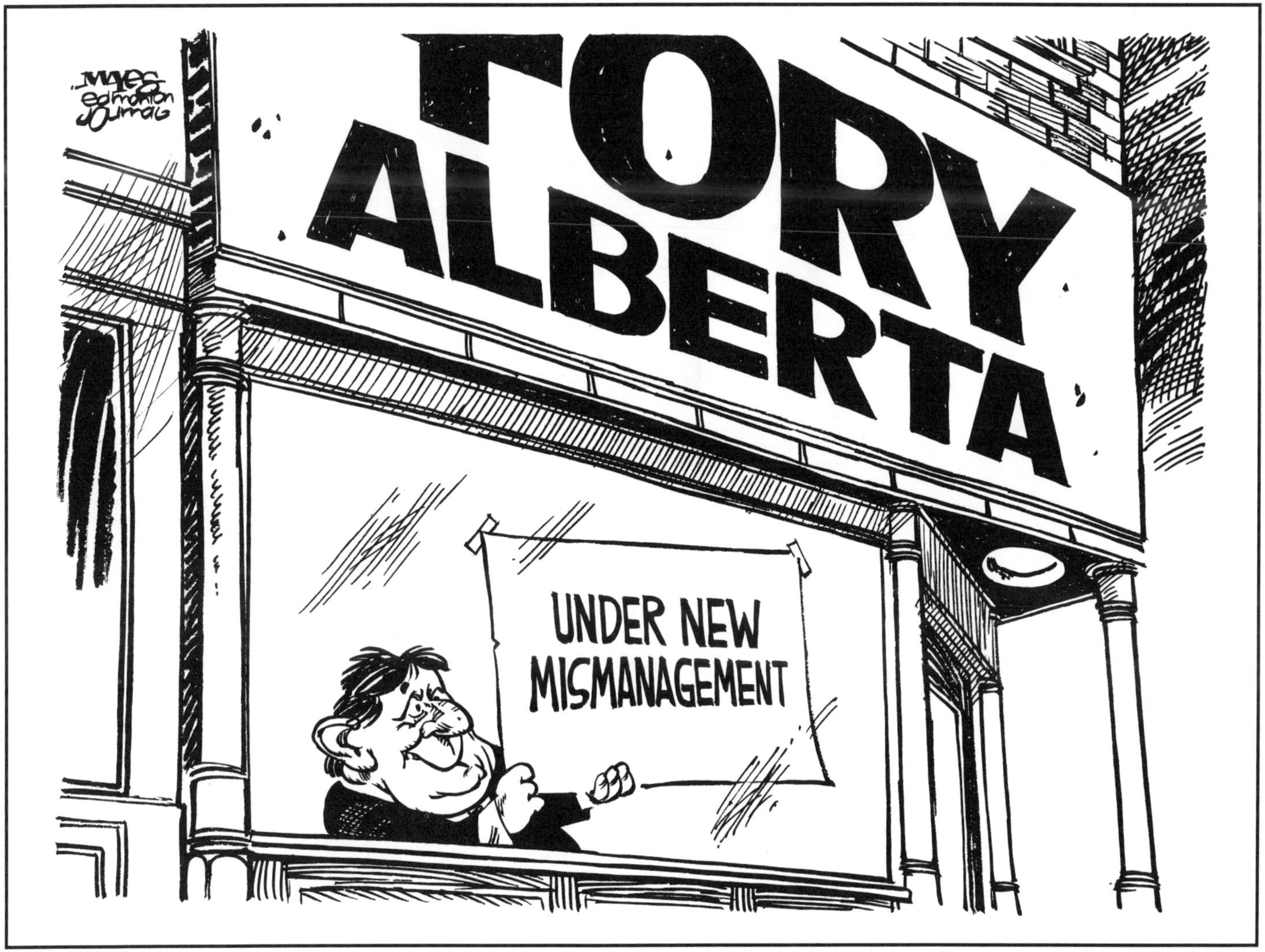
TORY ALBERTA
UNDER NEW MISMANAGEMENT

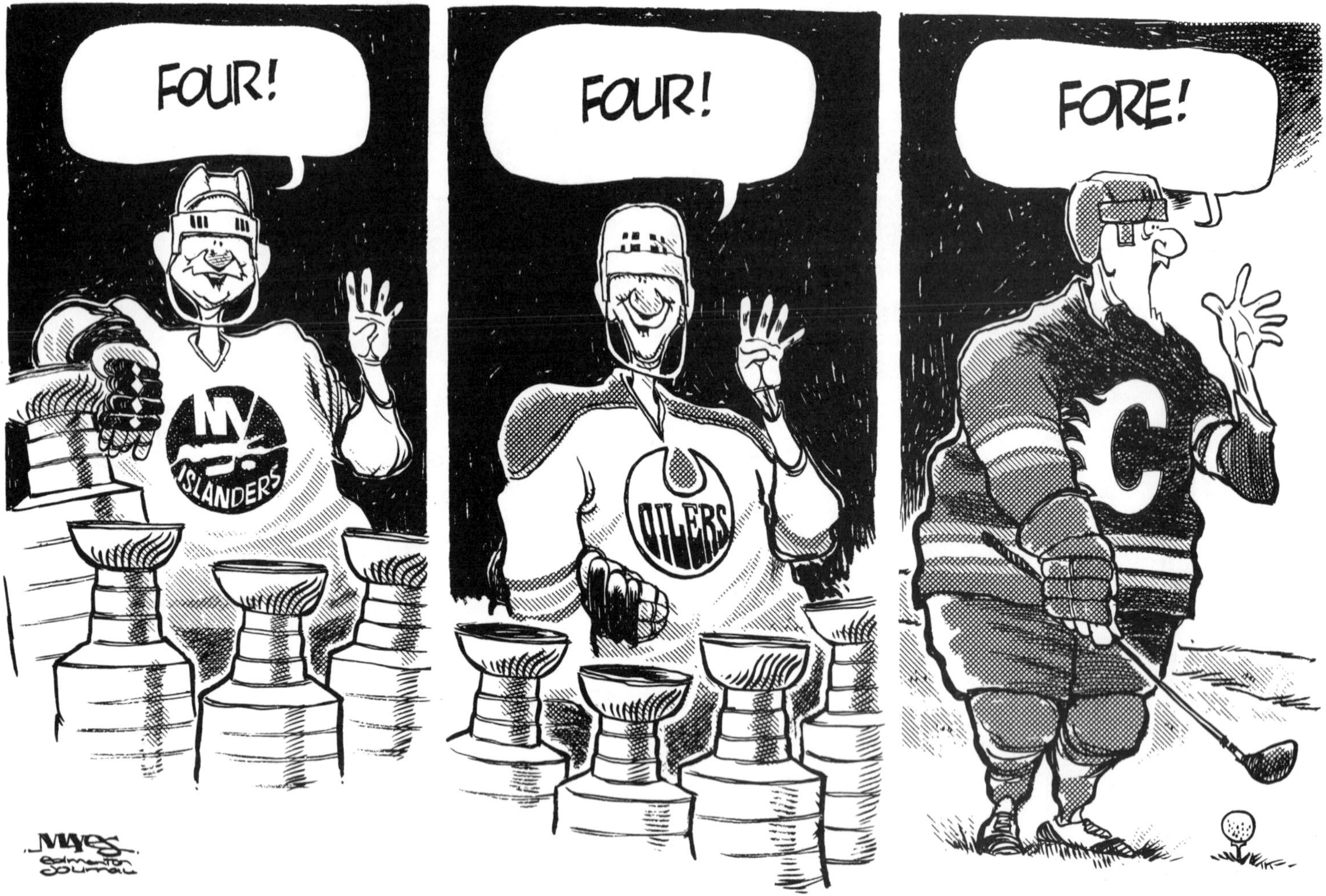
FOUR!
NY
ISLANDERS
FOUR!
OILERS
FORE!
MAYES
Edmonton Journal

Hockey Dynasties.

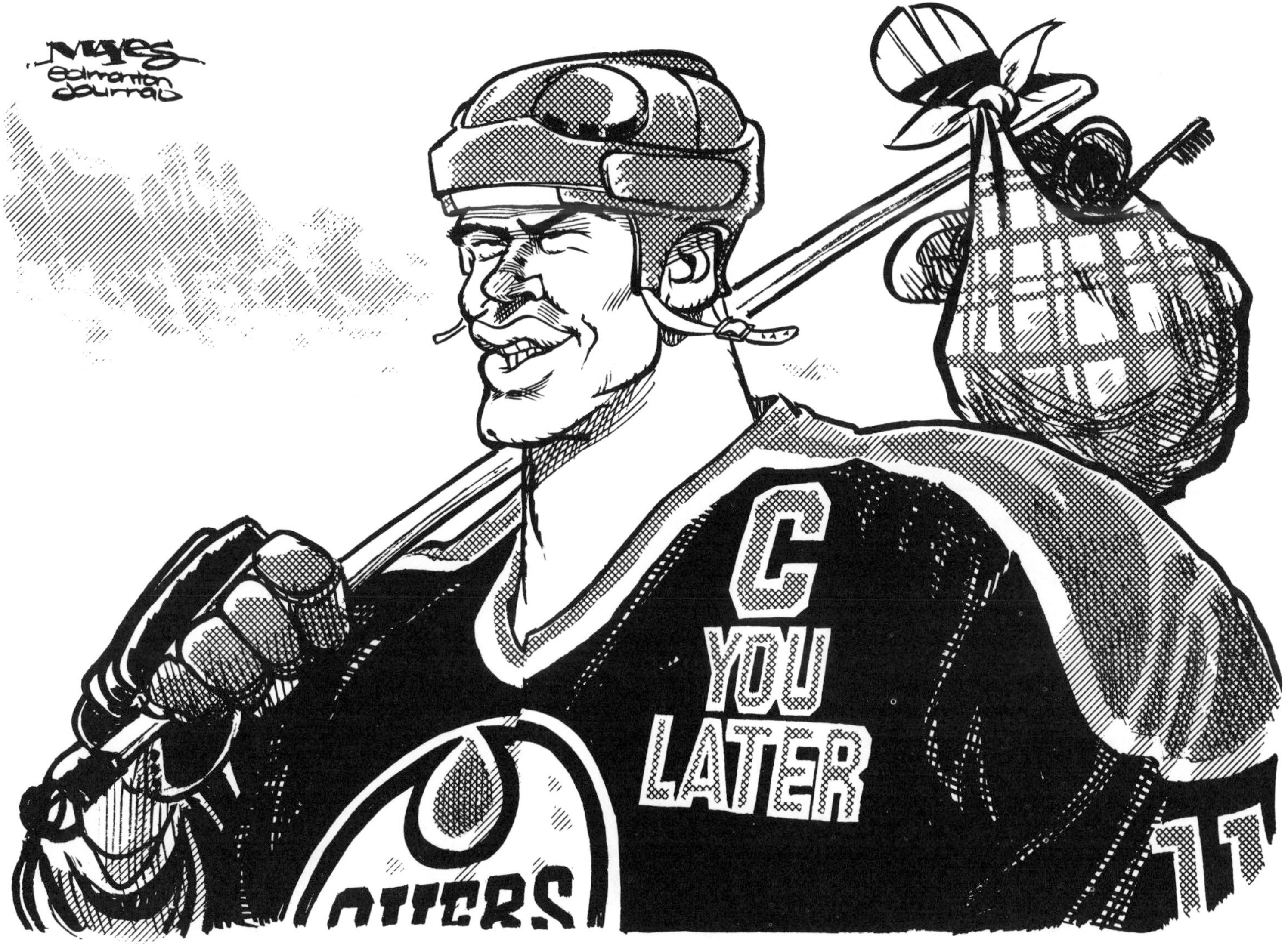
C
YOU
LATER

Edmonton's hockey stars leave for greener pasture$.

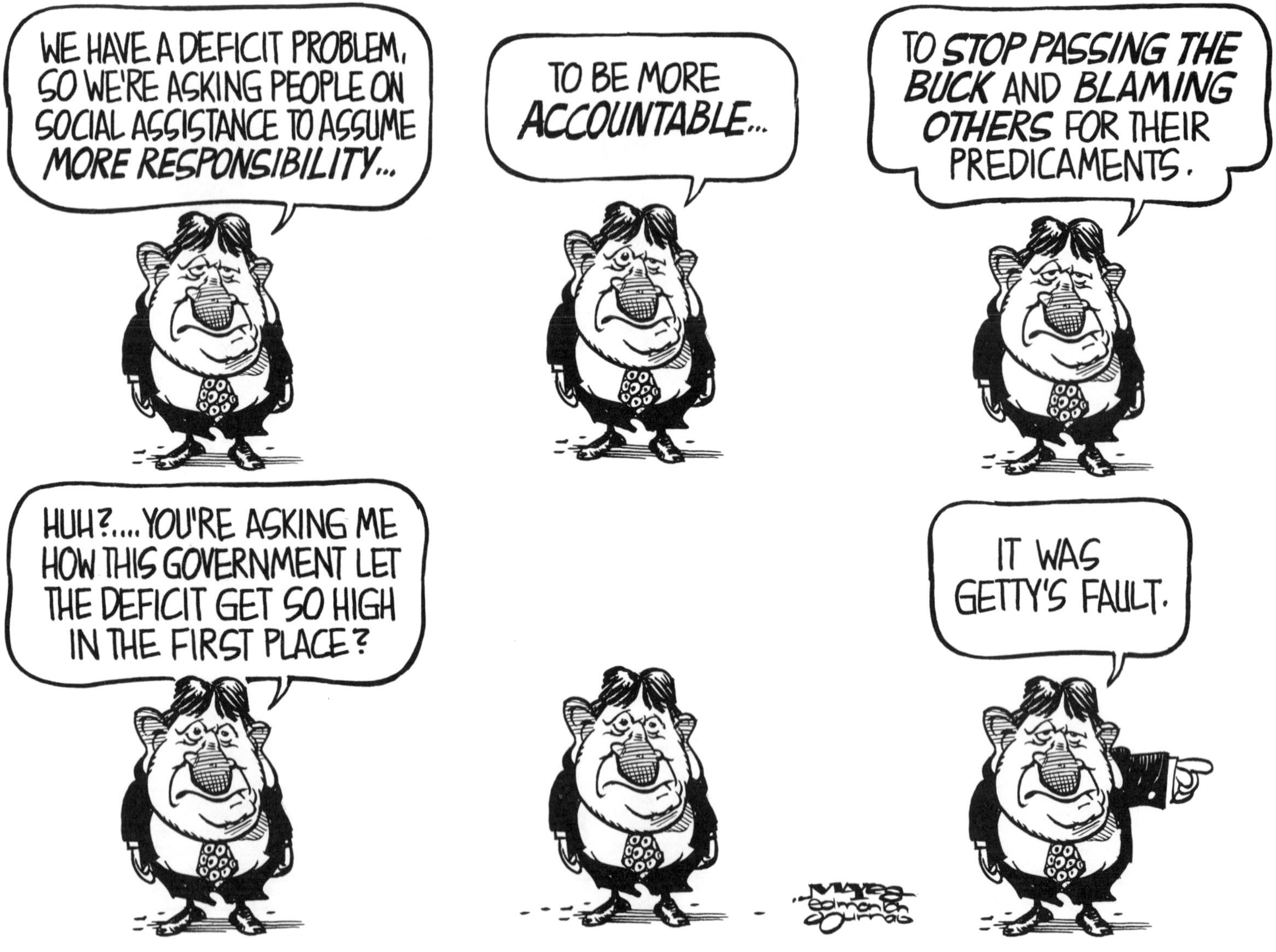
WE HAVE A DEFICIT PROBLEM, SO WE'RE ASKING PEOPLE ON SOCIAL ASSISTANCE TO ASSUME MORE RESPONSIBILITY...
TO BE MORE ACCOUNTABLE...
TO STOP PASSING THE BUCK AND BLAMING OTHERS FOR THEIR PREDICAMENTS.
HUH?.... YOU'RE ASKING ME HOW THIS GOVERNMENT LET THE DEFICIT GET SO HIGH IN THE FIRST PLACE?
IT WAS GETTY'S FAULT.
MAYES
Edmonton Journal

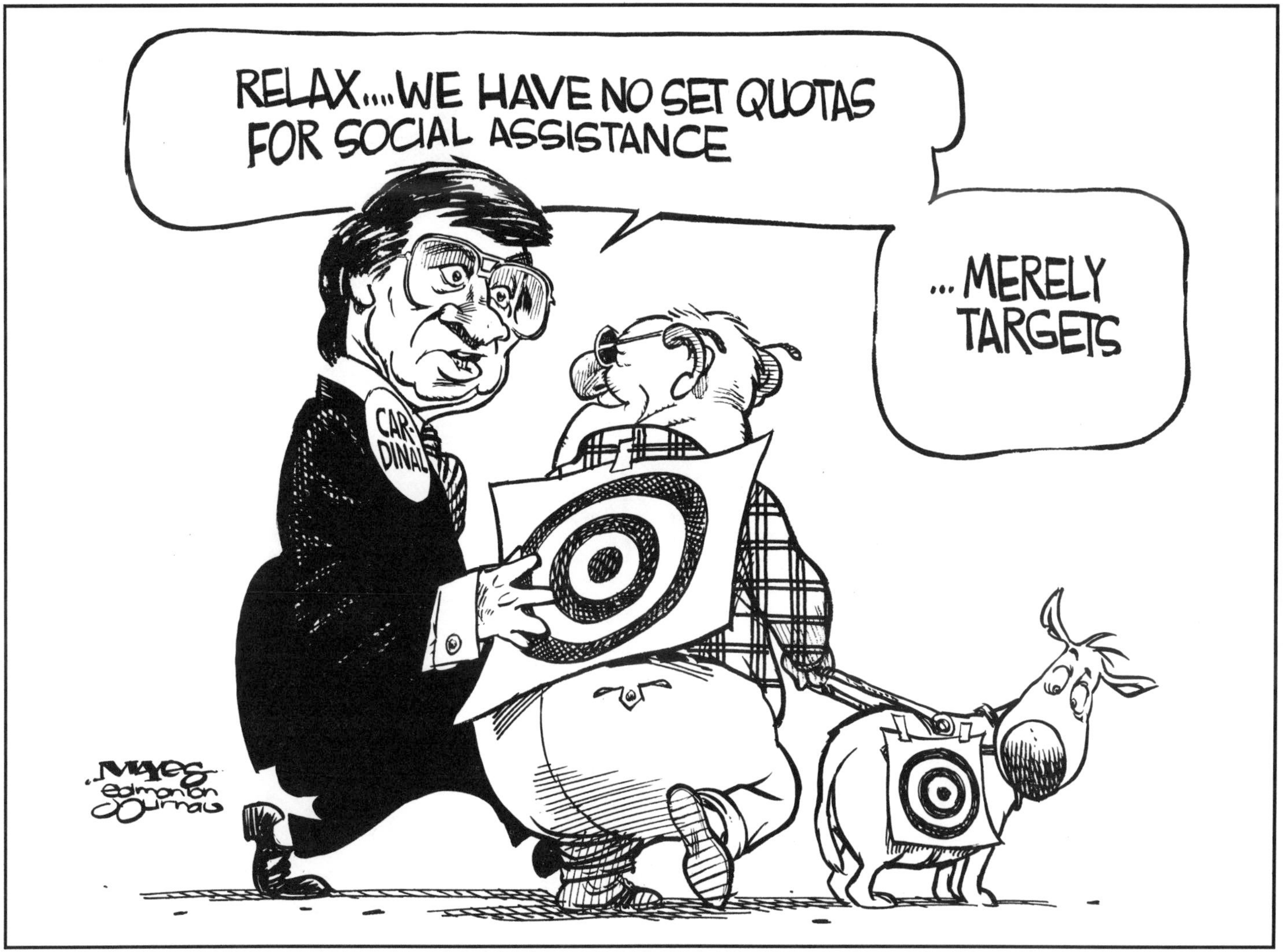
RELAX.... WE HAVE NO SET QUOTAS FOR SOCIAL ASSISTANCE
... MERELY TARGETS
CAR-DINAL
MAYES edmonton Journal

Alberta social services minister drops thousands of needy Albertans from welfare rolls.

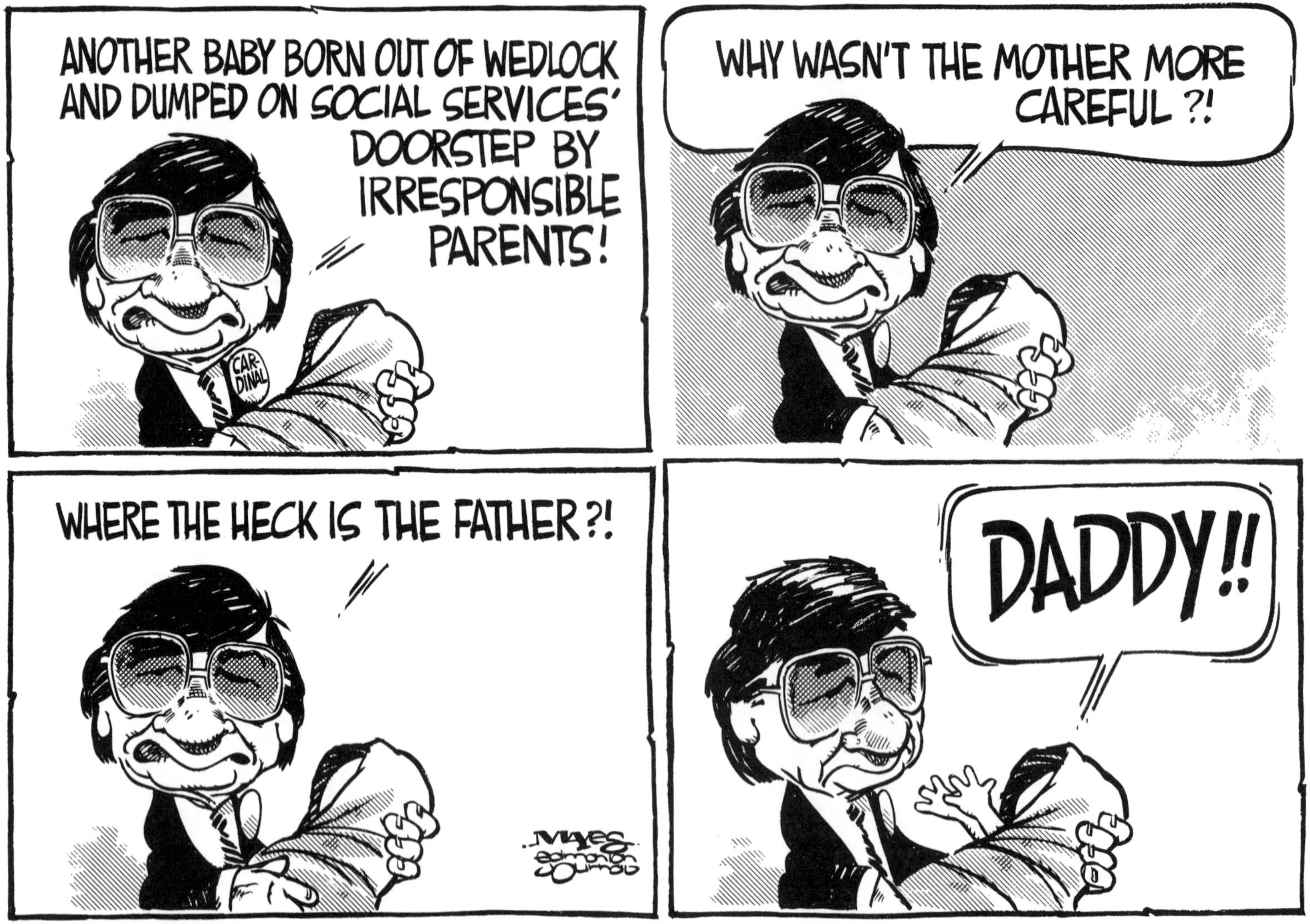
ANOTHER BABY BORN OUT OF WEDLOCK AND DUMPED ON SOCIAL SERVICES' DOORSTEP BY IRRESPONSIBLE PARENTS!
CAR-DINAL
WHY WASN'T THE MOTHER MORE CAREFUL ?!
WHERE THE HECK IS THE FATHER ?!
DADDY!!
Mayes edmonton journal

After attacking single parent families on welfare, Social Services Minister Mike Cardinal admits he abandoned his daughter and her mother years ago.

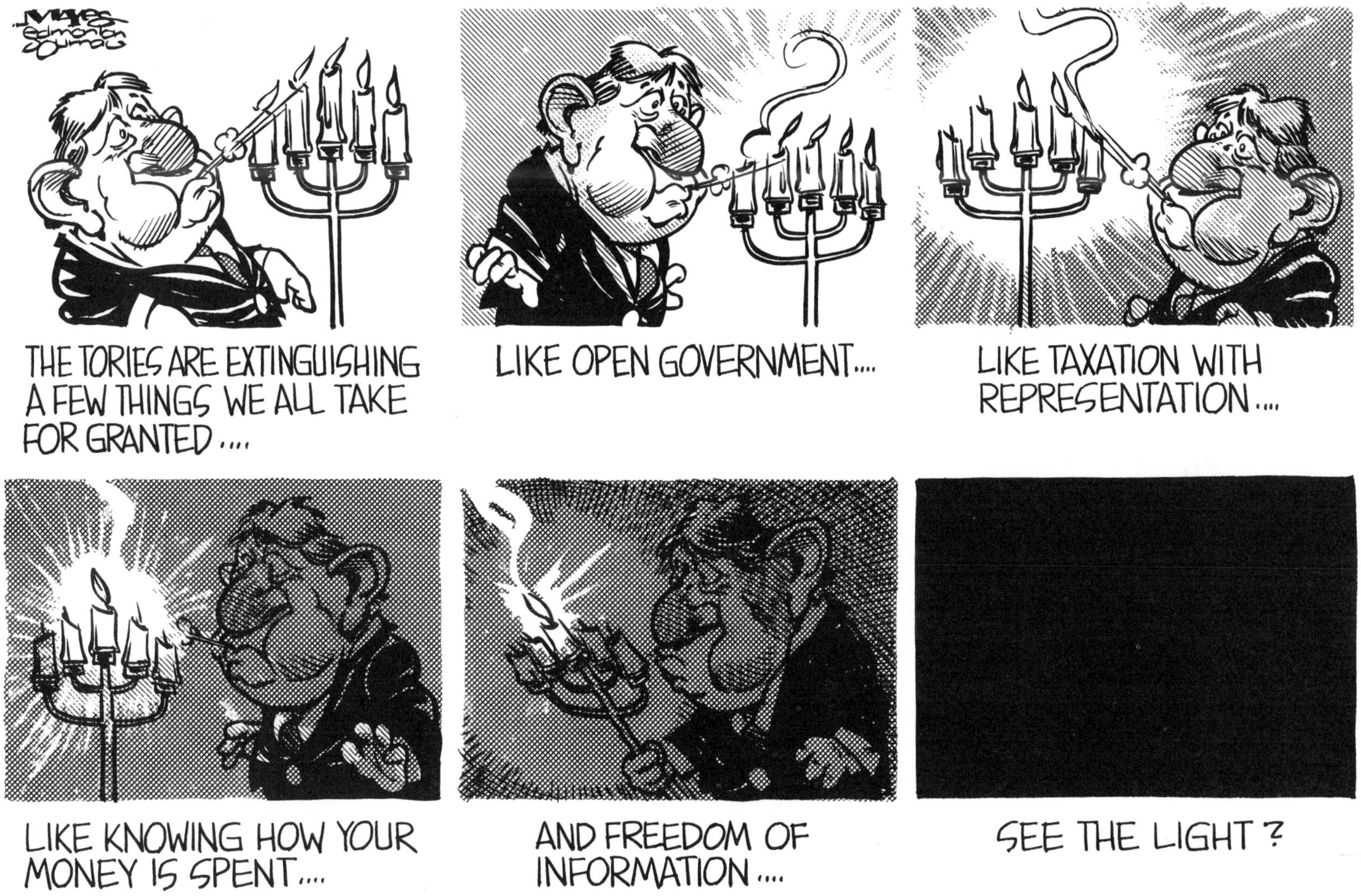
Mayes Edmonton Journal
THE TORIES ARE EXTINGUISHING A FEW THINGS WE ALL TAKE FOR GRANTED....
LIKE OPEN GOVERNMENT....
LIKE TAXATION WITH REPRESENTATION....
LIKE KNOWING HOW YOUR MONEY IS SPENT....
AND FREEDOM OF INFORMATION....
SEE THE LIGHT?

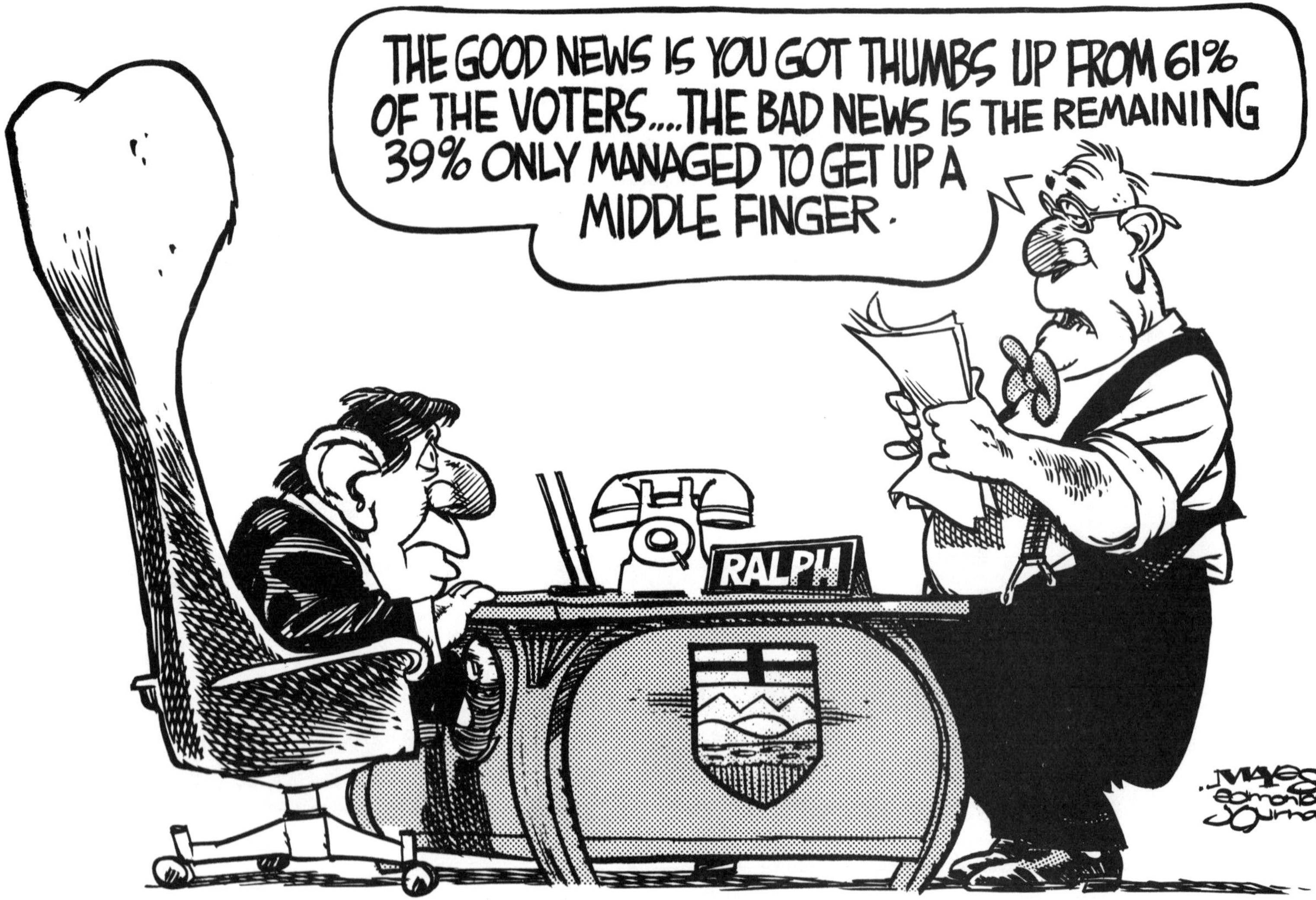
THE GOOD NEWS IS YOU GOT THUMBS UP FROM 61% OF THE VOTERS....THE BAD NEWS IS THE REMAINING 39% ONLY MANAGED TO GET UP A MIDDLE FINGER.
RALPH
MAYES
Edmonton Journal

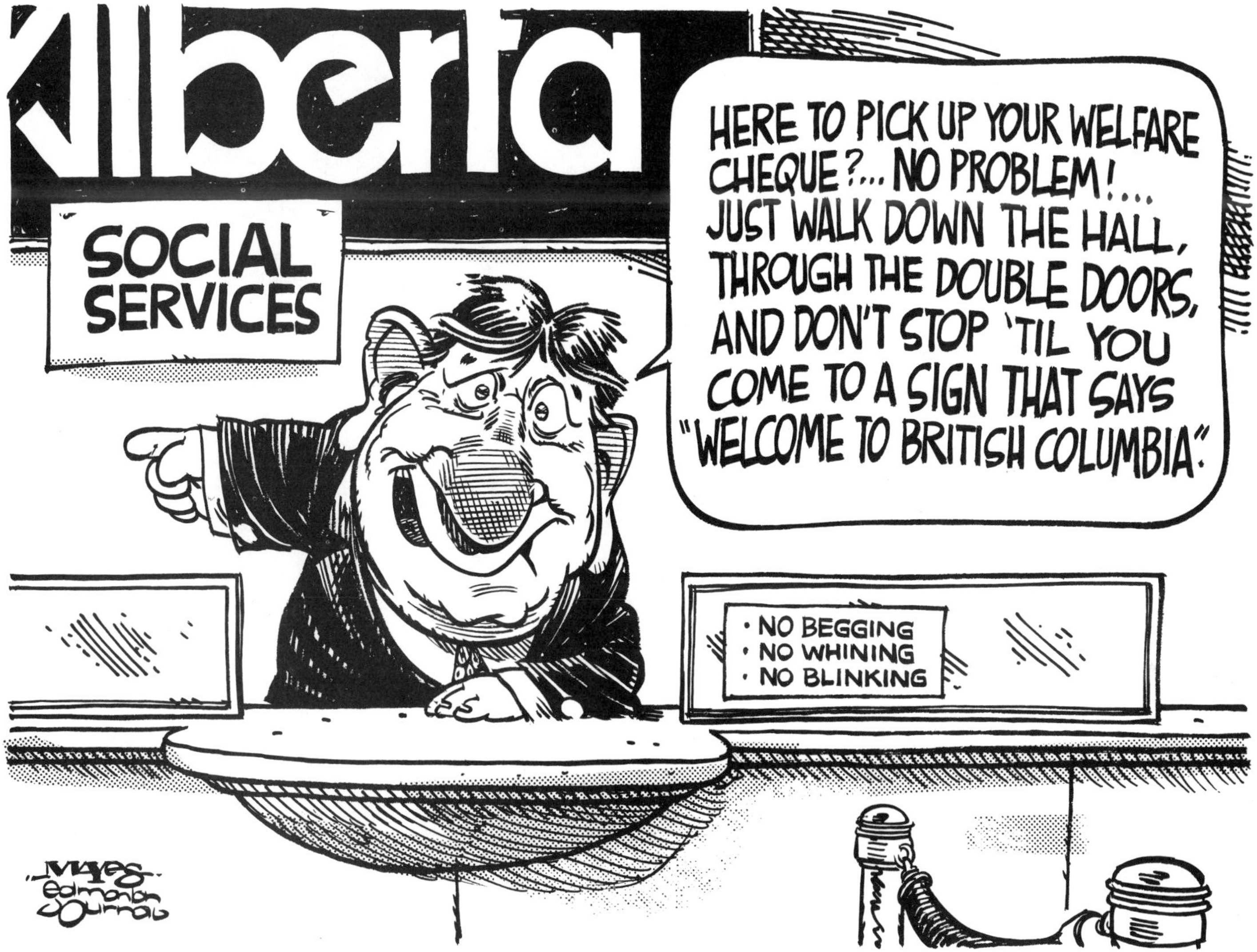
Alberta
SOCIAL SERVICES
HERE TO PICK UP YOUR WELFARE CHEQUE?... NO PROBLEM!... JUST WALK DOWN THE HALL, THROUGH THE DOUBLE DOORS, AND DON'T STOP 'TIL YOU COME TO A SIGN THAT SAYS "WELCOME TO BRITISH COLUMBIA".
• NO BEGGING
• NO WHINING
• NO BLINKING
Mayes Edmonton Journal

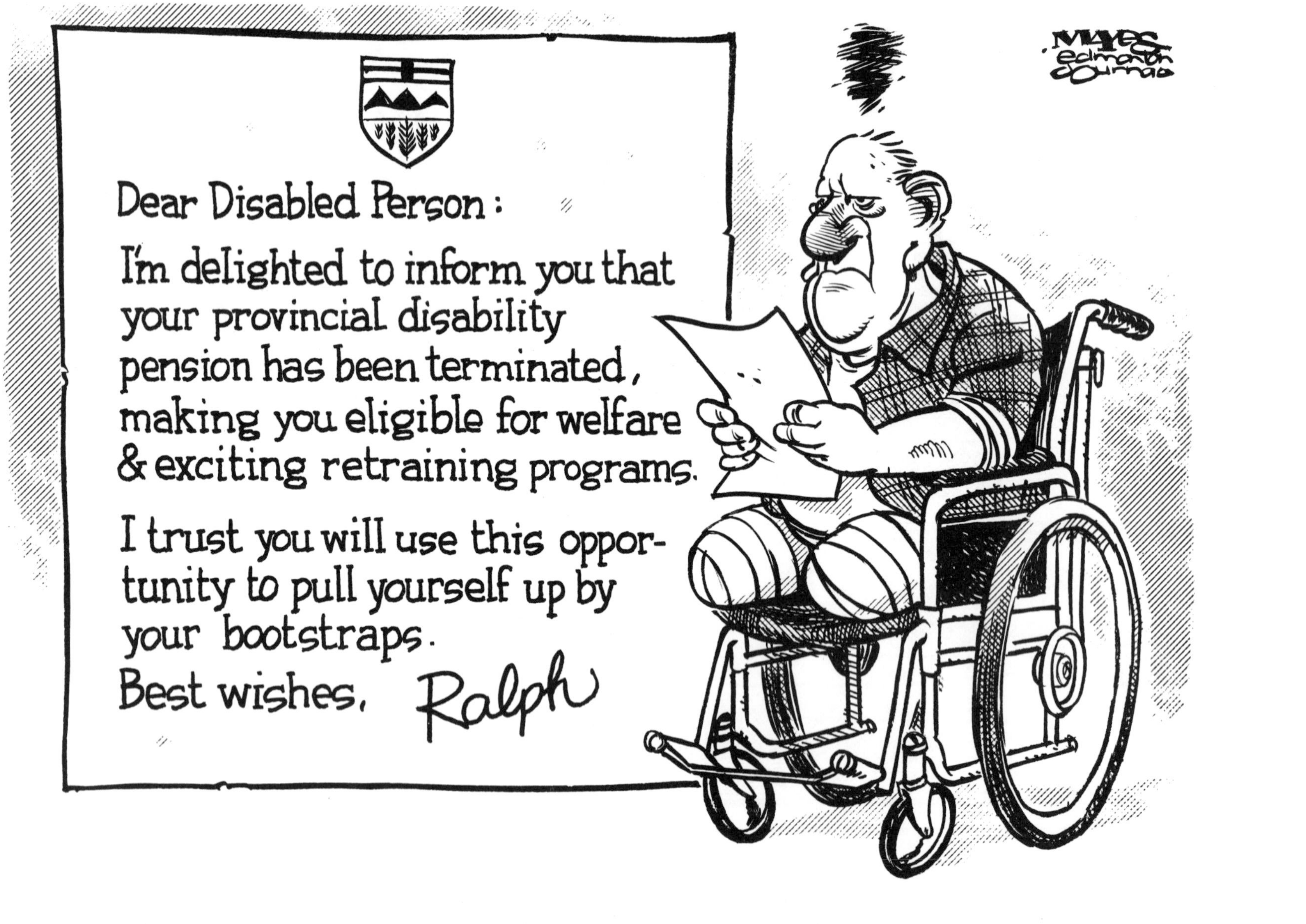
Dear Disabled Person:
I'm delighted to inform you that your provincial disability pension has been terminated, making you eligible for welfare & exciting retraining programs.
I trust you will use this opportunity to pull yourself up by your bootstraps.
Best wishes, Ralph
MAYES edmonton journal

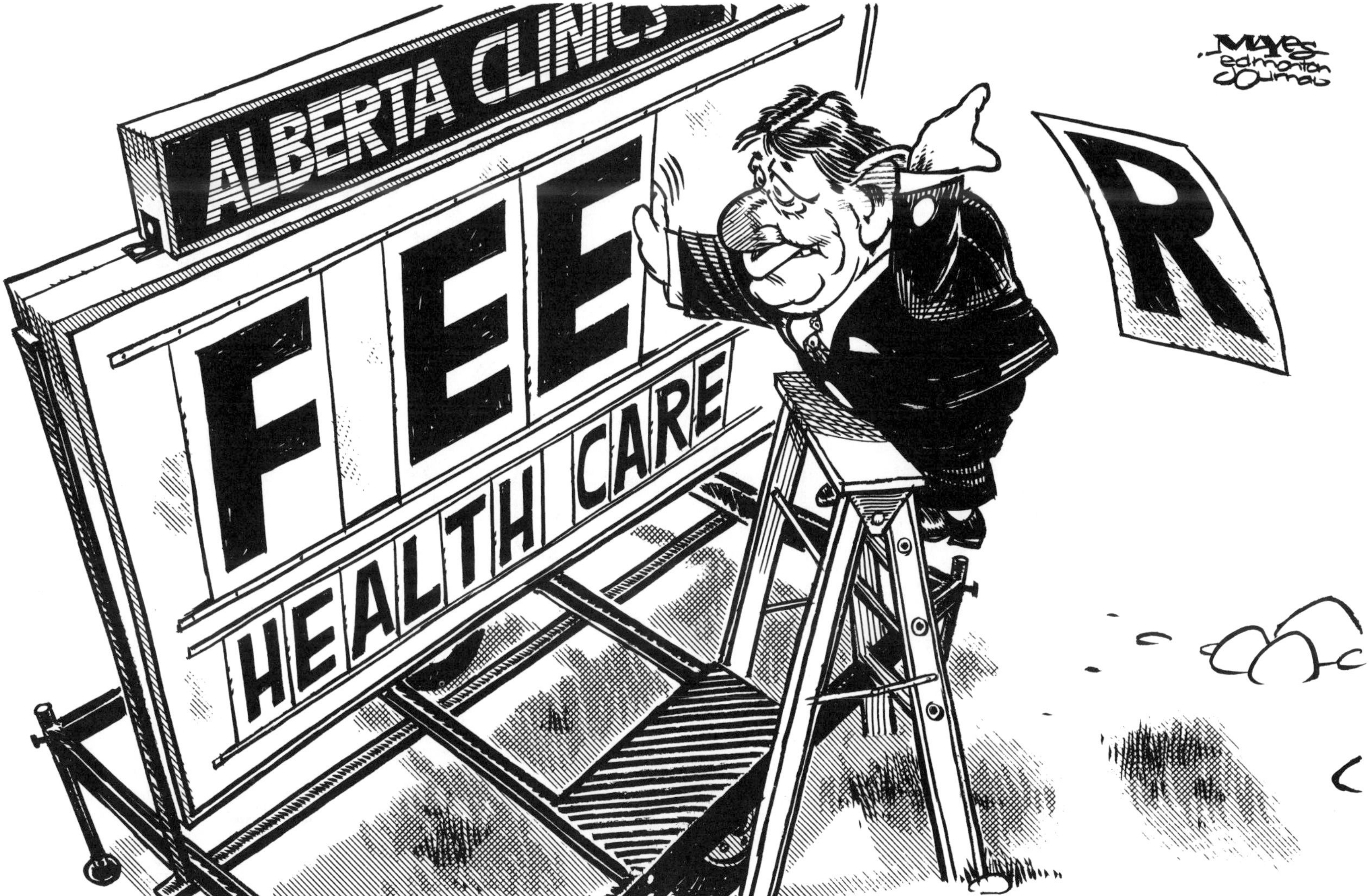

ALBERTA CLINICS
FEE
R
HEALTH CARE
MAYES
edmonton journal

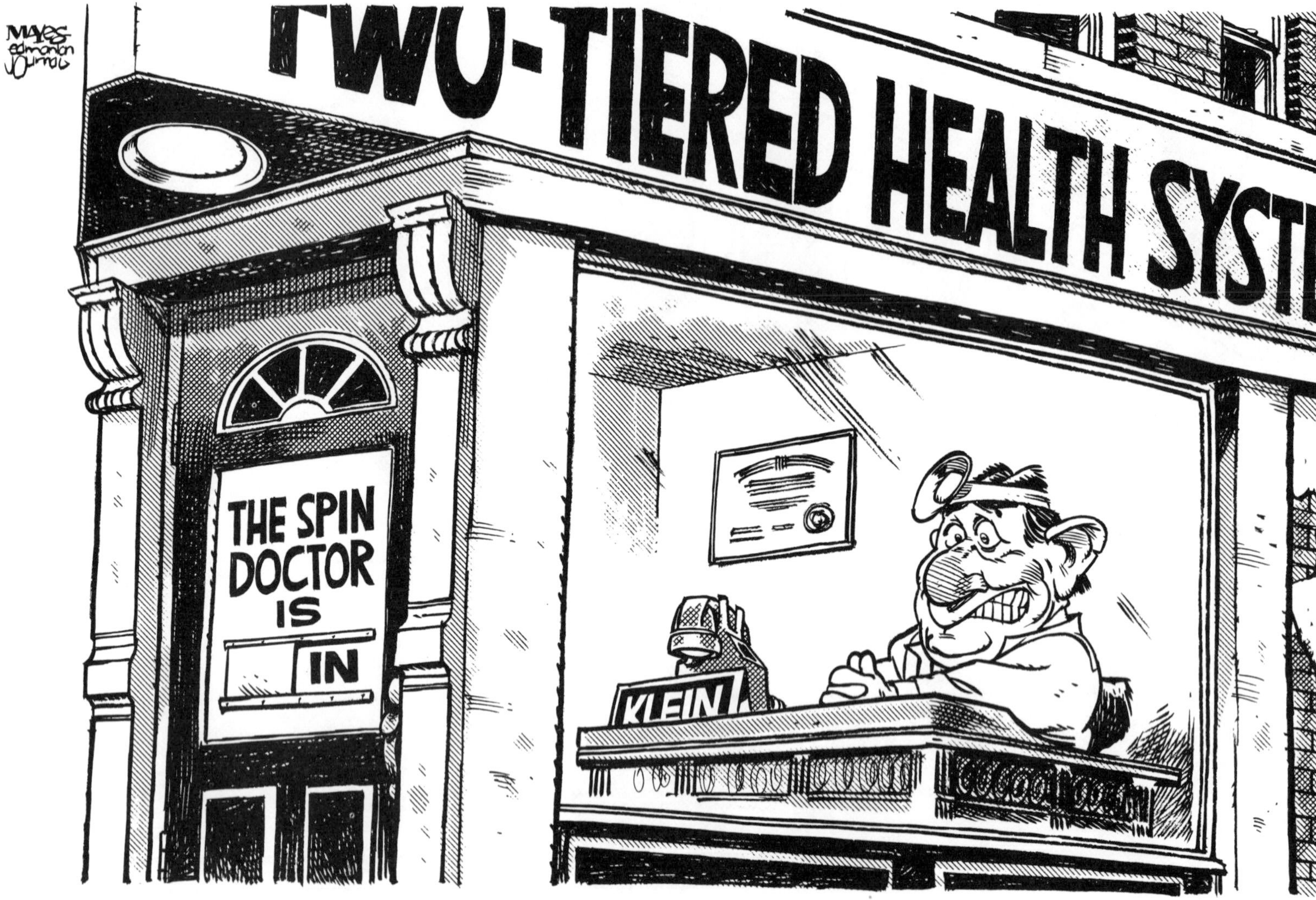
MAYES edmonton journal
TWO-TIERED HEALTH SYSTE
THE SPIN DOCTOR IS IN
KLEIN

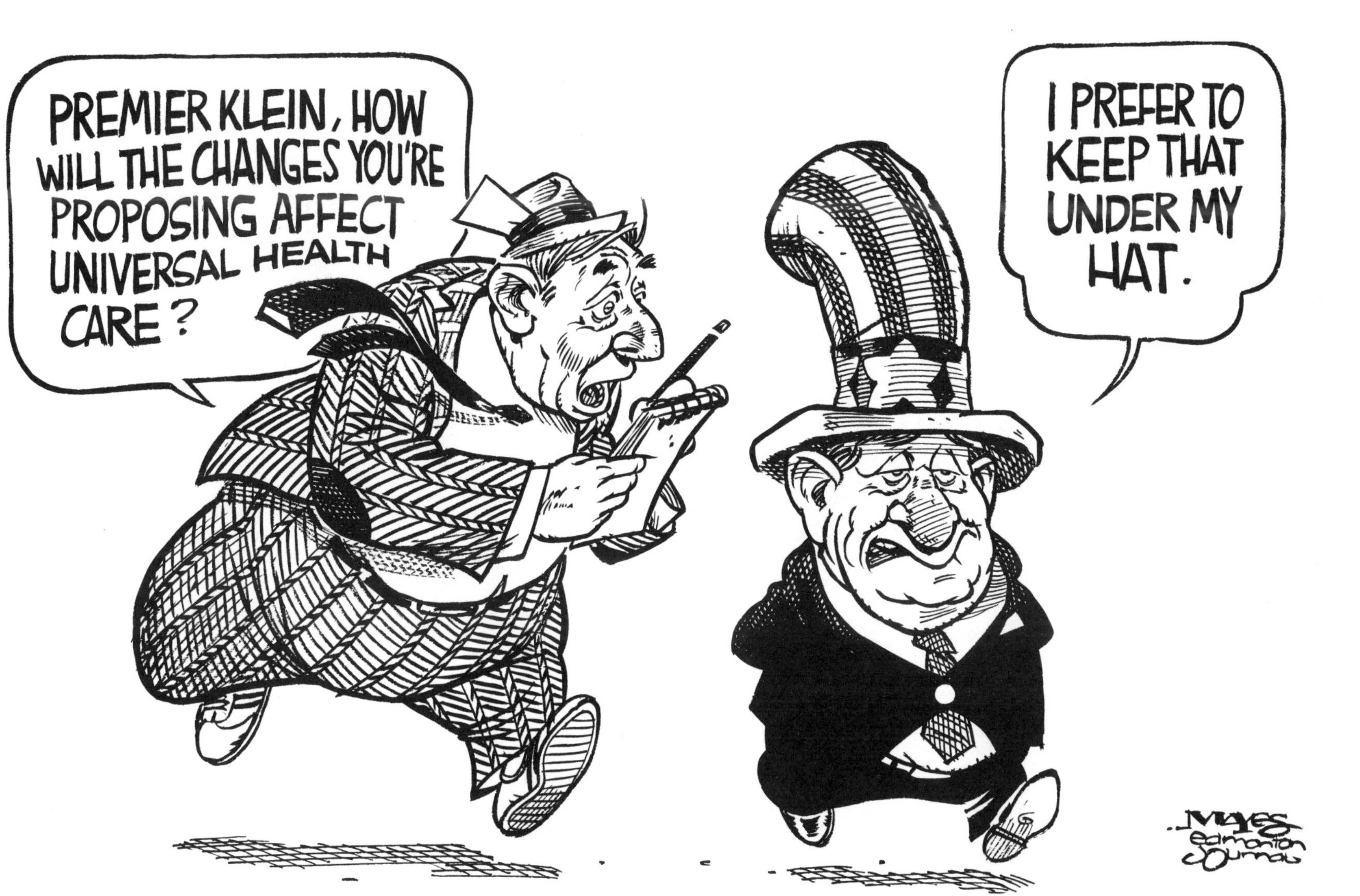
PREMIER KLEIN, HOW WILL THE CHANGES YOU'RE PROPOSING AFFECT UNIVERSAL HEALTH CARE?
I PREFER TO KEEP THAT UNDER MY HAT.
MAYES edmonton journal

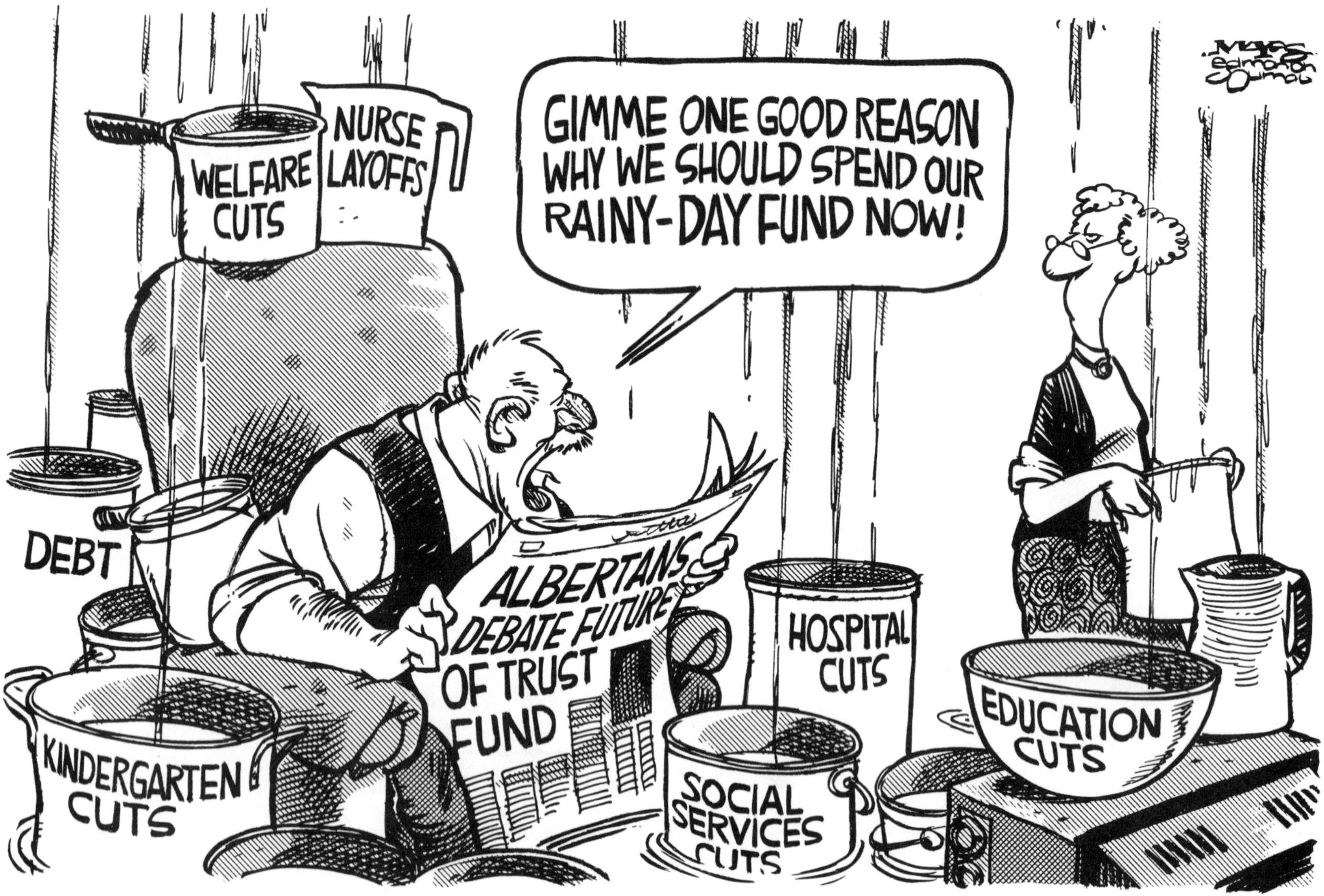

GIMME ONE GOOD REASON WHY WE SHOULD SPEND OUR RAINY-DAY FUND NOW!
WELFARE CUTS
NURSE LAYOFFS
DEBT
ALBERTANS DEBATE FUTURE OF TRUST FUND
HOSPITAL CUTS
EDUCATION CUTS
KINDERGARTEN CUTS
SOCIAL SERVICES CUTS

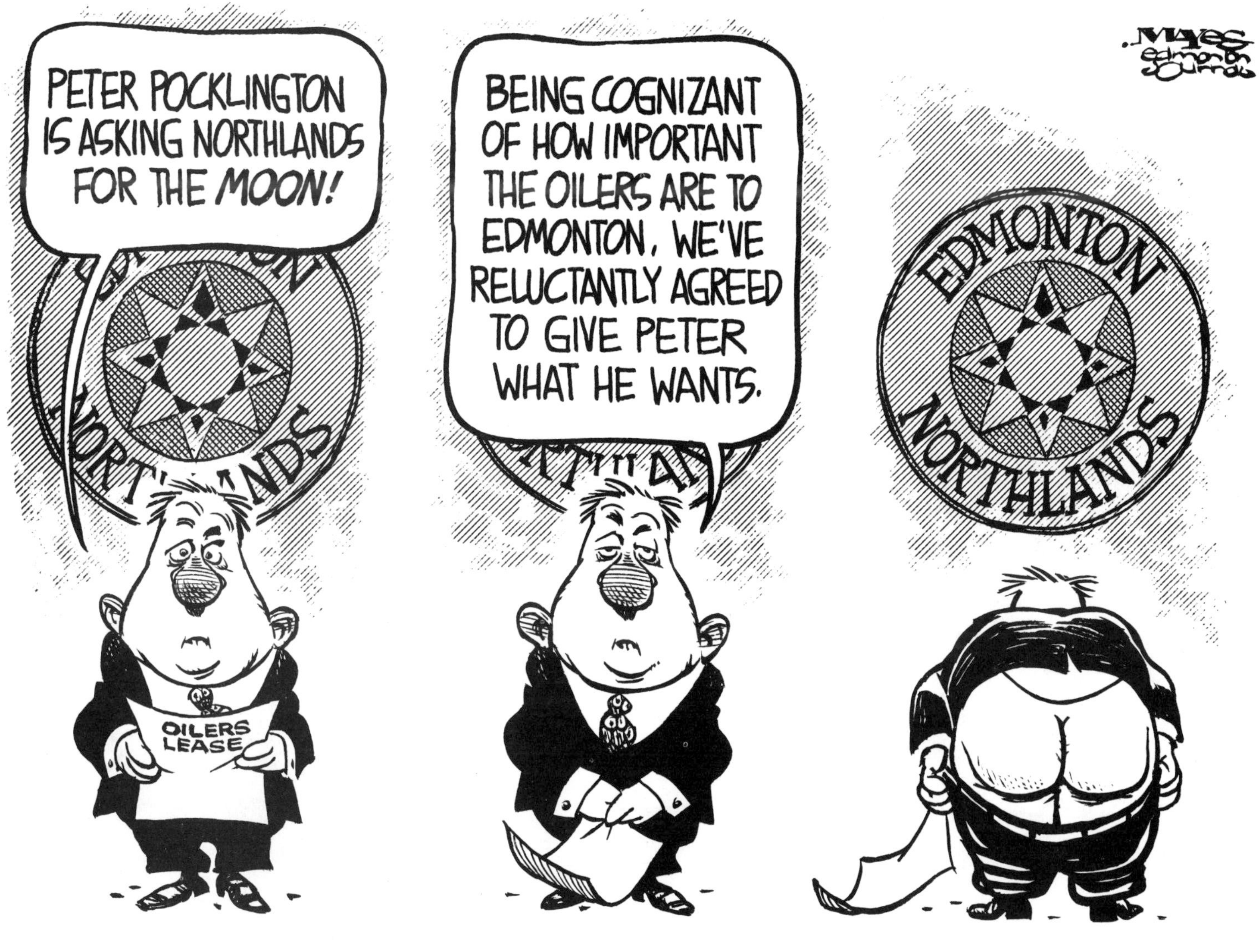
PETER POCKLINGTON IS ASKING NORTHLANDS FOR THE *MOON!*
BEING COGNIZANT OF HOW IMPORTANT THE OILERS ARE TO EDMONTON, WE'VE RELUCTANTLY AGREED TO GIVE PETER WHAT HE WANTS.
EDMONTON NORTHLANDS
OILERS LEASE
Mayes Edmonton Journal

Peter Pocklington threatens to move the Oilers unless he gets Northlands Coliseum for free.

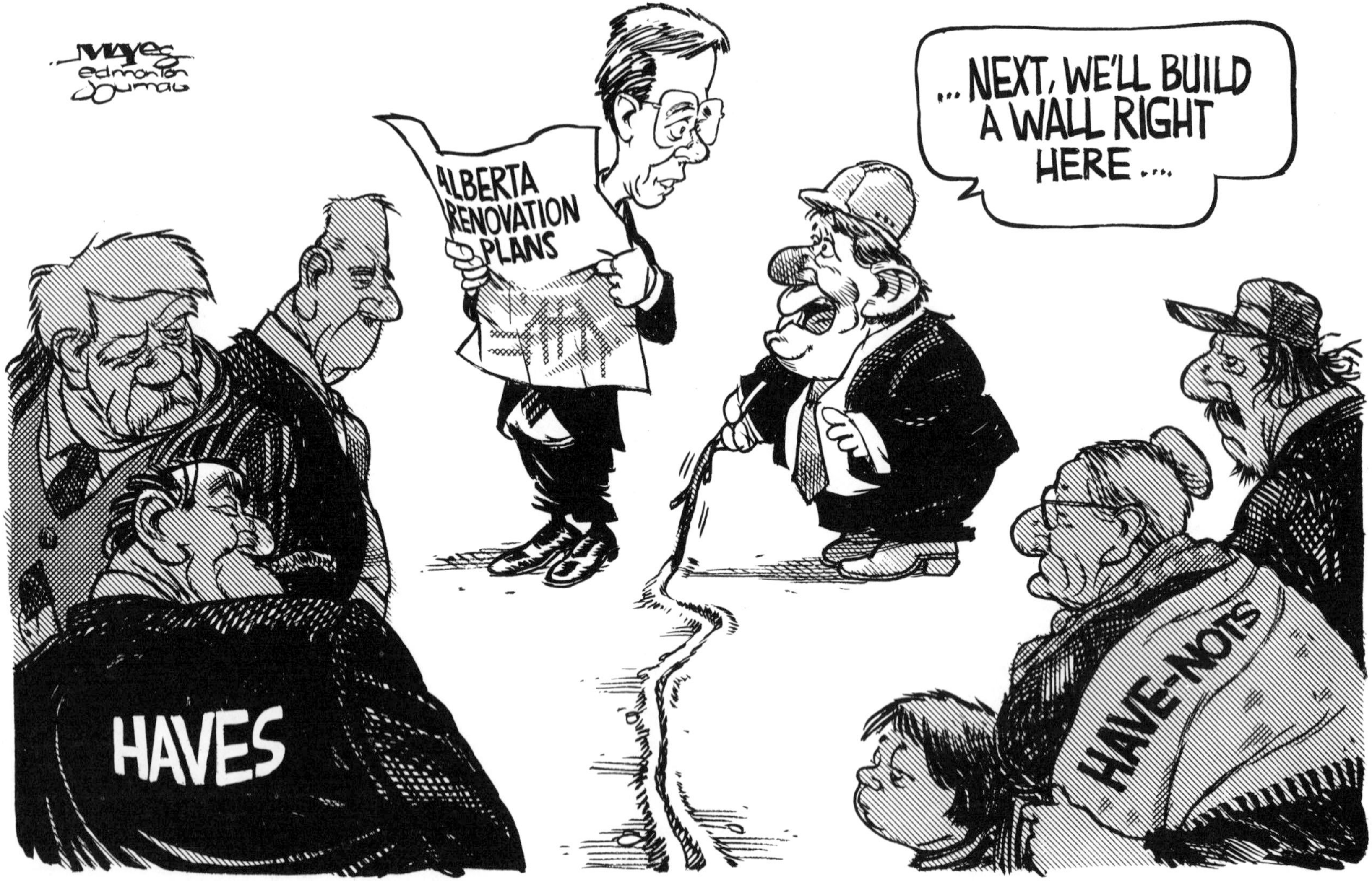
MAYES edmonton journal
ALBERTA RENOVATION PLANS
...NEXT, WE'LL BUILD A WALL RIGHT HERE....
HAVES
HAVE-NOTS

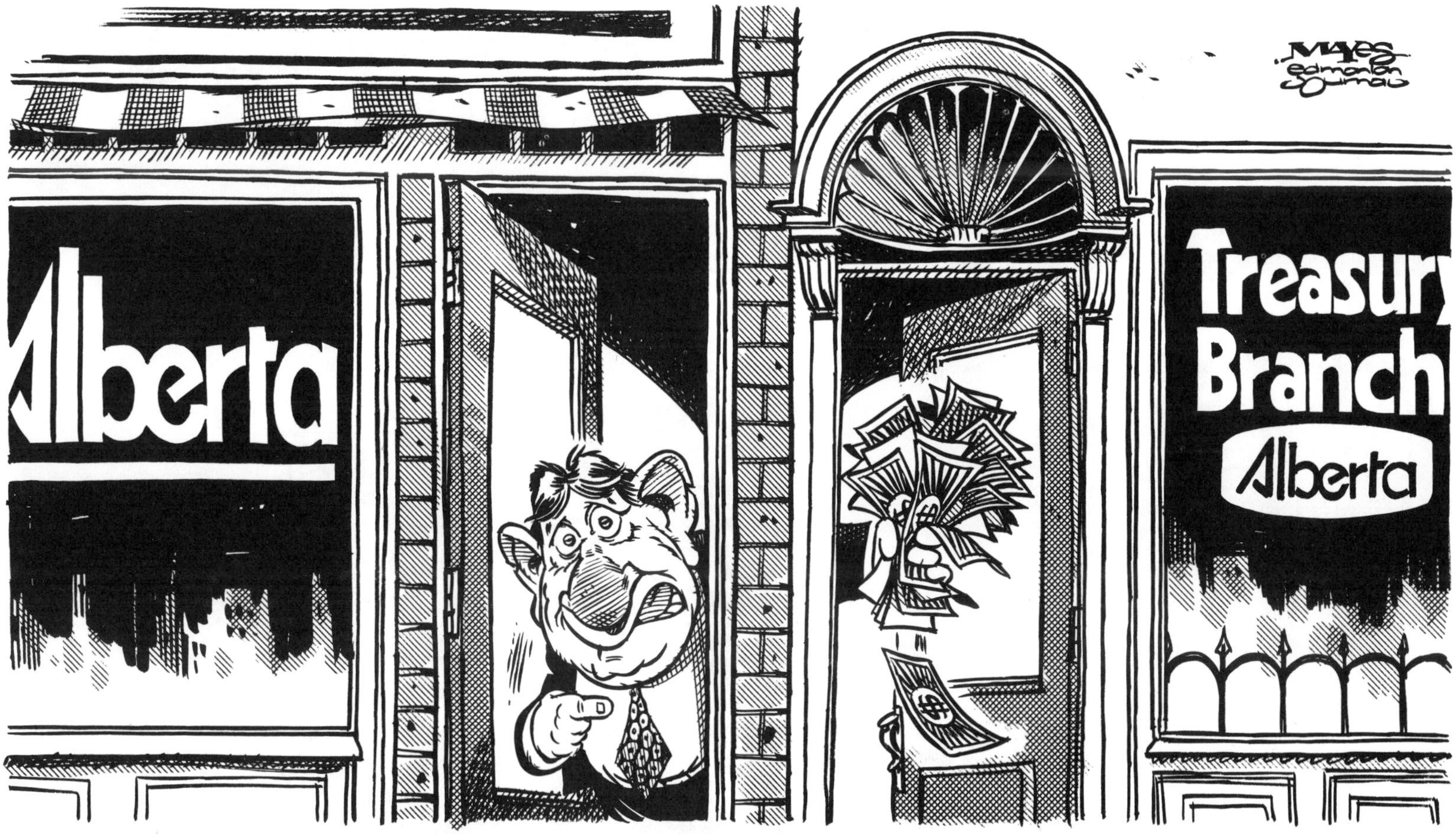
MAYES edmonton journal
Alberta
Treasury Branch
Alberta

"SORRY, WE DON'T PROVIDE LOAN GUARANTEES TO PRIVATE BUSINESS ANY MORE.....
HOWEVER, YOU MIGHT WANT TO TRY NEXT DOOR."

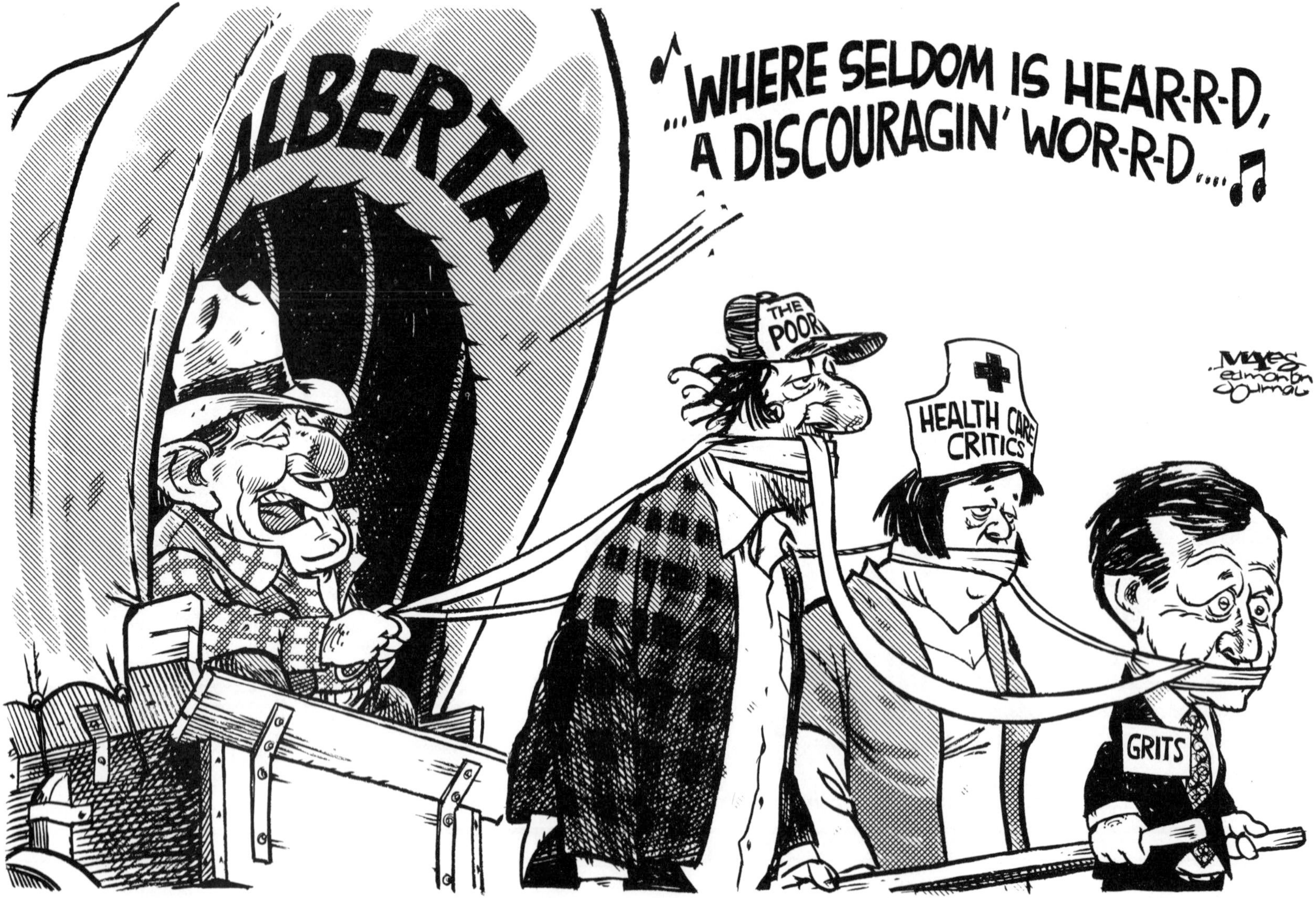

ALBERTA
...WHERE SELDOM IS HEAR-R-D, A DISCOURAGIN' WOR-R-D....
THE POOR
HEALTH CARE CRITICS
GRITS
MAYES EDMONTON JOURNAL

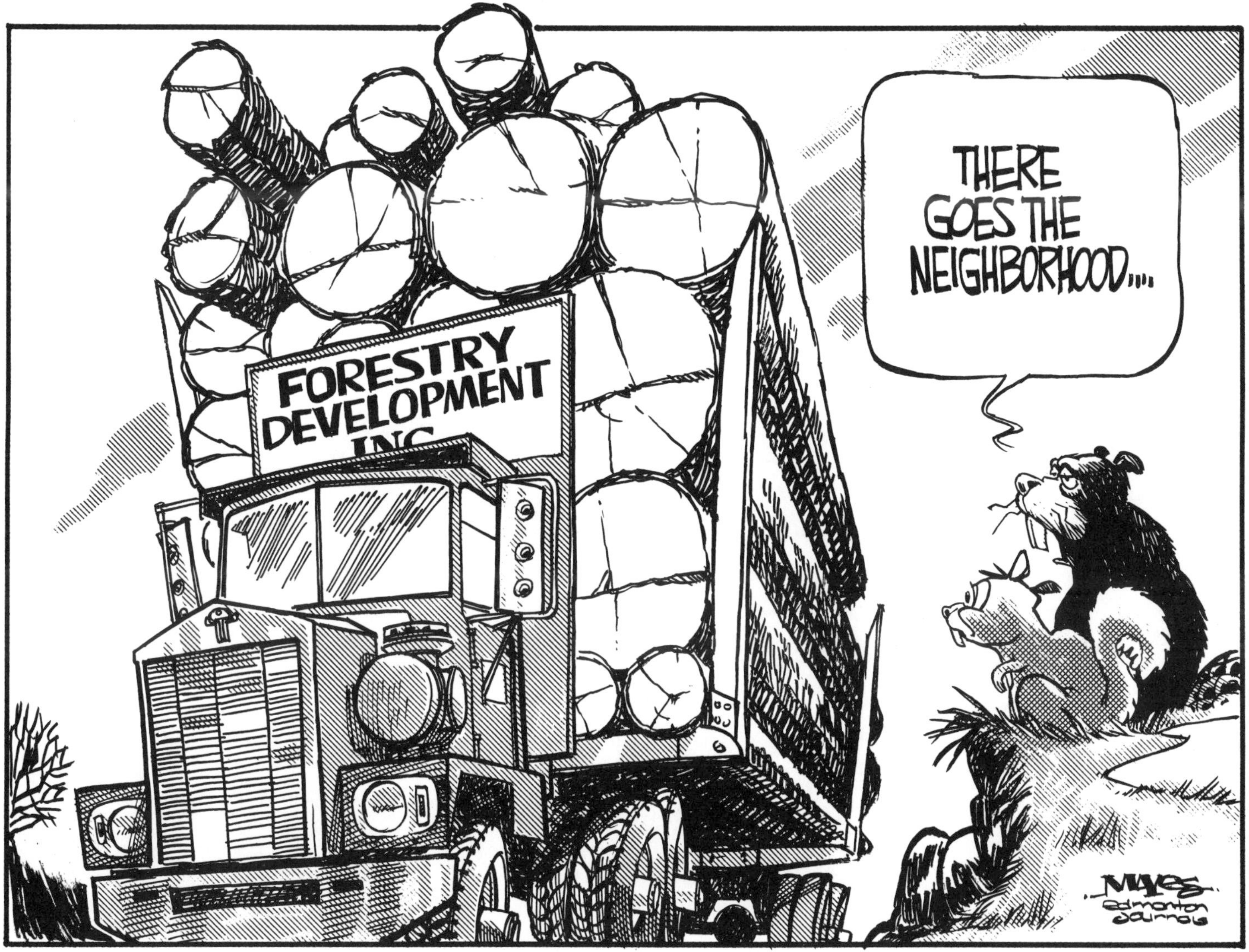
FORESTRY DEVELOPMENT INC
THERE GOES THE NEIGHBORHOOD....
MAYES Edmonton Journal

MY CANADA INCLUDES . . .

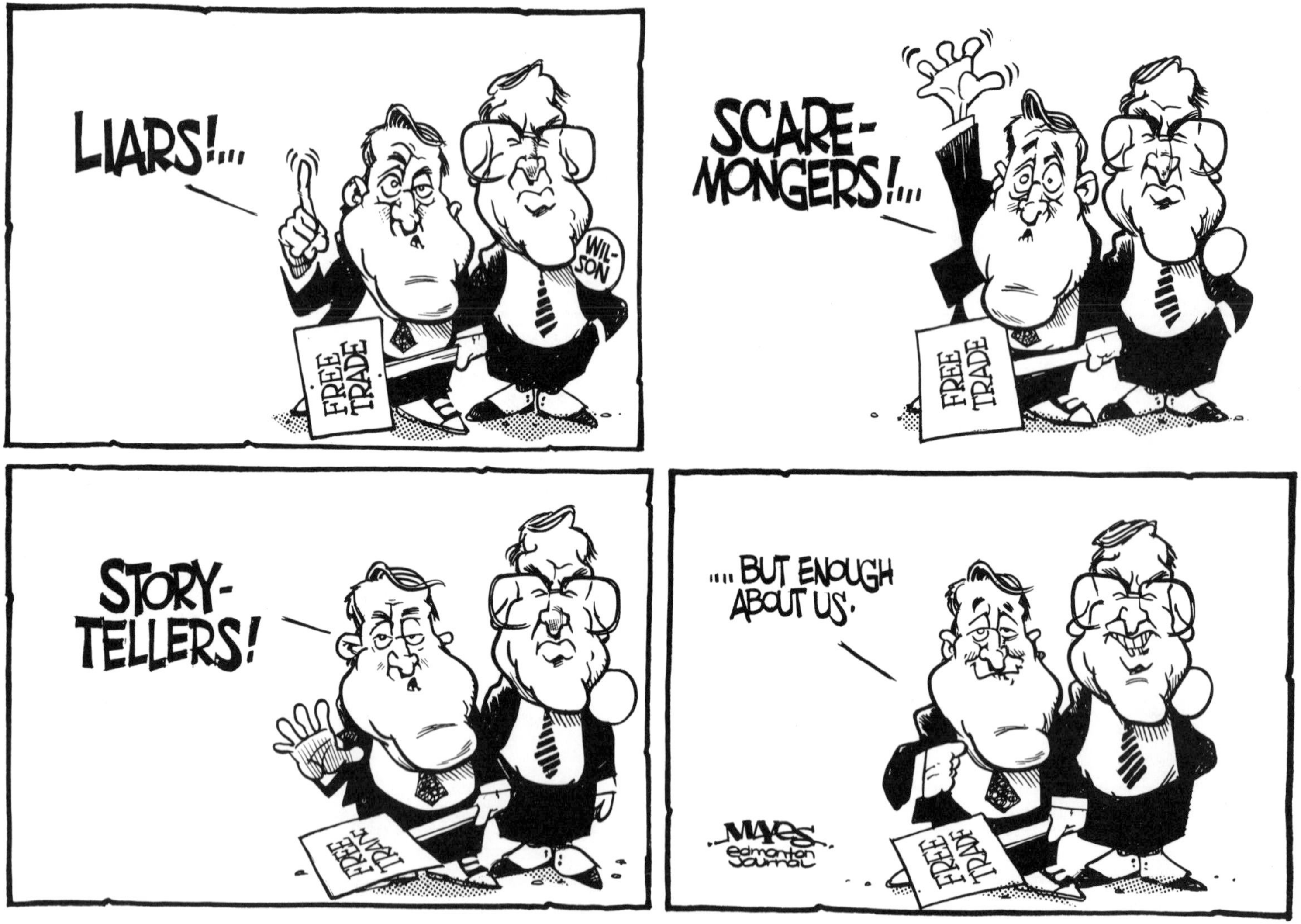
LIARS!...
WIL-SON
FREE TRADE
SCARE-MONGERS!...
FREE TRADE
STORY-TELLERS!
FREE TRADE
.... BUT ENOUGH ABOUT US.
FREE TRADE
MAYES
edmonton journal

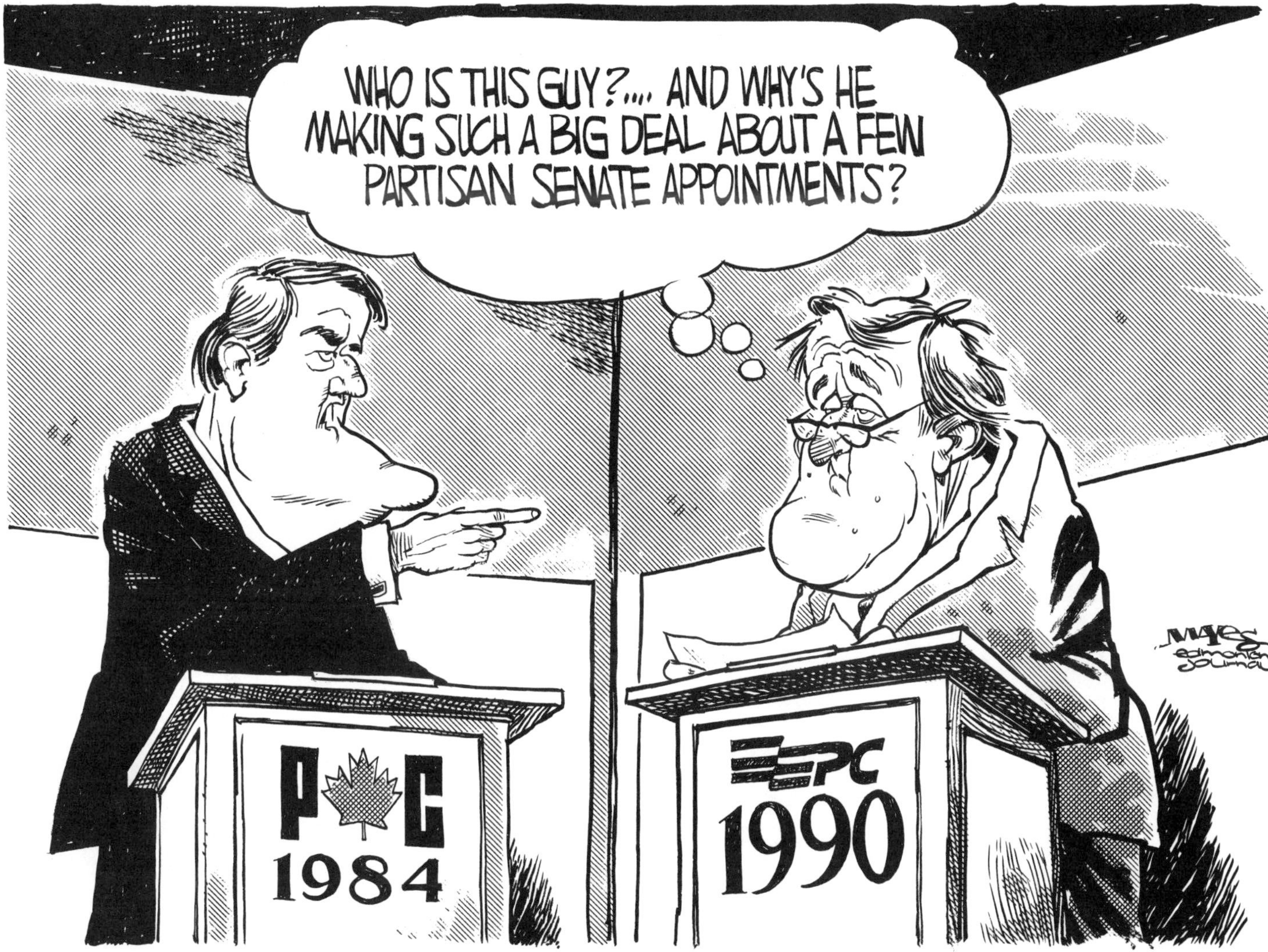
WHO IS THIS GUY?.... AND WHY'S HE MAKING SUCH A BIG DEAL ABOUT A FEW PARTISAN SENATE APPOINTMENTS?
PC
1984
PC
1990
MAYES
Edmonton Journal

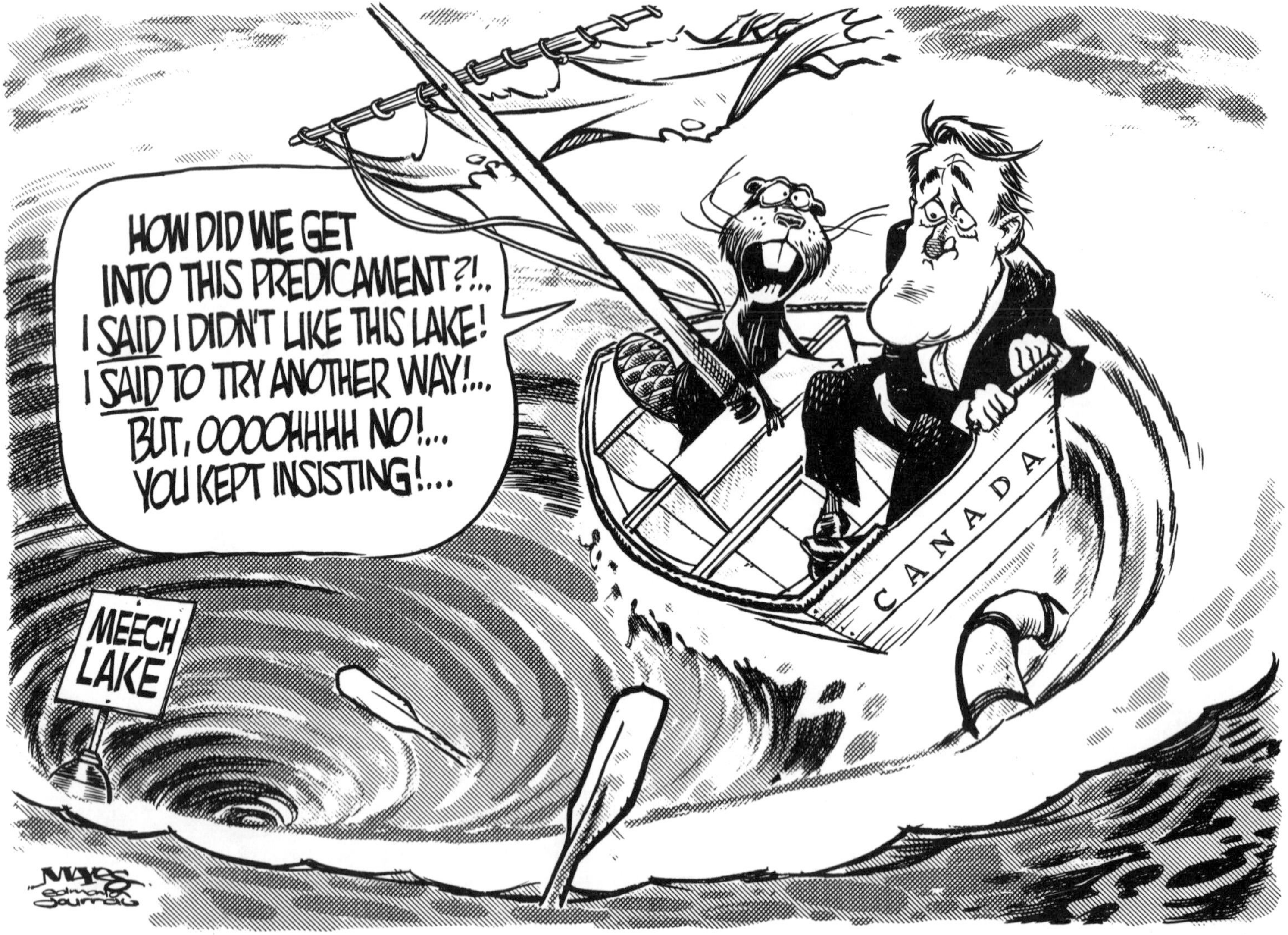
HOW DID WE GET INTO THIS PREDICAMENT?!... I SAID I DIDN'T LIKE THIS LAKE! I SAID TO TRY ANOTHER WAY!... BUT, OOOOHHHH NO!... YOU KEPT INSISTING!...
CANADA
MEECH LAKE
MAYES edmonton journal

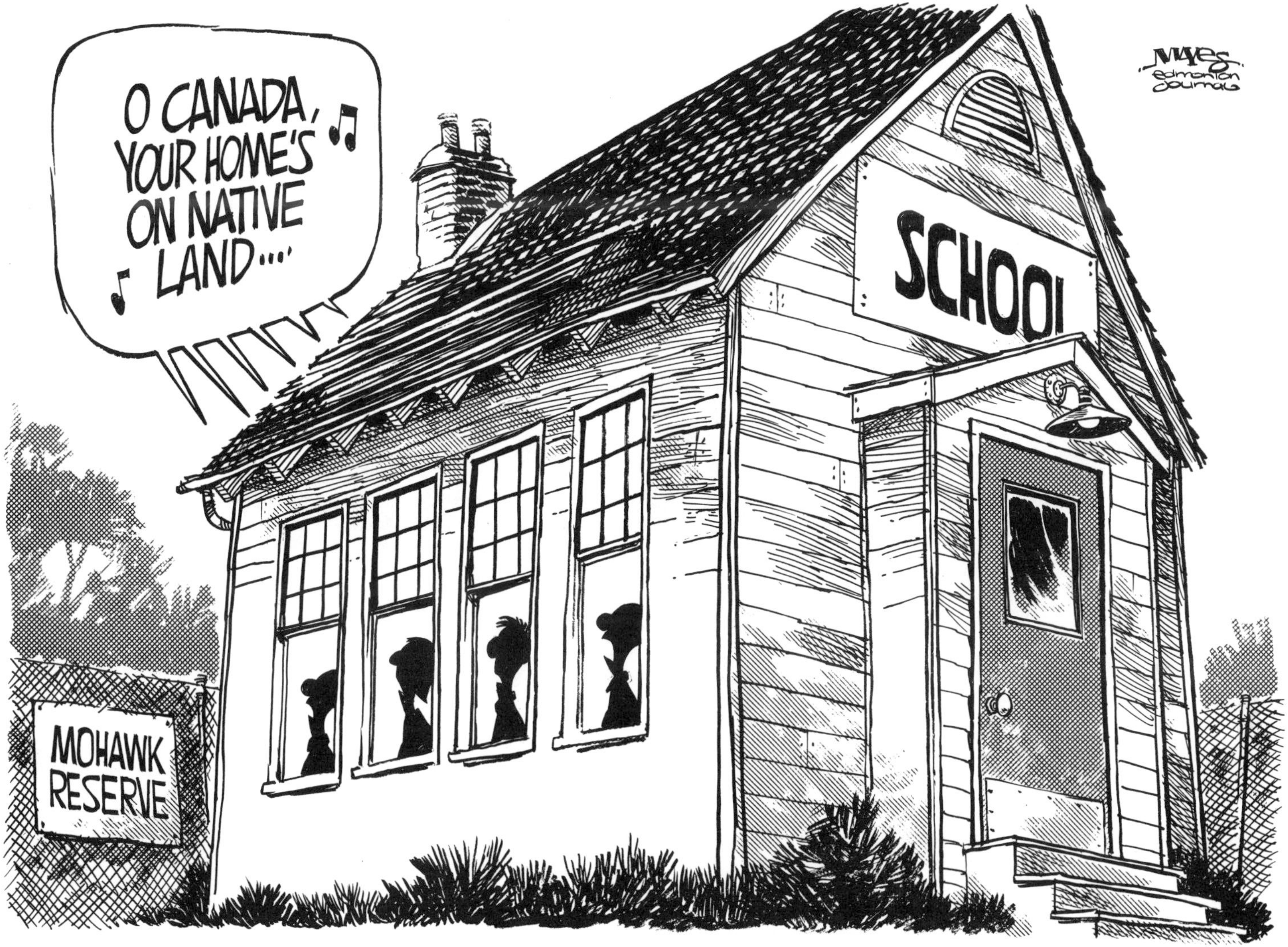
O CANADA, YOUR HOME'S ON NATIVE LAND....
SCHOOl
MOHAWK RESERVE
edmonton journal

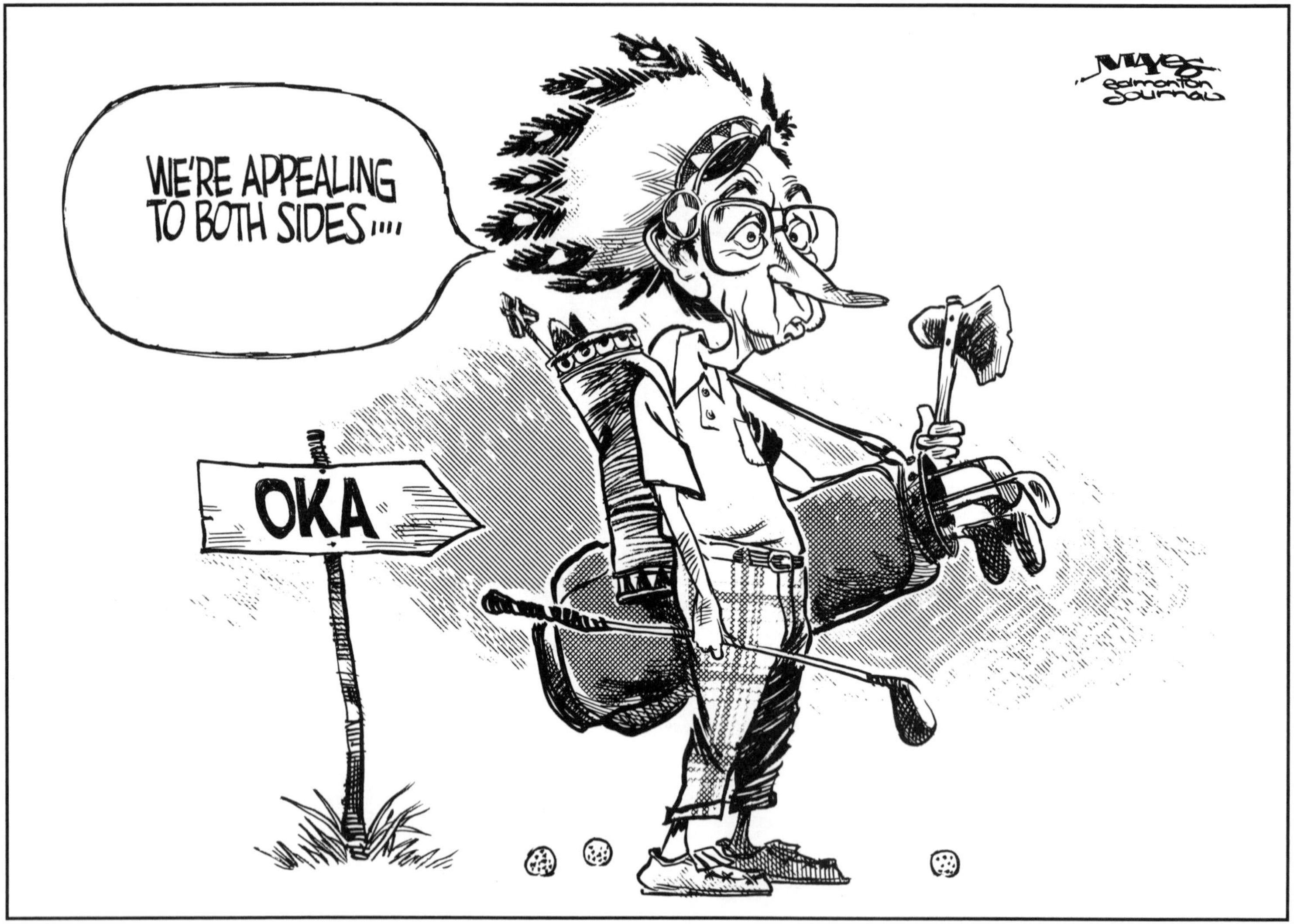
WE'RE APPEALING TO BOTH SIDES....
OKA
MAYES
edmonton journal

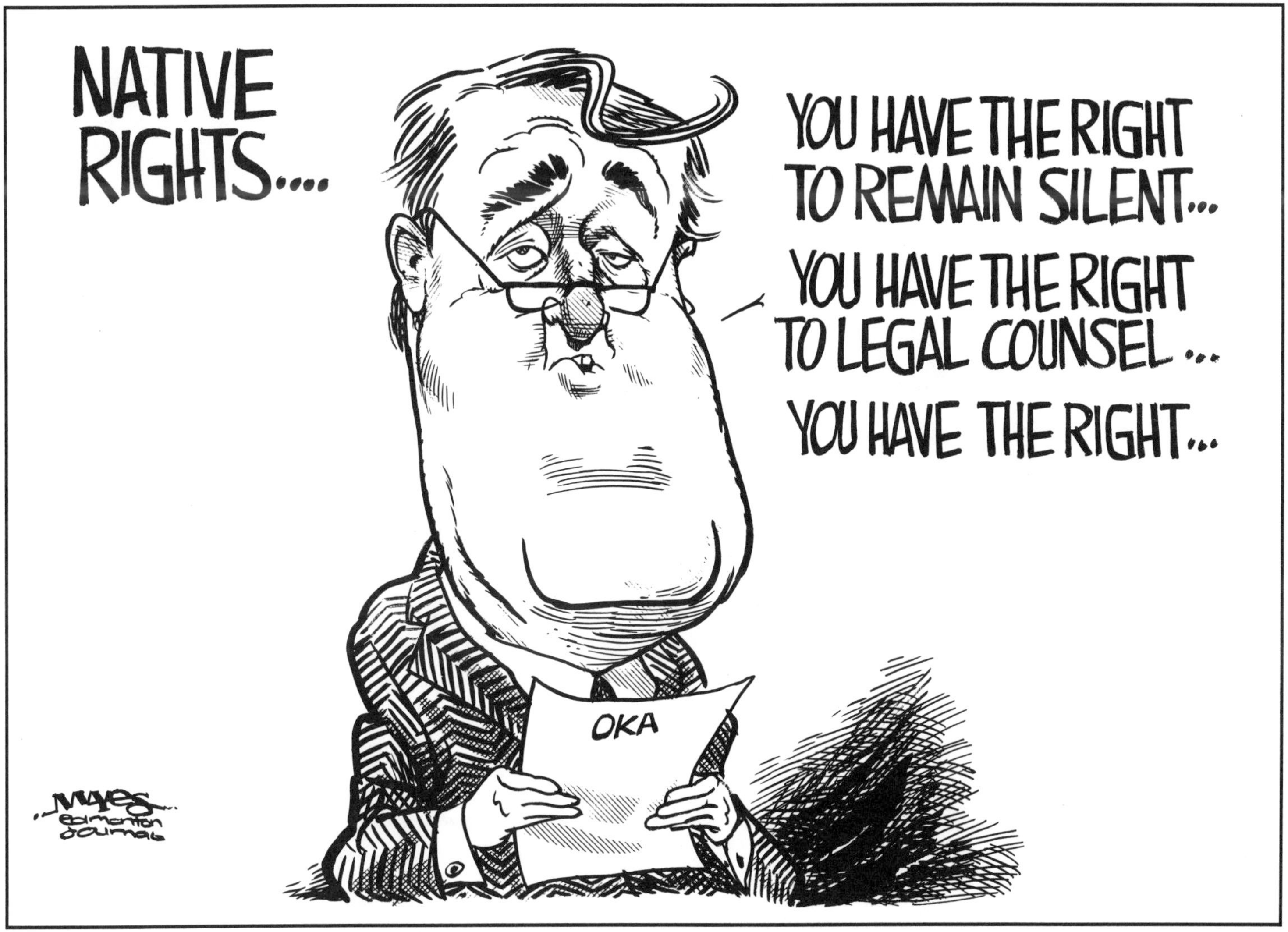
NATIVE RIGHTS....
YOU HAVE THE RIGHT TO REMAIN SILENT...
YOU HAVE THE RIGHT TO LEGAL COUNSEL ...
YOU HAVE THE RIGHT...
OKA
MAYES
Edmonton Journal

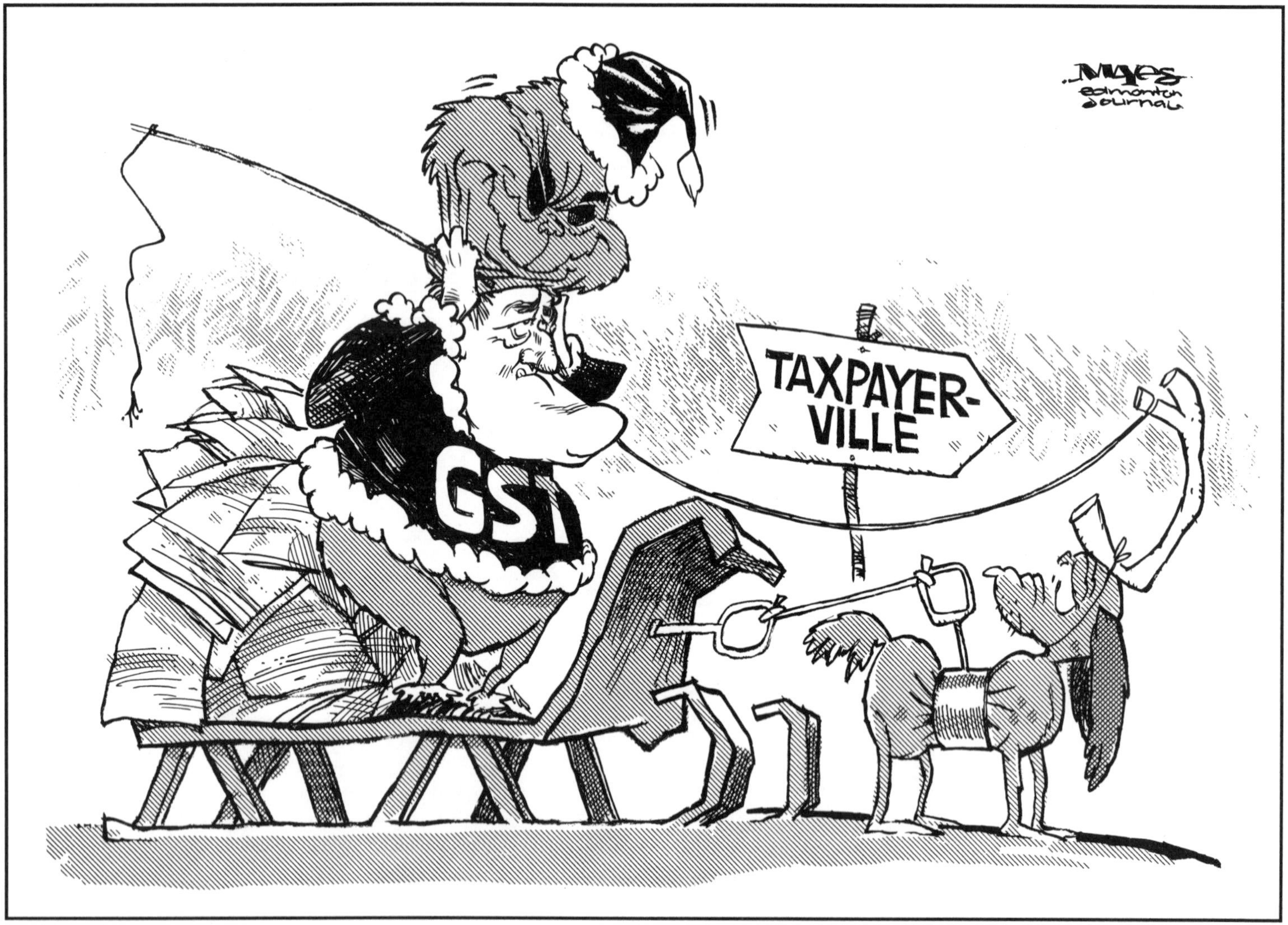

MAYES
edmonton journal
TAXPAYER-
VILLE
GST

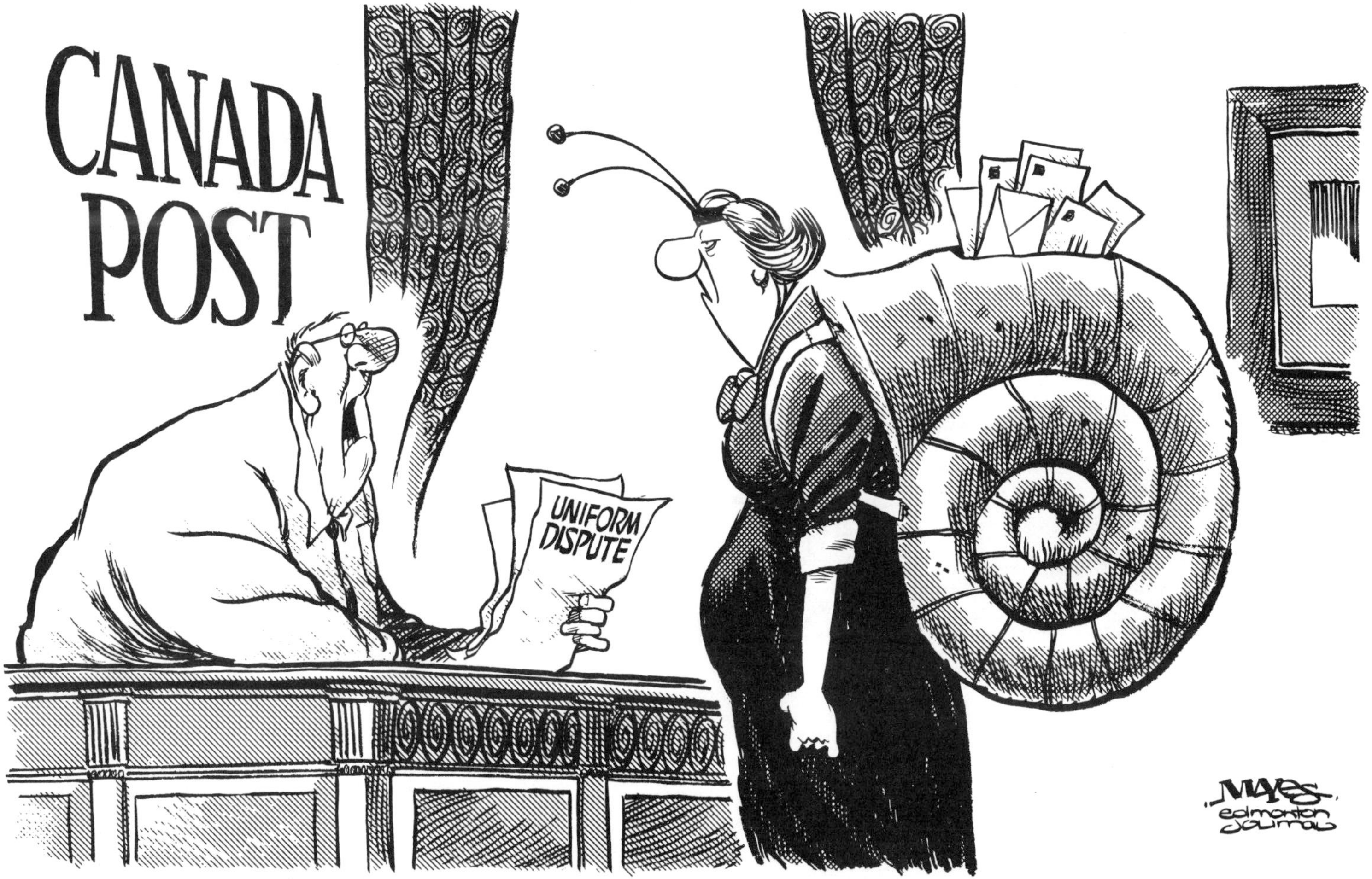
CANADA POST
UNIFORM DISPUTE
MAYES edmonton journal

" LOOK SMITH .... YOU'RE THE ONE WHO INSISTED ON UNIFORMS MORE BEFITTING A POSTAL WORKER ...."

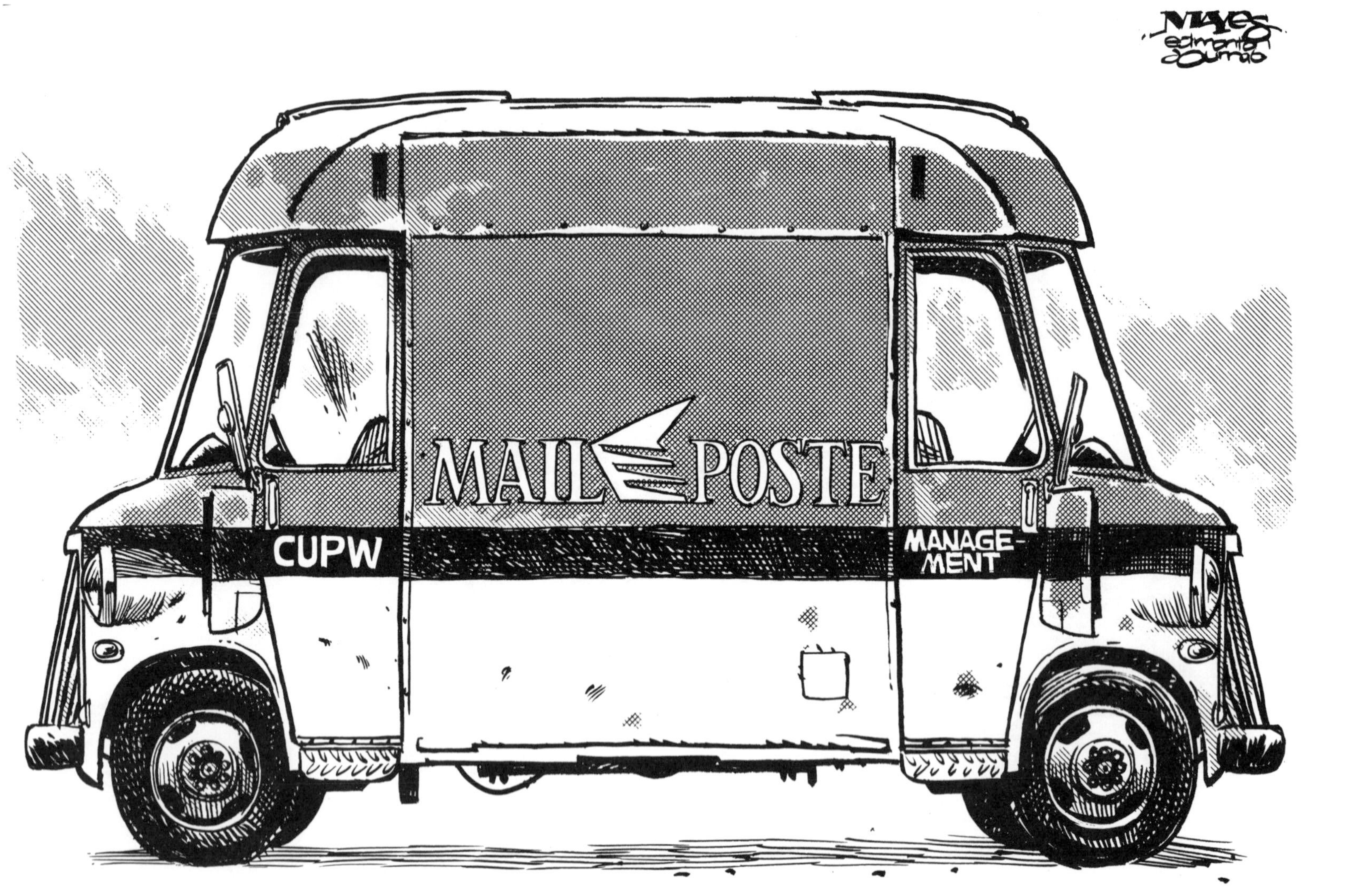
MAIL POSTE
CUPW
MANAGE-
MENT
MAYES
edmonton
journal

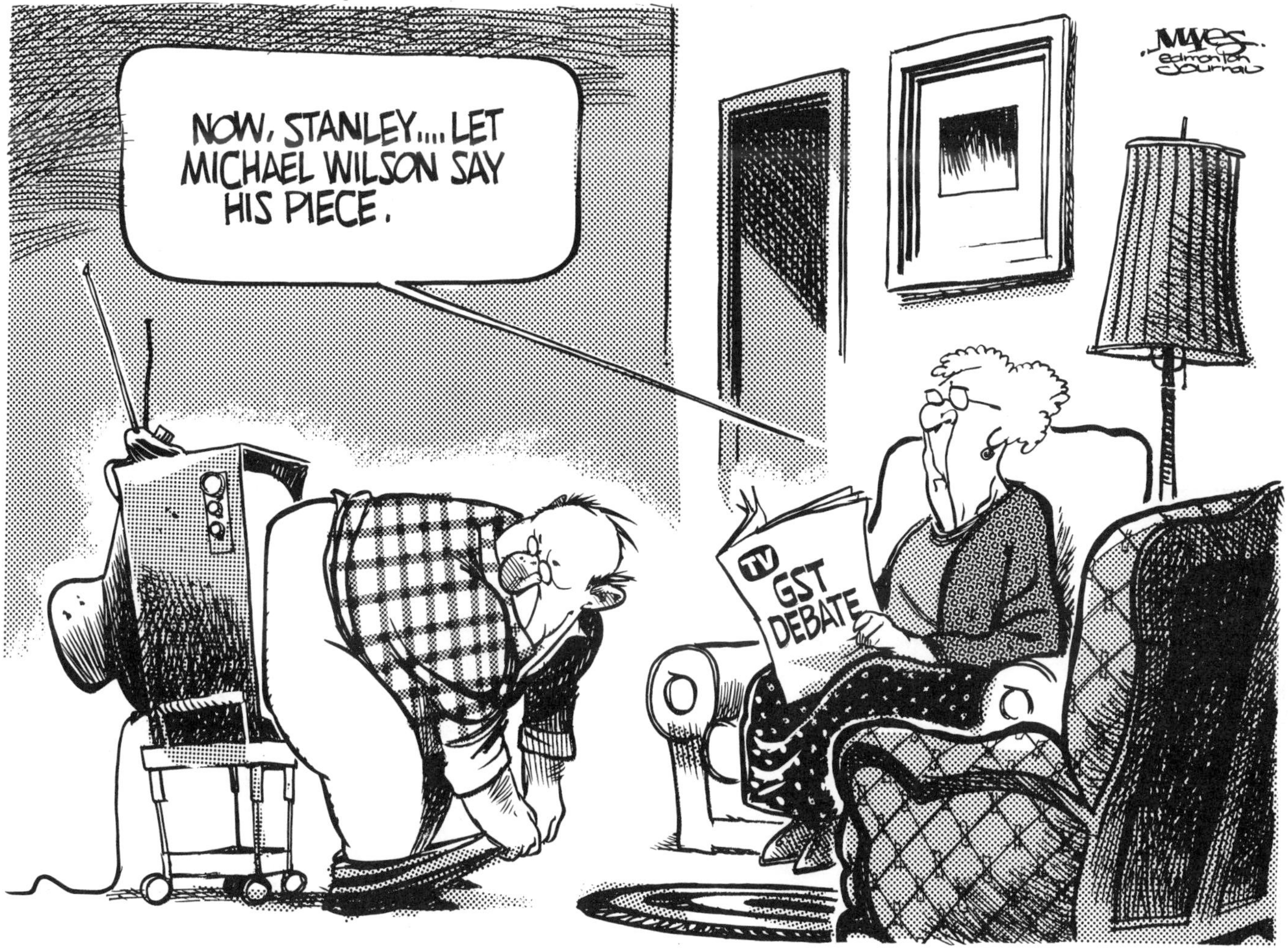

NOW, STANLEY.... LET MICHAEL WILSON SAY HIS PIECE.
TV GST DEBATE
MAYES edmonton Journal

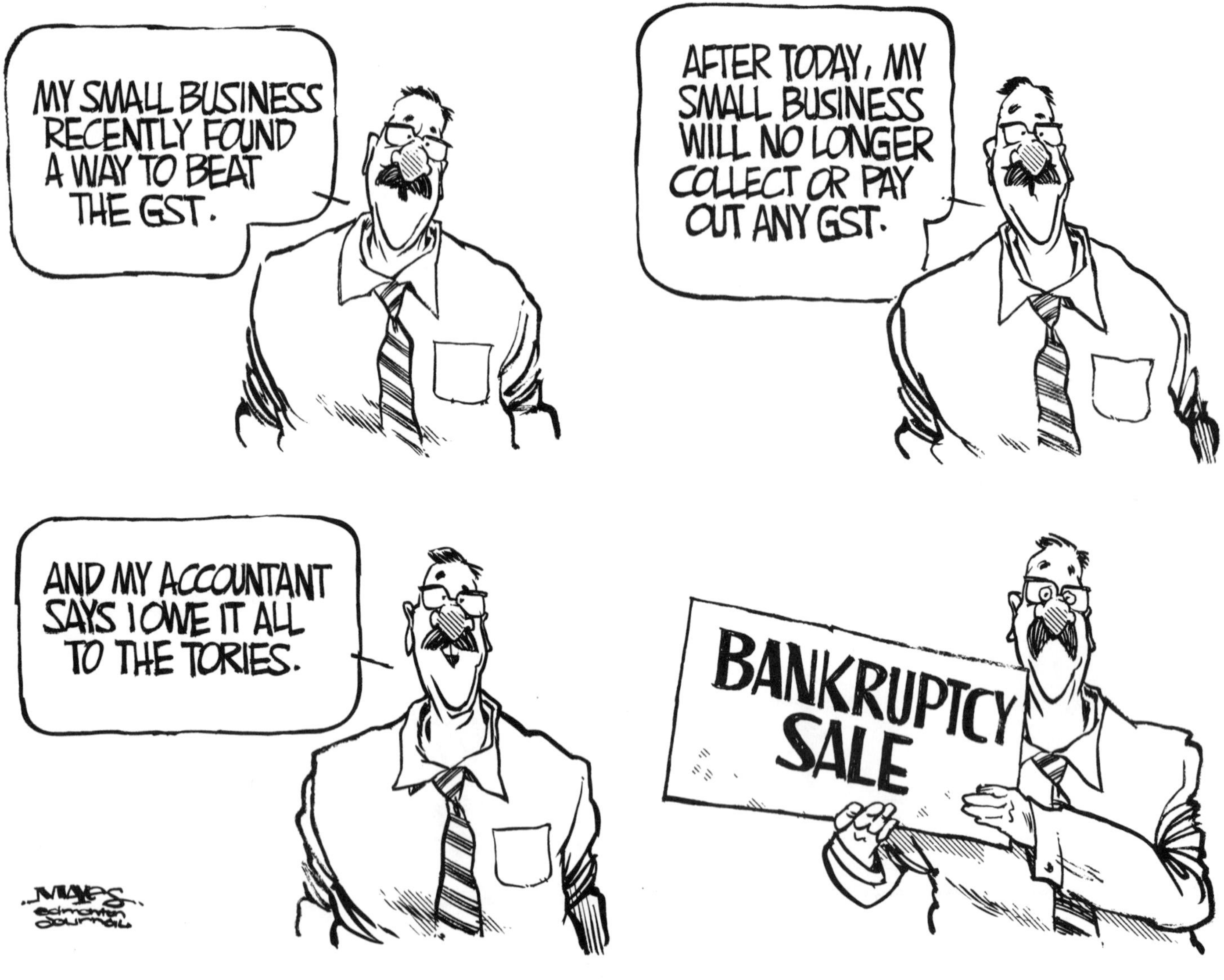
MY SMALL BUSINESS RECENTLY FOUND A WAY TO BEAT THE GST.
AFTER TODAY, MY SMALL BUSINESS WILL NO LONGER COLLECT OR PAY OUT ANY GST.
AND MY ACCOUNTANT SAYS I OWE IT ALL TO THE TORIES.
BANKRUPTCY SALE
MAYES
edmonton journal

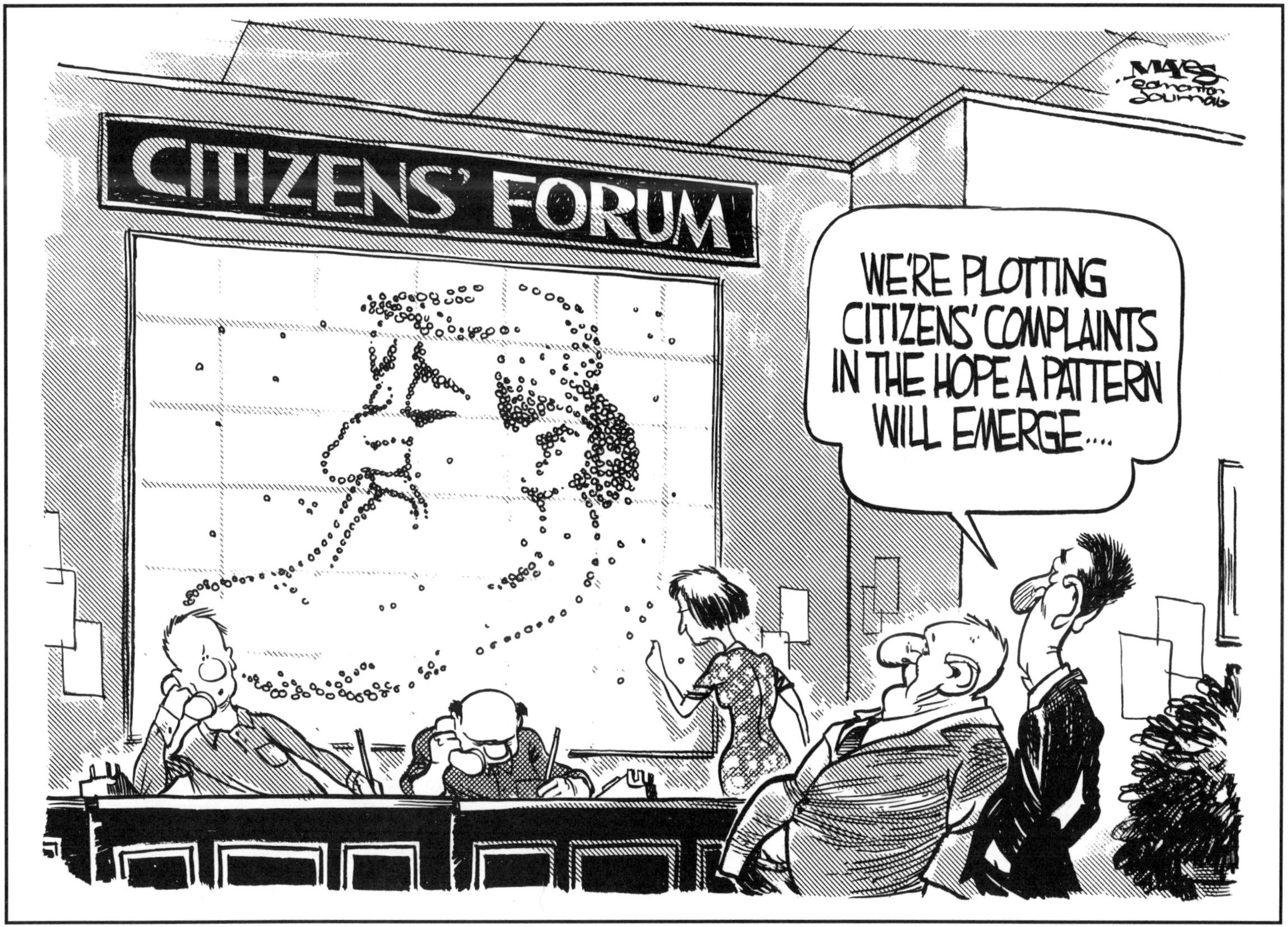
CITIZENS' FORUM
WE'RE PLOTTING CITIZENS' COMPLAINTS IN THE HOPE A PATTERN WILL EMERGE....
MAYES Edmonton Journal

The Spicer Commission finds a "fury in the land."

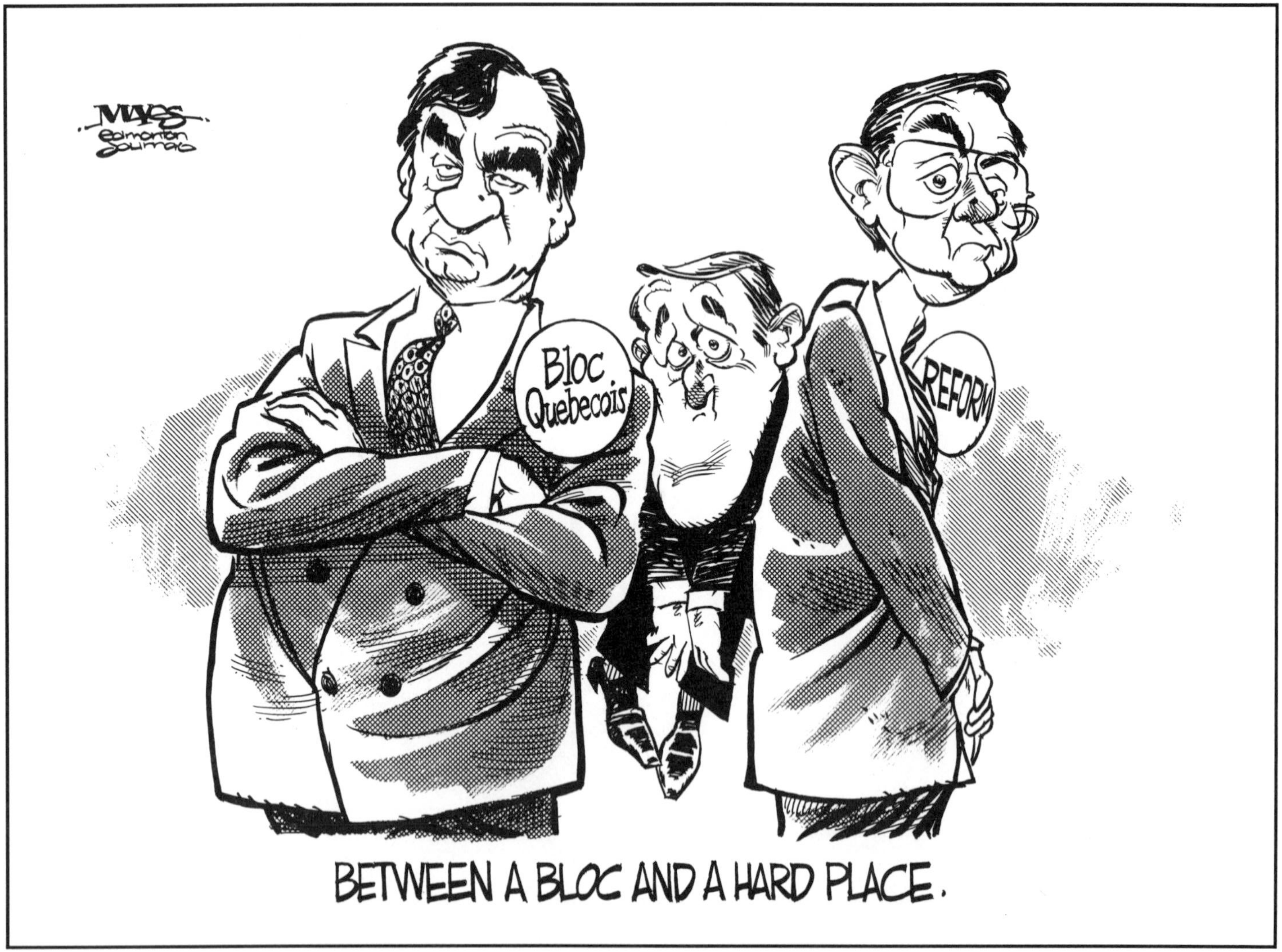
MAYES edmonton journal
Bloc Quebecois
REFORM
BETWEEN A BLOC AND A HARD PLACE.

New political forces squeeze out the Tories.

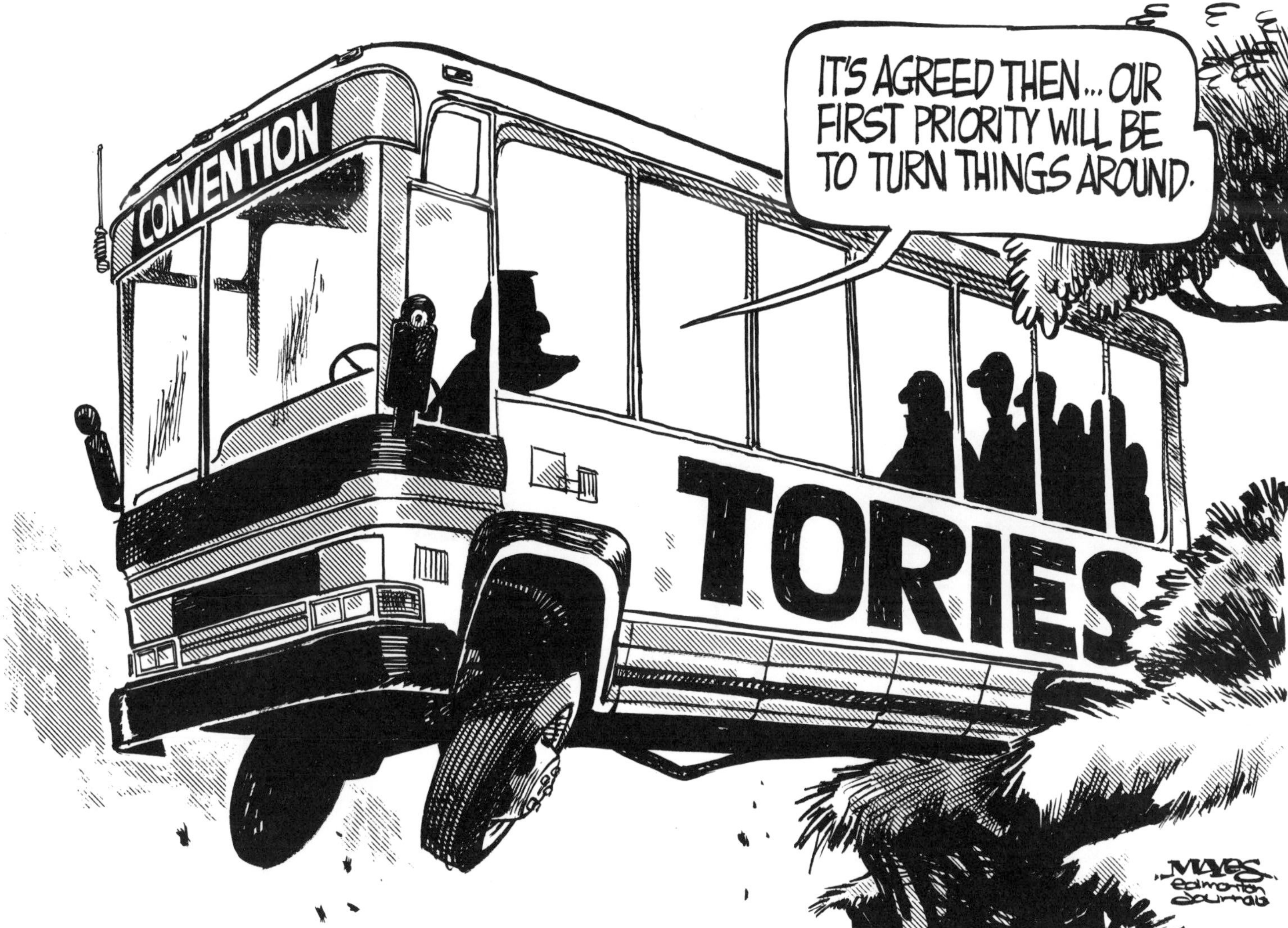
CONVENTION
IT'S AGREED THEN... OUR FIRST PRIORITY WILL BE TO TURN THINGS AROUND.
TORIES
MAYES
Edmonton Journal

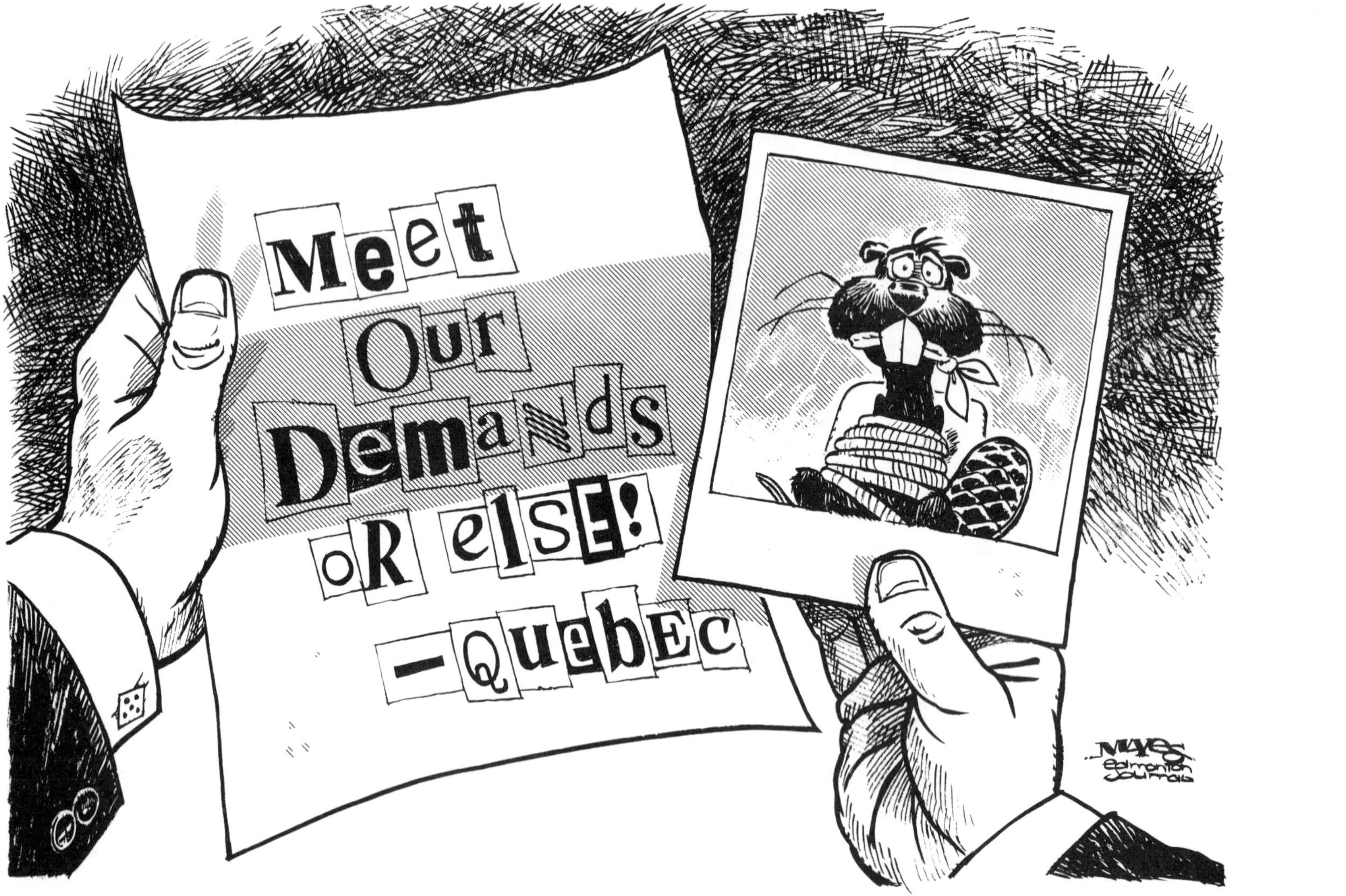
Meet Our Demands or else!
—Quebec
Mayes
Edmonton Journal

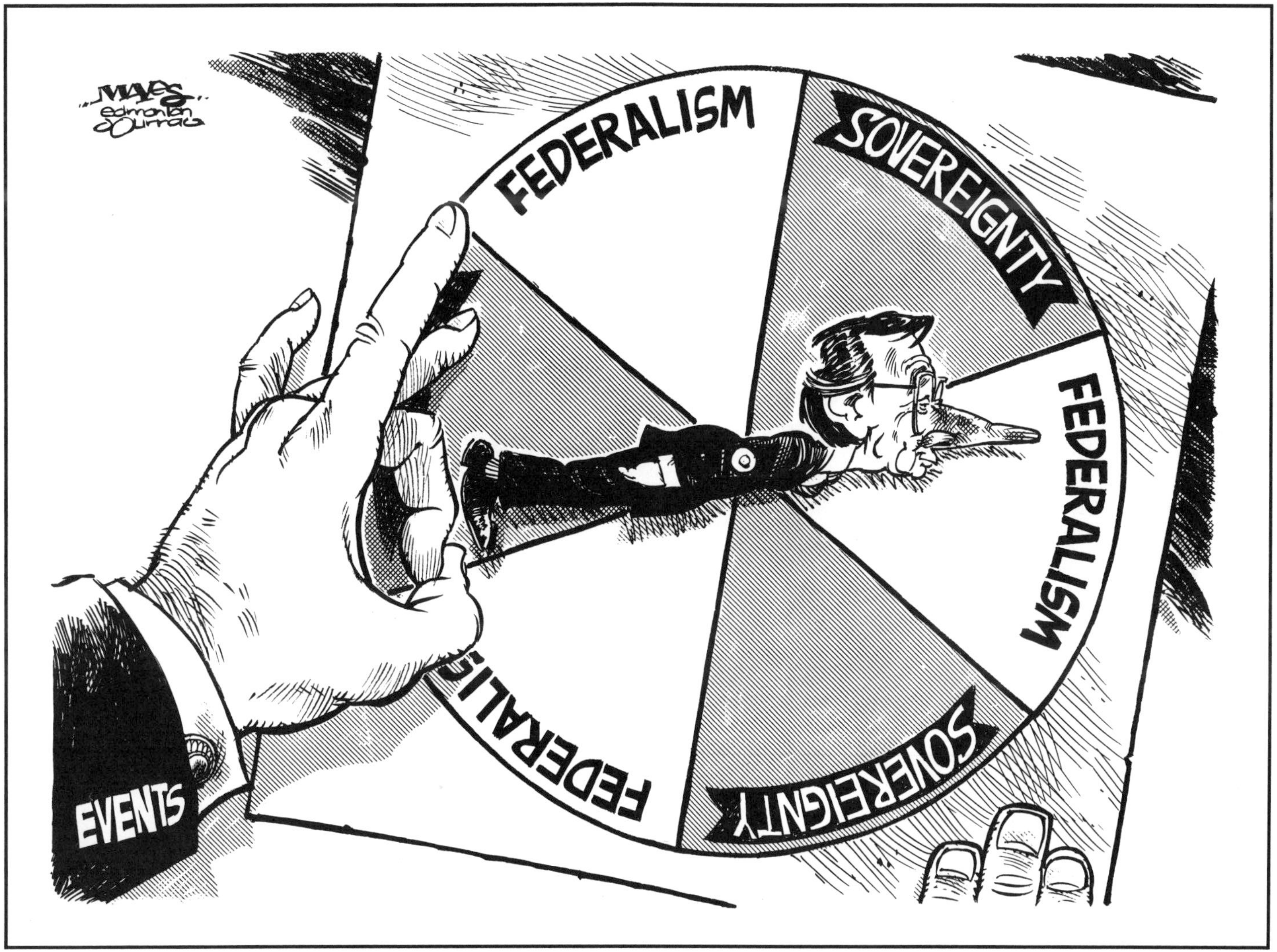
FEDERALISM
SOVEREIGNTY
FEDERALISM
SOVEREIGNTY
FEDERALIS
EVENTS

Bourassa makes his position clear.

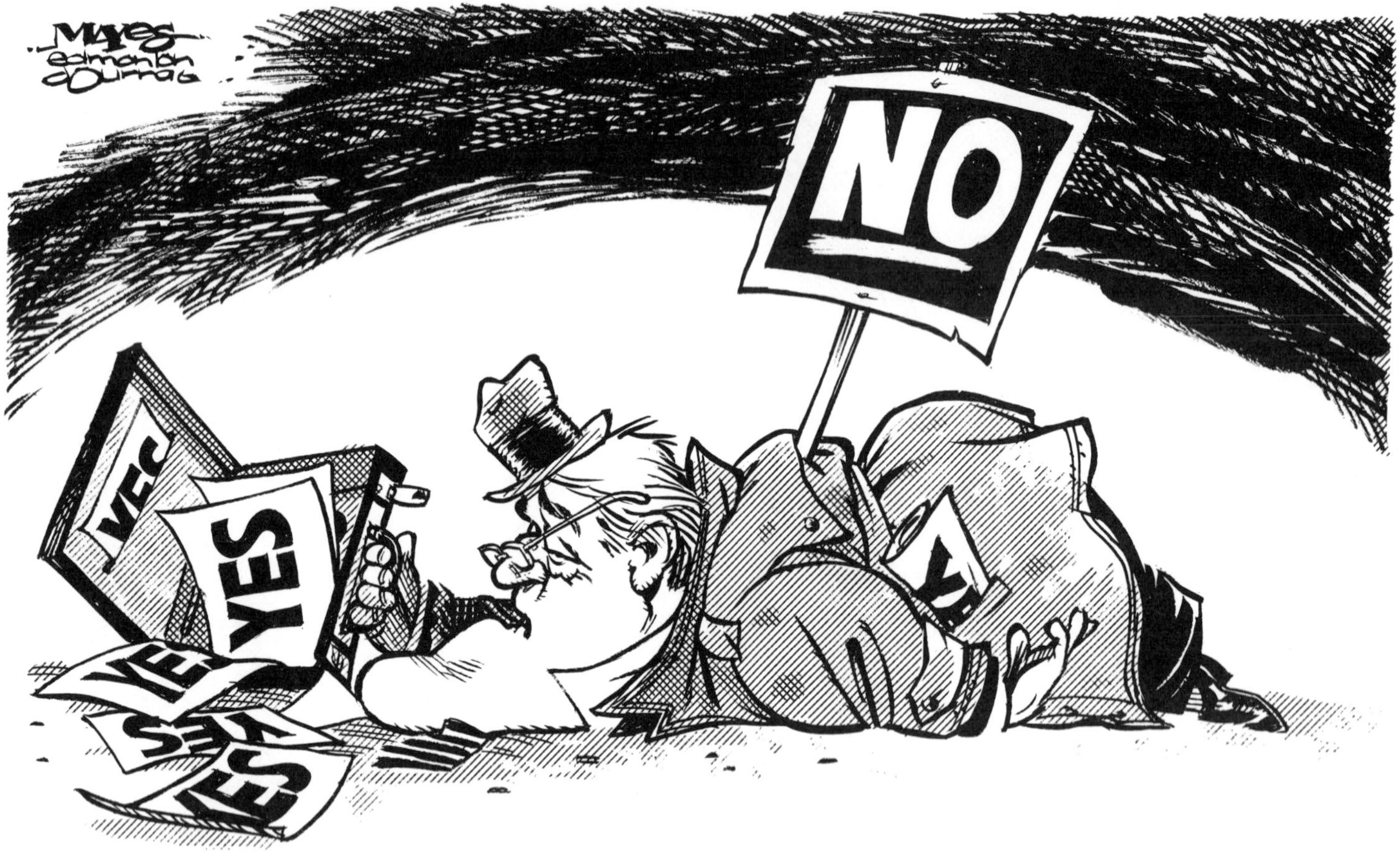
NO
YES
YES

Death of a Salesman.

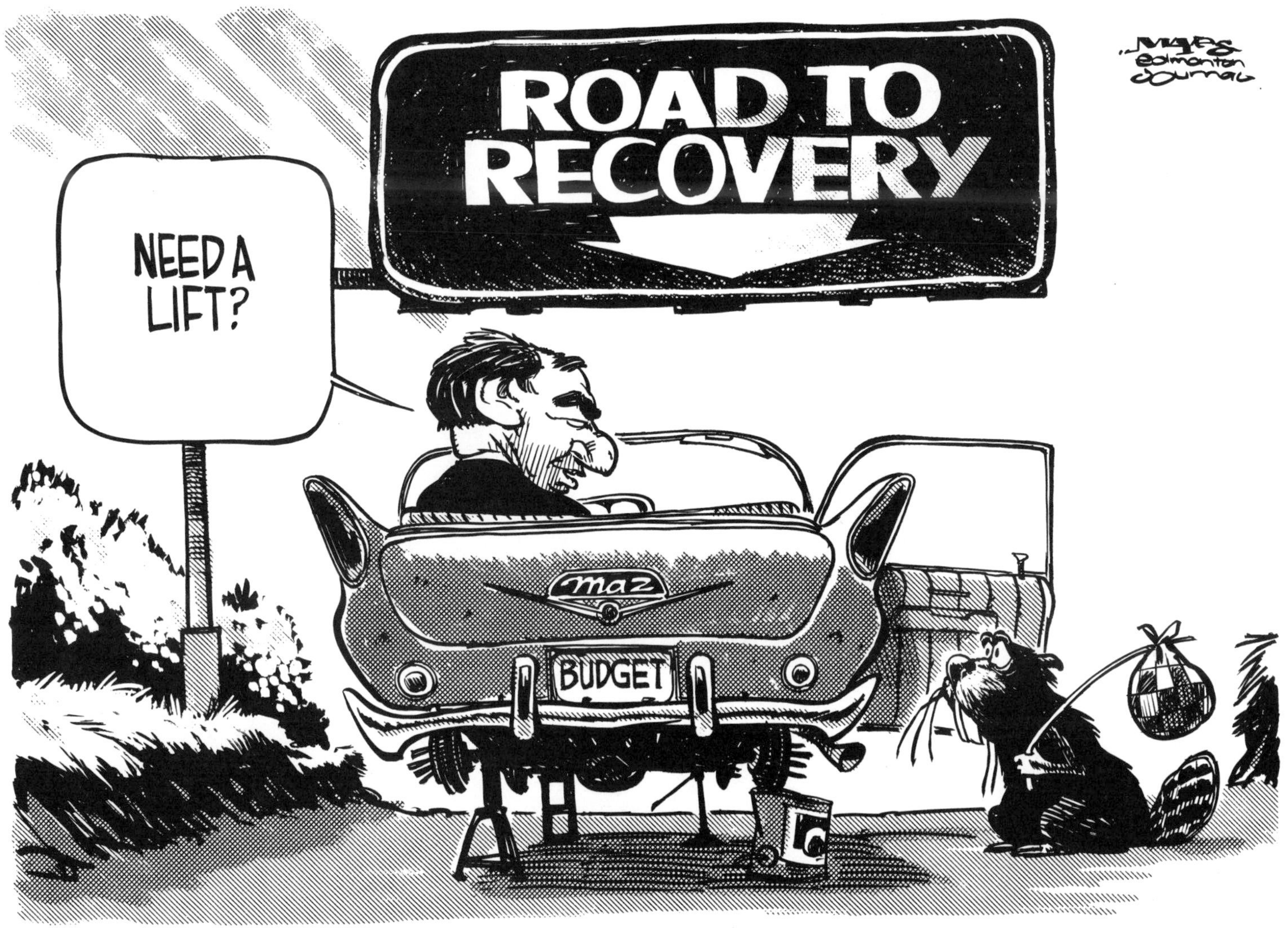
ROAD TO RECOVERY
NEED A LIFT?
MAZ
BUDGET

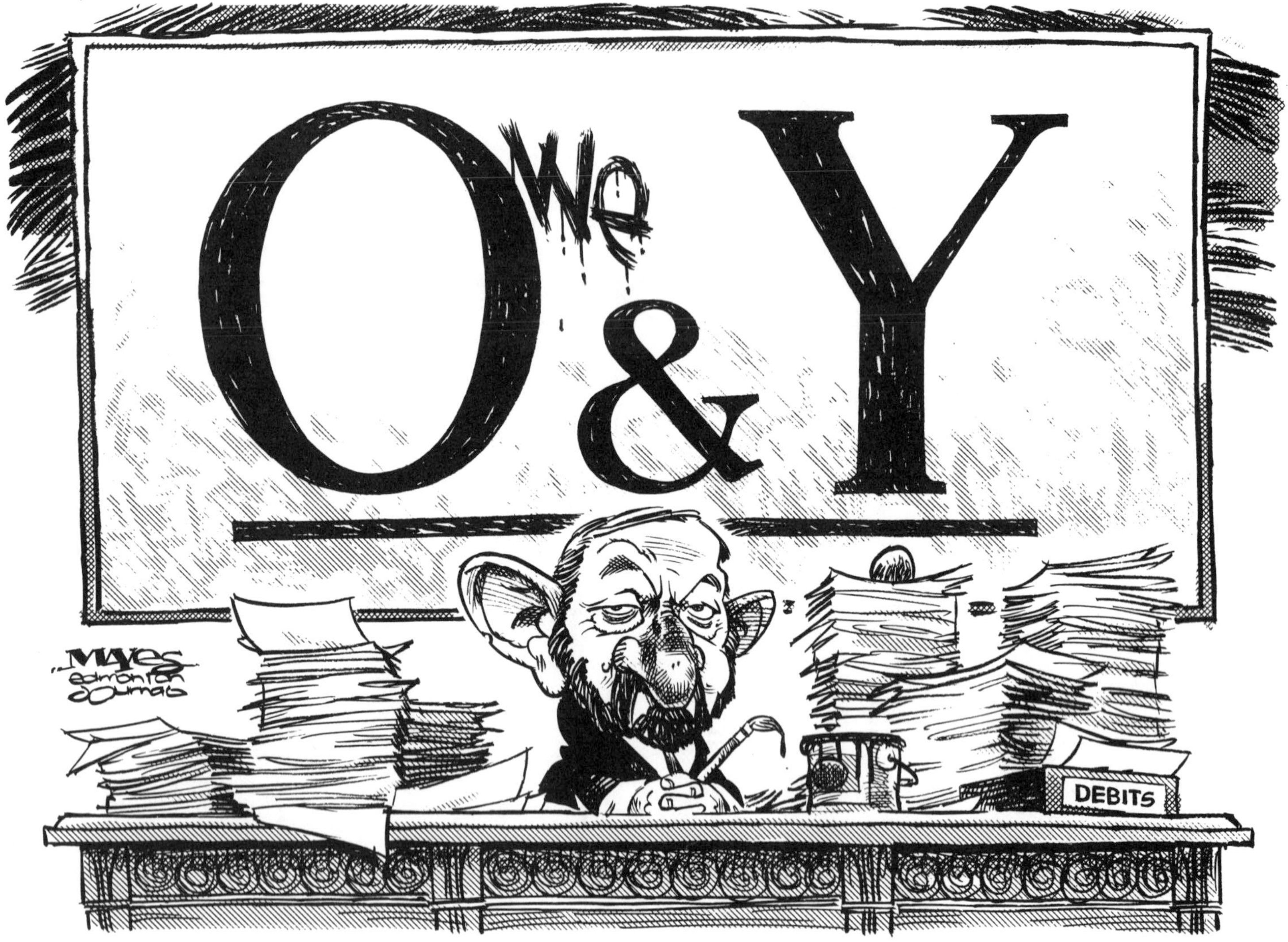
O we & Y
MAYES
edmonton journal
DEBITS

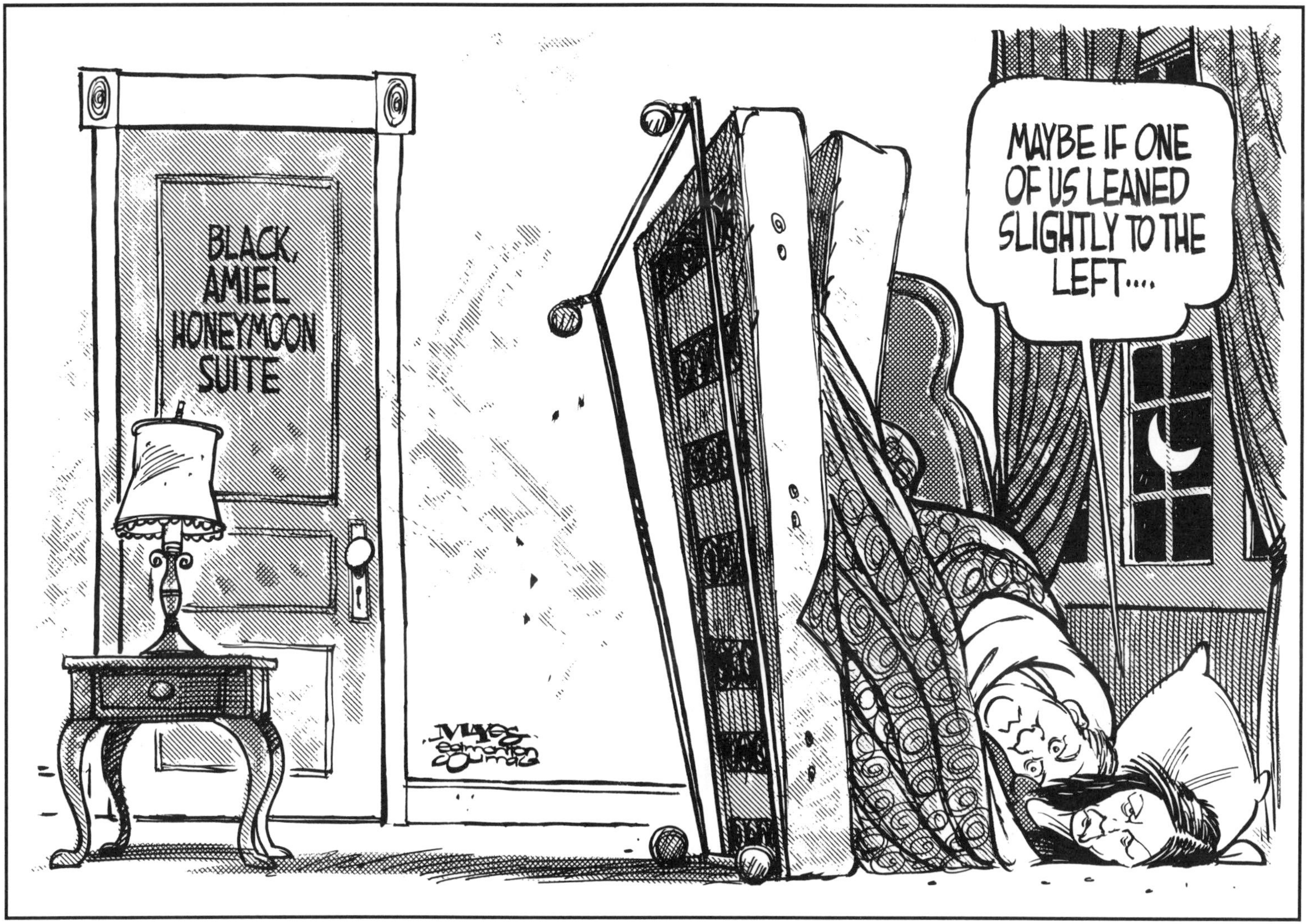
BLACK, AMIEL HONEYMOON SUITE
MAYBE IF ONE OF US LEANED SLIGHTLY TO THE LEFT....
MAYES Edmonton Journal

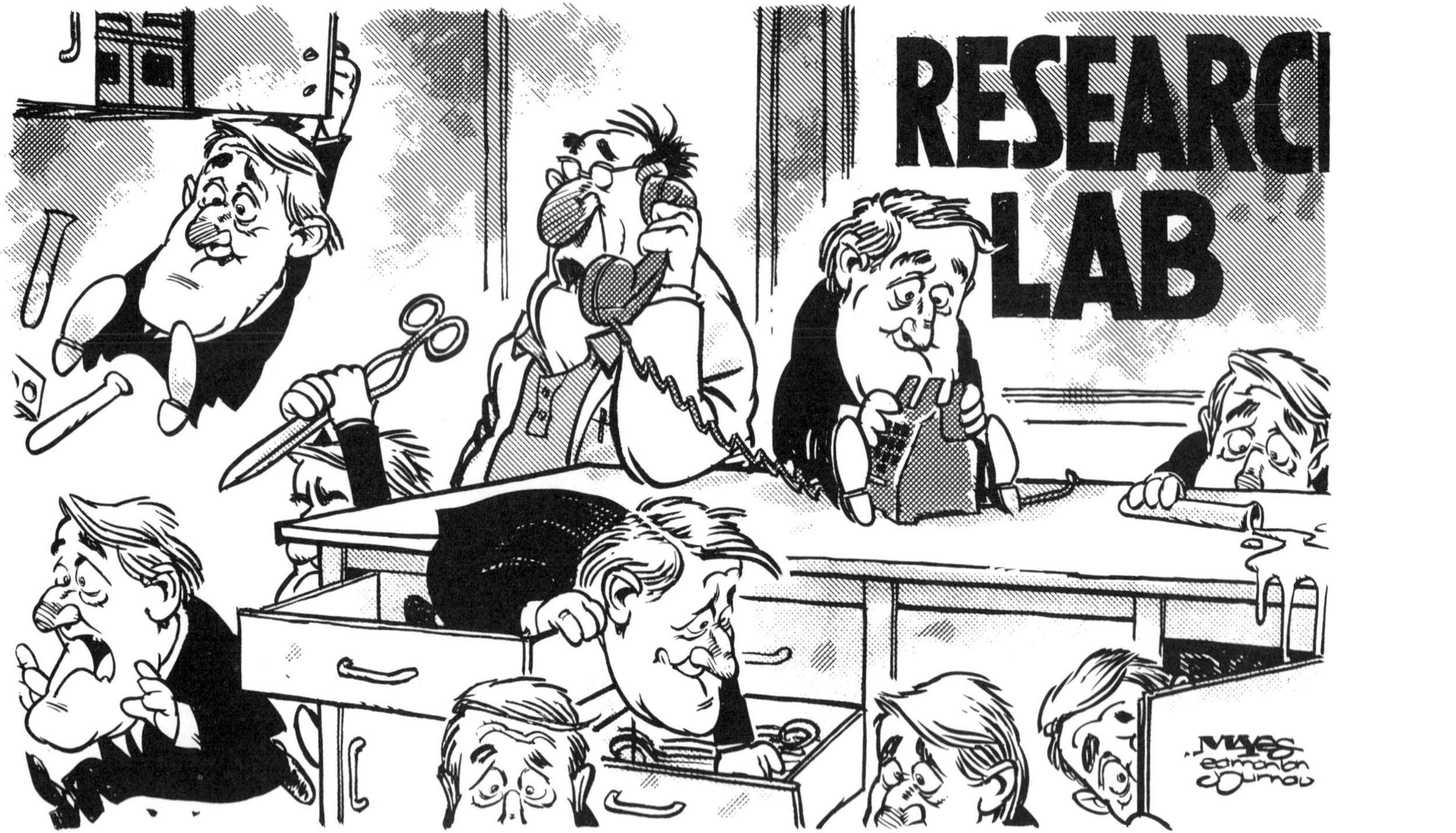
RESEARC
LAB
MAYES edmonton journal

"OH YES, THERE ARE DOZENS OF REASONS WHY CANADA SHOULD RESTRICT CLONING...,
WOULD YOU LIKE TO SPEAK TO ONE OF THEM?...."

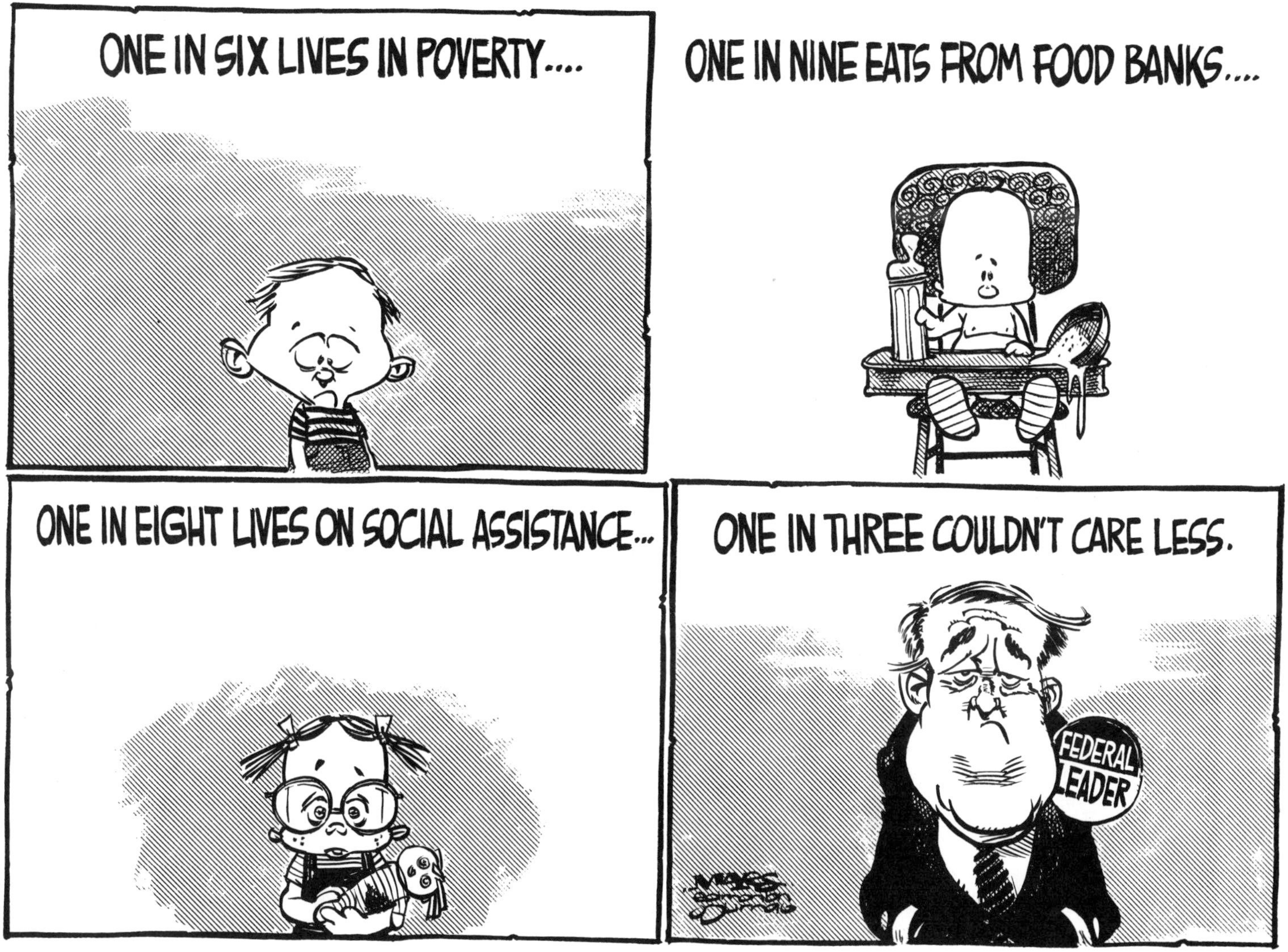
ONE IN SIX LIVES IN POVERTY....
ONE IN NINE EATS FROM FOOD BANKS....
ONE IN EIGHT LIVES ON SOCIAL ASSISTANCE...
ONE IN THREE COULDN'T CARE LESS.
FEDERAL LEADER

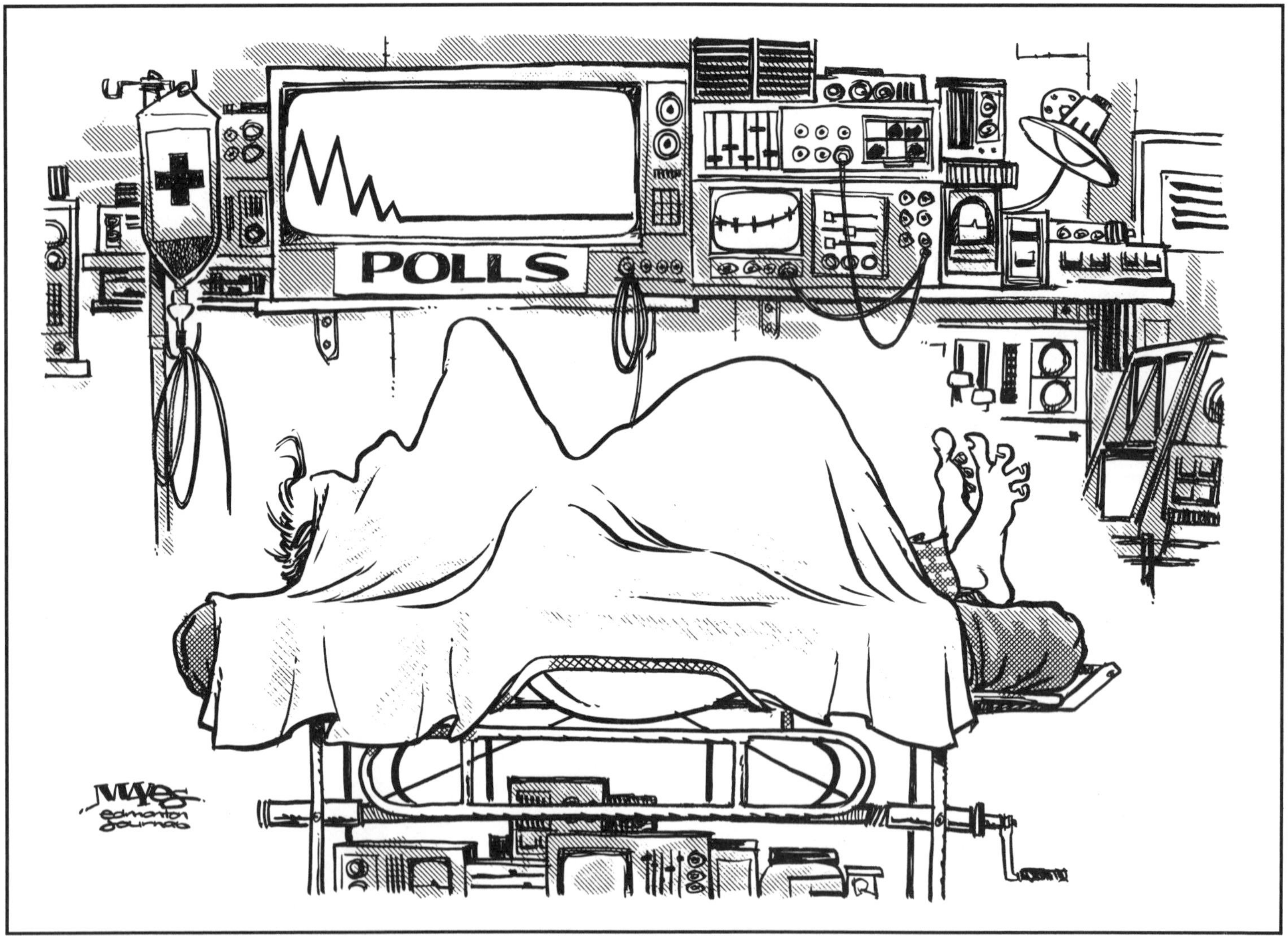
POLLS
Mayes
edmonton journal

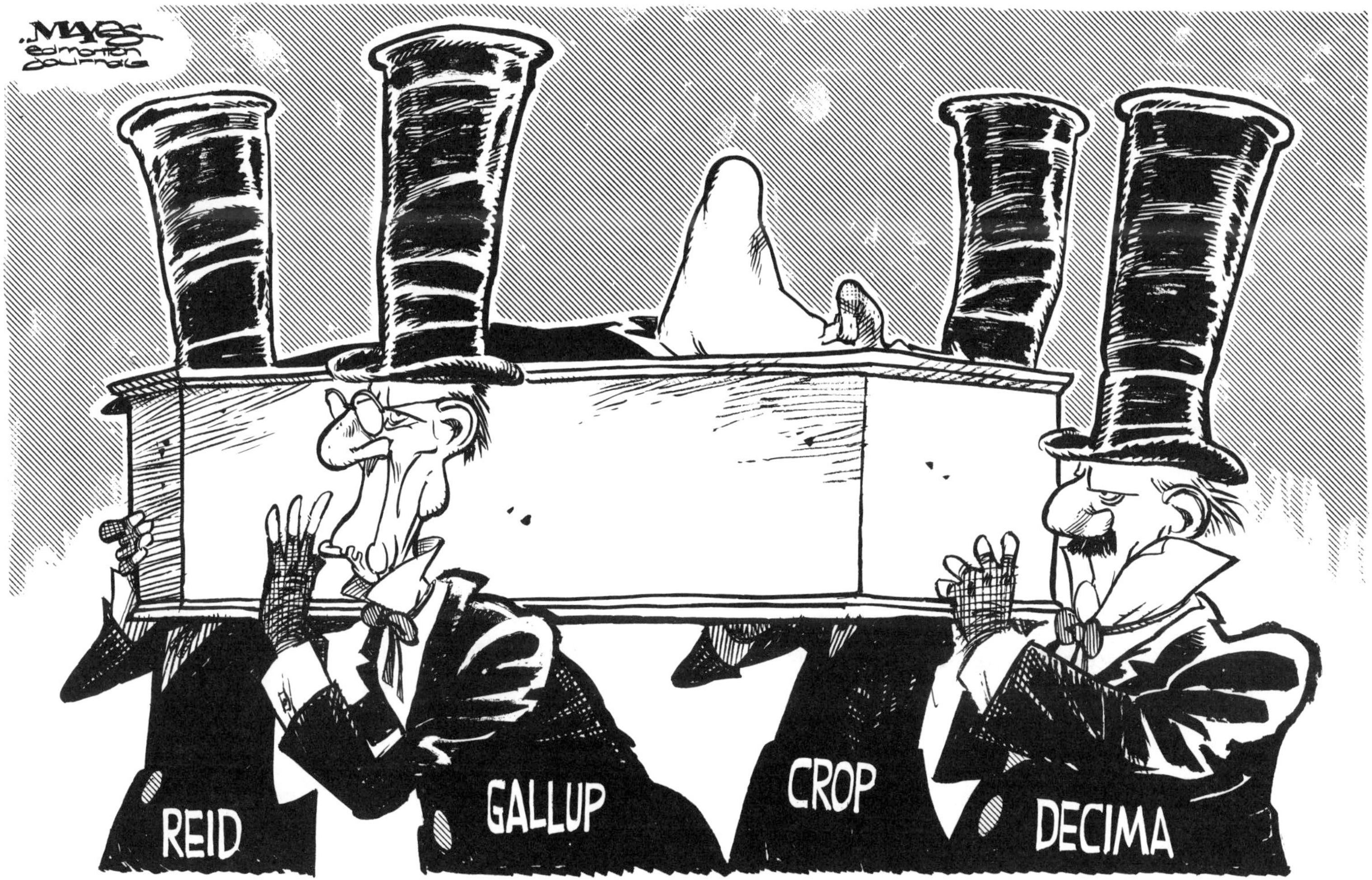
MAYES
edmonton journal
REID
GALLUP
CROP
DECIMA

POLLBEARERS.

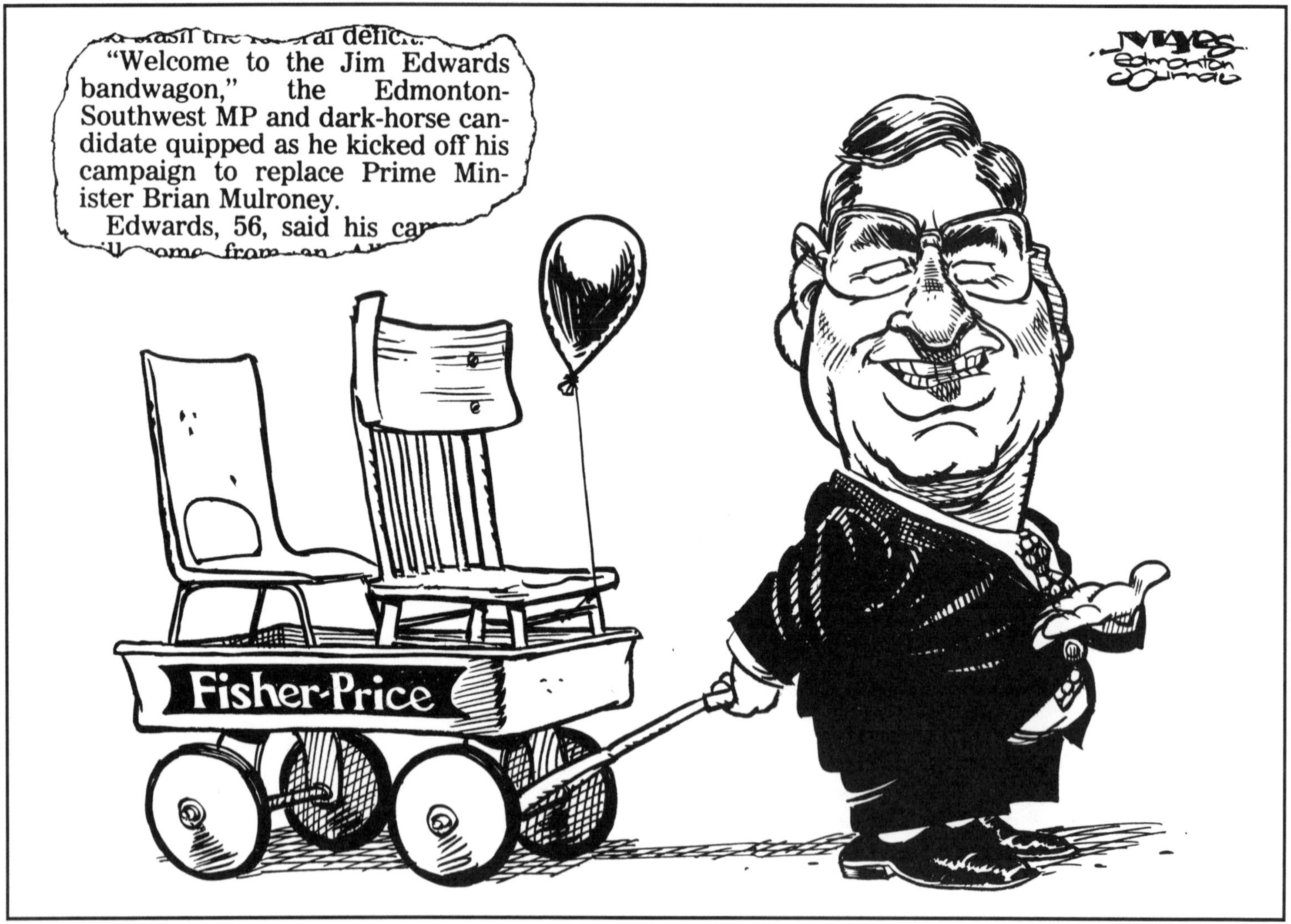
"Welcome to the Jim Edwards bandwagon," the Edmonton-Southwest MP and dark-horse candidate quipped as he kicked off his campaign to replace Prime Minister Brian Mulroney.
Edwards, 56, said his ca
Fisher-Price
MAYES
Edmonton Journal

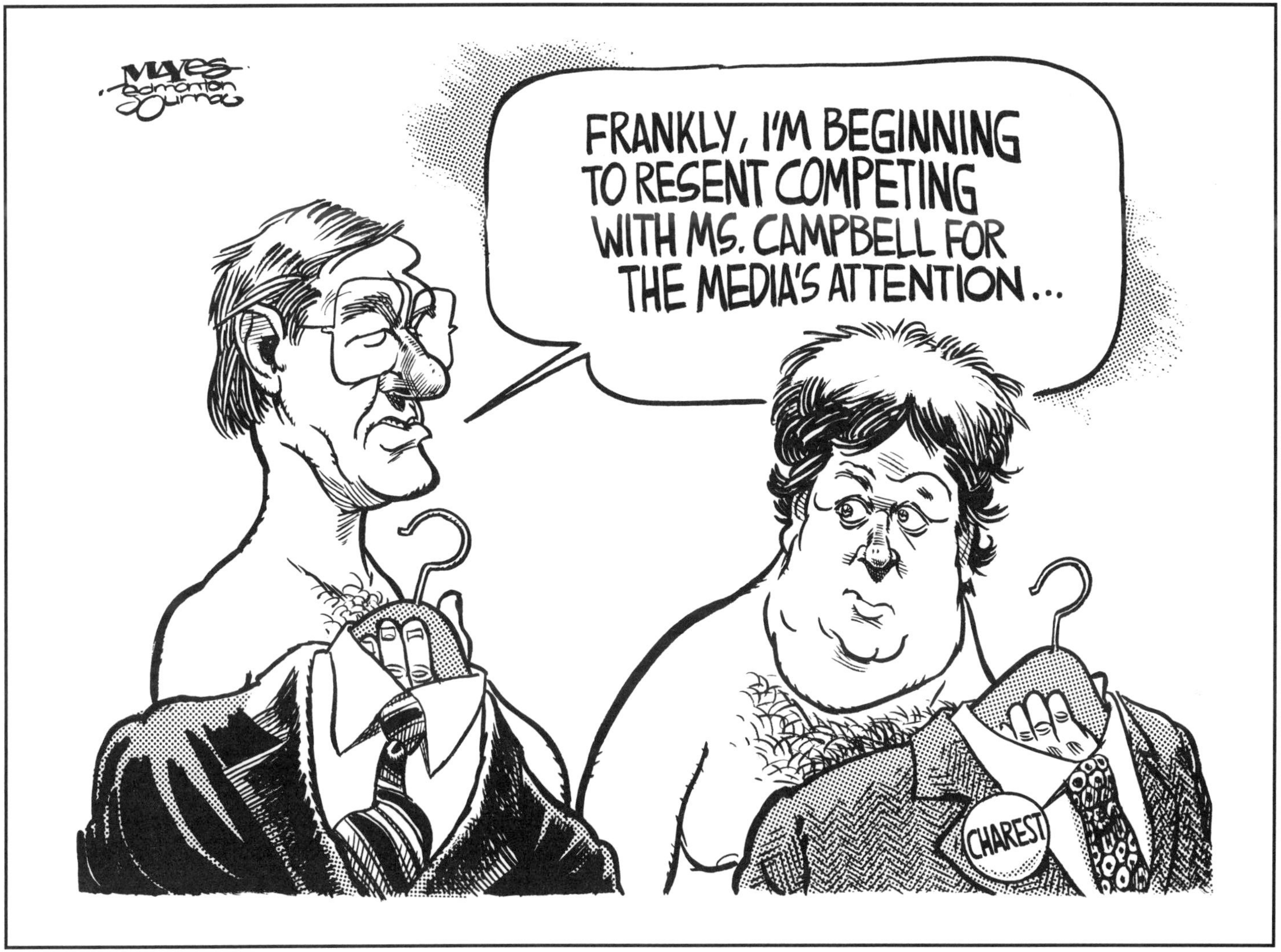
MAYES Edmonton Journal
FRANKLY, I'M BEGINNING TO RESENT COMPETING WITH MS. CAMPBELL FOR THE MEDIA'S ATTENTION...
CHAREST

Photo of bare-shouldered Kim Campbell excites Tories.

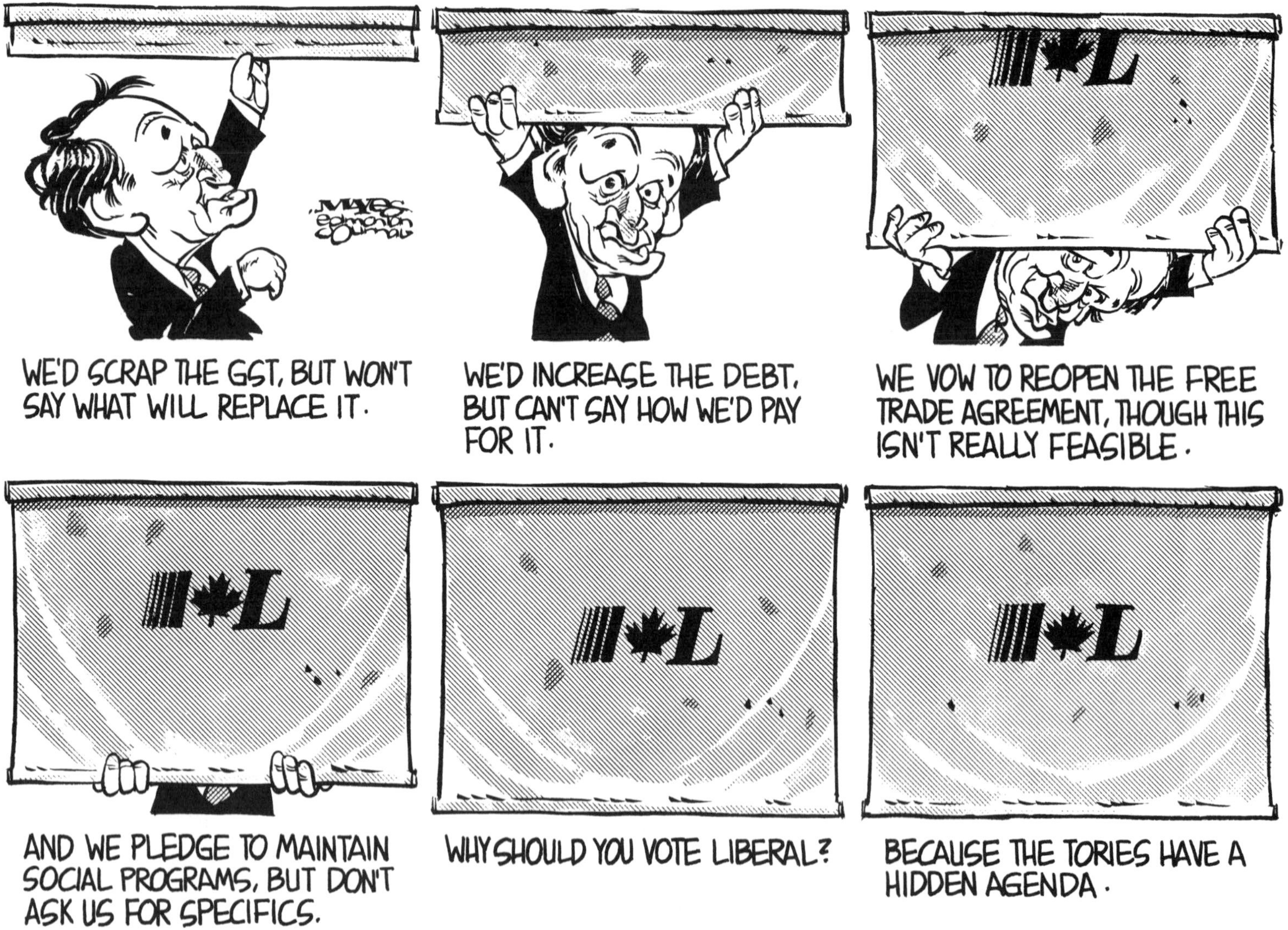
MAYES edmonton journal
WE'D SCRAP THE GST, BUT WON'T SAY WHAT WILL REPLACE IT.
WE'D INCREASE THE DEBT, BUT CAN'T SAY HOW WE'D PAY FOR IT.
WE VOW TO REOPEN THE FREE TRADE AGREEMENT, THOUGH THIS ISN'T REALLY FEASIBLE.
AND WE PLEDGE TO MAINTAIN SOCIAL PROGRAMS, BUT DON'T ASK US FOR SPECIFICS.
WHY SHOULD YOU VOTE LIBERAL?
BECAUSE THE TORIES HAVE A HIDDEN AGENDA.

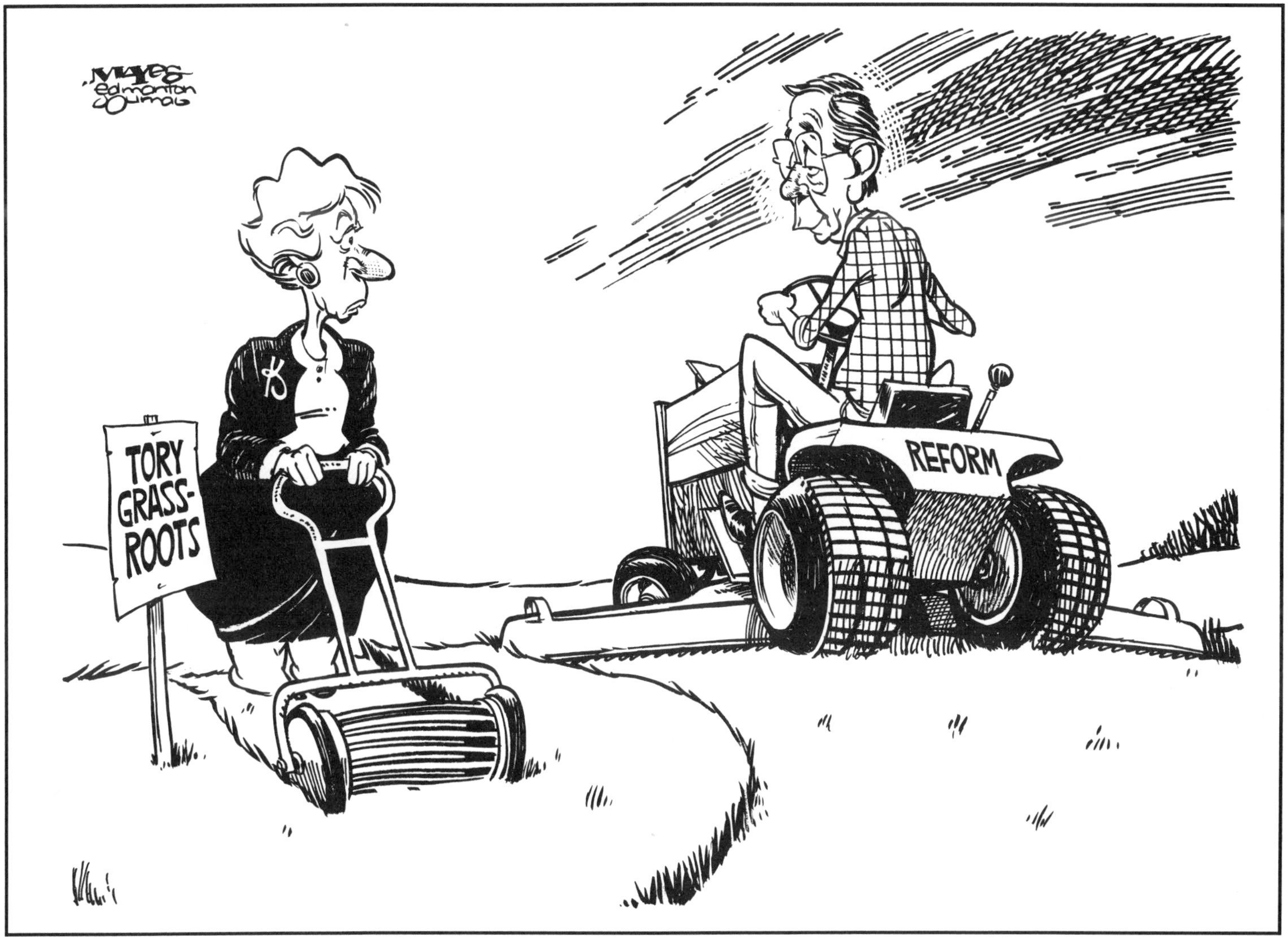
MAYES edmonton journal
TORY GRASS-ROOTS
REFORM

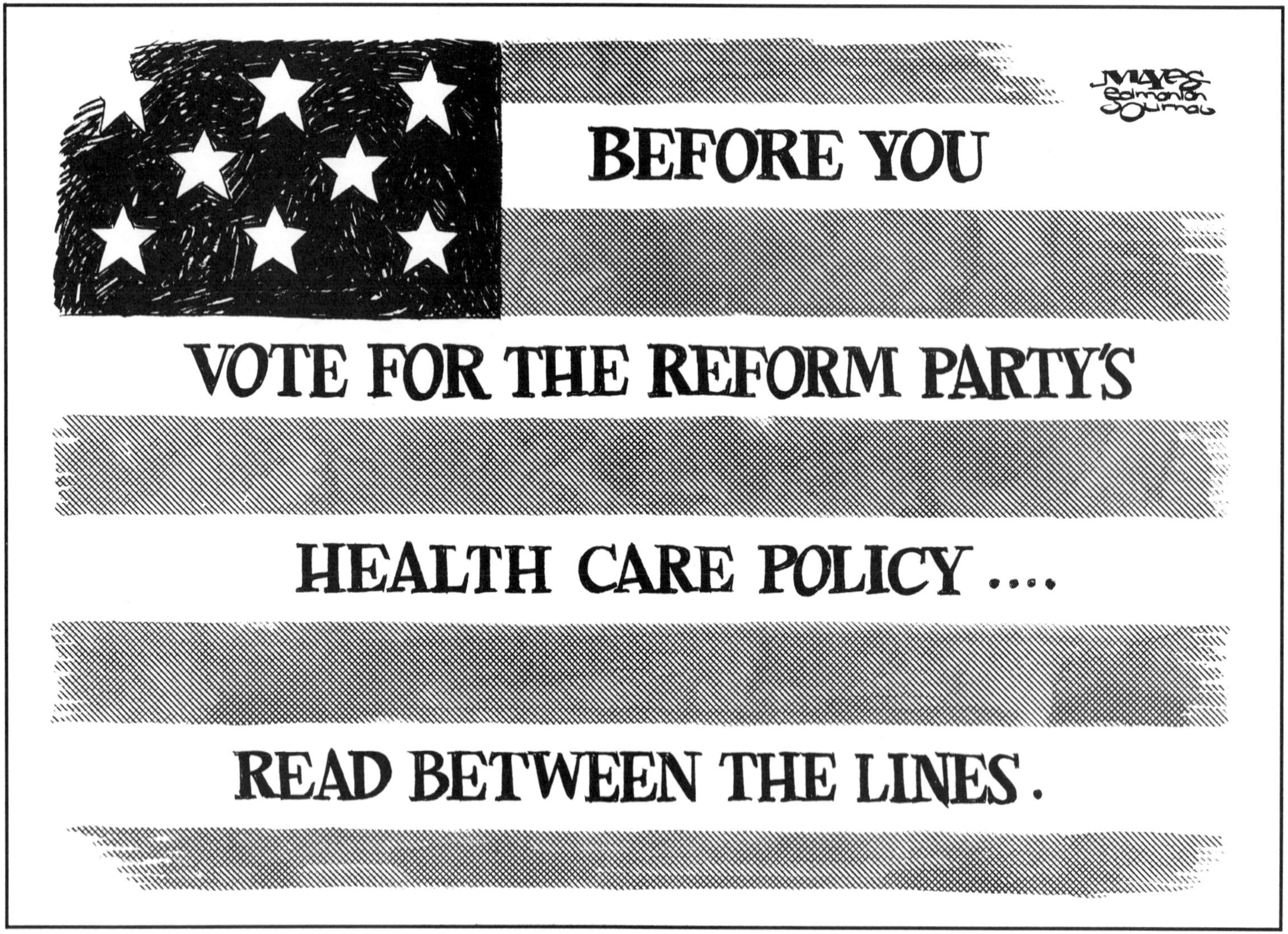
MAYES
Edmonton Journal
BEFORE YOU
VOTE FOR THE REFORM PARTY'S
HEALTH CARE POLICY ....
READ BETWEEN THE LINES.

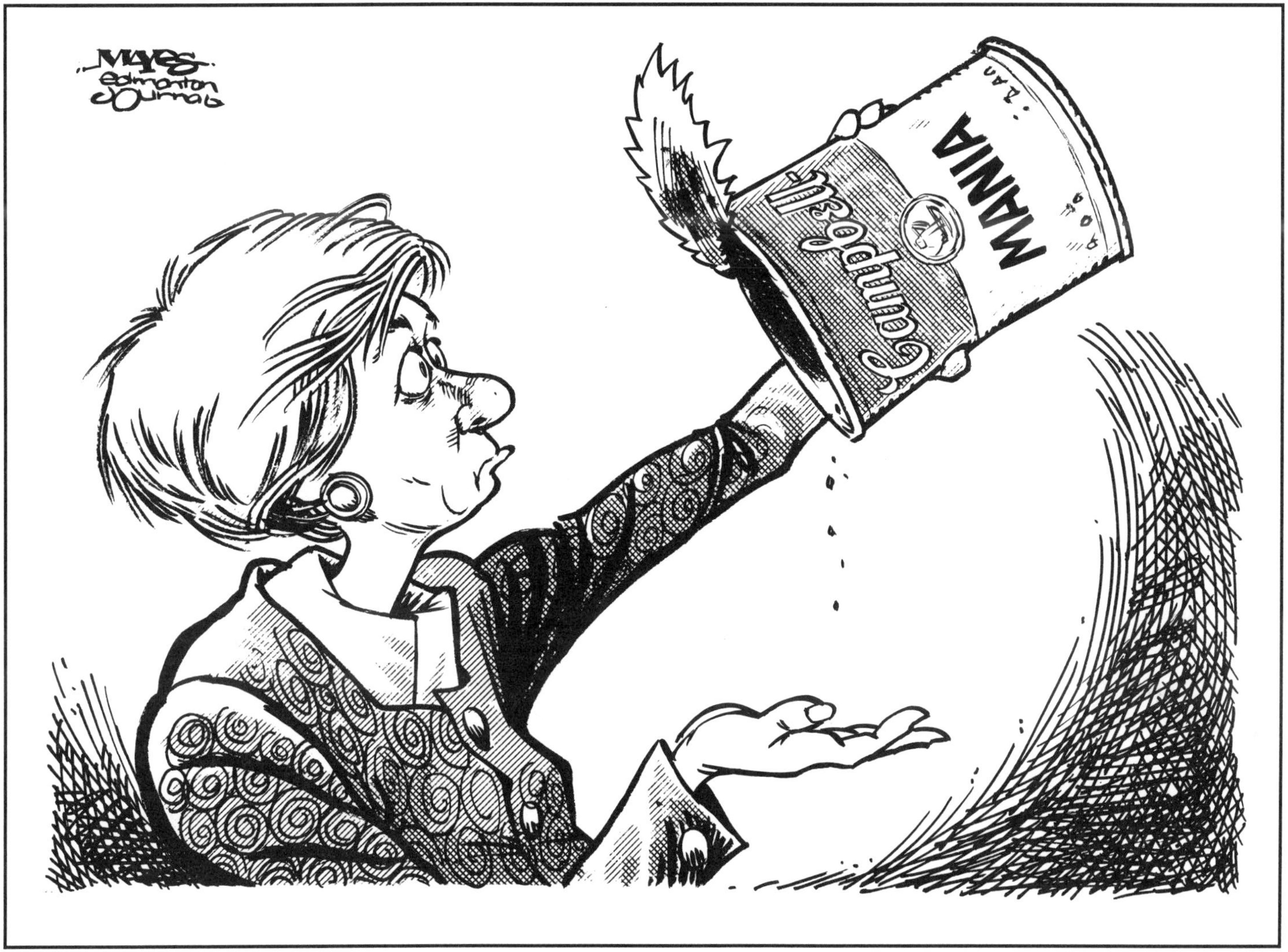
MAYES
Edmonton Journal
Campbell
MANIA

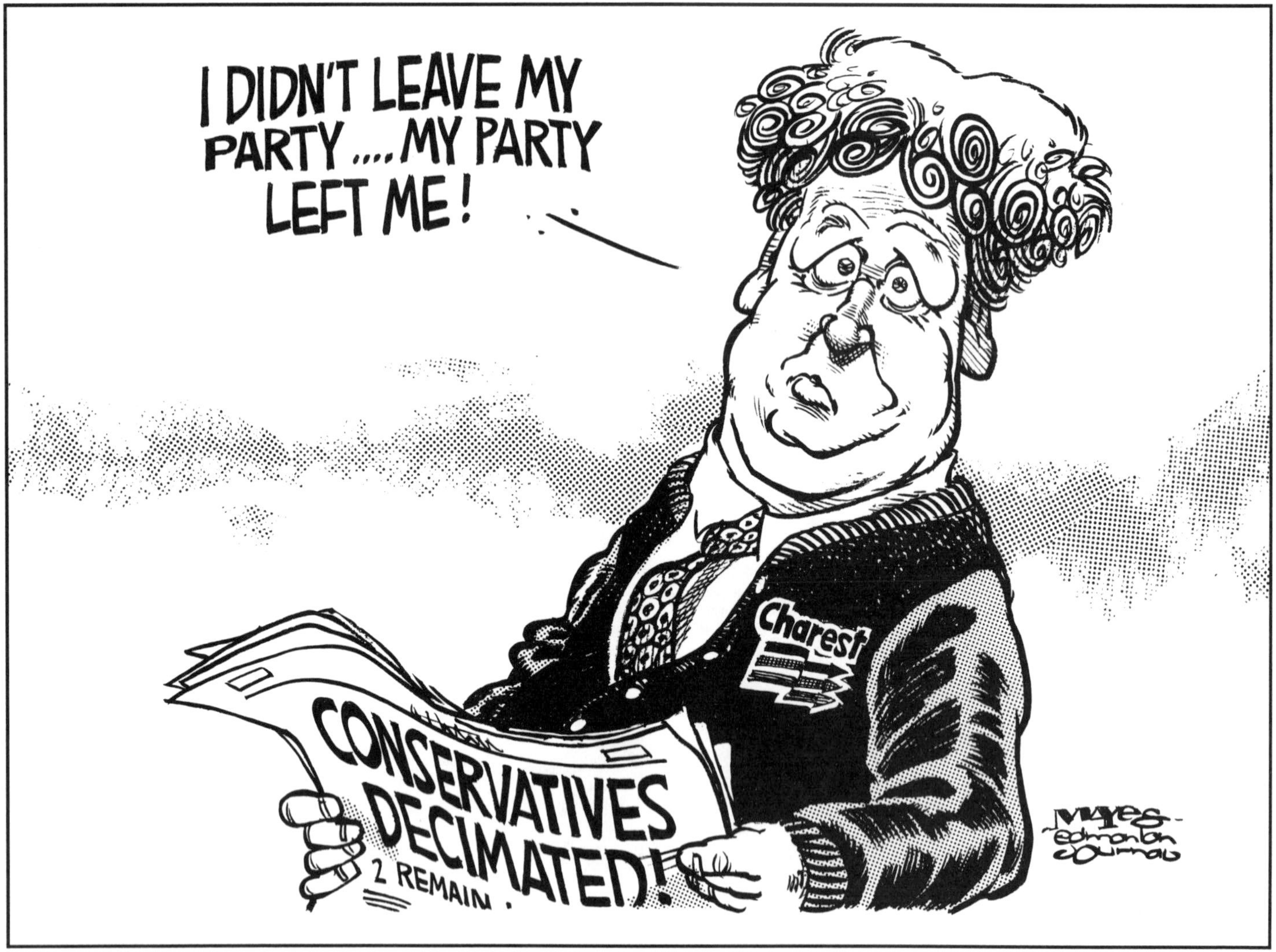
I DIDN'T LEAVE MY PARTY .... MY PARTY LEFT ME !
Charest
CONSERVATIVES DECIMATED!
2 REMAIN.
MAYES - EDMONTON JOURNAL

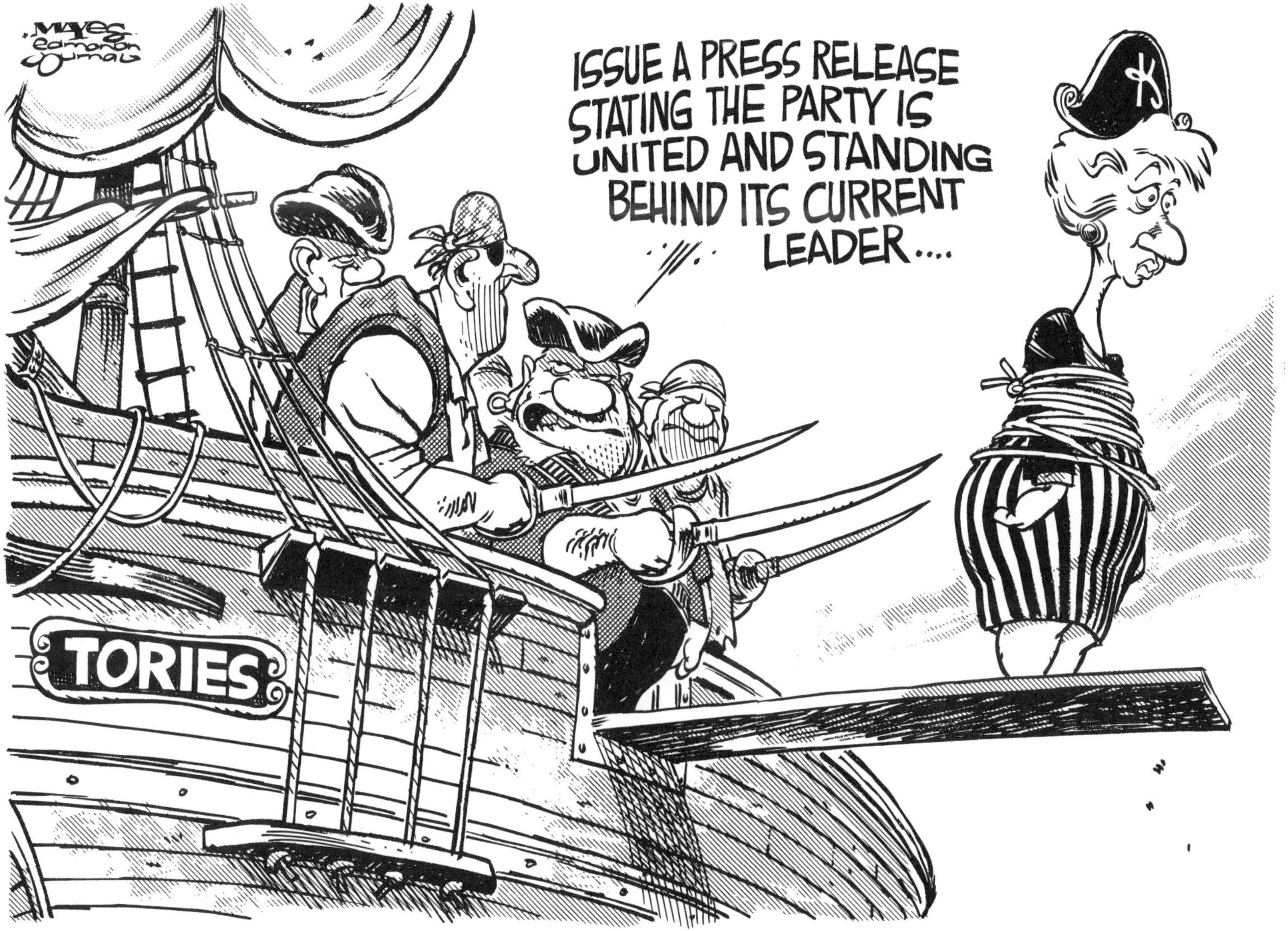
ISSUE A PRESS RELEASE STATING THE PARTY IS UNITED AND STANDING BEHIND ITS CURRENT LEADER....
TORIES

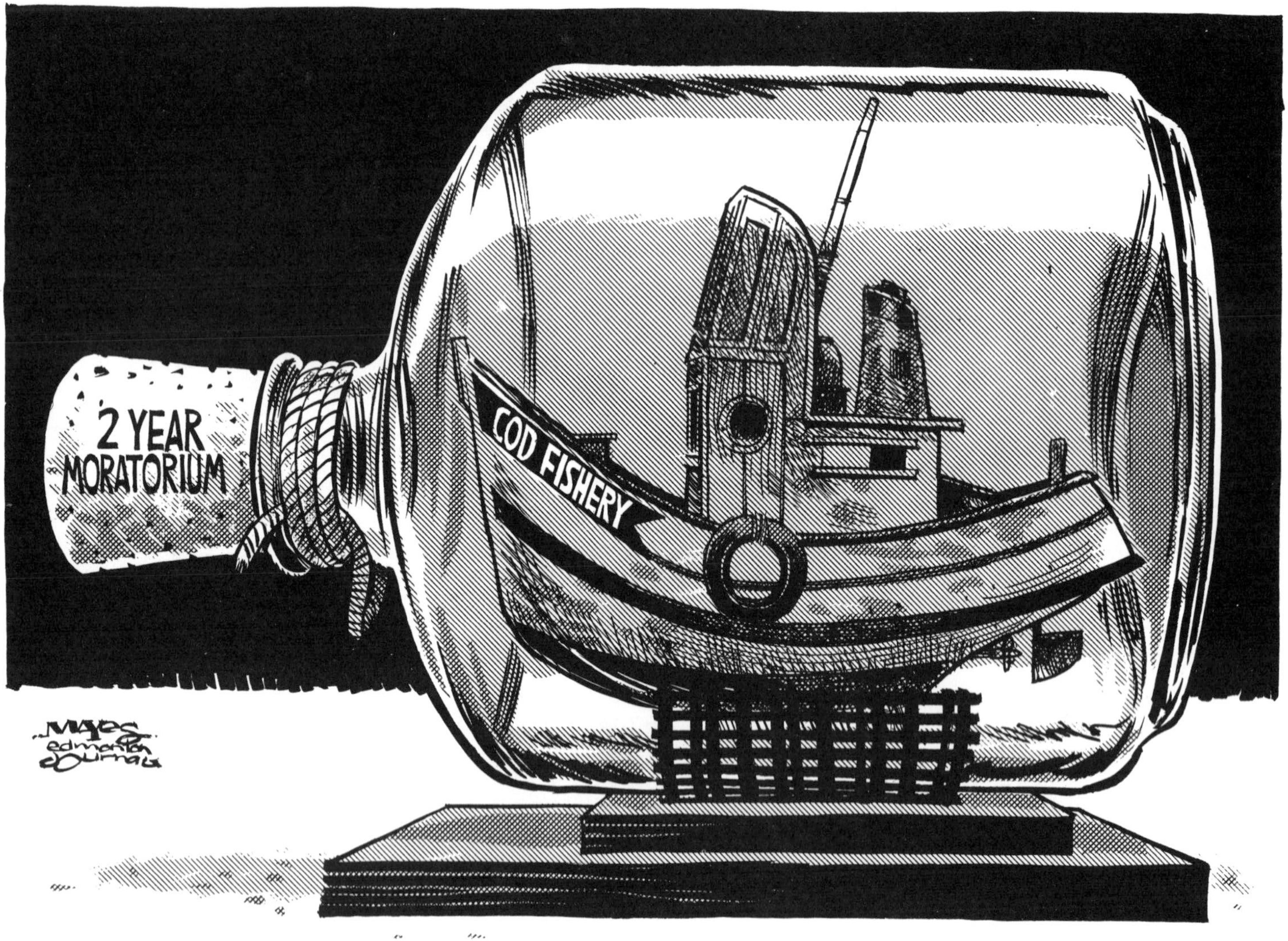
2 YEAR
MORATORIUM
COD FISHERY
MAYES
edmonton
journal

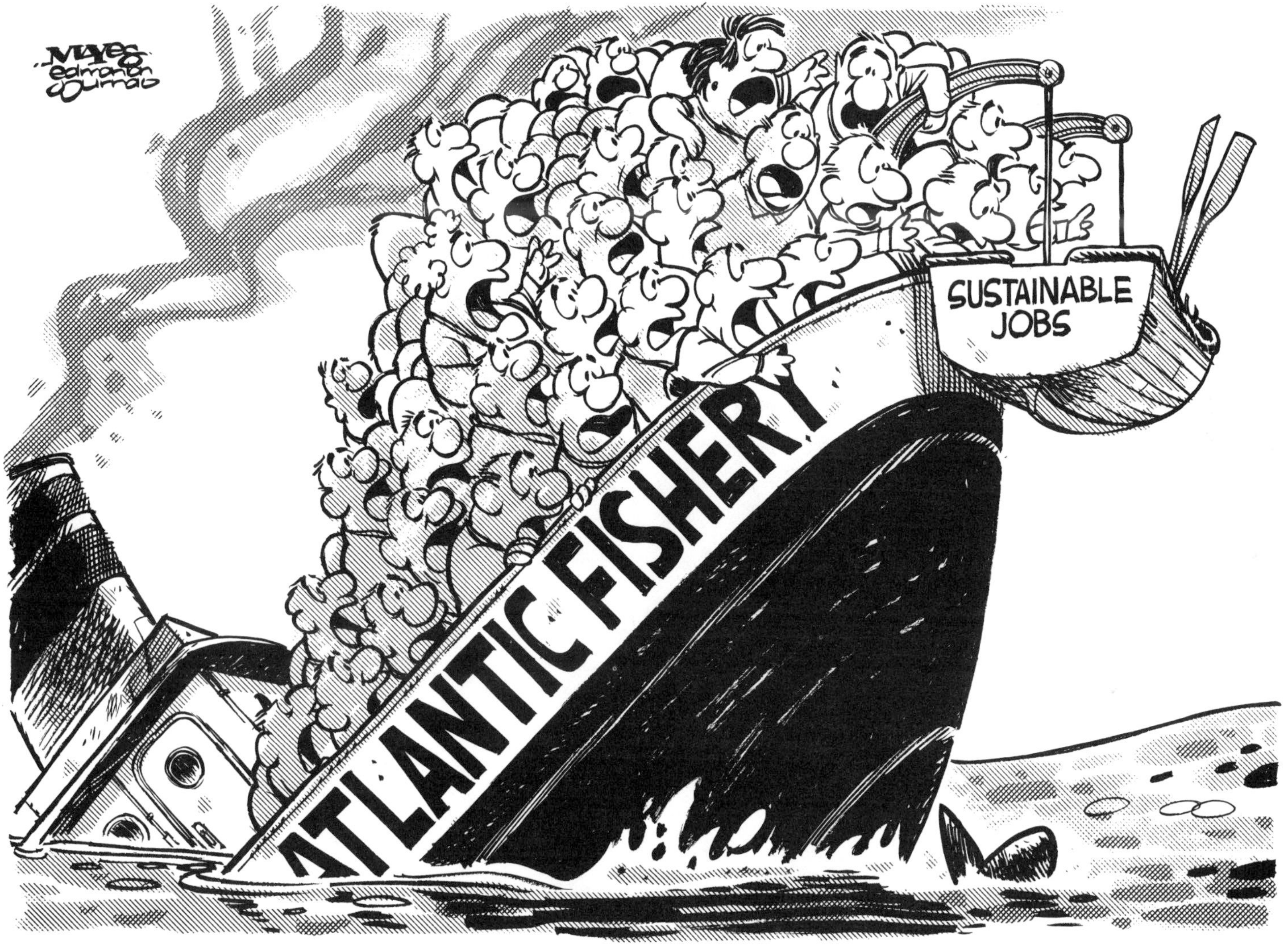
ATLANTIC FISHERY
SUSTAINABLE JOBS

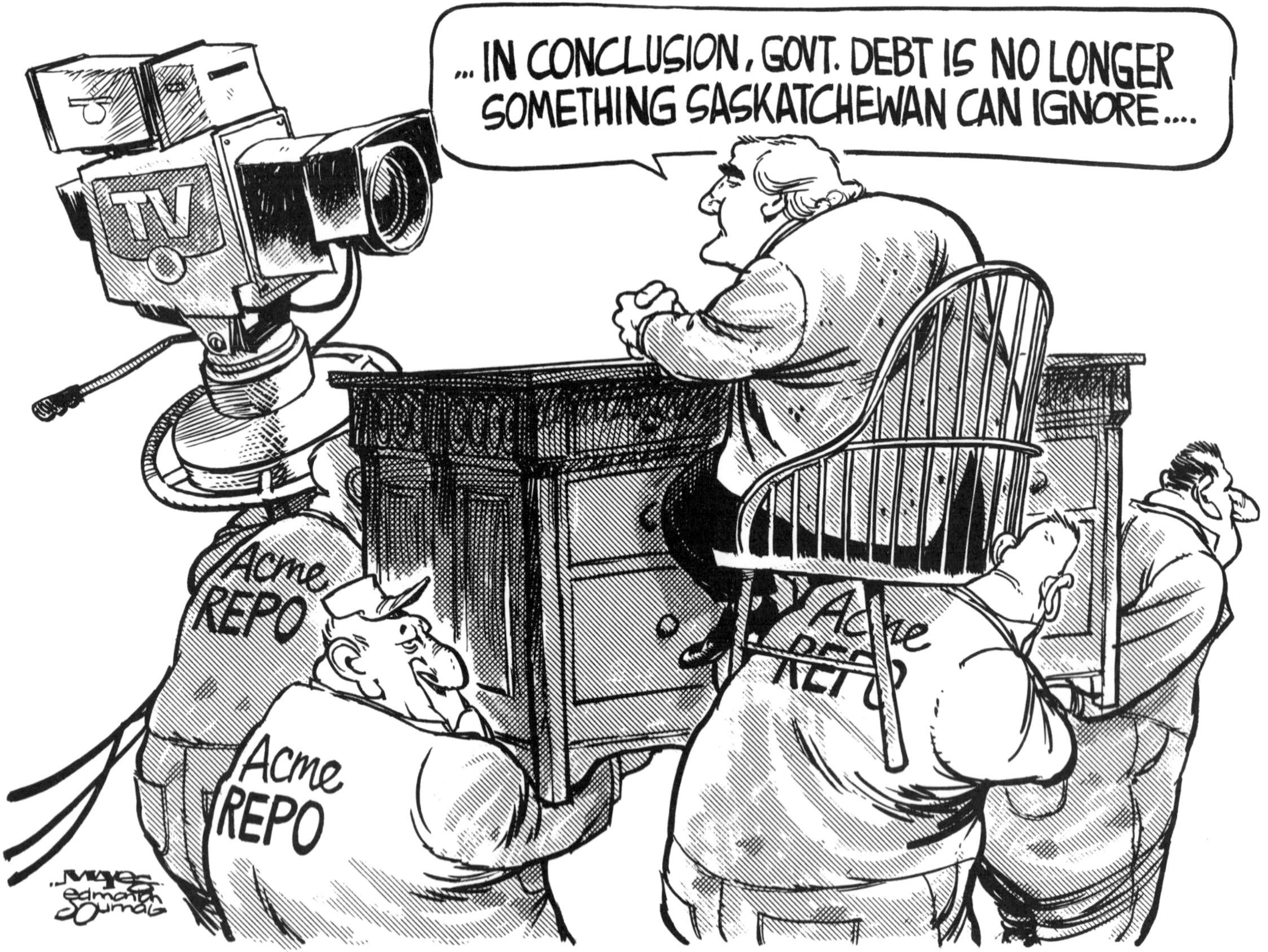
...IN CONCLUSION, GOVT. DEBT IS NO LONGER SOMETHING SASKATCHEWAN CAN IGNORE....
TV
Acme REPO
Acme REPO
Acme REPO

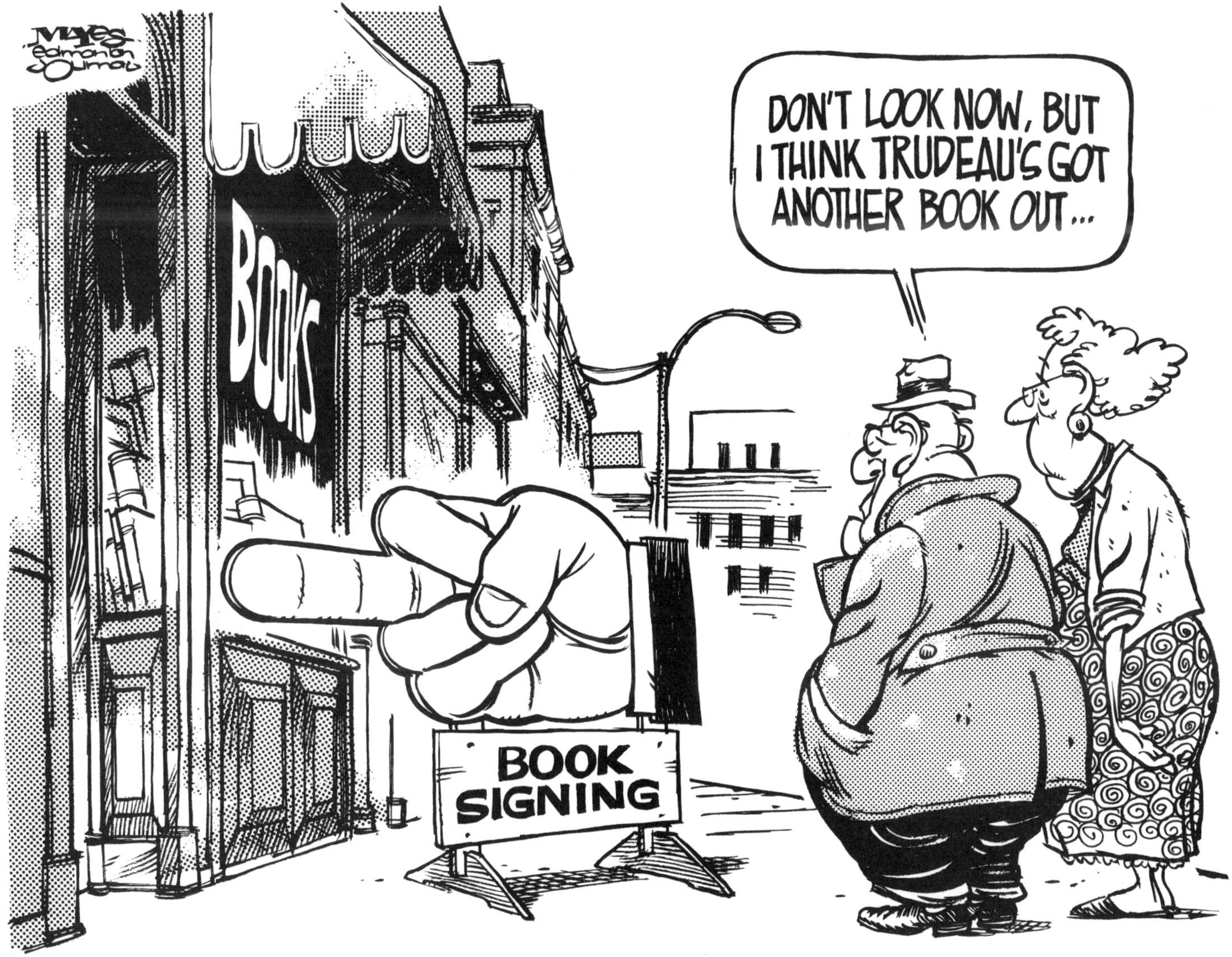

Mayes
Edmonton Journal
BOOKS
DON'T LOOK NOW, BUT
I THINK TRUDEAU'S GOT
ANOTHER BOOK OUT...
BOOK
SIGNING

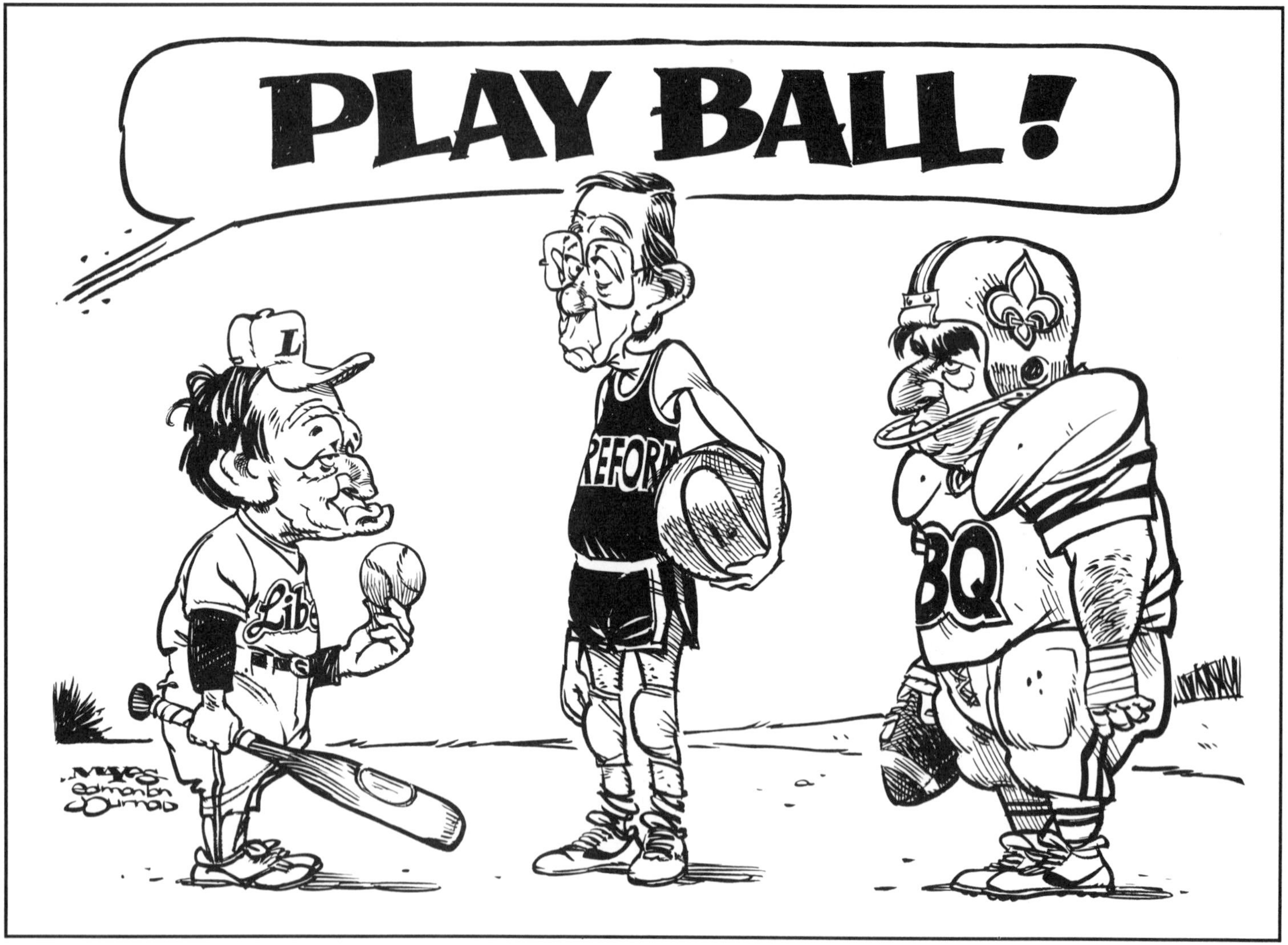
PLAY BALL!
L
Lib
REFOR
BQ

At last, the election's over and Parliament gets down to business.

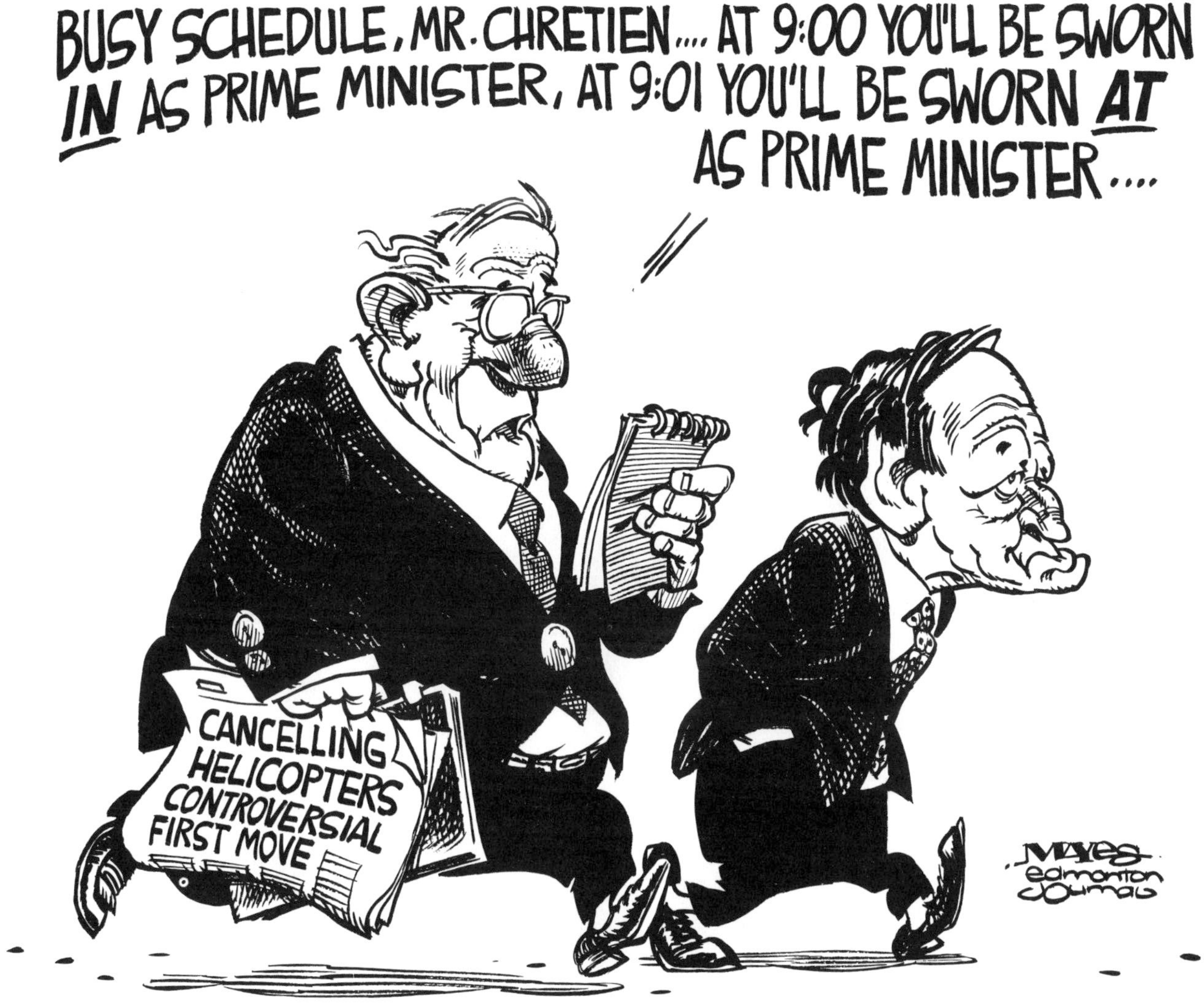
BUSY SCHEDULE, MR. CHRETIEN.... AT 9:00 YOU'LL BE SWORN IN AS PRIME MINISTER, AT 9:01 YOU'LL BE SWORN AT AS PRIME MINISTER....
CANCELLING HELICOPTERS CONTROVERSIAL FIRST MOVE
MAYES
edmonton journal

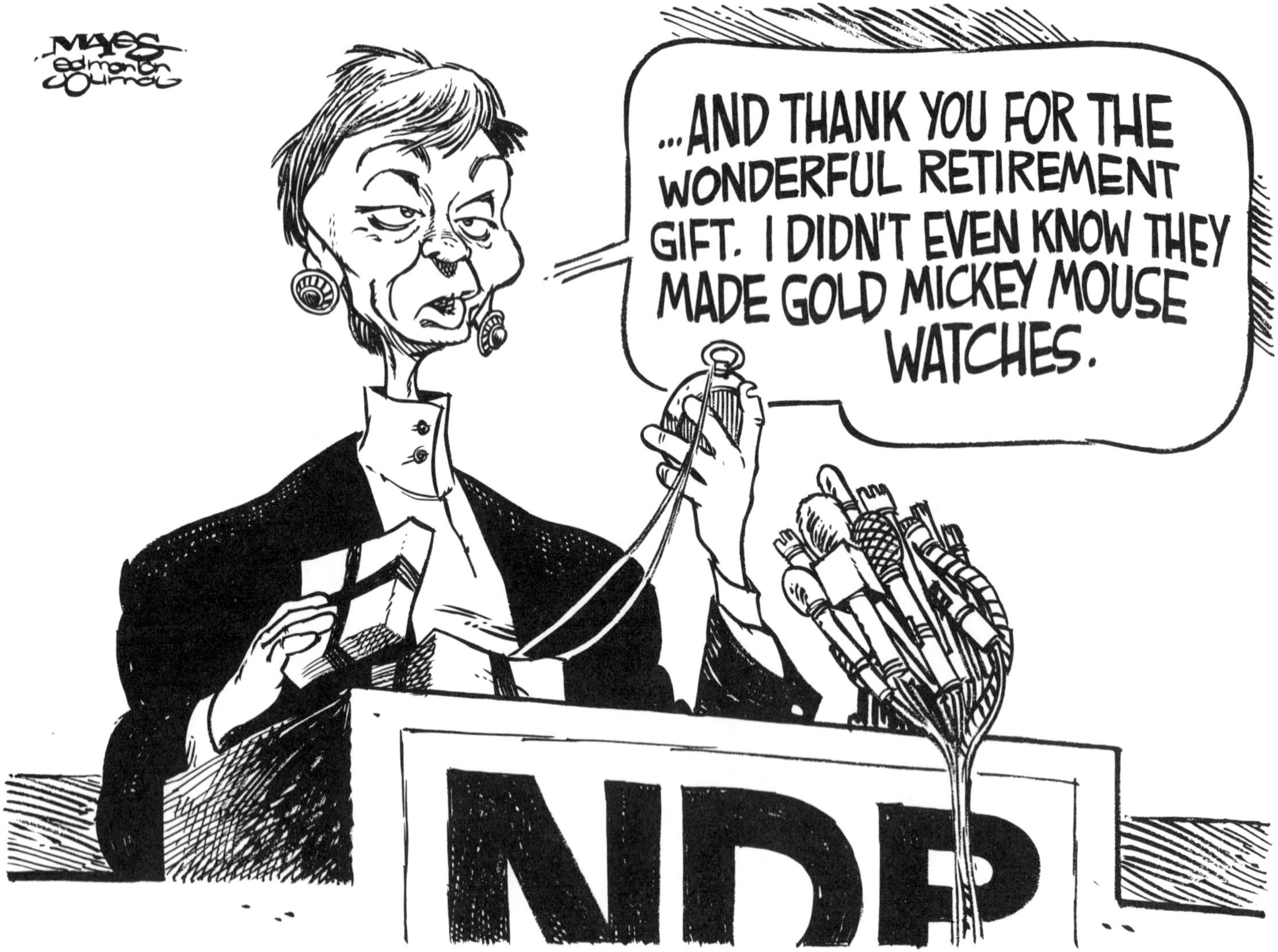
MAYES edmonton journal
...AND THANK YOU FOR THE WONDERFUL RETIREMENT GIFT. I DIDN'T EVEN KNOW THEY MADE GOLD MICKEY MOUSE WATCHES.
NDP

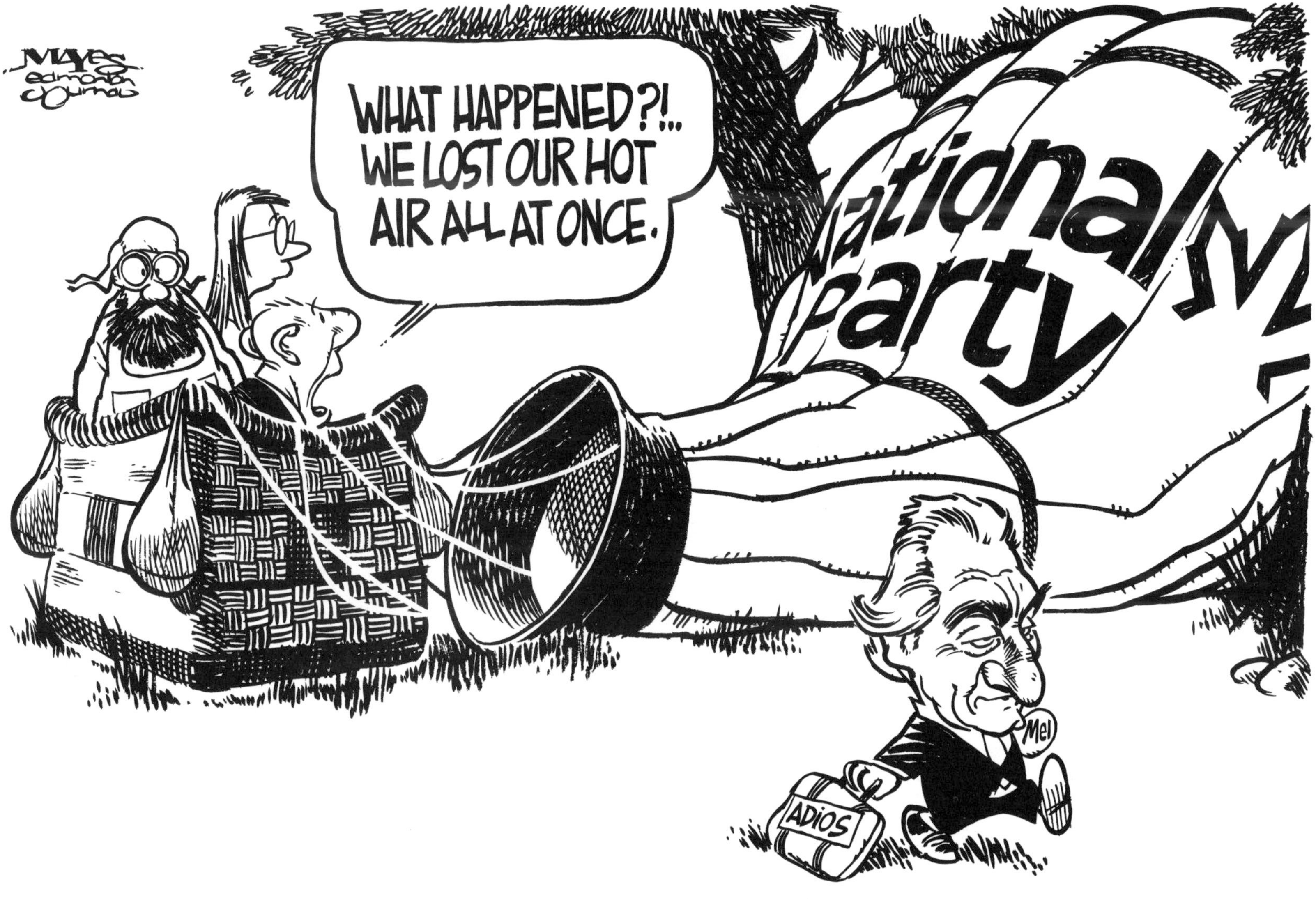
MAYES edmonton journal
WHAT HAPPENED?!.. WE LOST OUR HOT AIR ALL AT ONCE.
National Party
Mel
ADIOS

Founder Mel Hurtig abandons the National Party.

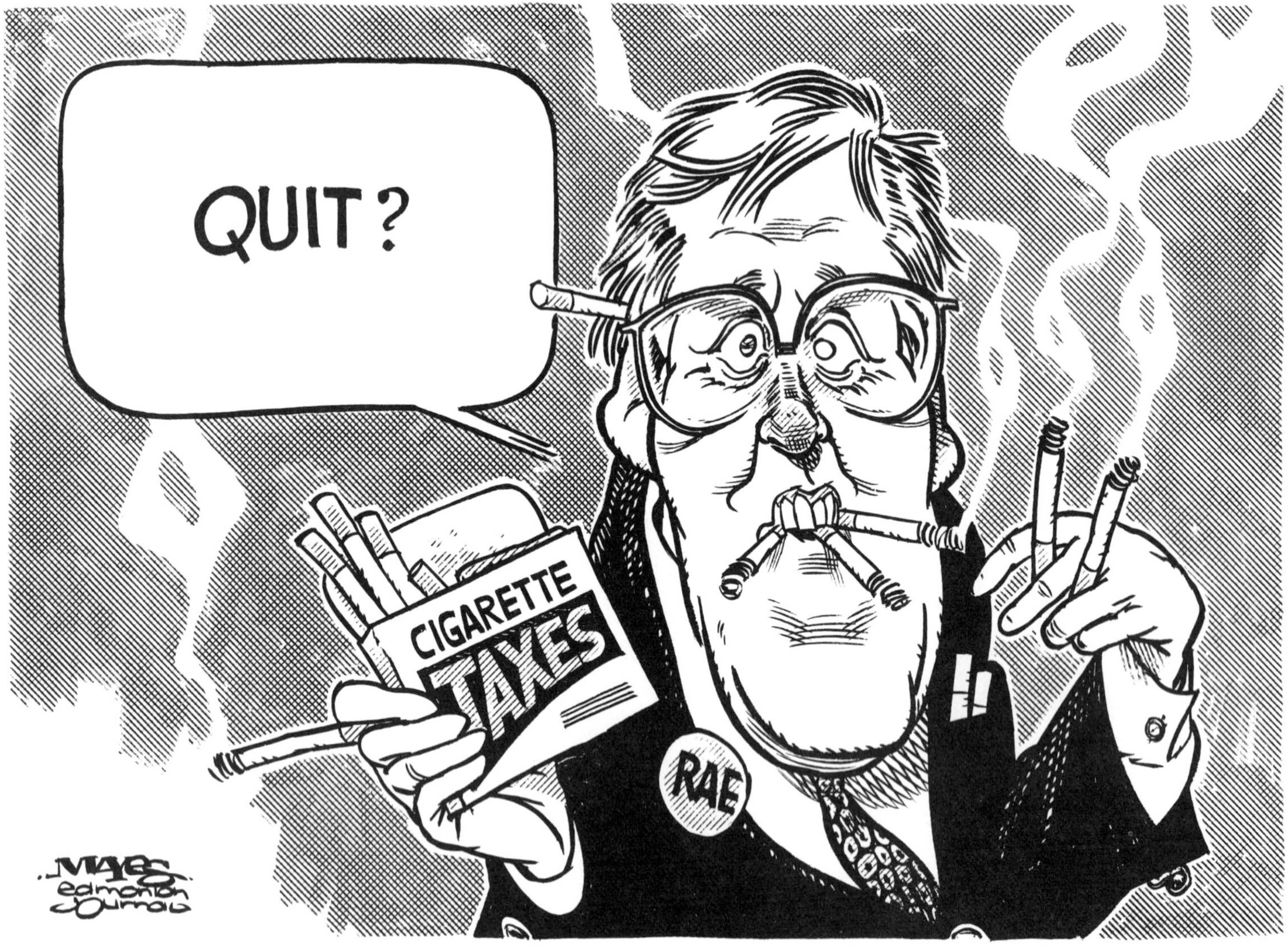
QUIT?
CIGARETTE TAXES
RAE
MAYES edmonton journal

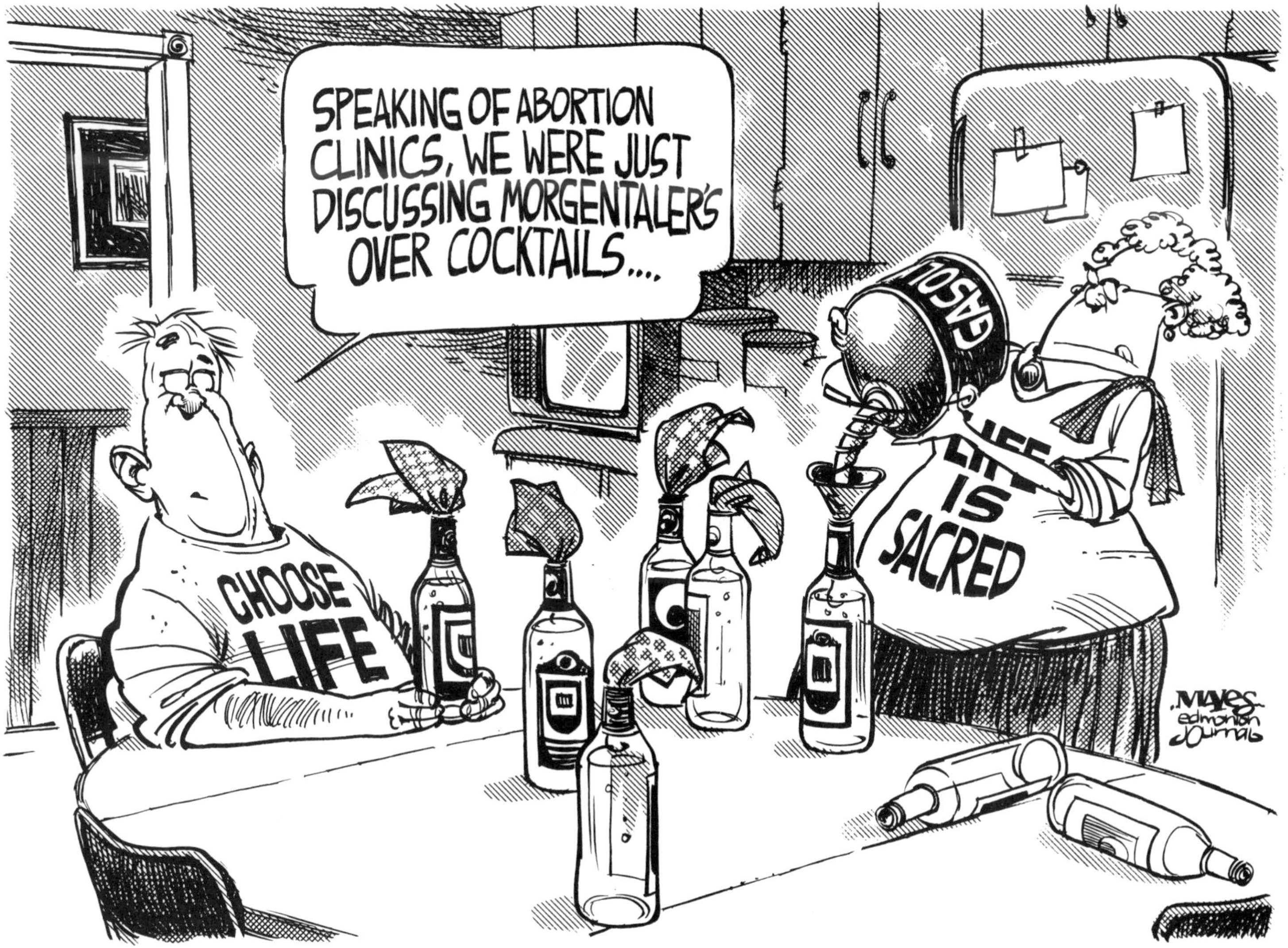
SPEAKING OF ABORTION CLINICS, WE WERE JUST DISCUSSING MORGENTALER'S OVER COCKTAILS....
CHOOSE LIFE
LIFE IS SACRED
MAYES
edmonton journal

Morgentaler abortion clinic is bombed.

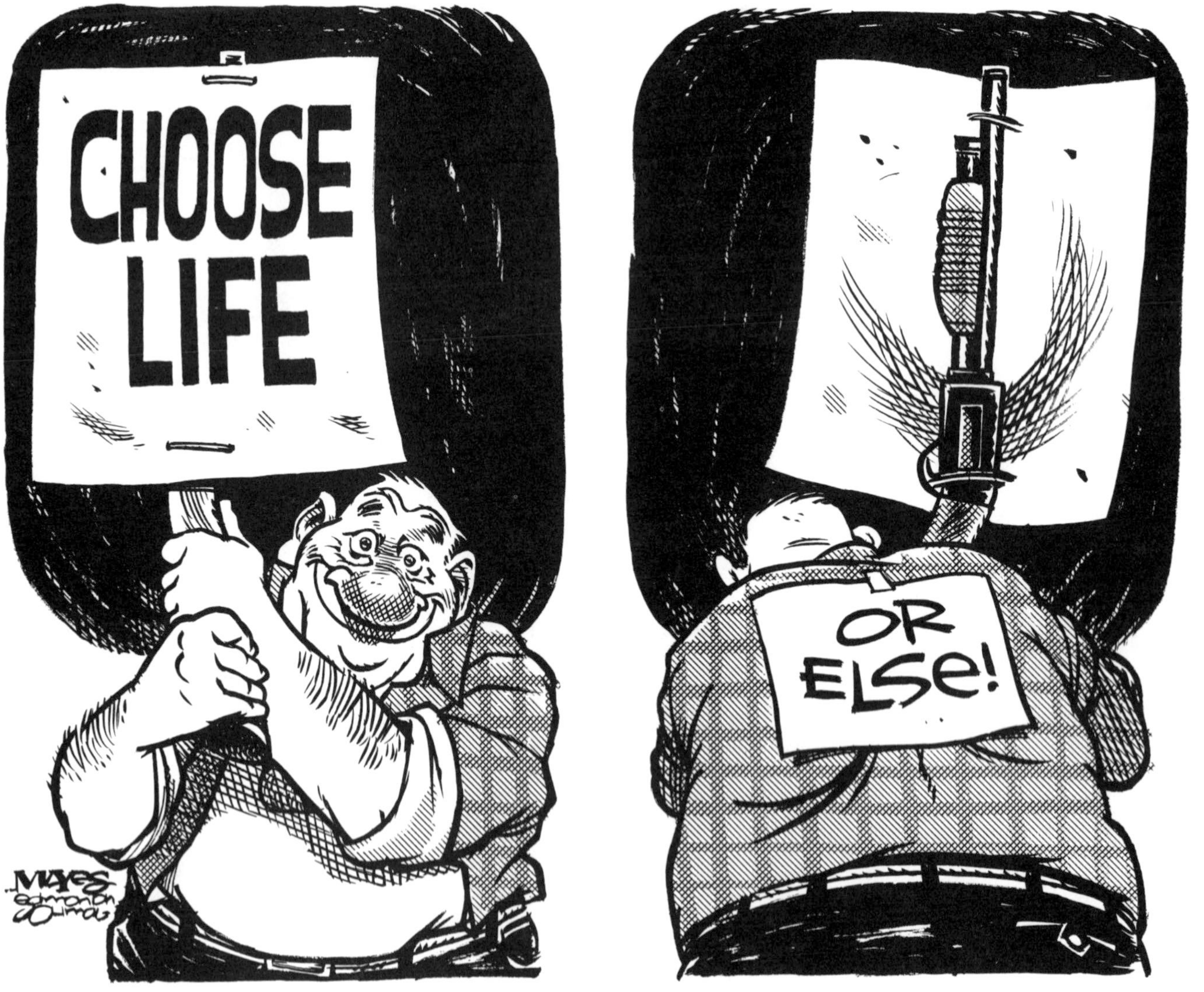
CHOOSE LIFE
OR ELSE!
MAYES

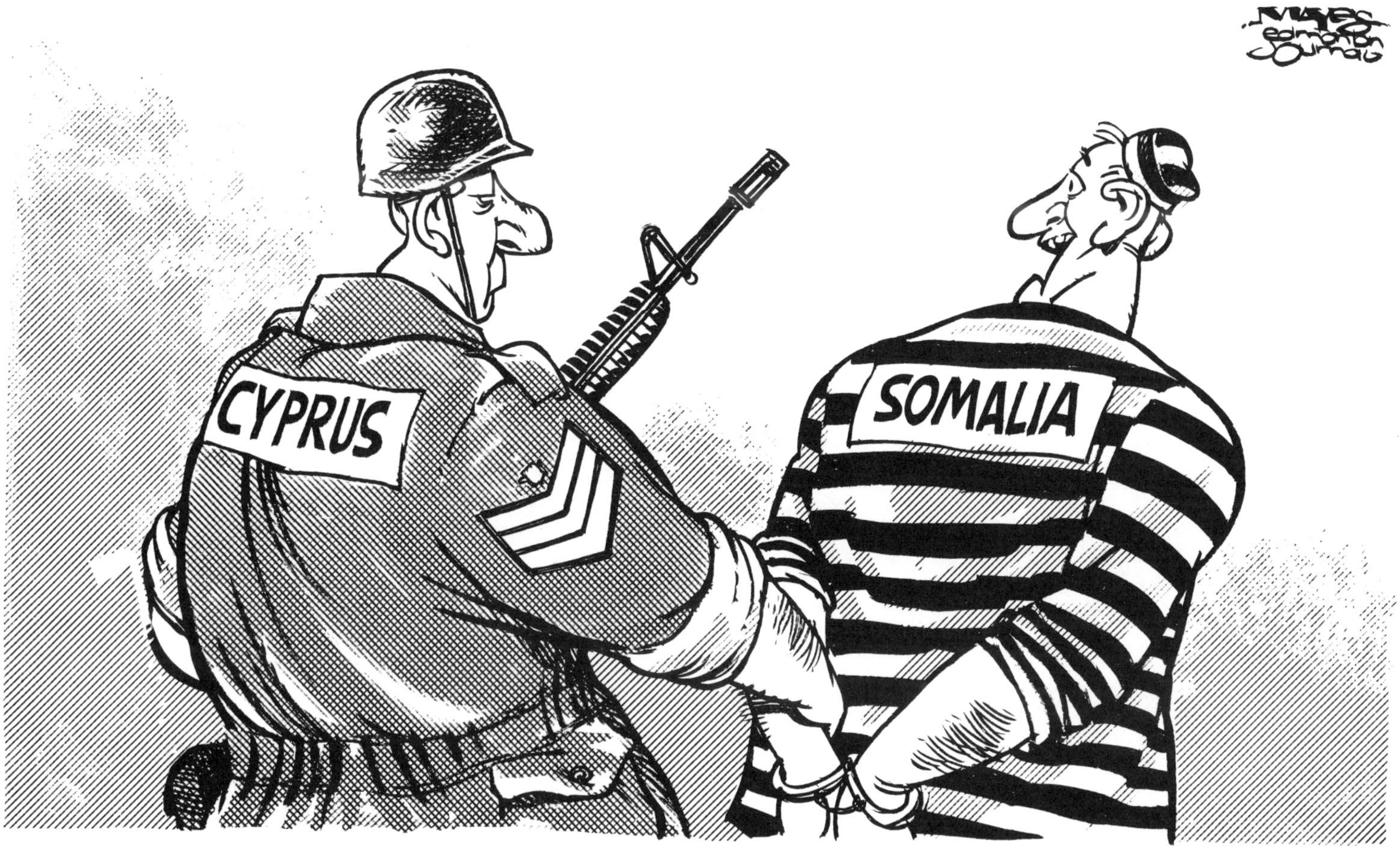
CYPRUS
SOMALIA

"HOW ABOUT THAT, EH?.... WE'RE BOTH CANADIAN, BOTH SOLDIERS, AND BOTH EARNED OUR STRIPES ON A PEACEKEEPING MISSION!...."

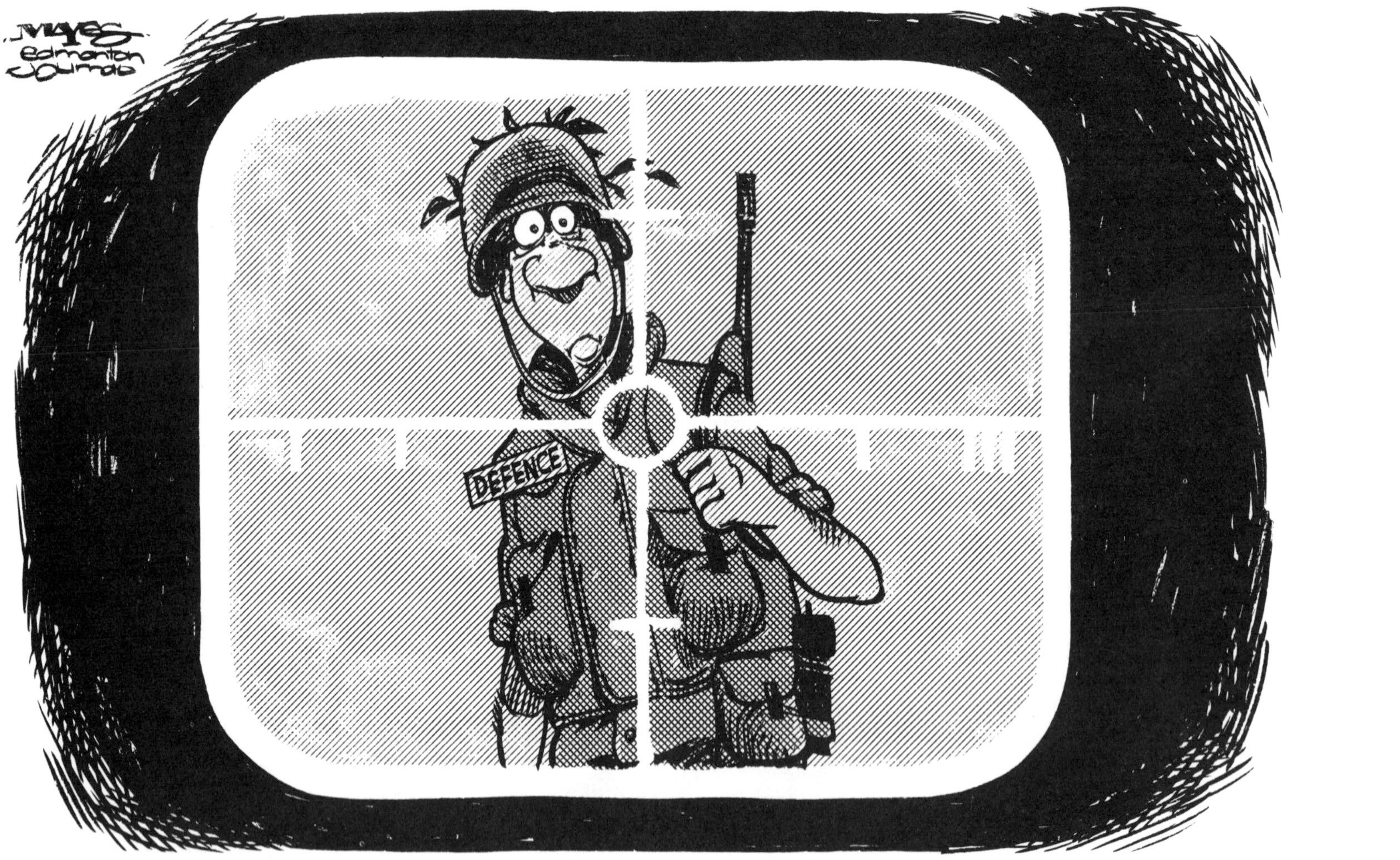
MAYES
edmonton journal
DEFENCE

PAUL MARTIN'S 1994 DEFICIT REDUCTION TARGET.

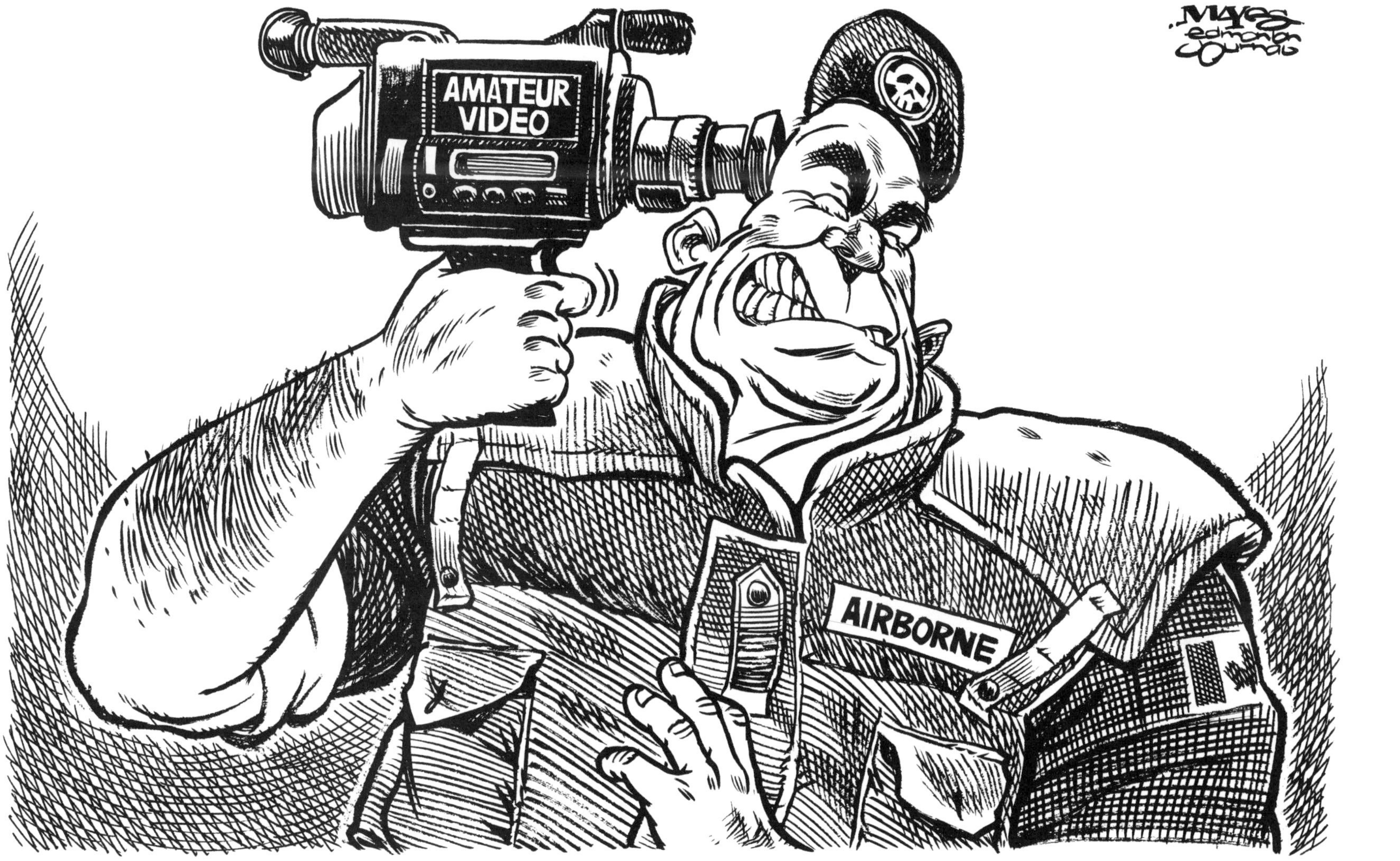
AMATEUR VIDEO
AIRBORNE
Mayes
edmonton journal

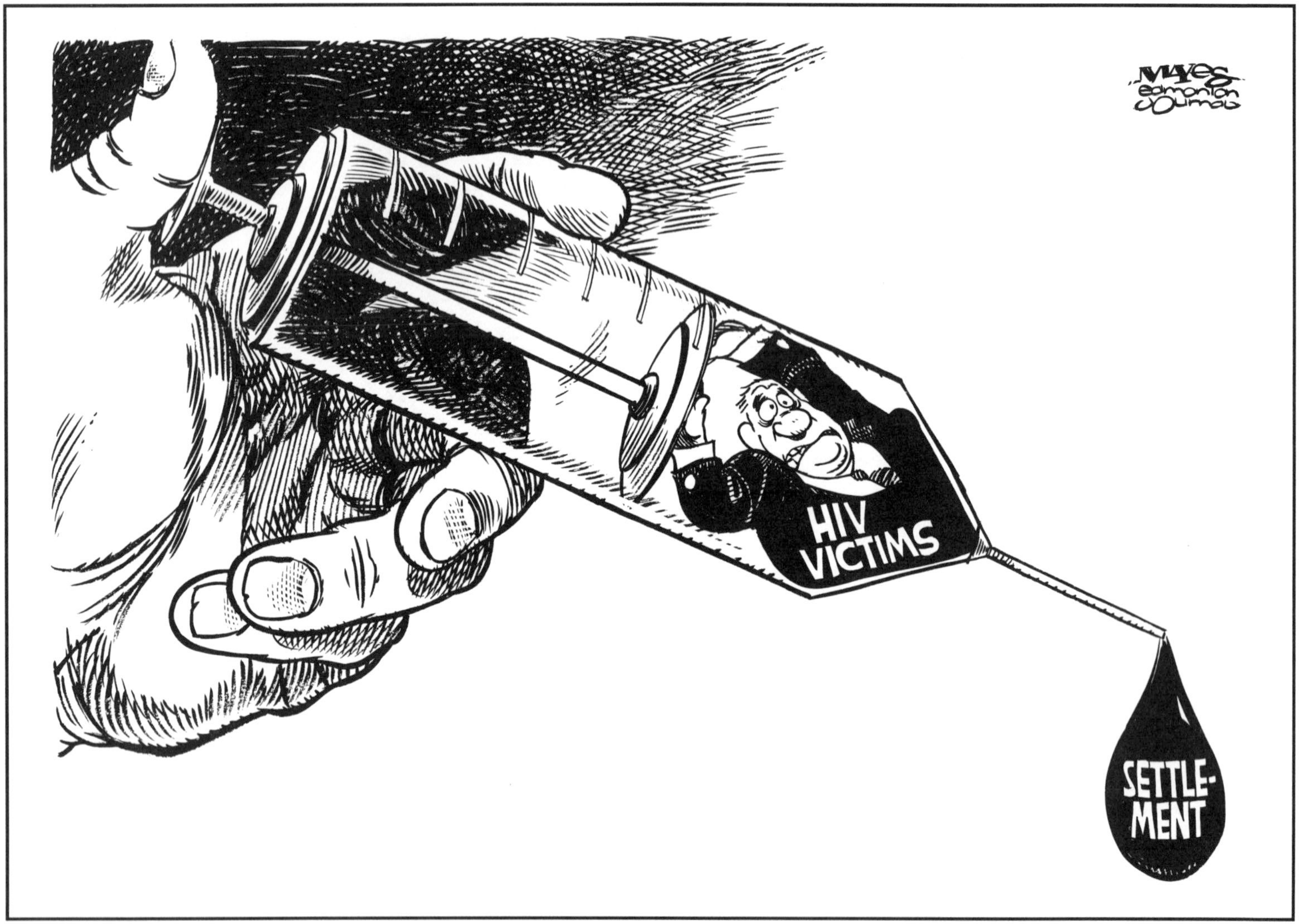
Mayes
edmonton
journal
HIV
VICTIMS
SETTLE-
MENT

Tainted Red Cross blood supply infected many Canadians with HIV.

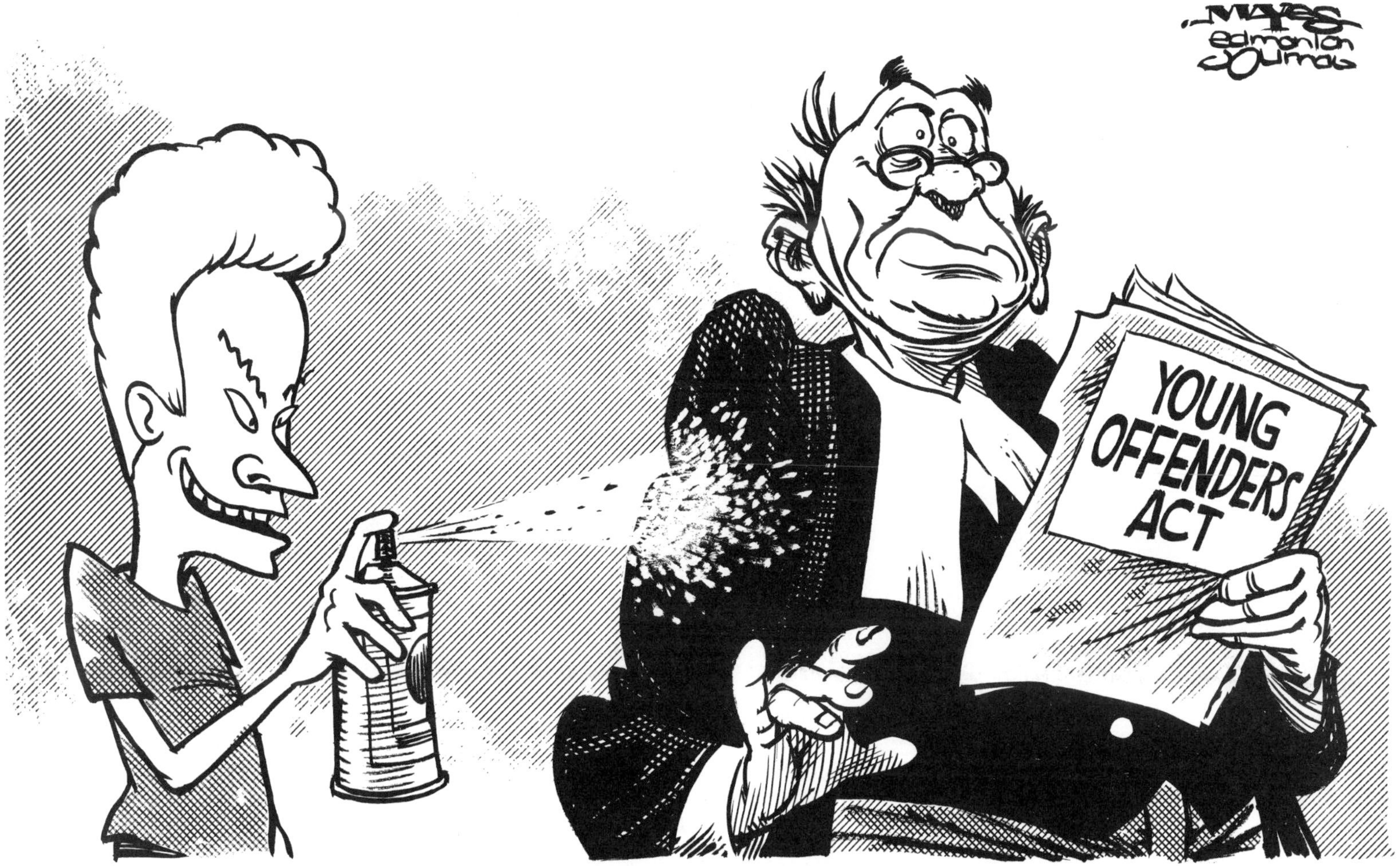
MAYES
edmonton journal
YOUNG OFFENDERS ACT

BEAVIS AND BUTT-HEAD.

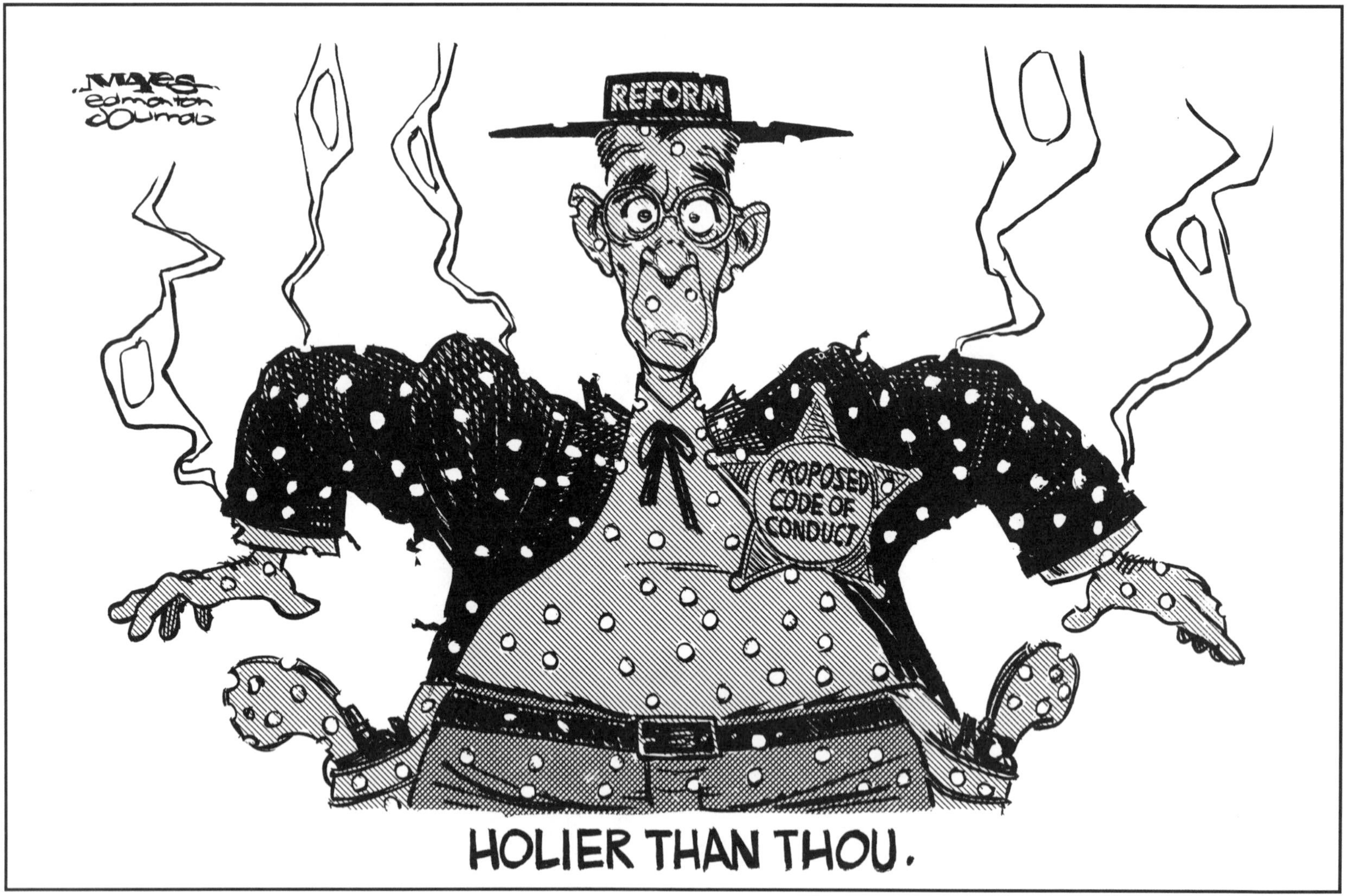
MAYES edmonton journal
REFORM
PROPOSED CODE OF CONDUCT
HOLIER THAN THOU.

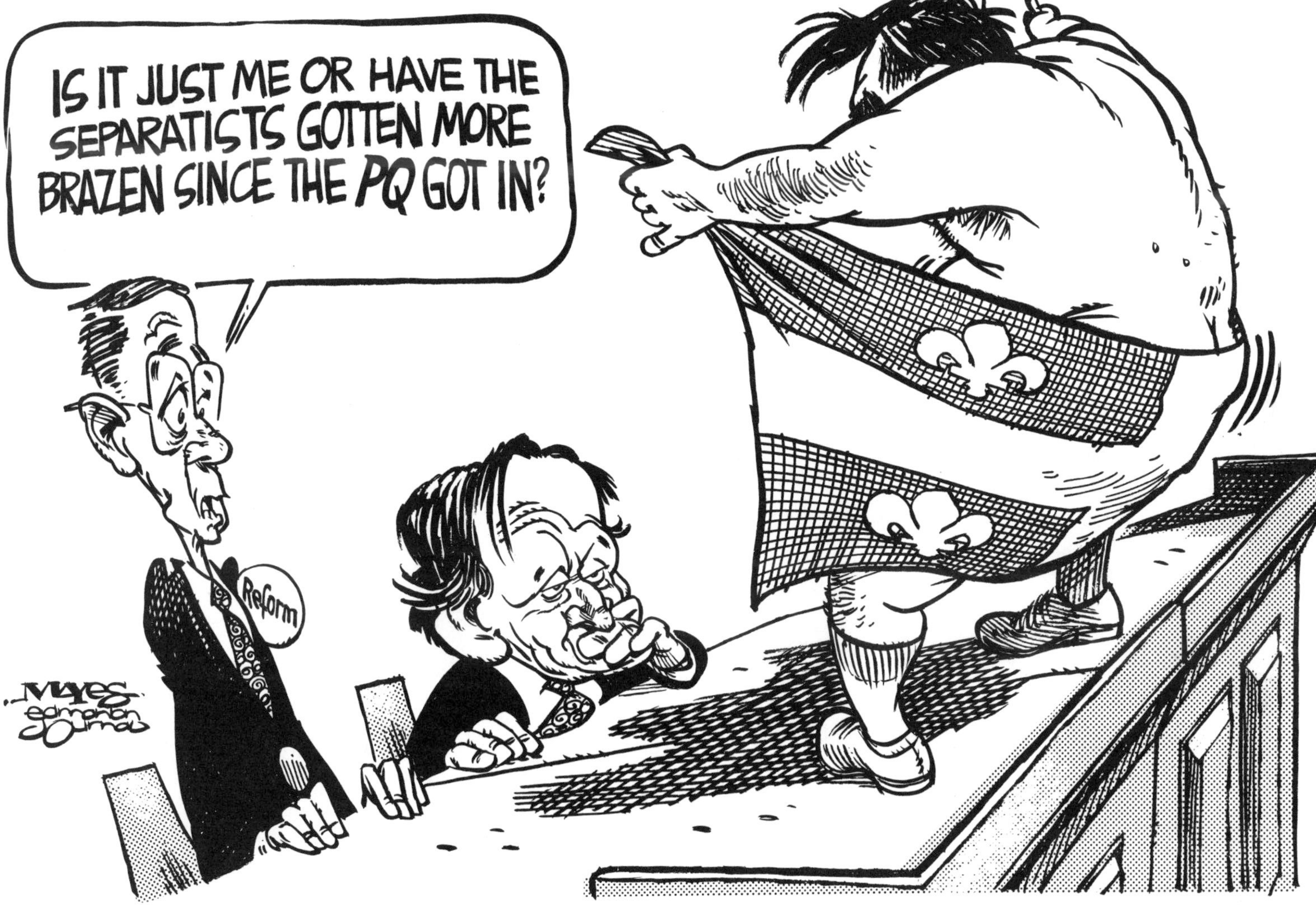
IS IT JUST ME OR HAVE THE SEPARATISTS GOTTEN MORE BRAZEN SINCE THE PQ GOT IN?
Reform
MAYES
edmonton journal

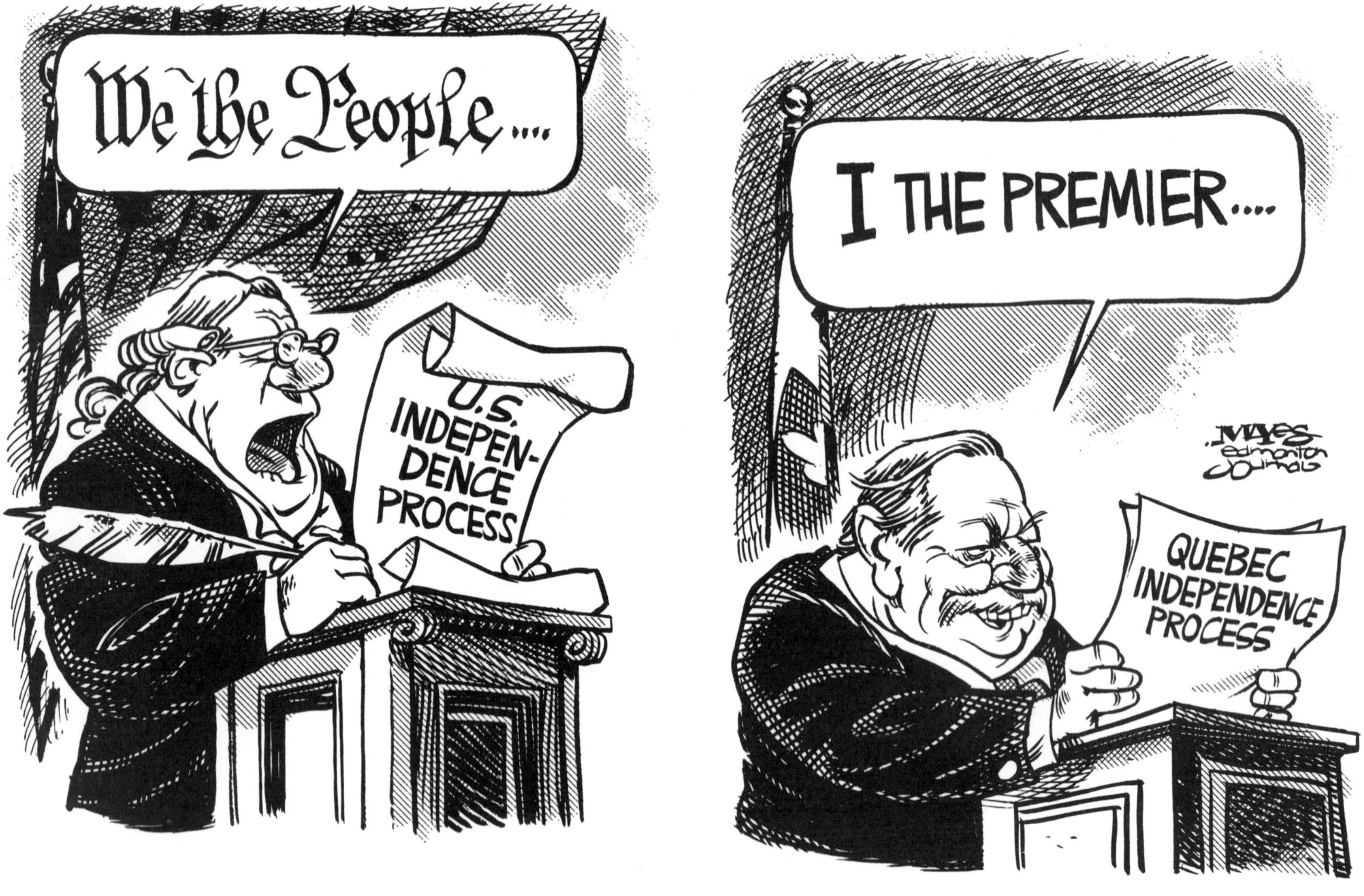
We the People....
U.S.
INDEPEN-
DENCE
PROCESS
I THE PREMIER....
MAYES
QUEBEC
INDEPENDENCE
PROCESS

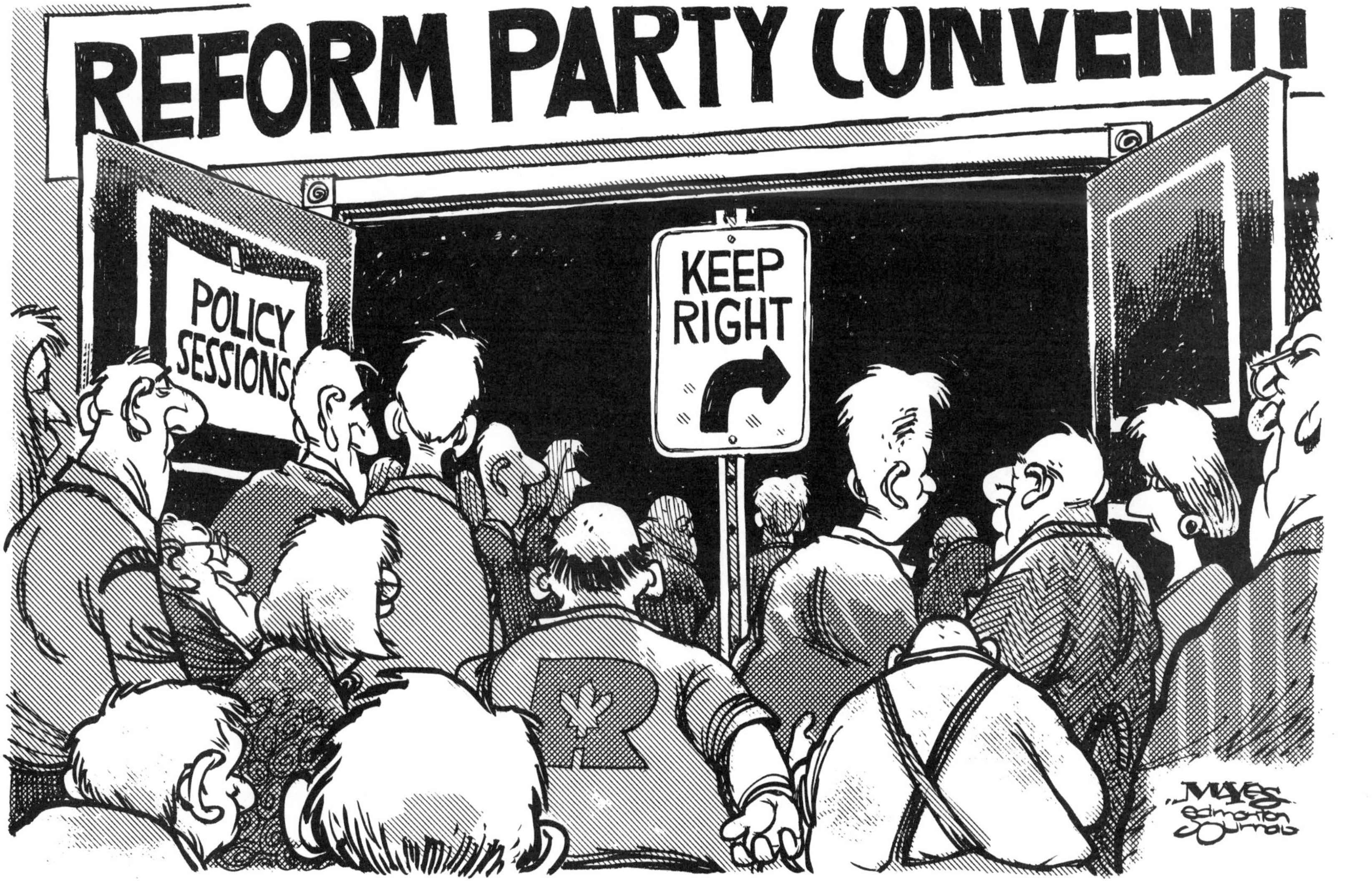
REFORM PARTY CONVENT
POLICY SESSIONS
KEEP RIGHT
MAYES edmonton journal

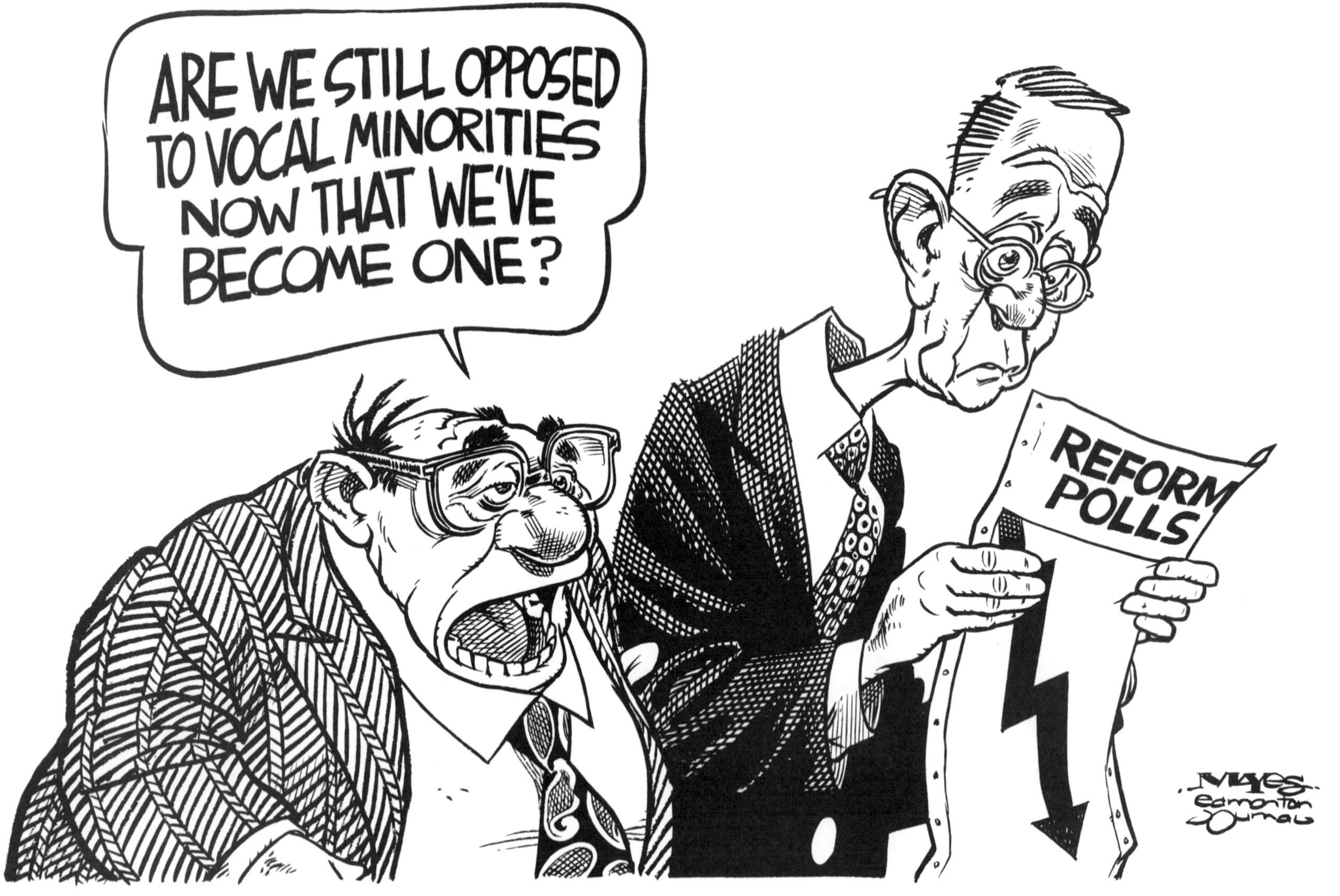
ARE WE STILL OPPOSED TO VOCAL MINORITIES NOW THAT WE'VE BECOME ONE?
REFORM POLLS
MAYES
Edmonton Journal

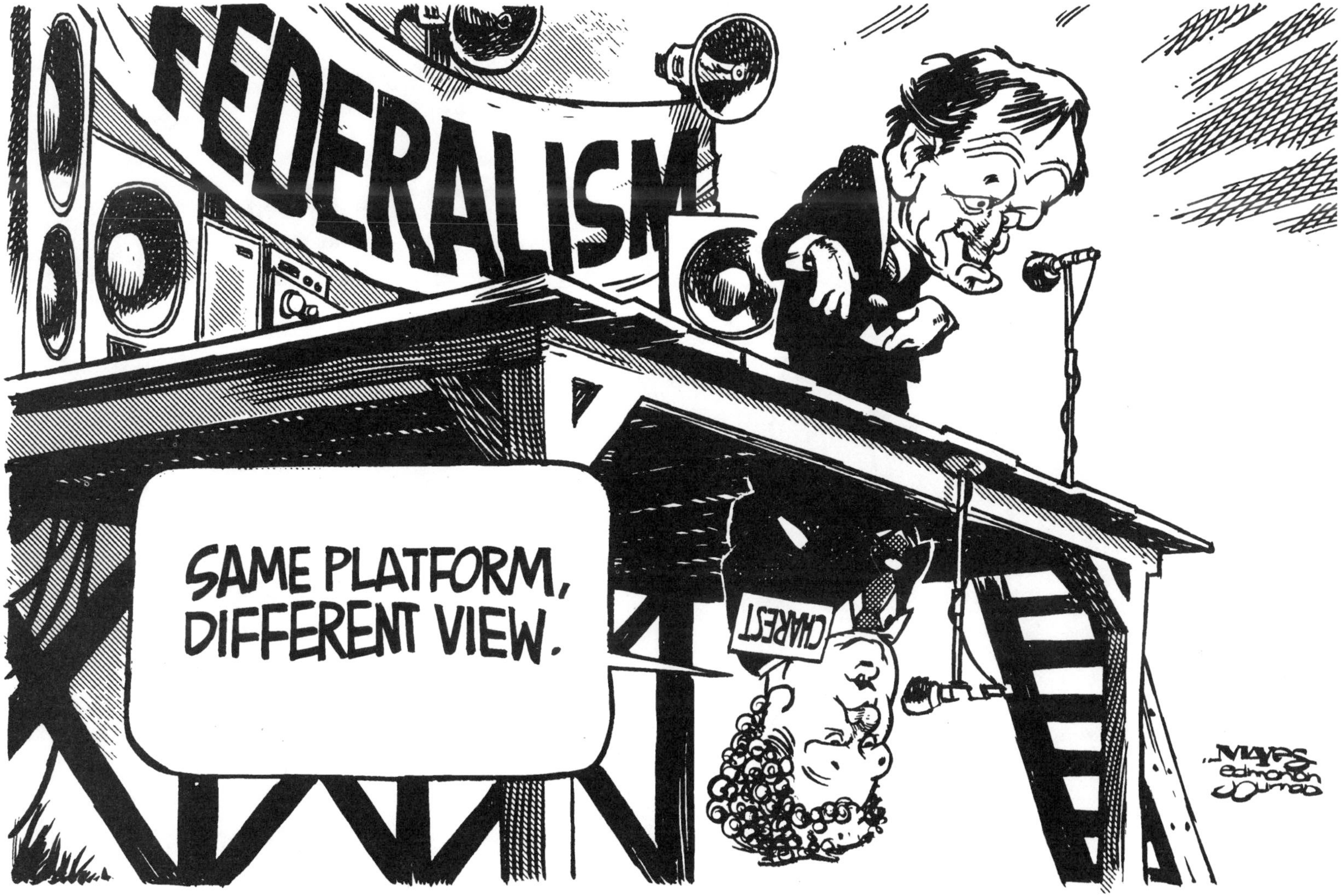
FEDERALISM
SAME PLATFORM, DIFFERENT VIEW.
CHAREST
MAYES edmonton journal

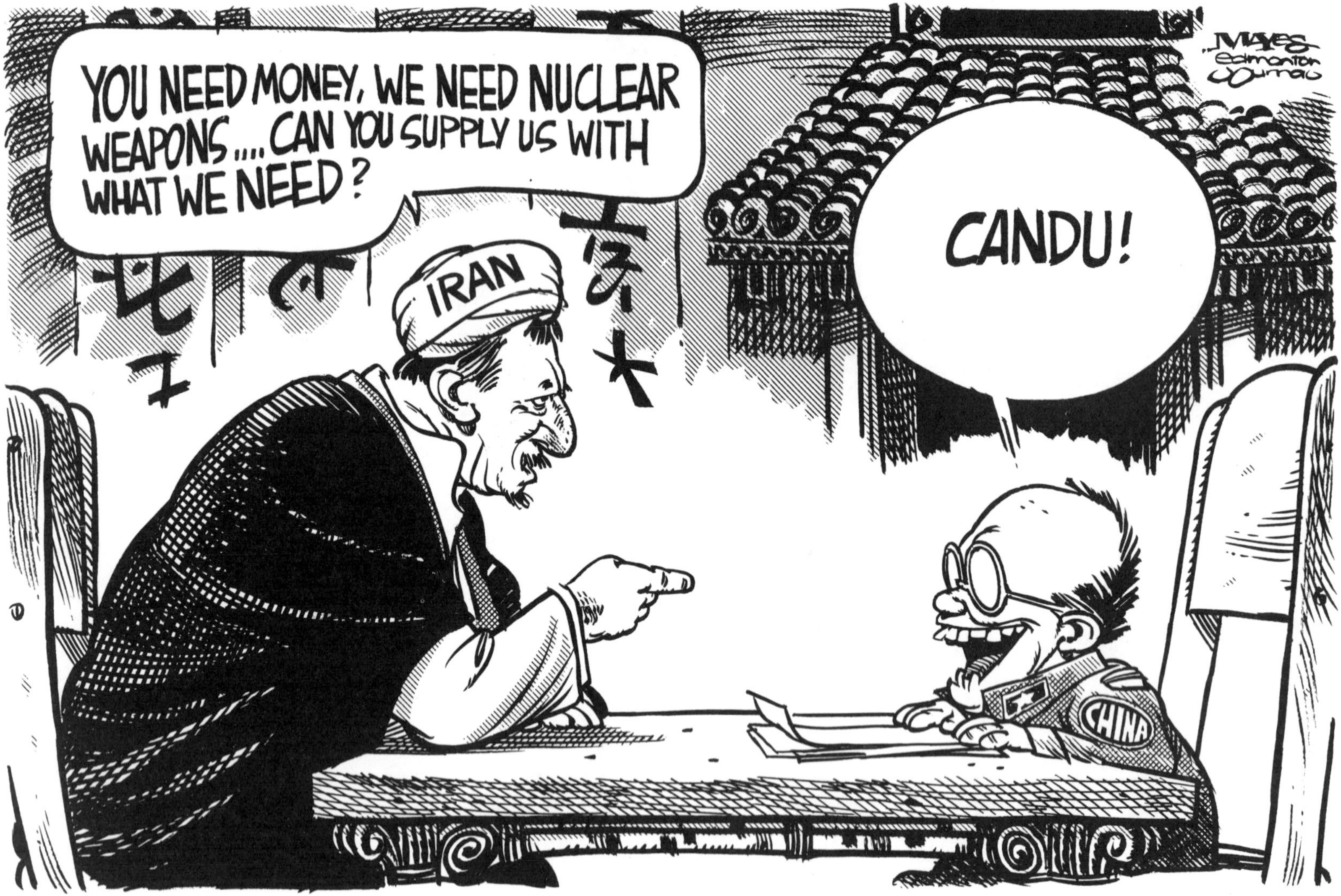
YOU NEED MONEY, WE NEED NUCLEAR WEAPONS.... CAN YOU SUPPLY US WITH WHAT WE NEED?
CANDU!
IRAN
CHINA
MAYES Edmonton Journal

Canada sells nuclear reactors to China.

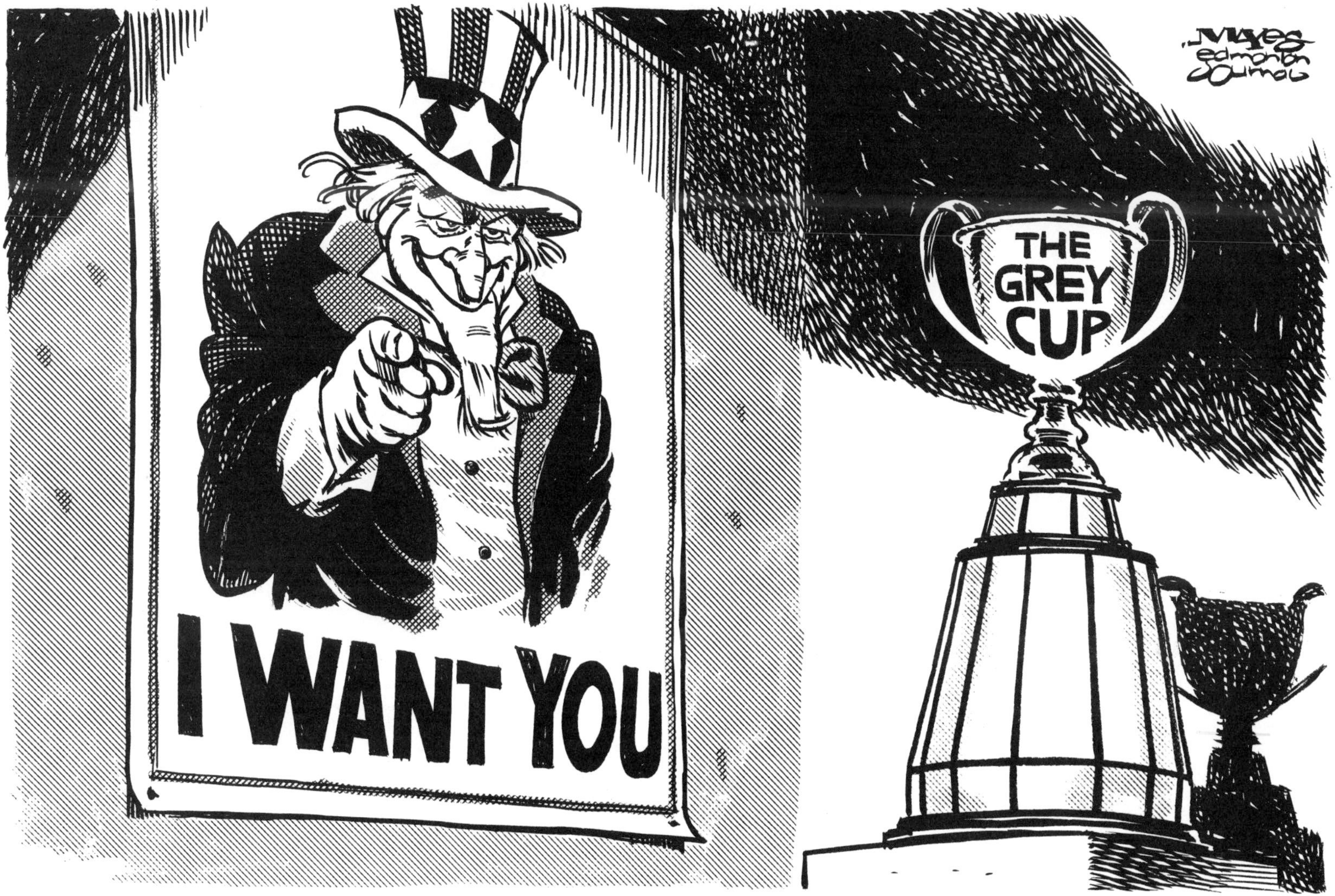
I WANT YOU
THE GREY CUP
Mayes edmonton Journal

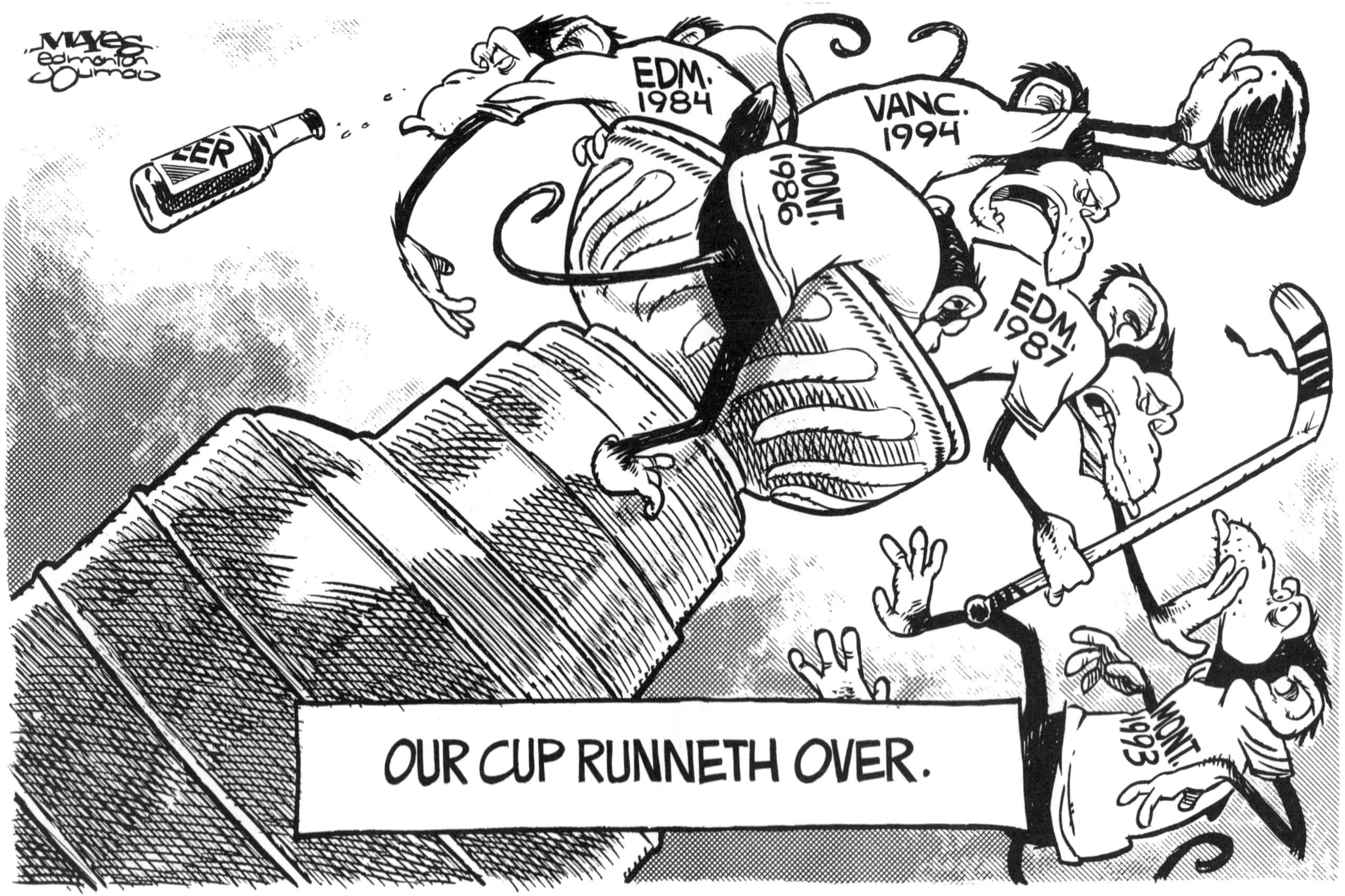
MAYES
edmonton journal
BEER
EDM. 1984
VANC. 1994
MONT. 1986
EDM. 1987
MONT. 1993
OUR CUP RUNNETH OVER.

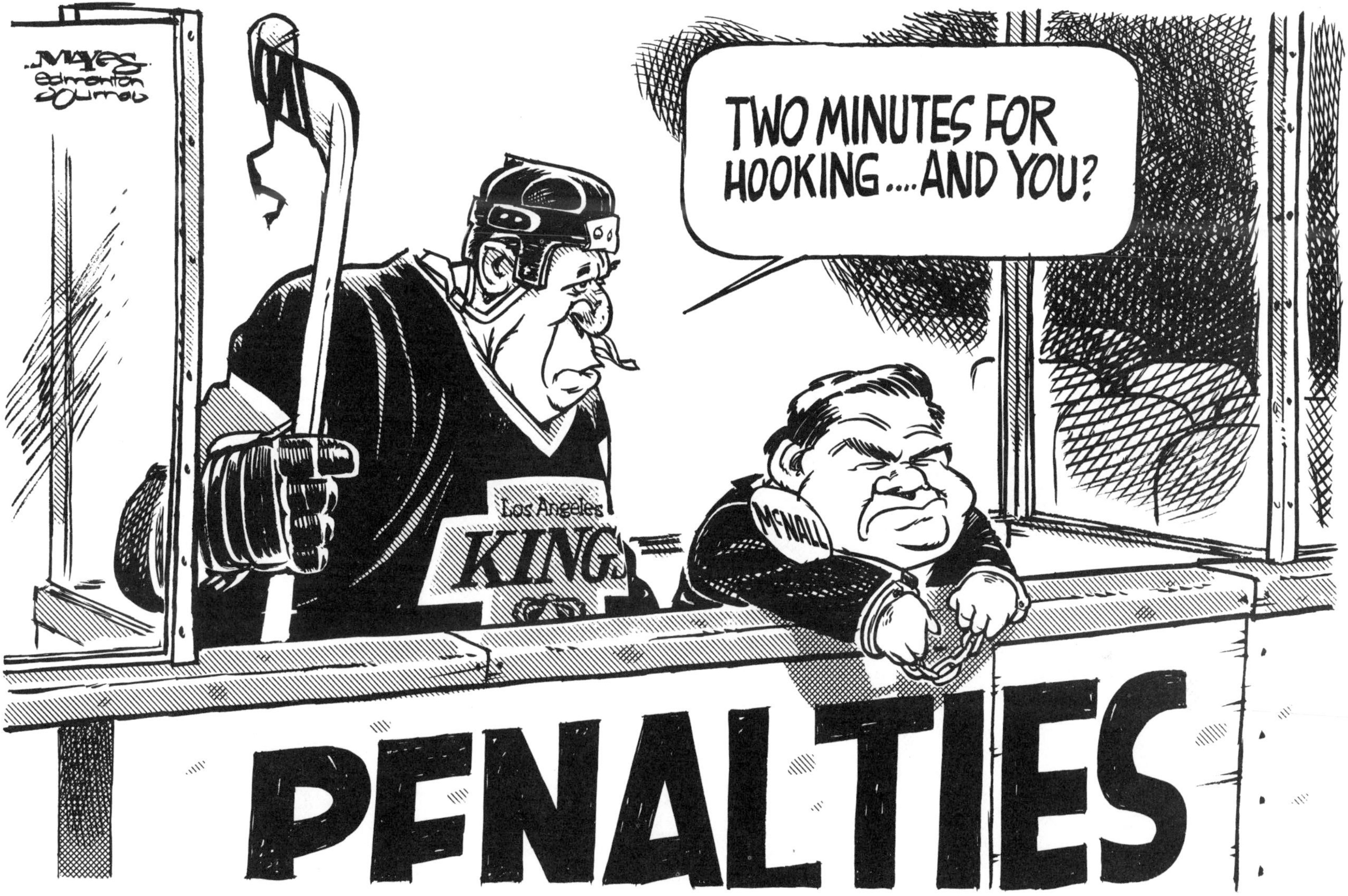
MAYES
Edmonton Journal
TWO MINUTES FOR HOOKING....AND YOU?
Los Angeles
KINGS
McNALL
PENALTIES

LA Kings owner Bruce McNall convicted of fraud.

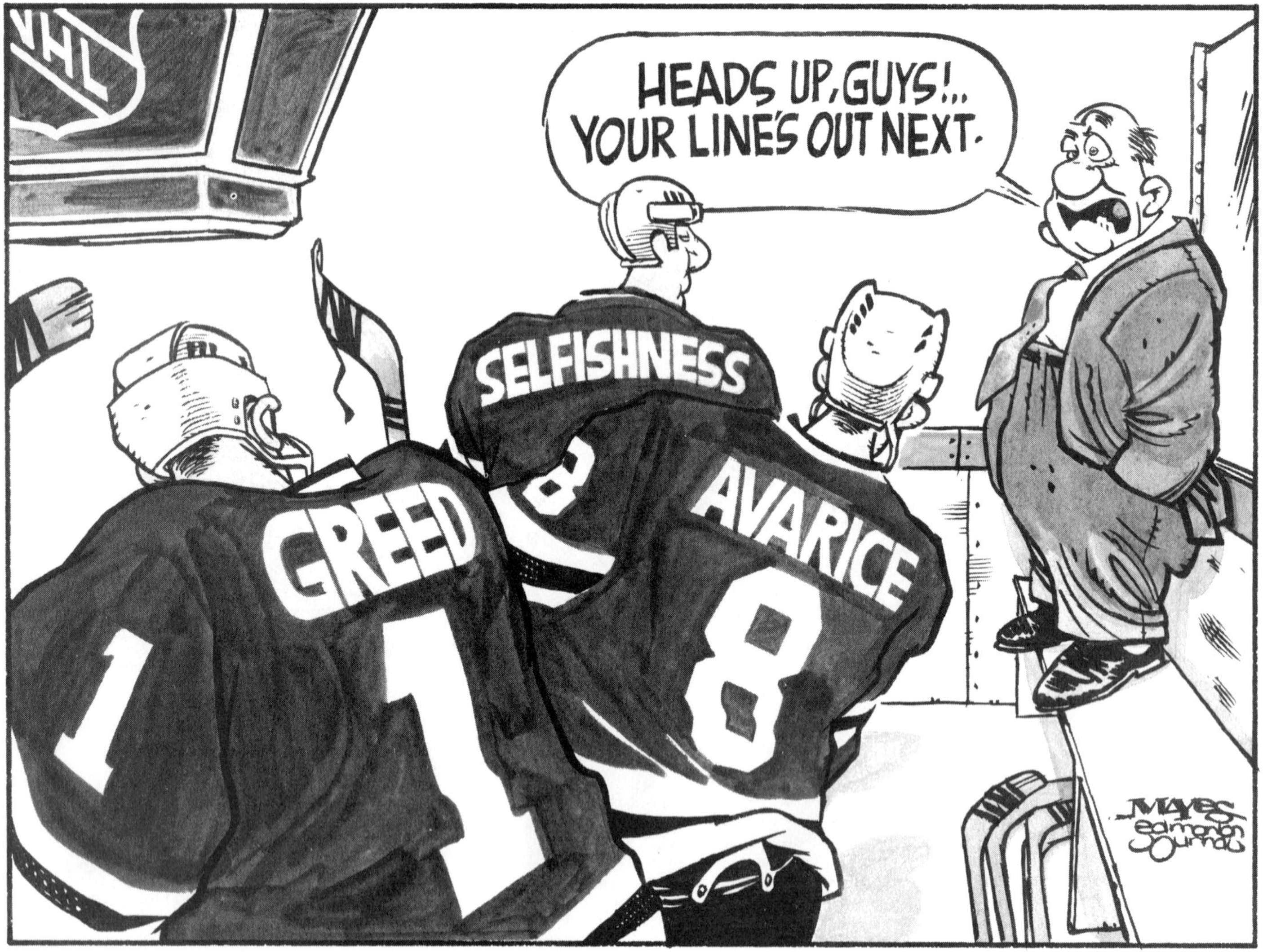
NHL
HEADS UP, GUYS!..
YOUR LINE'S OUT NEXT.
SELFISHNESS
GREED
1
AVARICE
8
MAYES
edmonton journal

NHL pay dispute cuts hockey season in half.

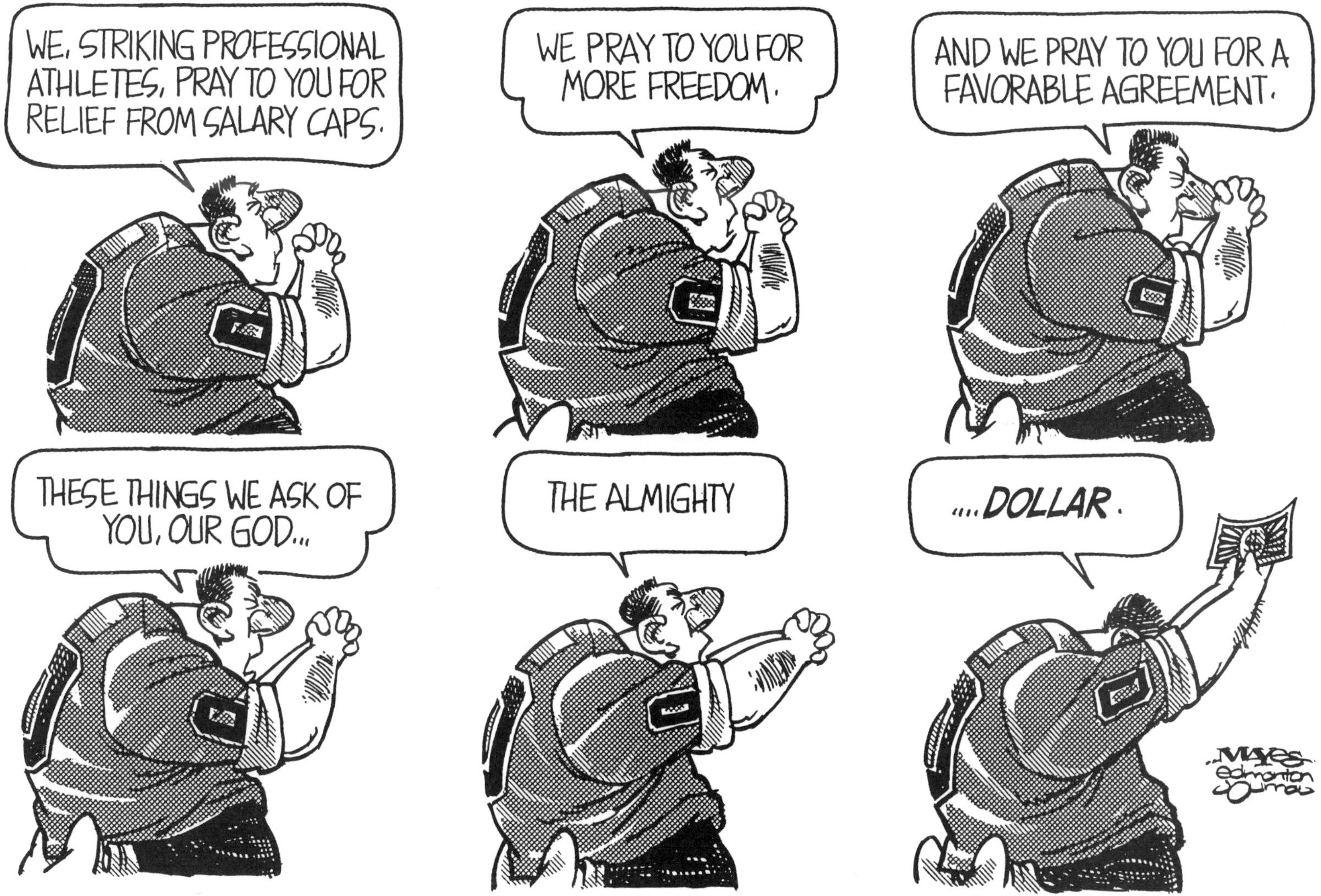
WE, STRIKING PROFESSIONAL ATHLETES, PRAY TO YOU FOR RELIEF FROM SALARY CAPS.
WE PRAY TO YOU FOR MORE FREEDOM.
AND WE PRAY TO YOU FOR A FAVORABLE AGREEMENT.
THESE THINGS WE ASK OF YOU, OUR GOD...
THE ALMIGHTY
....DOLLAR.
MAYES
edmonton journal

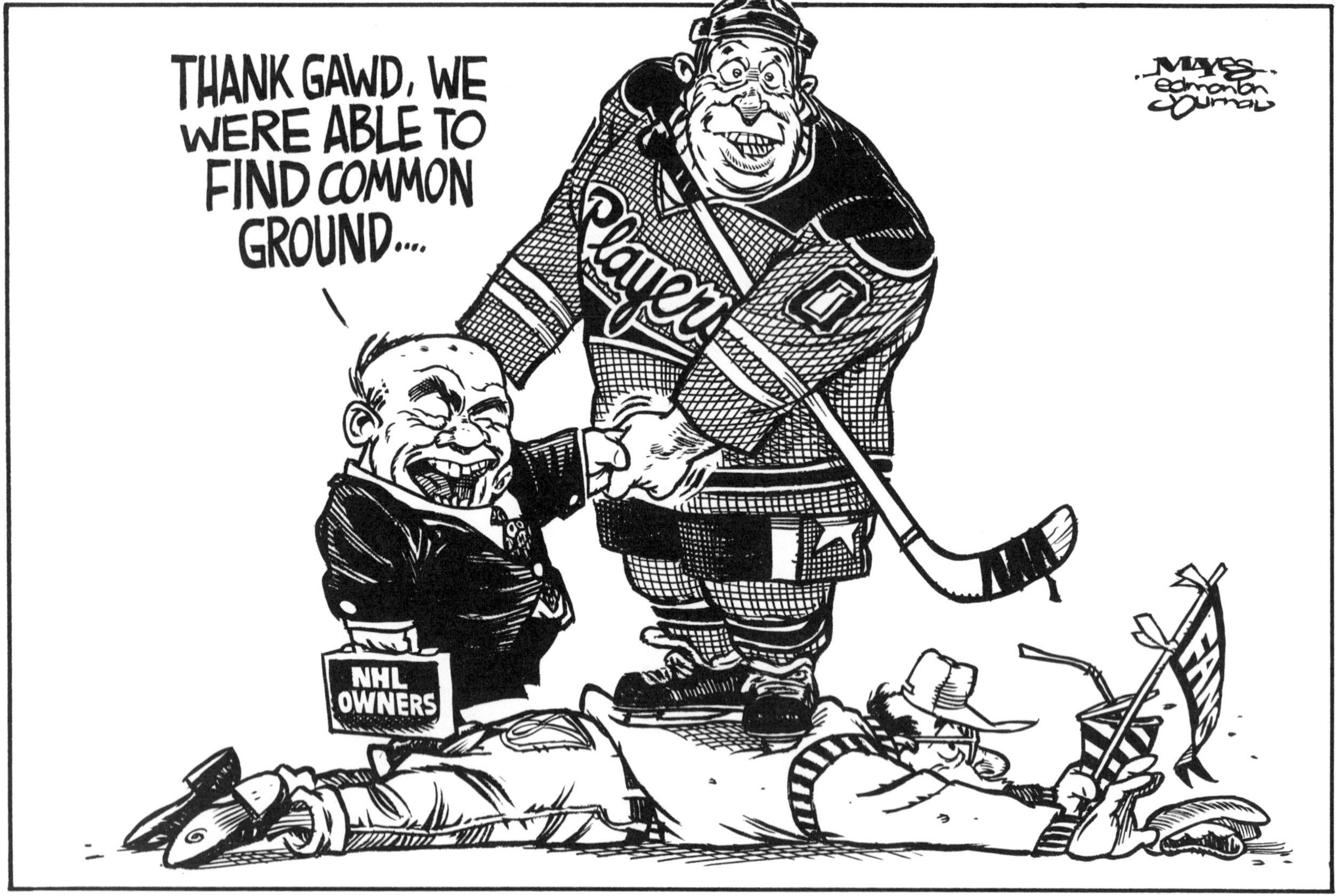

THANK GAWD, WE WERE ABLE TO FIND COMMON GROUND....
MAYES edmonton journal
Players
NHL OWNERS
FANS

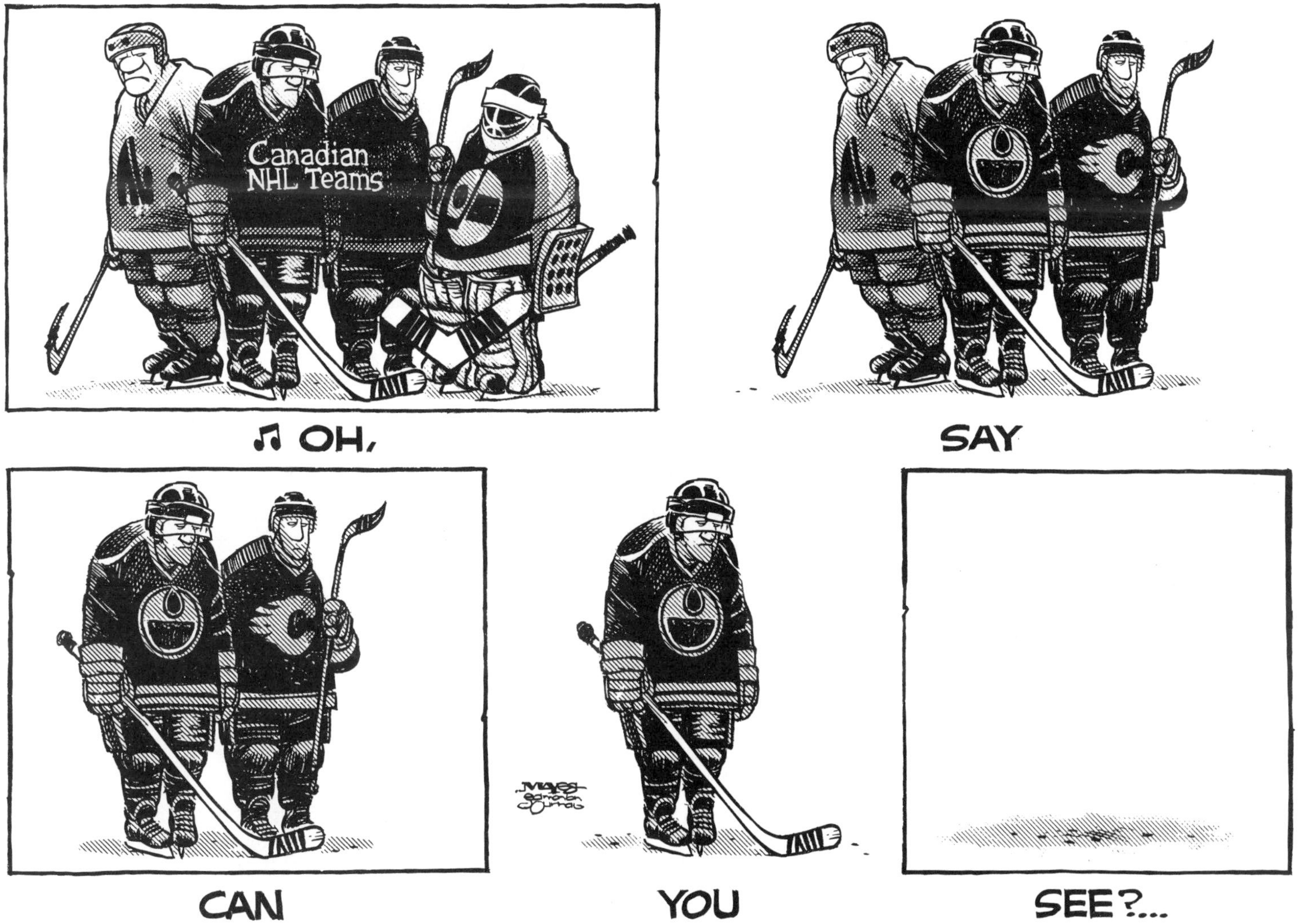
Canadian NHL Teams
♫ OH,
SAY
CAN
YOU
SEE?...

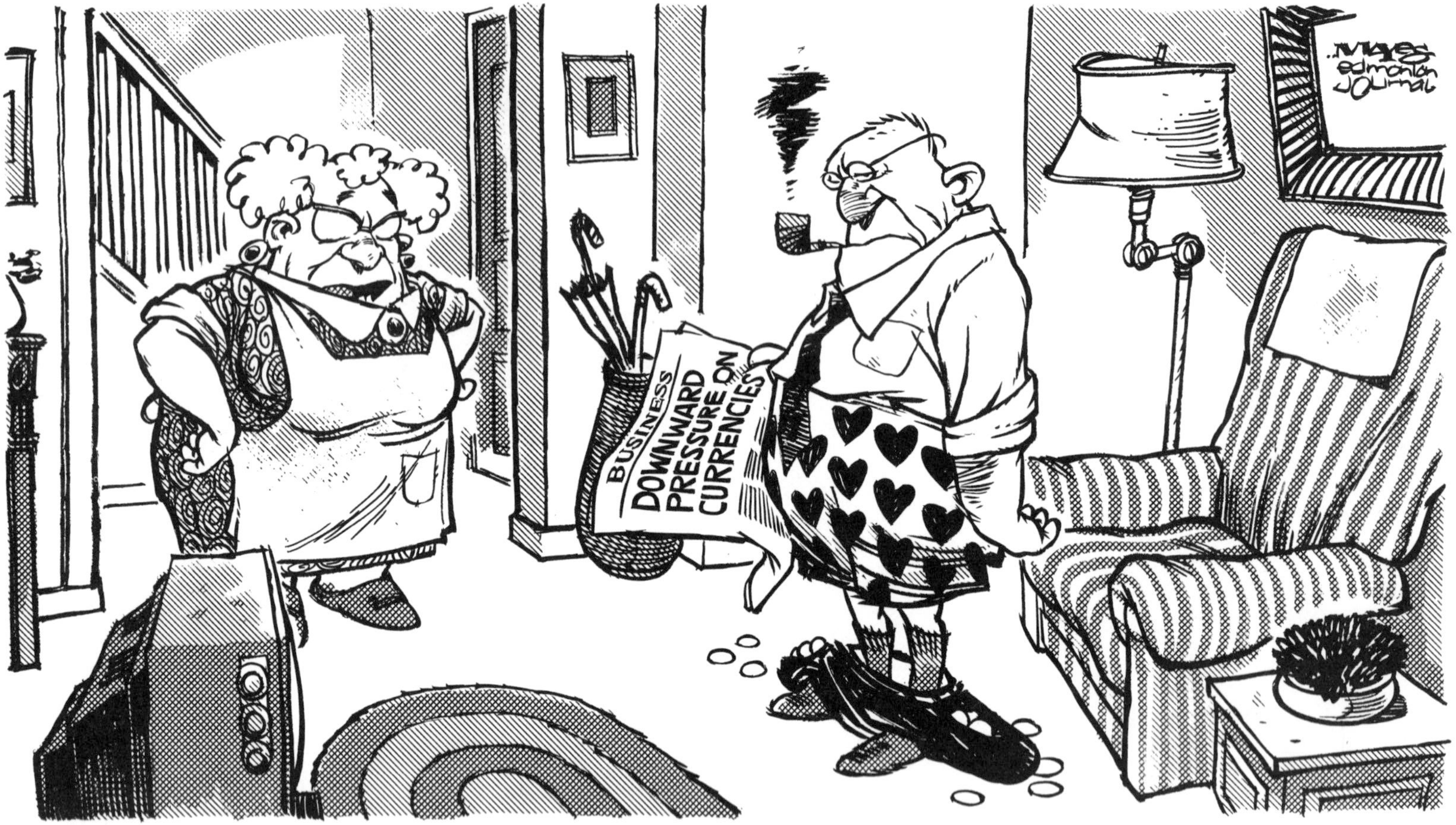
MAYES
edmonton
journal
BUSINESS
DOWNWARD PRESSURE ON CURRENCIES

"WELL, FOR HEAVEN'S SAKE, NO WONDER THEY WON'T STAY UP!.... YOU'VE GOT MEXICAN PESOS IN ONE POCKET AND CANADIAN DOLLARS IN THE OTHER!"

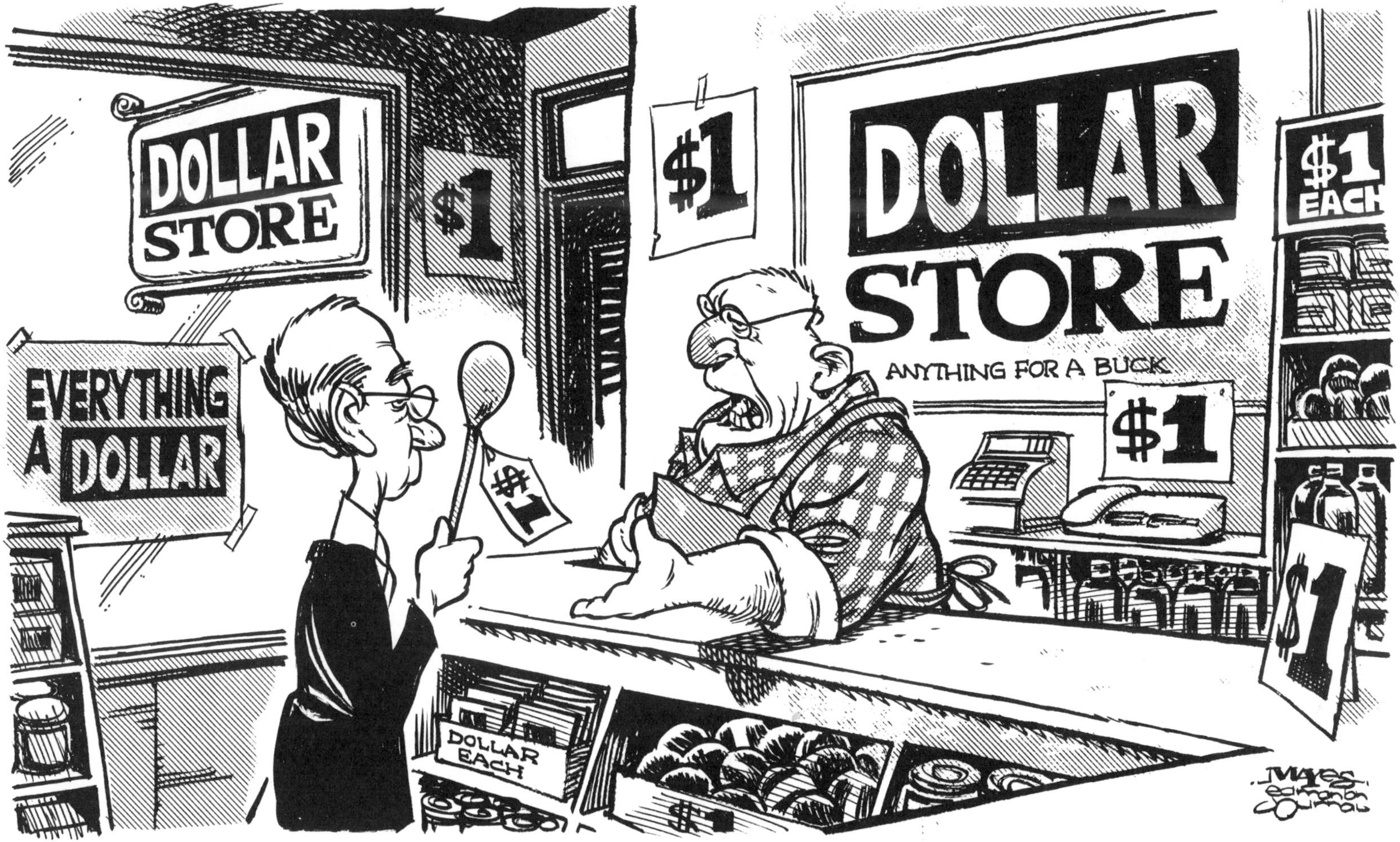
DOLLAR STORE
$1
$1
DOLLAR STORE
ANYTHING FOR A BUCK
$1 EACH
EVERYTHING A DOLLAR
$1
$1
$1
DOLLAR EACH
$1
MAYES
Edmonton Journal

" THAT'LL BE 70¢."

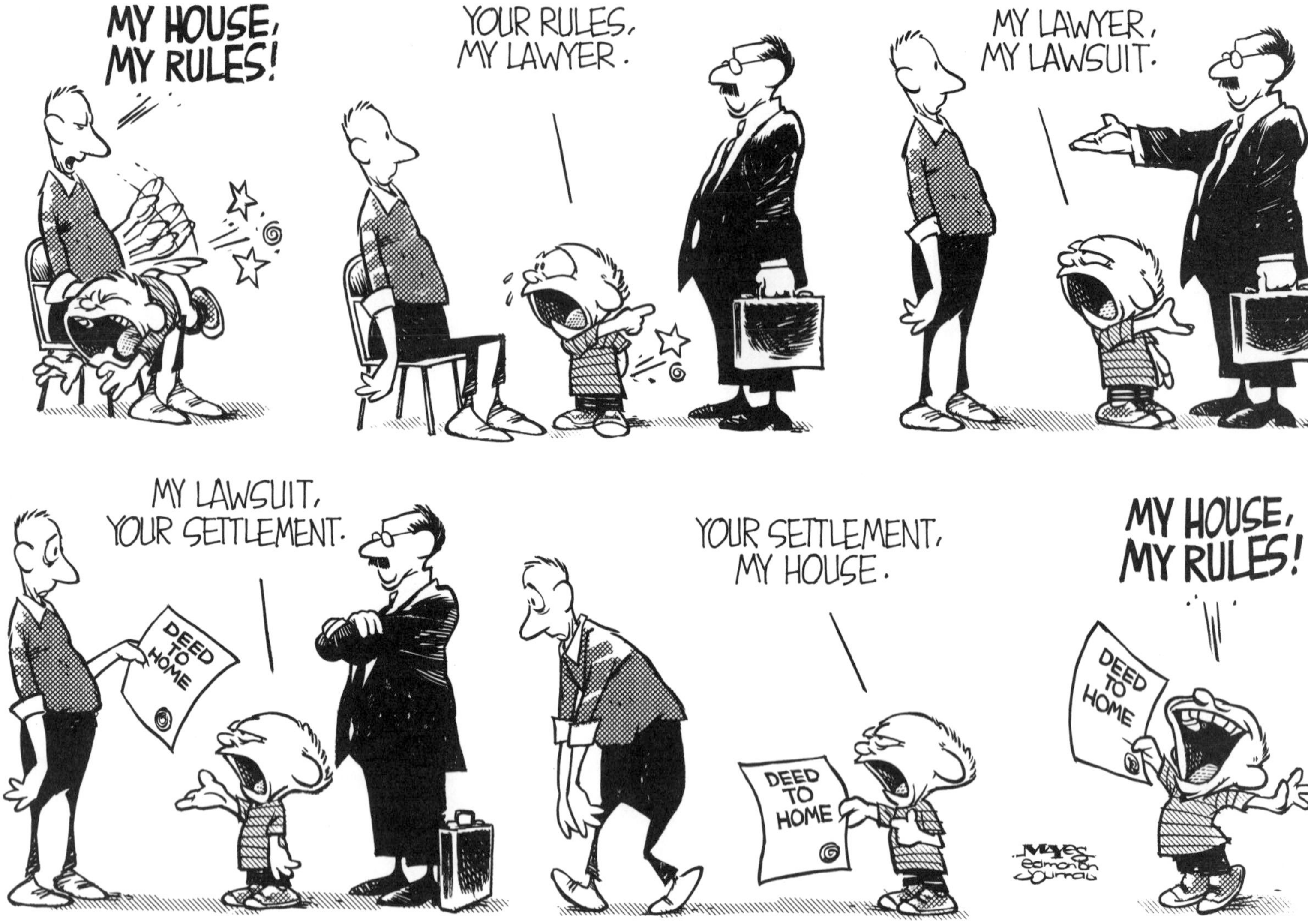
MY HOUSE, MY RULES!
YOUR RULES, MY LAWYER.
MY LAWYER, MY LAWSUIT.
MY LAWSUIT, YOUR SETTLEMENT.
DEED TO HOME
YOUR SETTLEMENT, MY HOUSE.
DEED TO HOME
MAYES edmonton journal
DEED TO HOME
MY HOUSE, MY RULES!

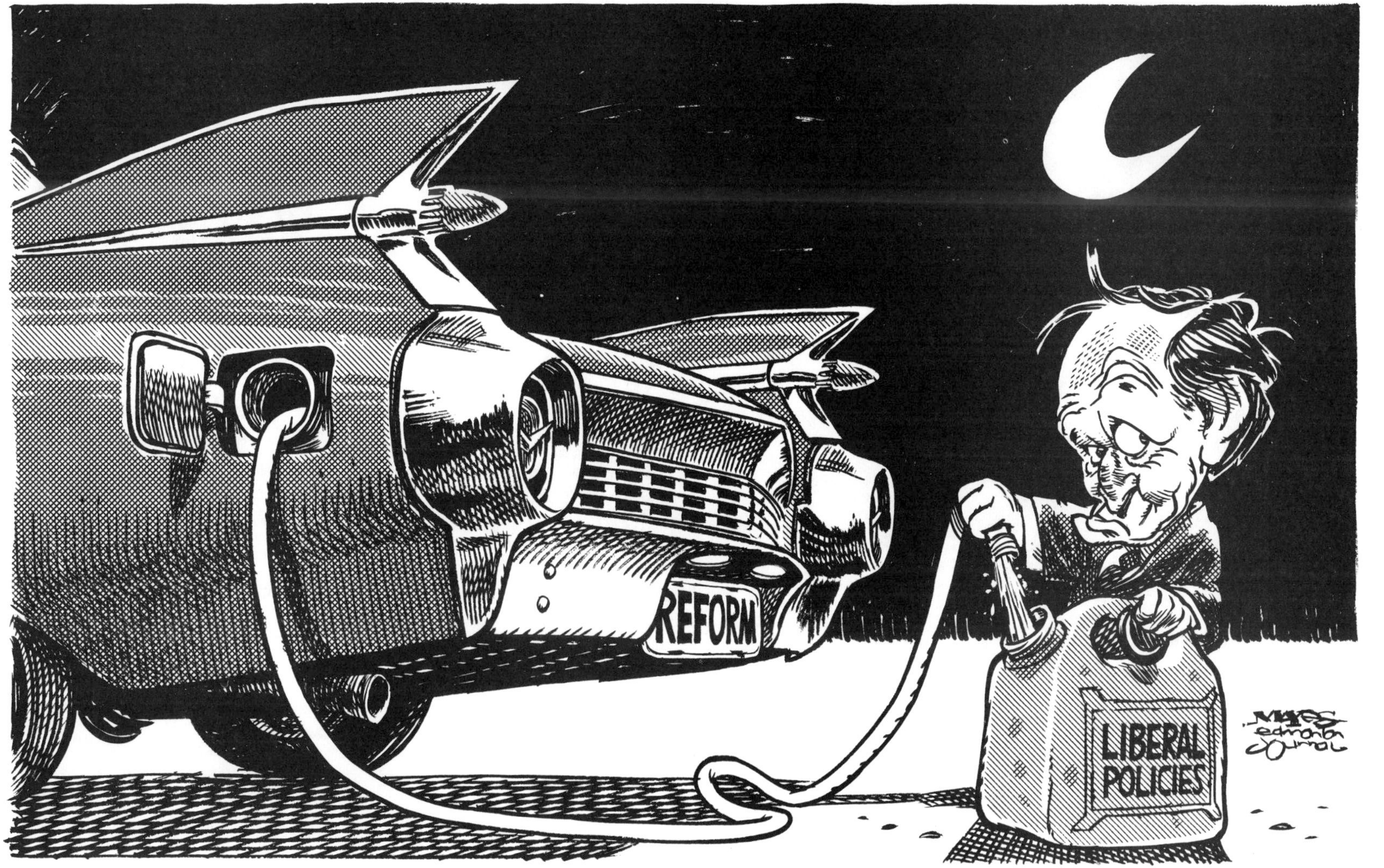
REFORM
LIBERAL POLICIES

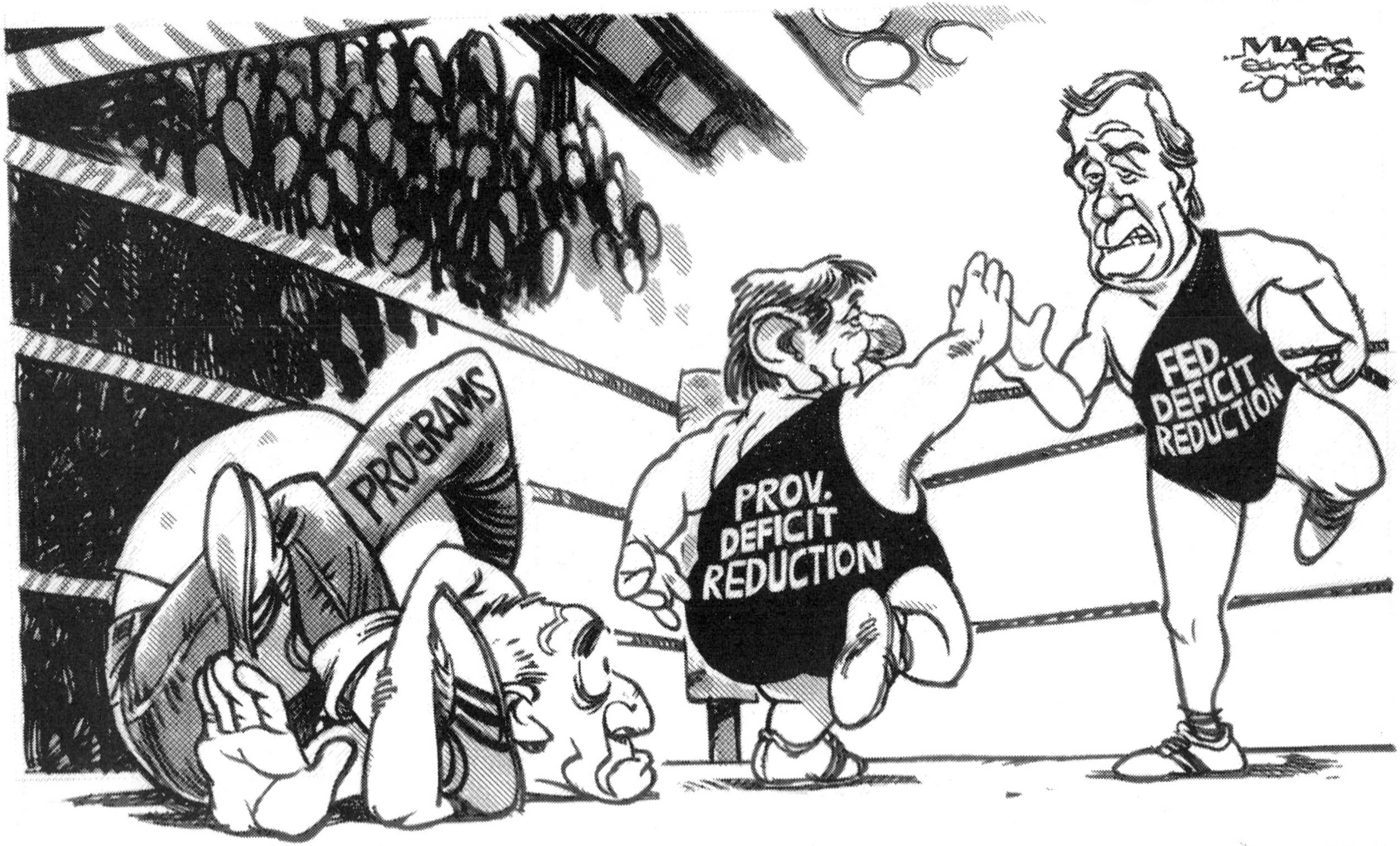
PROGRAMS
PROV. DEFICIT REDUCTION
FED. DEFICIT REDUCTION

TAG TEAM.

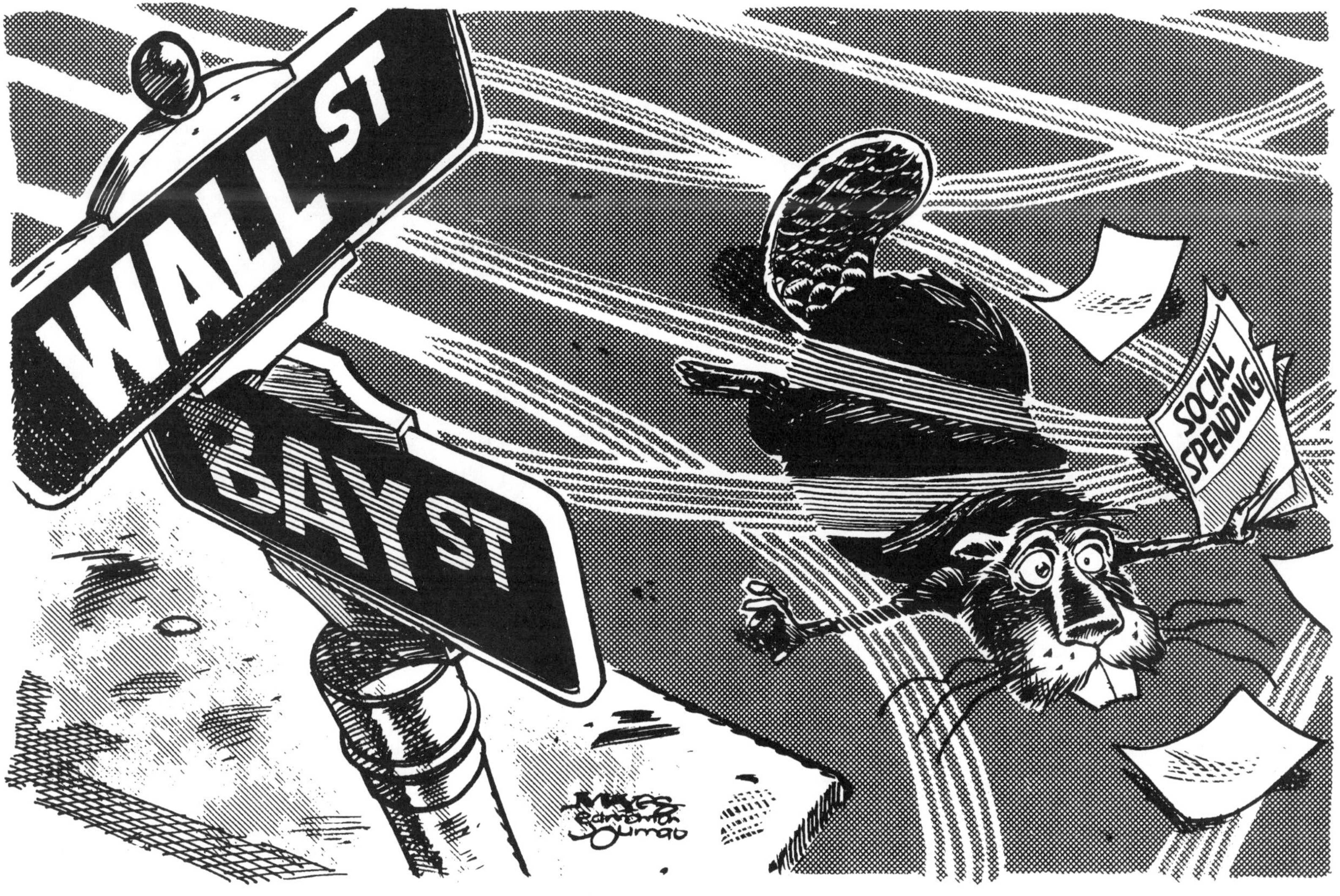
WALL ST
BAY ST
SOCIAL SPENDING

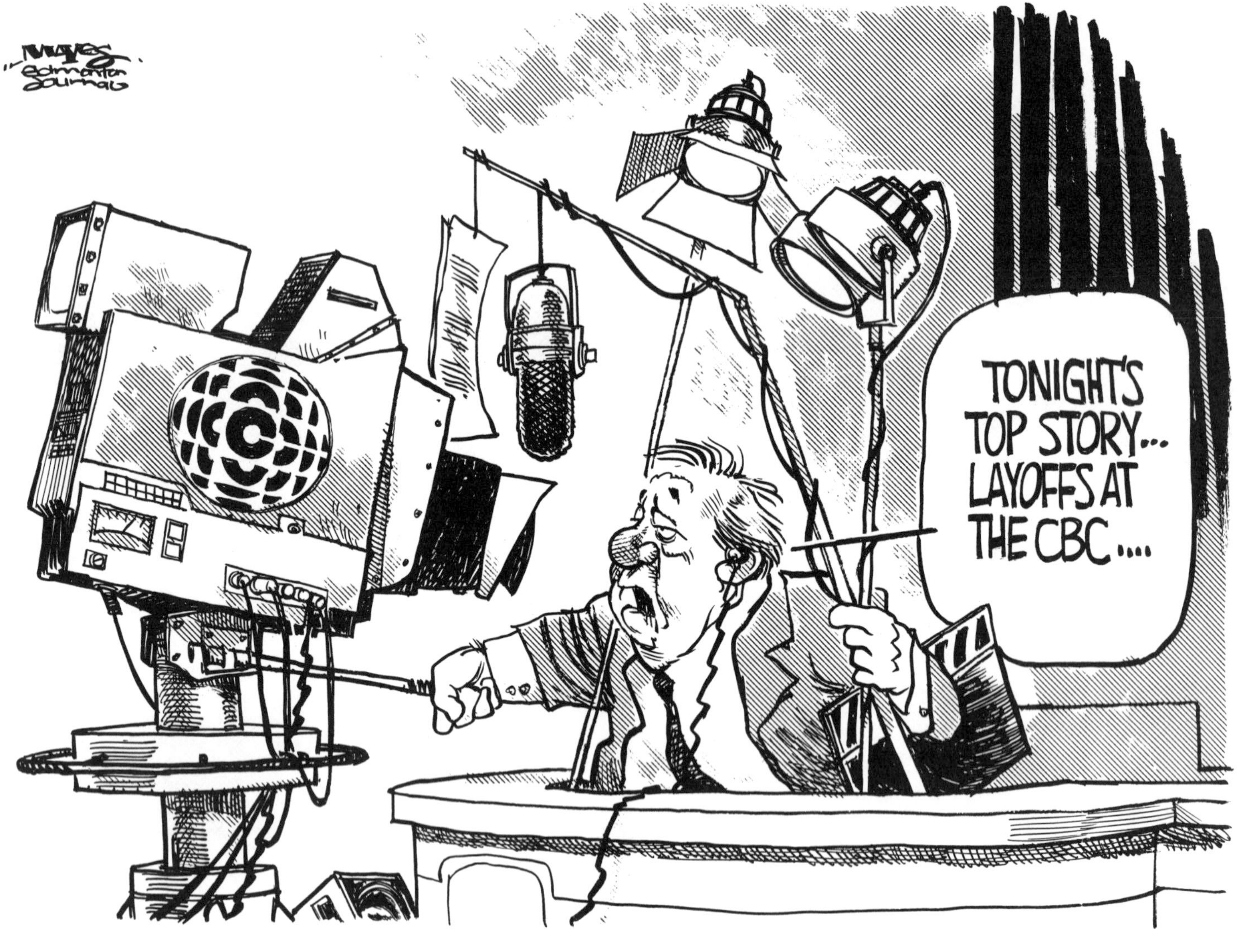
TONIGHT'S TOP STORY... LAYOFFS AT THE CBC ....

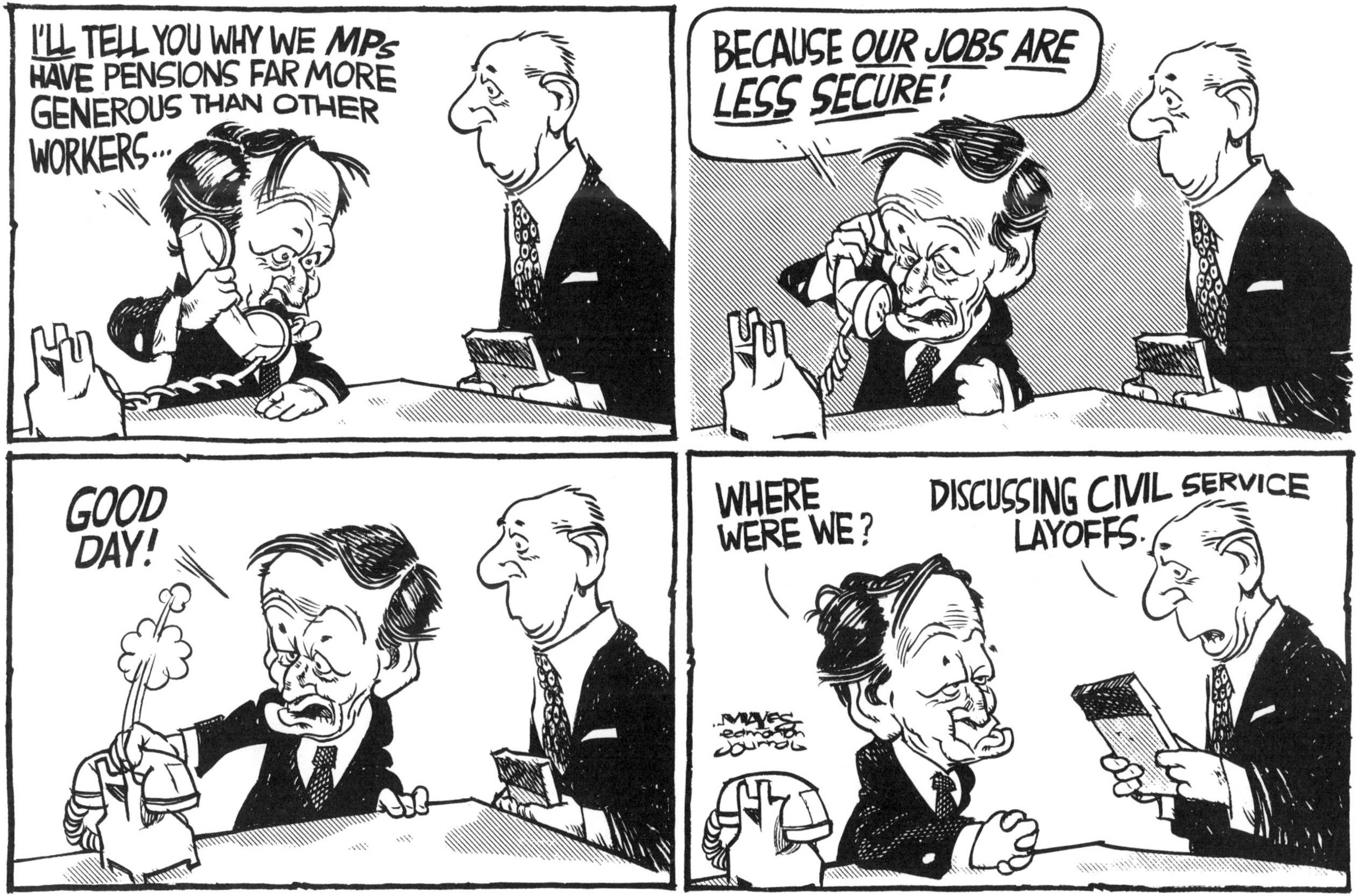
I'LL TELL YOU WHY WE MPs HAVE PENSIONS FAR MORE GENEROUS THAN OTHER WORKERS...
BECAUSE OUR JOBS ARE LESS SECURE!
GOOD DAY!
WHERE WERE WE?
DISCUSSING CIVIL SERVICE LAYOFFS.
MAYES edmonton journal

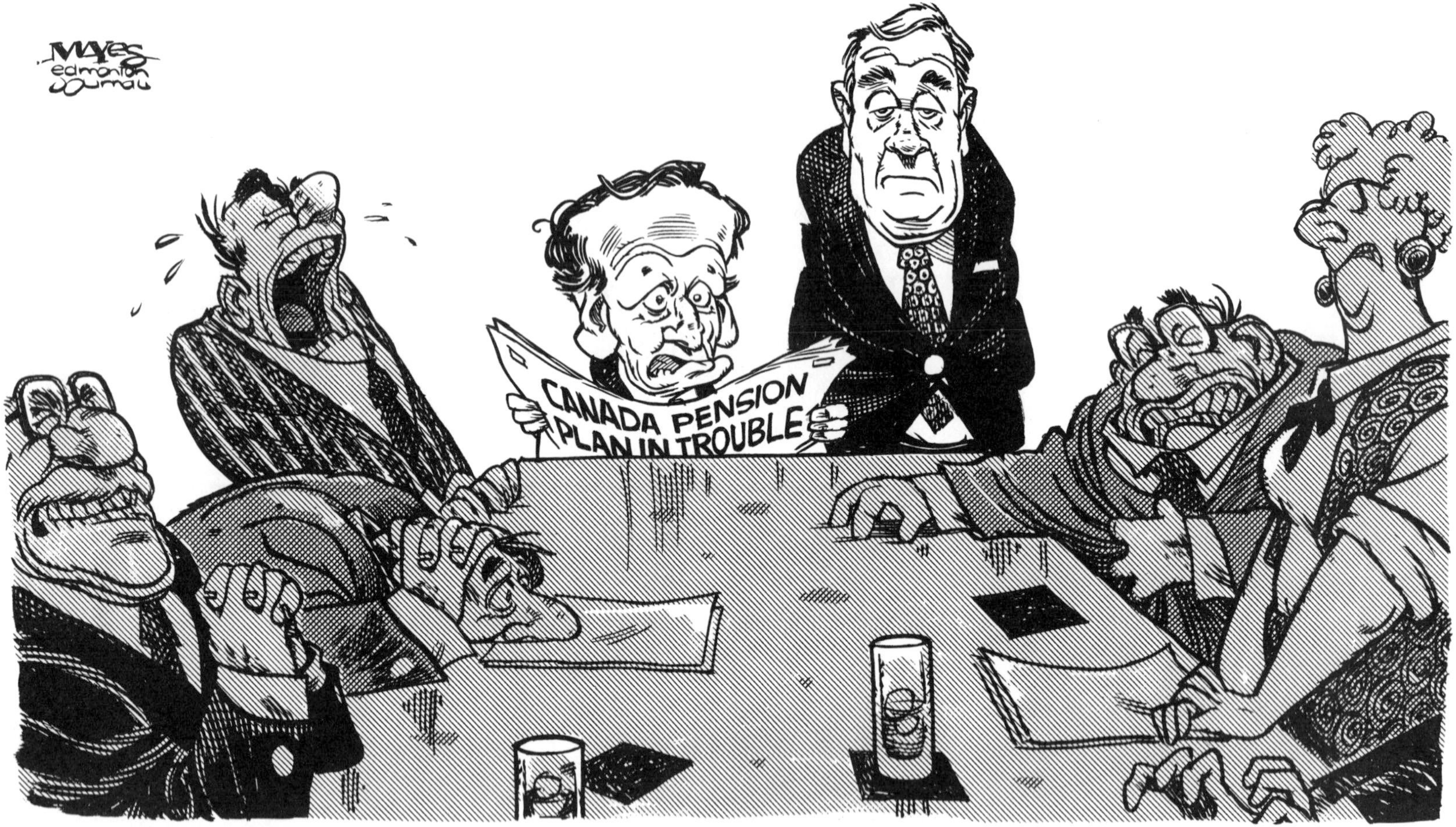
MAYES
edmonton journal
CANADA PENSION PLAN IN TROUBLE

"***RELAX, EVERYONE***.... WHEN PAUL SAID OUR MPs' PENSION PLAN WAS BANKRUPT TOO —— .. HE MEANT ***MORALLY***."

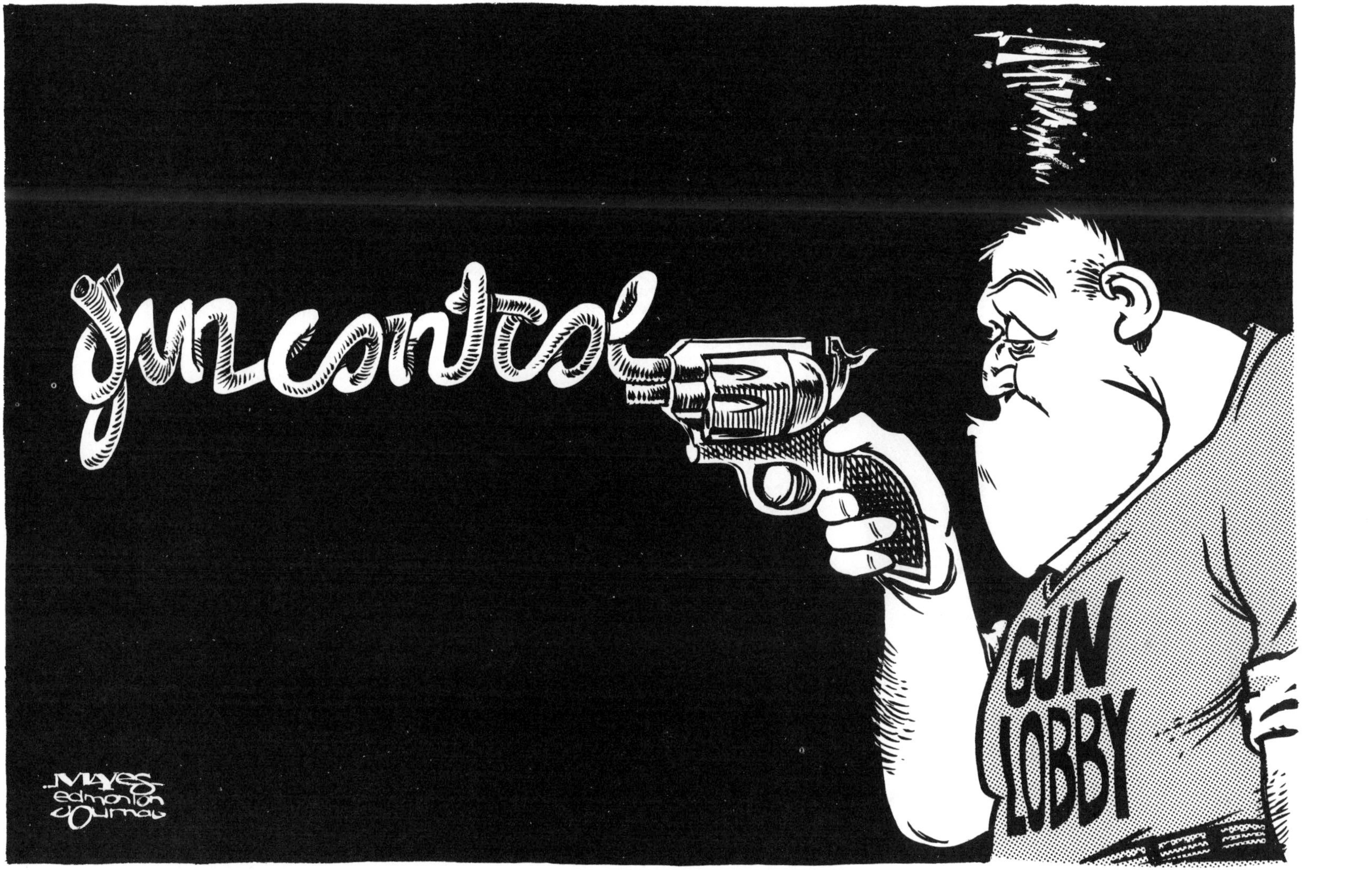

gun control
GUN LOBBY
MAYES
edmonton journal

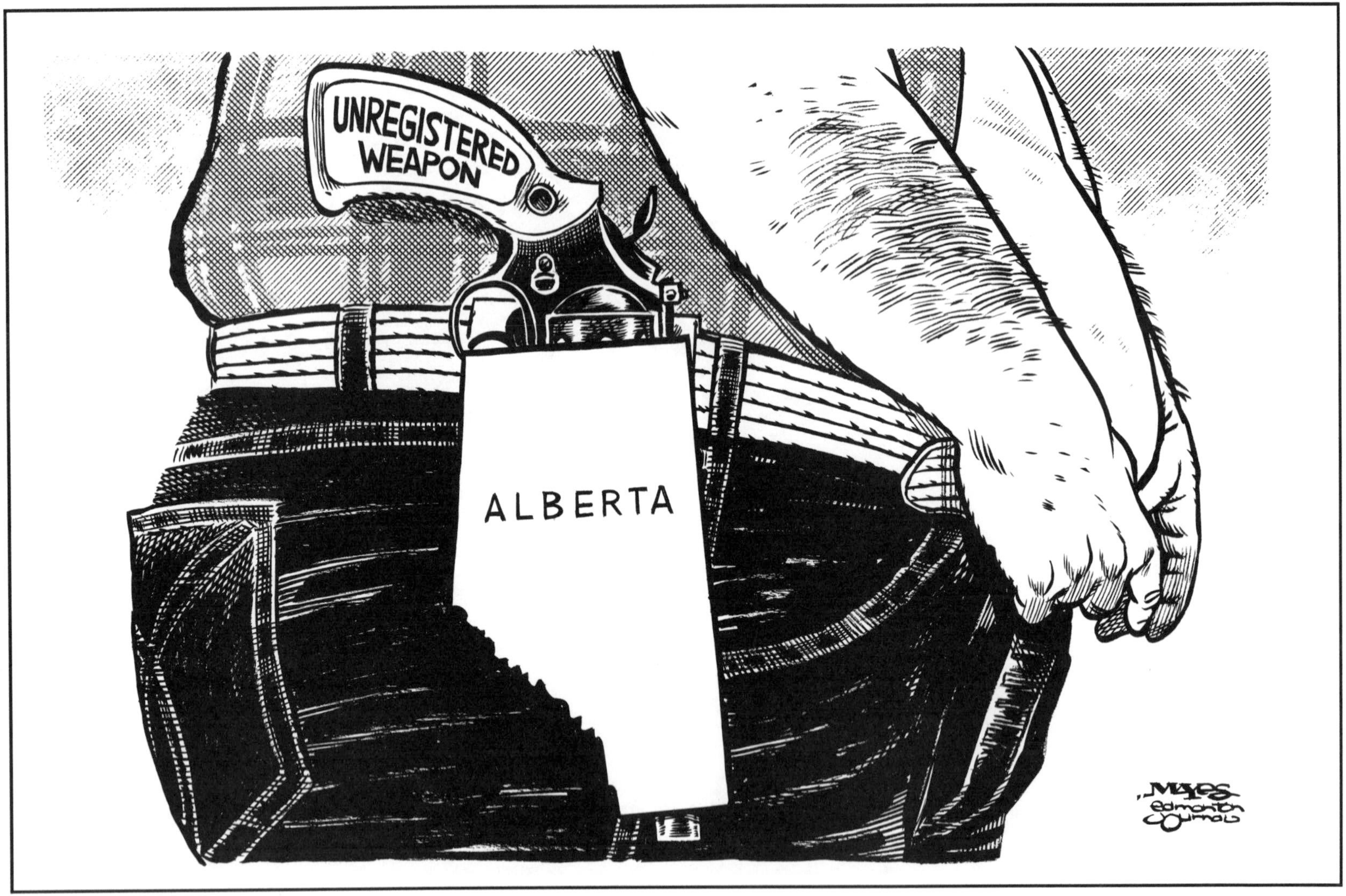
UNREGISTERED WEAPON
ALBERTA
MAYES Edmonton Journal

Province vows to fight federal gun registry.

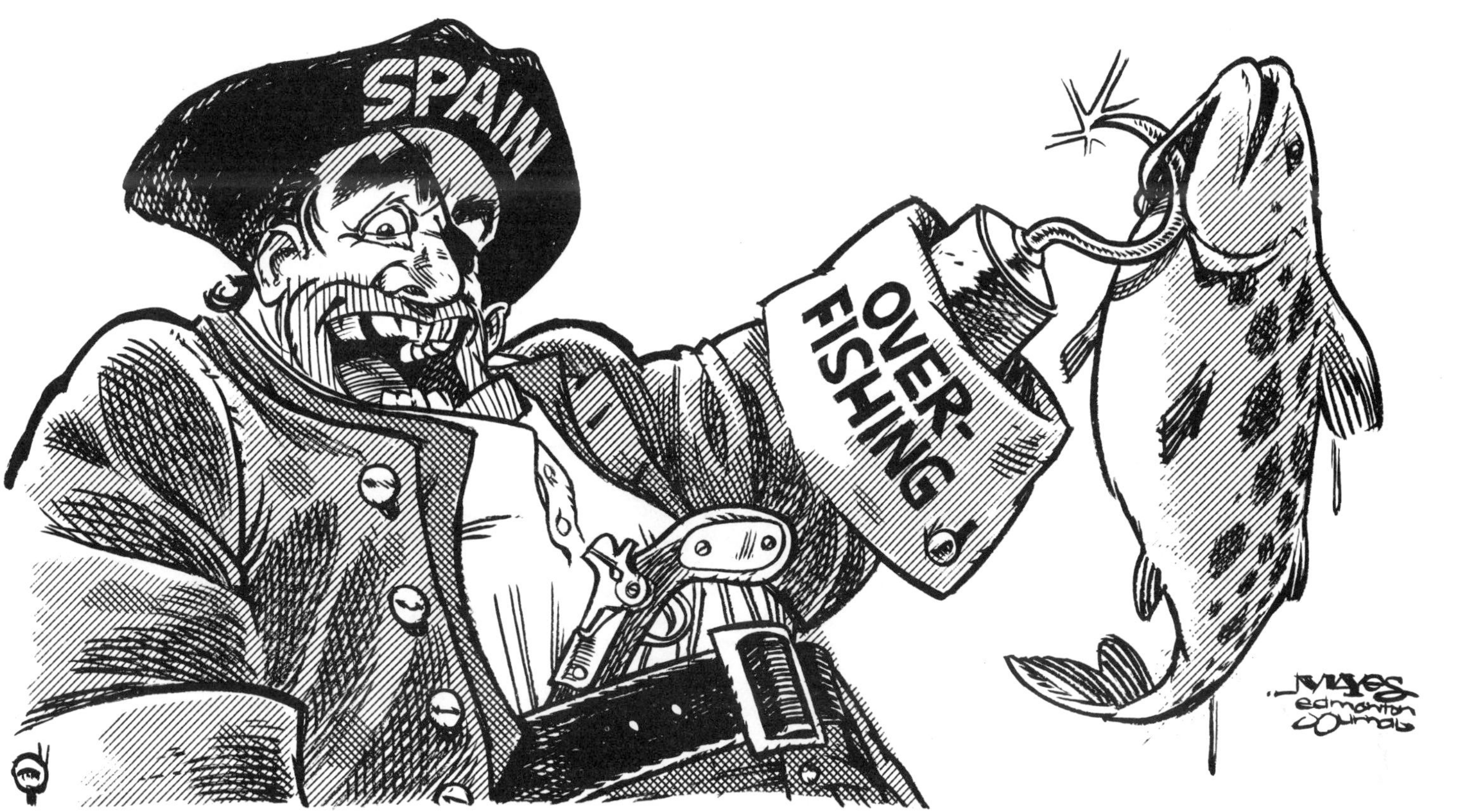
SPAIN
OVER-FISHING
MAYES
edmonton journal

"THERE MUST BE SOME MISUNDERSTANDING....I'M JUST A SIMPLE FISHERMAN WITH A SINGLE HOOK."

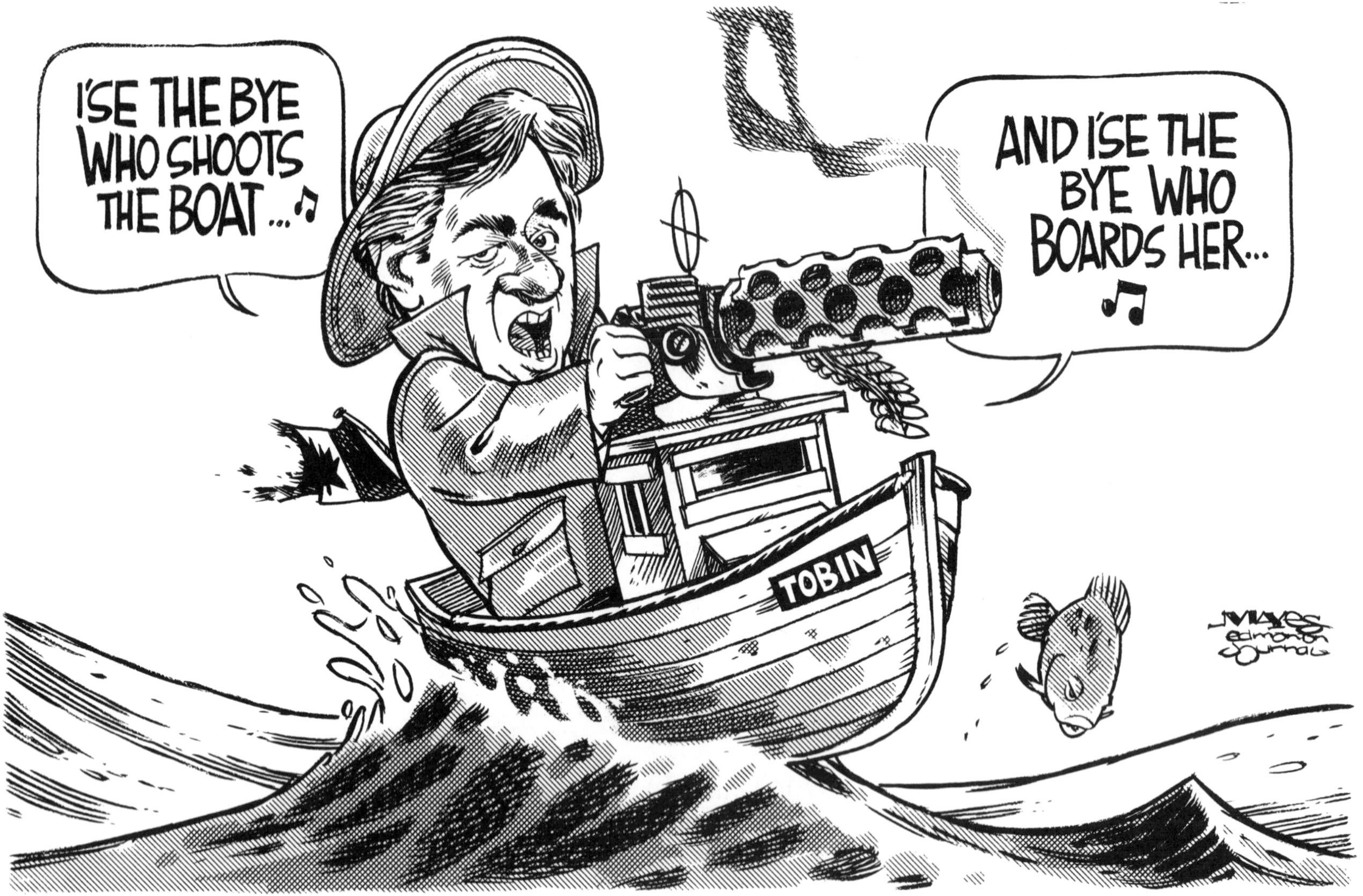
I'SE THE BYE WHO SHOOTS THE BOAT ...♪
AND I'SE THE BYE WHO BOARDS HER... ♪
TOBIN
MAYES
edmonton journal

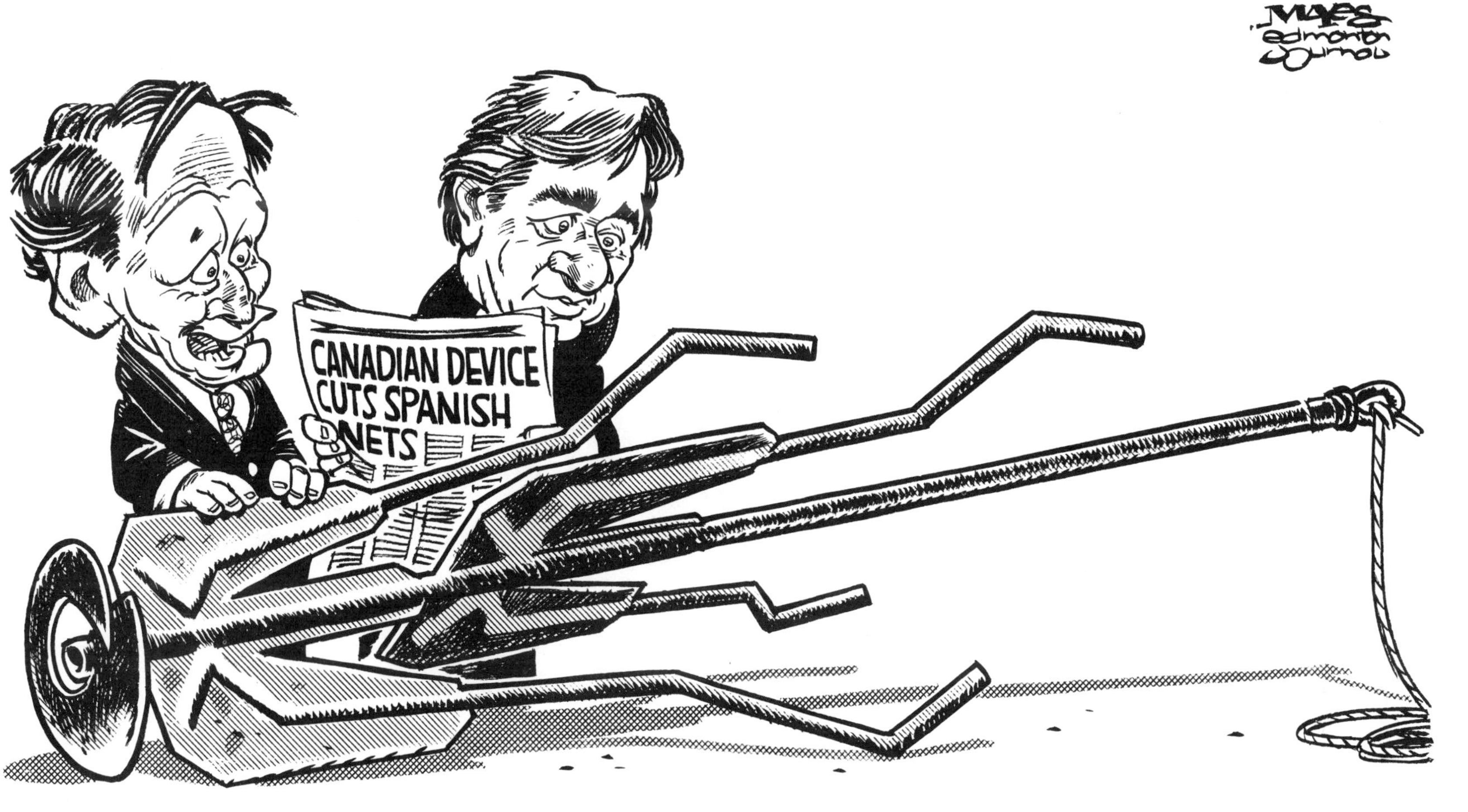
MAYES
Edmonton Journal
CANADIAN DEVICE CUTS SPANISH NETS

"INGENIOUS, TOBIN!... DOES IT WORK ON SOCIAL SAFETY NETS TOO?!..."

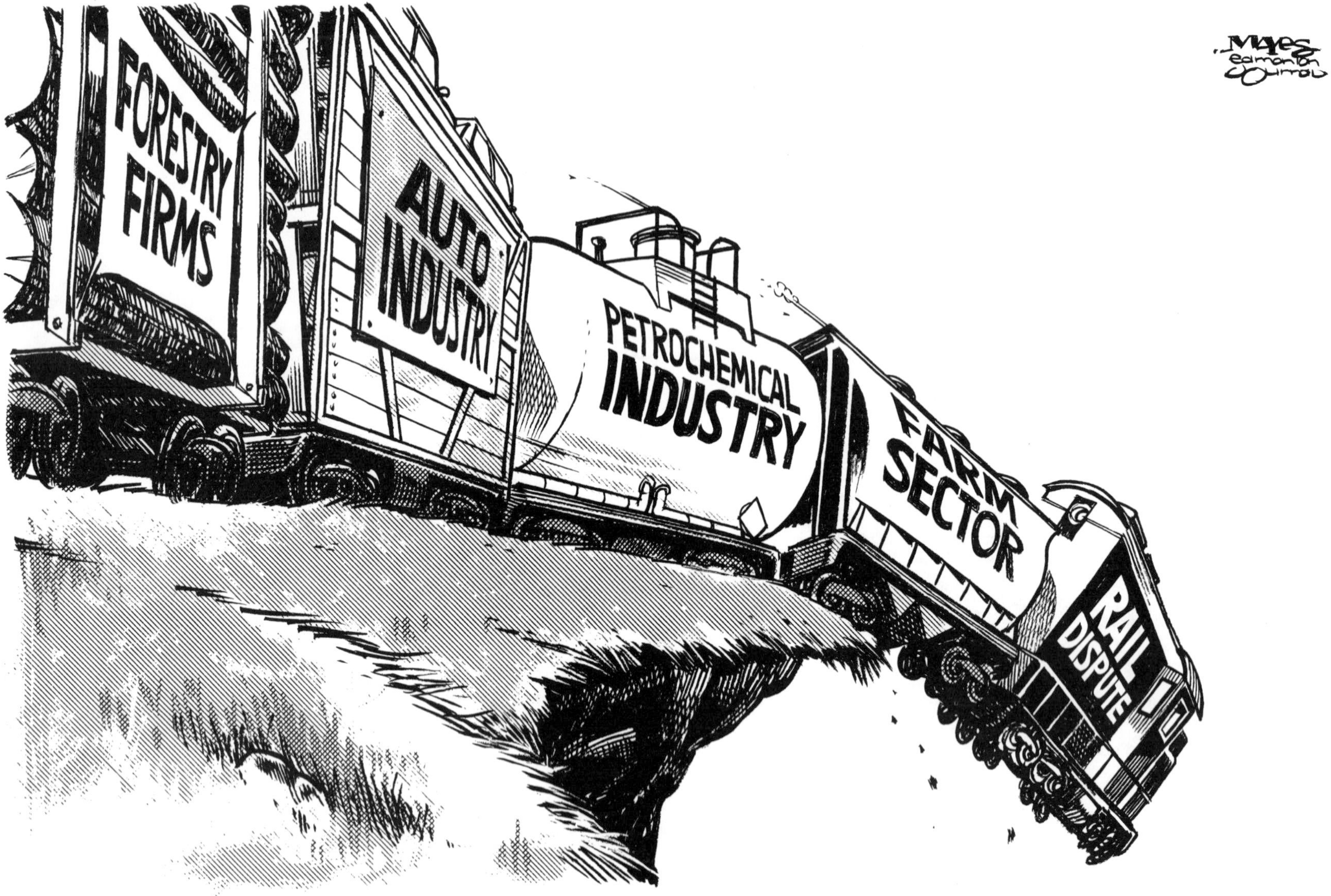
FORESTRY FIRMS
AUTO INDUSTRY
PETROCHEMICAL INDUSTRY
FARM SECTOR
RAIL DISPUTE
Mayes Edmonton Journal

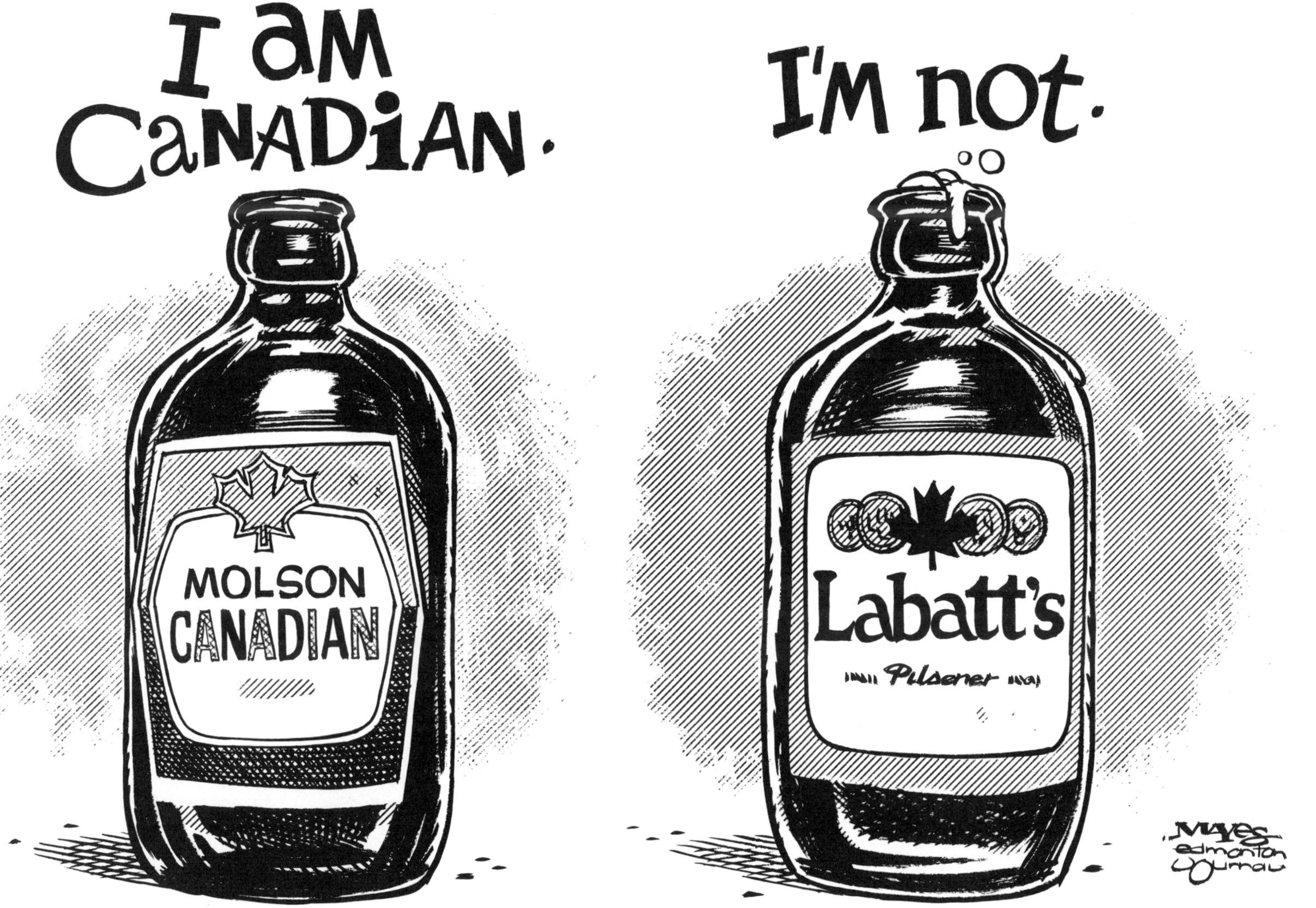
I am CANADIAN.
I'M not.
MOLSON CANADIAN
Labatt's
Pilsener
MAYES
edmonton journal

A Canadian institution is sold to foreigners.

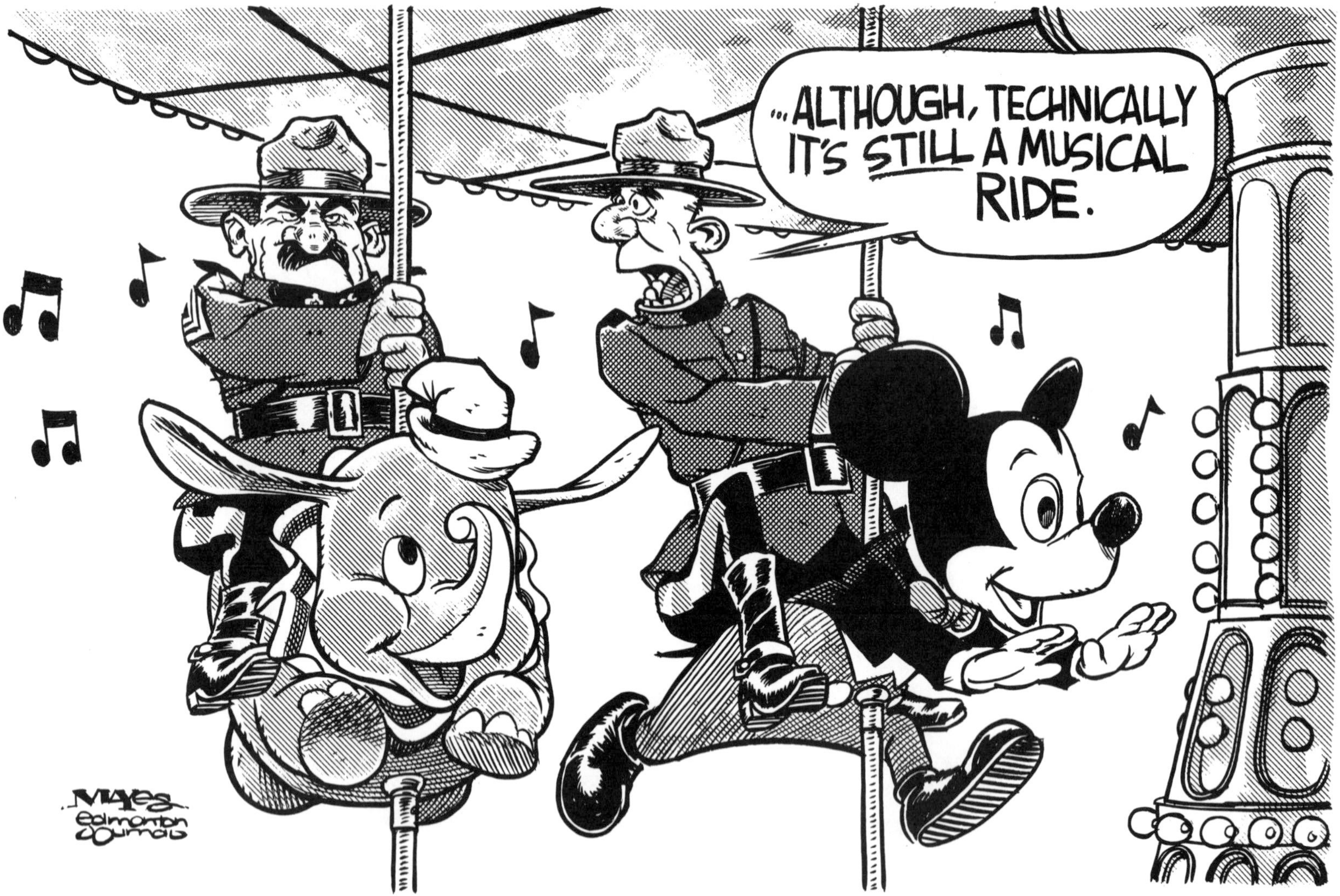
...ALTHOUGH, TECHNICALLY IT'S STILL A MUSICAL RIDE.
MAYES
edmonton journal

RCMP marketing rights sold to Disney.

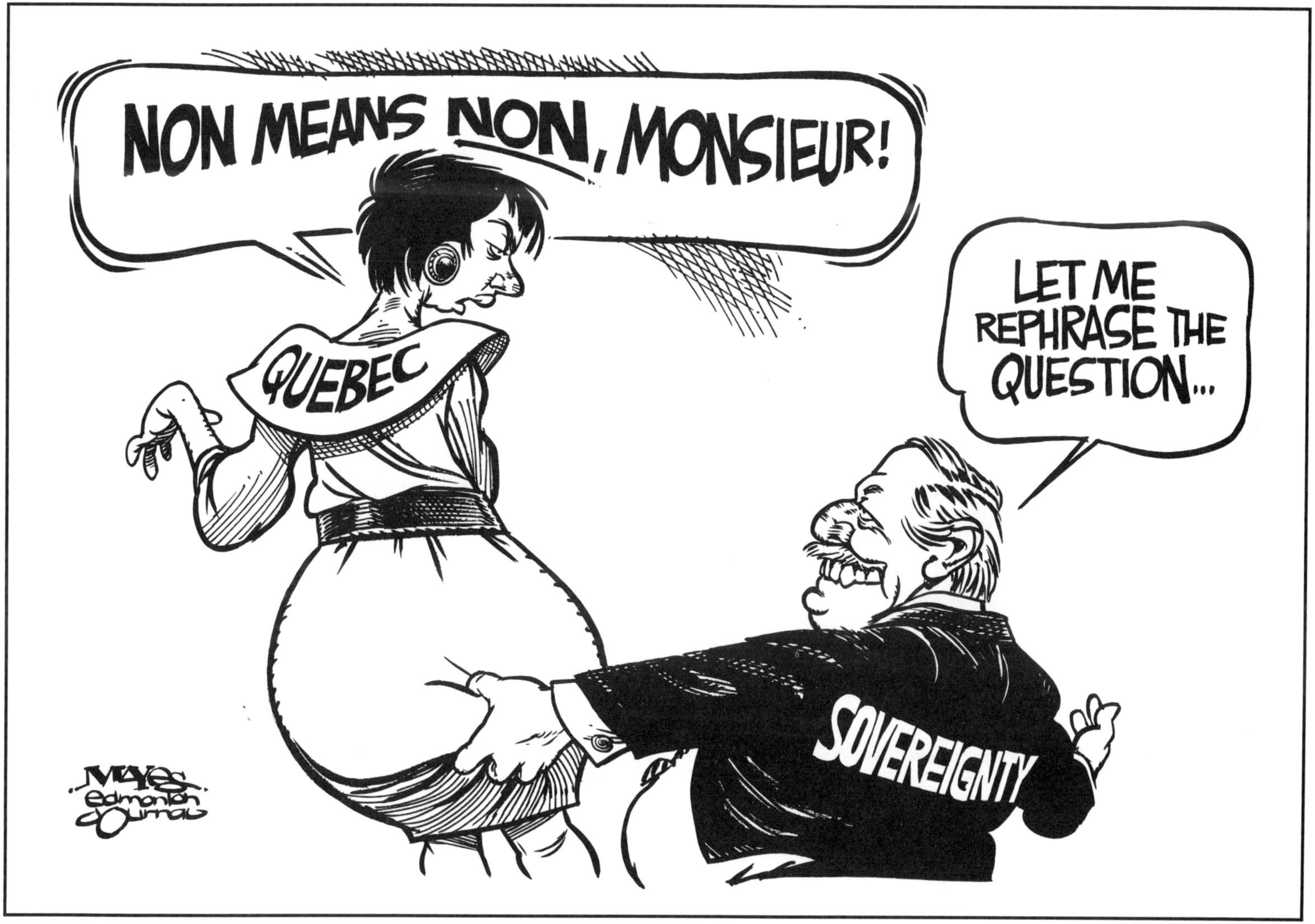
NON MEANS NON, MONSIEUR!
LET ME REPHRASE THE QUESTION...
QUEBEC
SOVEREIGNTY
MAYES Edmonton Journal

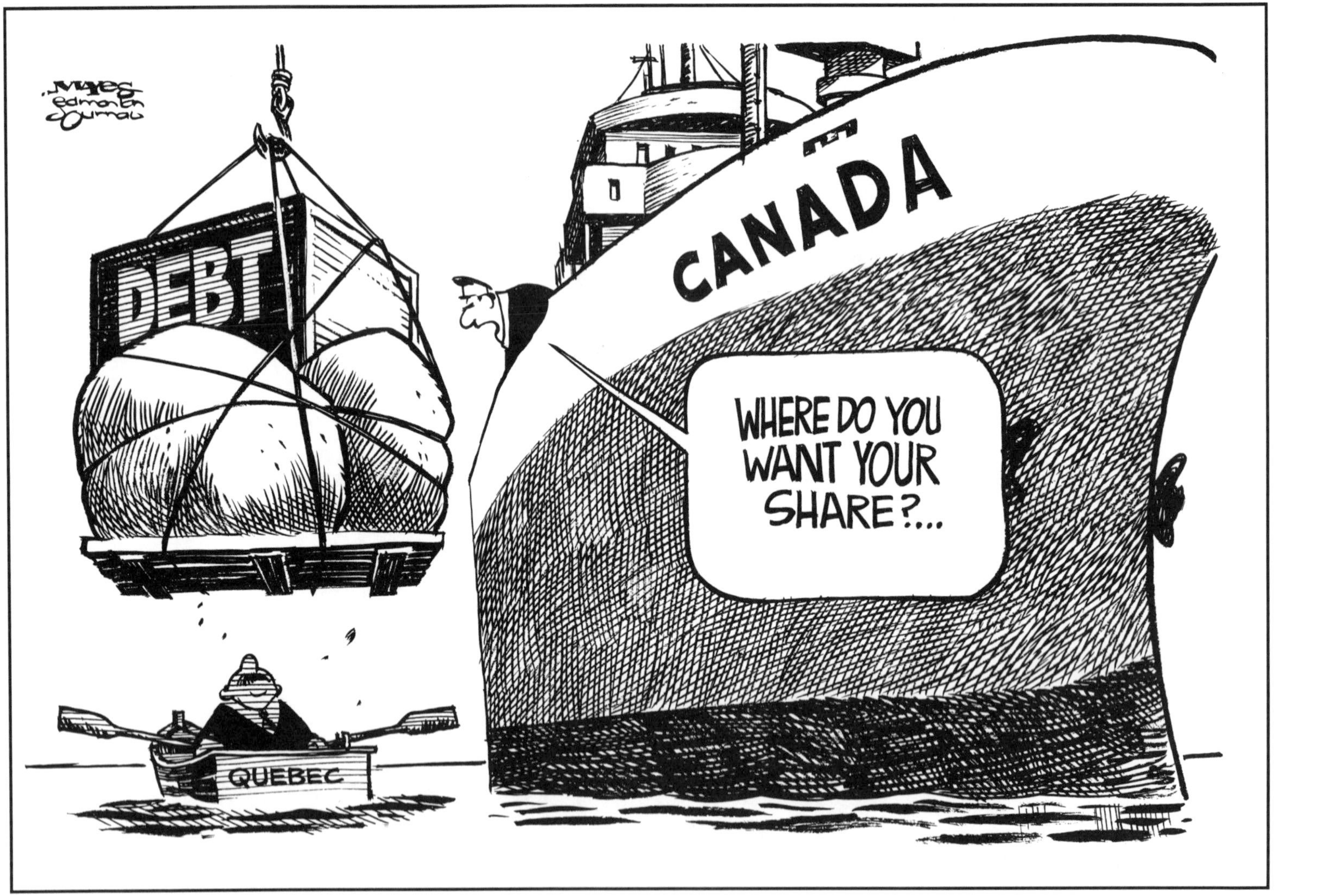
Mayes
Edmonton Journal
DEBT
CANADA
WHERE DO YOU WANT YOUR SHARE?...
QUEBEC

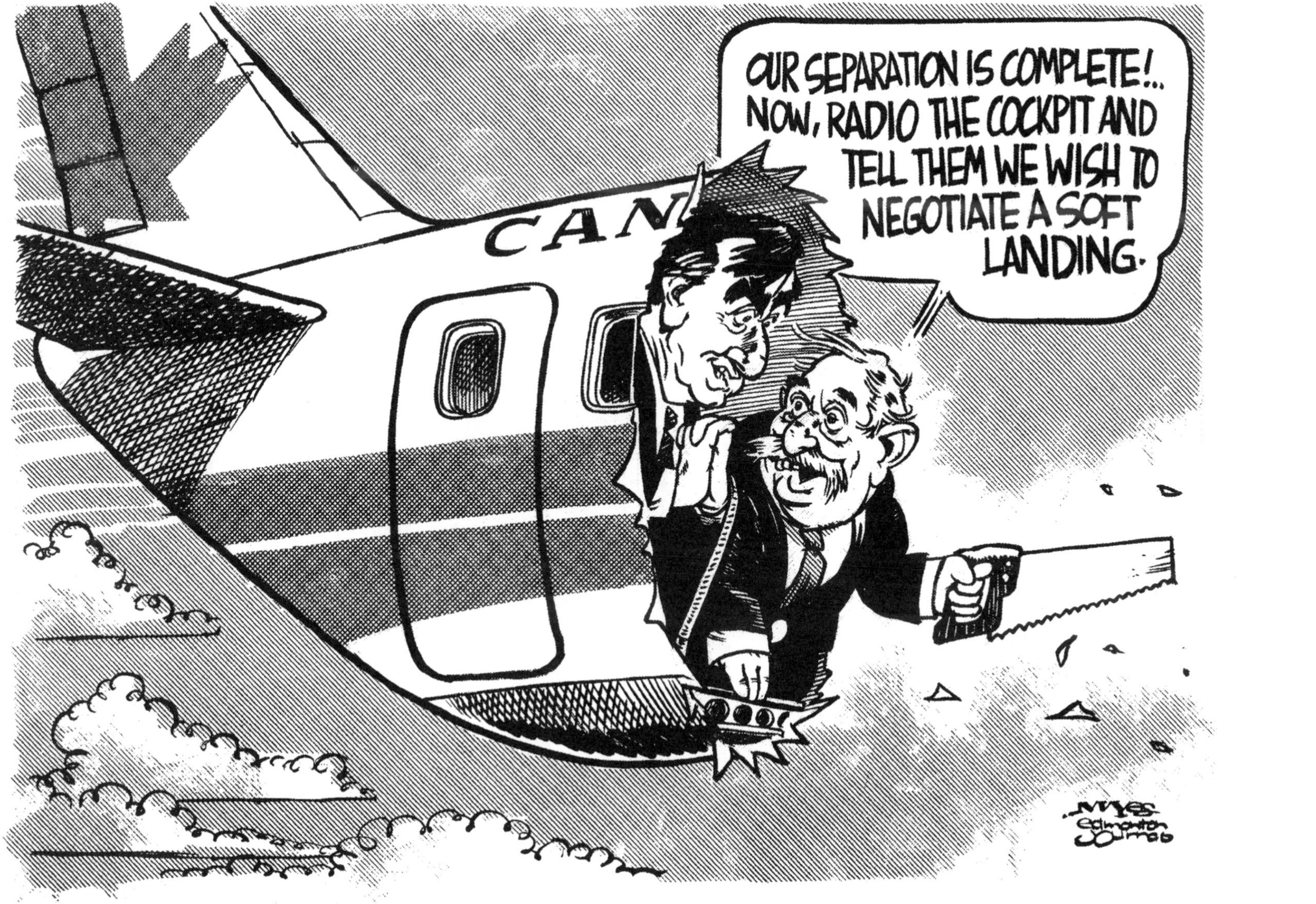
OUR SEPARATION IS COMPLETE!.. NOW, RADIO THE COCKPIT AND TELL THEM WE WISH TO NEGOTIATE A SOFT LANDING.
CAN
MYERS
edmonton journal

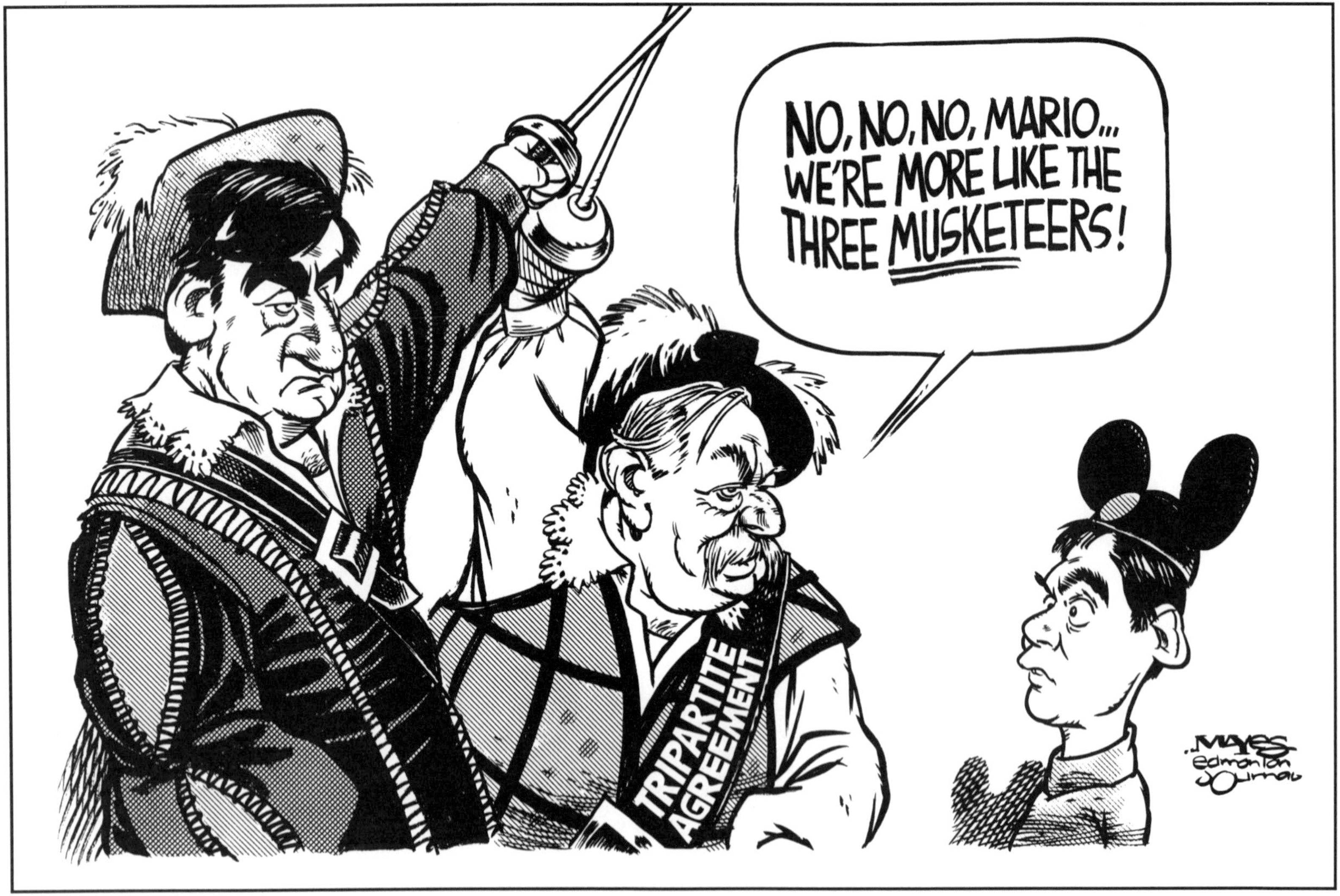

NO, NO, NO, MARIO...
WE'RE MORE LIKE THE
THREE MUSKETEERS!
TRIPARTITE AGREEMENT
MAYES
Edmonton Journal

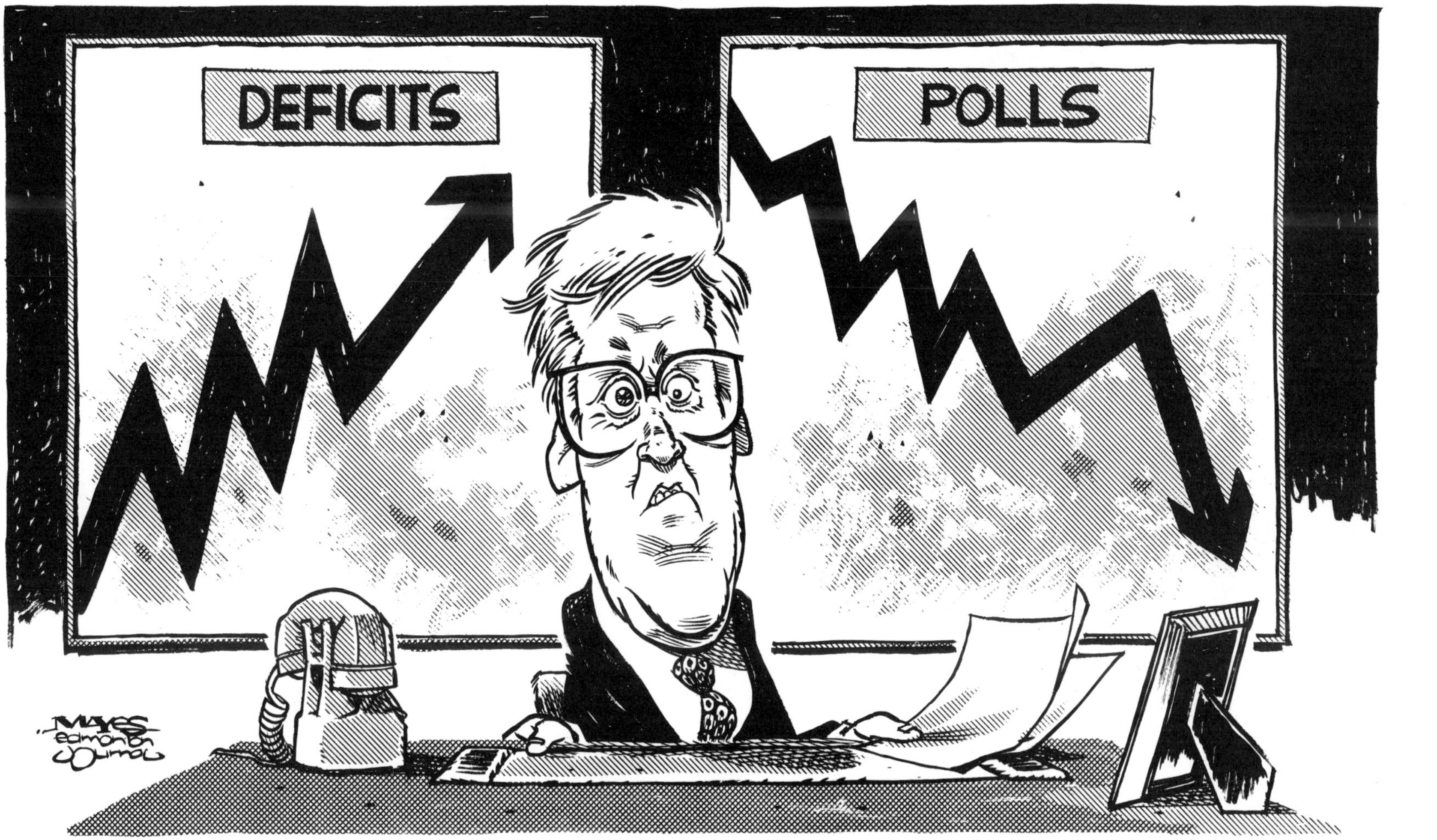
DEFICITS
POLLS
MAYES
edmonton journal

THE RISE AND FALL OF THE ONTARIO NDP.

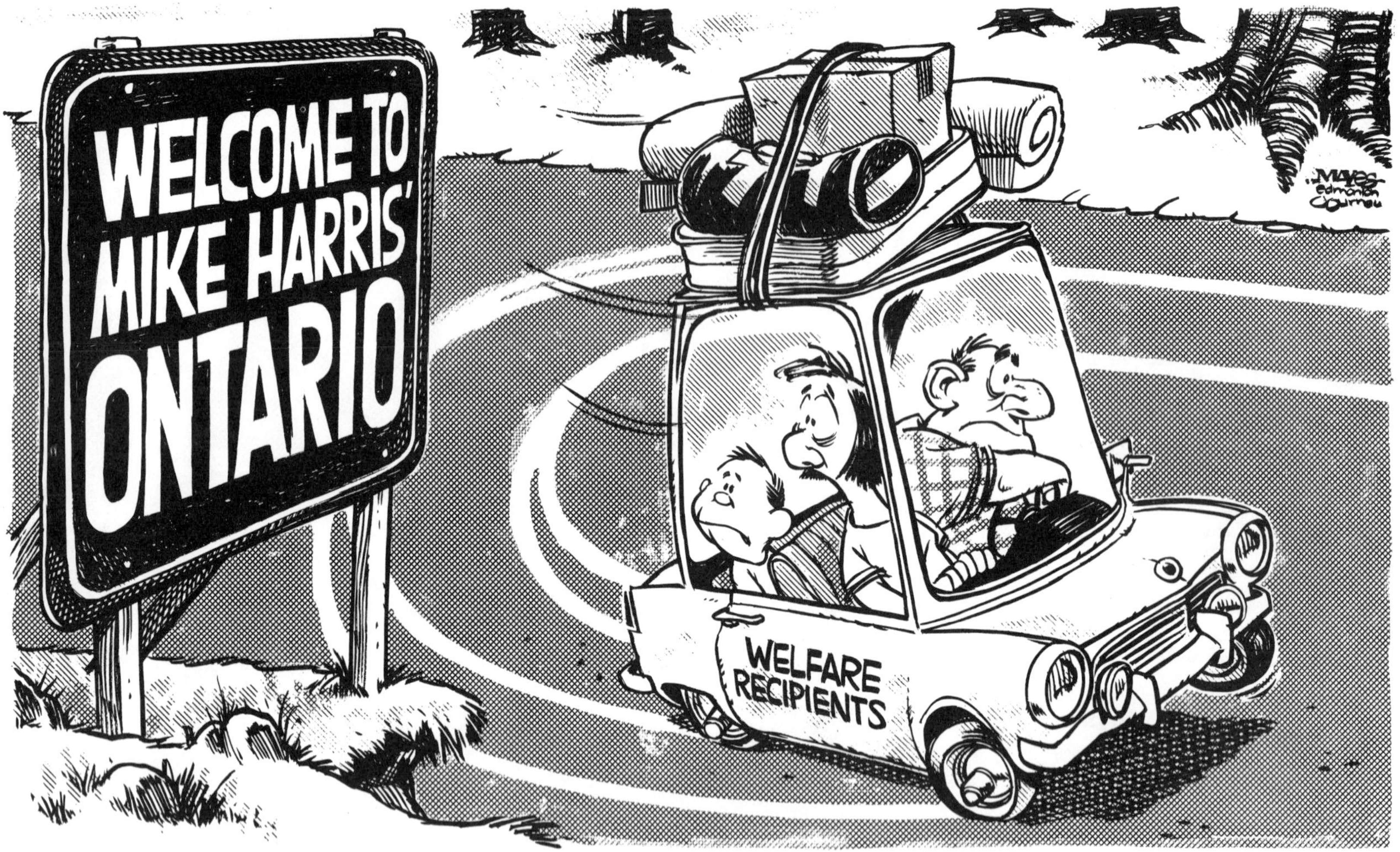
WELCOME TO
MIKE HARRIS'
ONTARIO
WELFARE
RECIPIENTS

A COMMON SENSE REVOLUTION.

A Mad Mad World

AQ

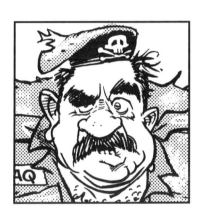

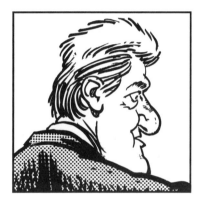

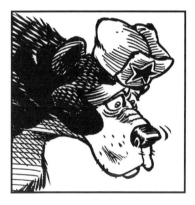

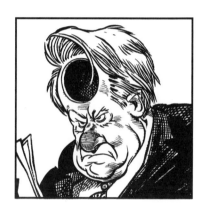

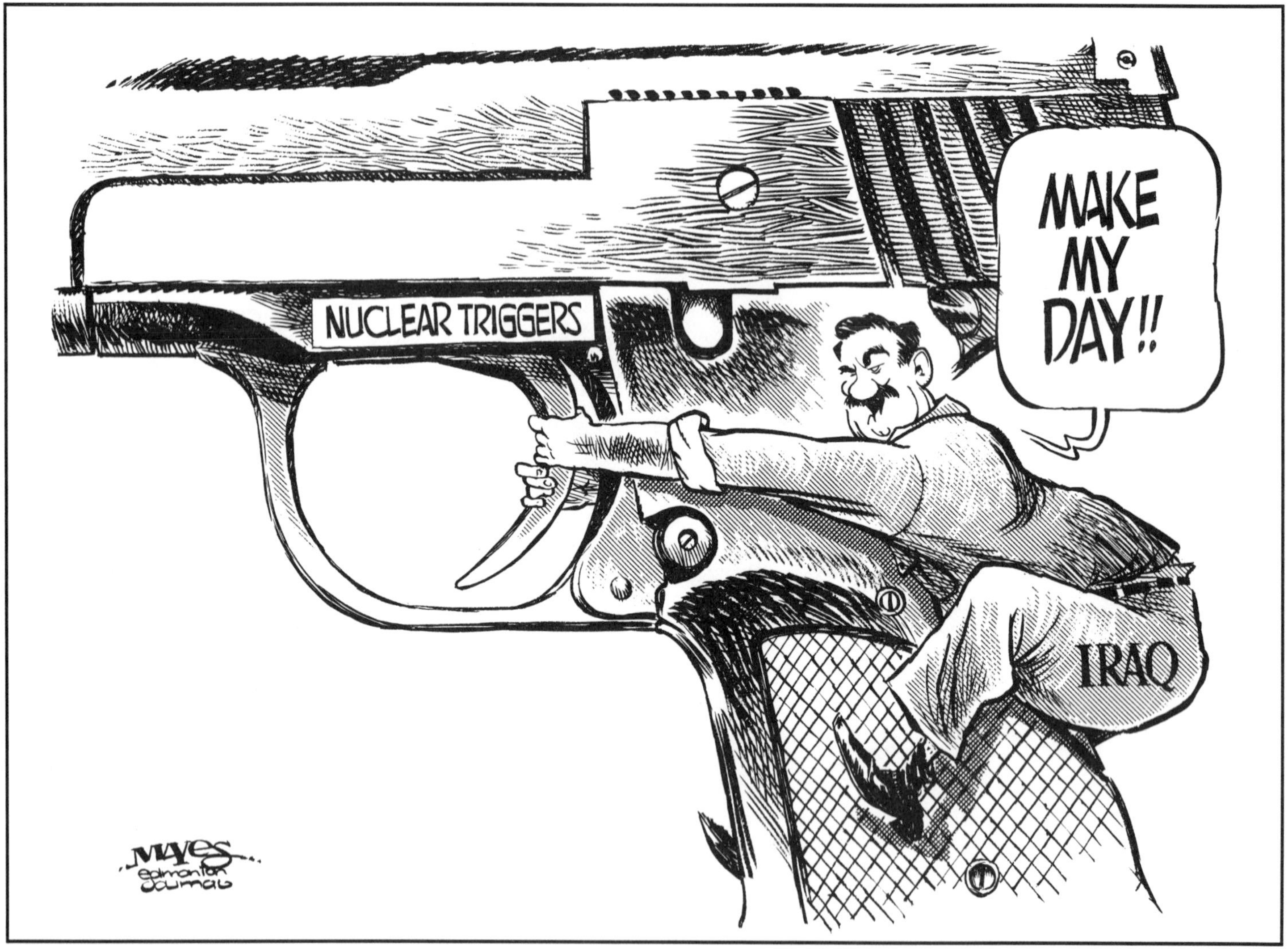
NUCLEAR TRIGGERS
MAKE MY DAY!!
IRAQ
MAYES
edmonton journal

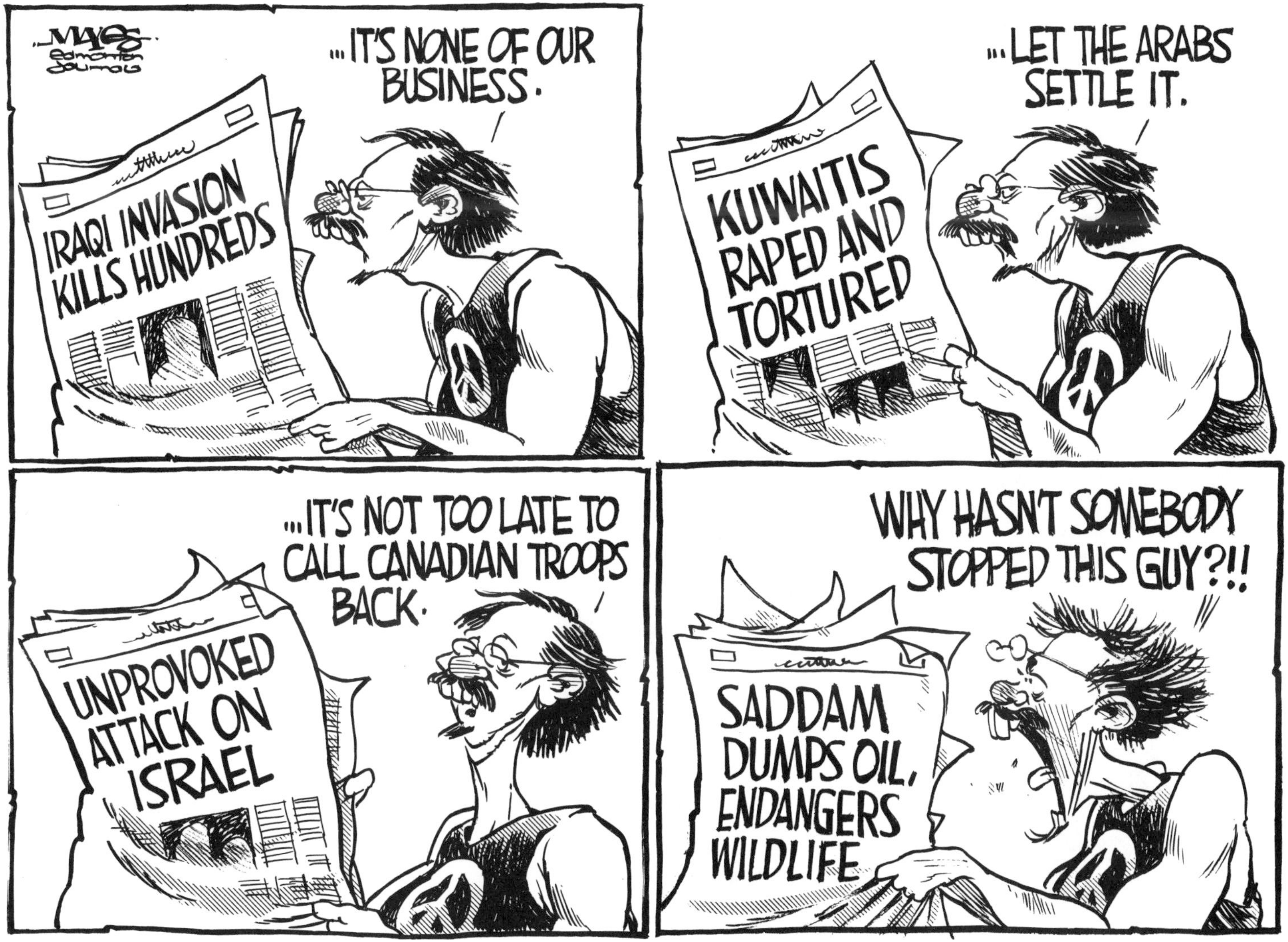
MAYES Edmonton Journal
...IT'S NONE OF OUR BUSINESS.
IRAQI INVASION KILLS HUNDREDS
...LET THE ARABS SETTLE IT.
KUWAITIS RAPED AND TORTURED
...IT'S NOT TOO LATE TO CALL CANADIAN TROOPS BACK.
UNPROVOKED ATTACK ON ISRAEL
WHY HASN'T SOMEBODY STOPPED THIS GUY?!!
SADDAM DUMPS OIL, ENDANGERS WILDLIFE

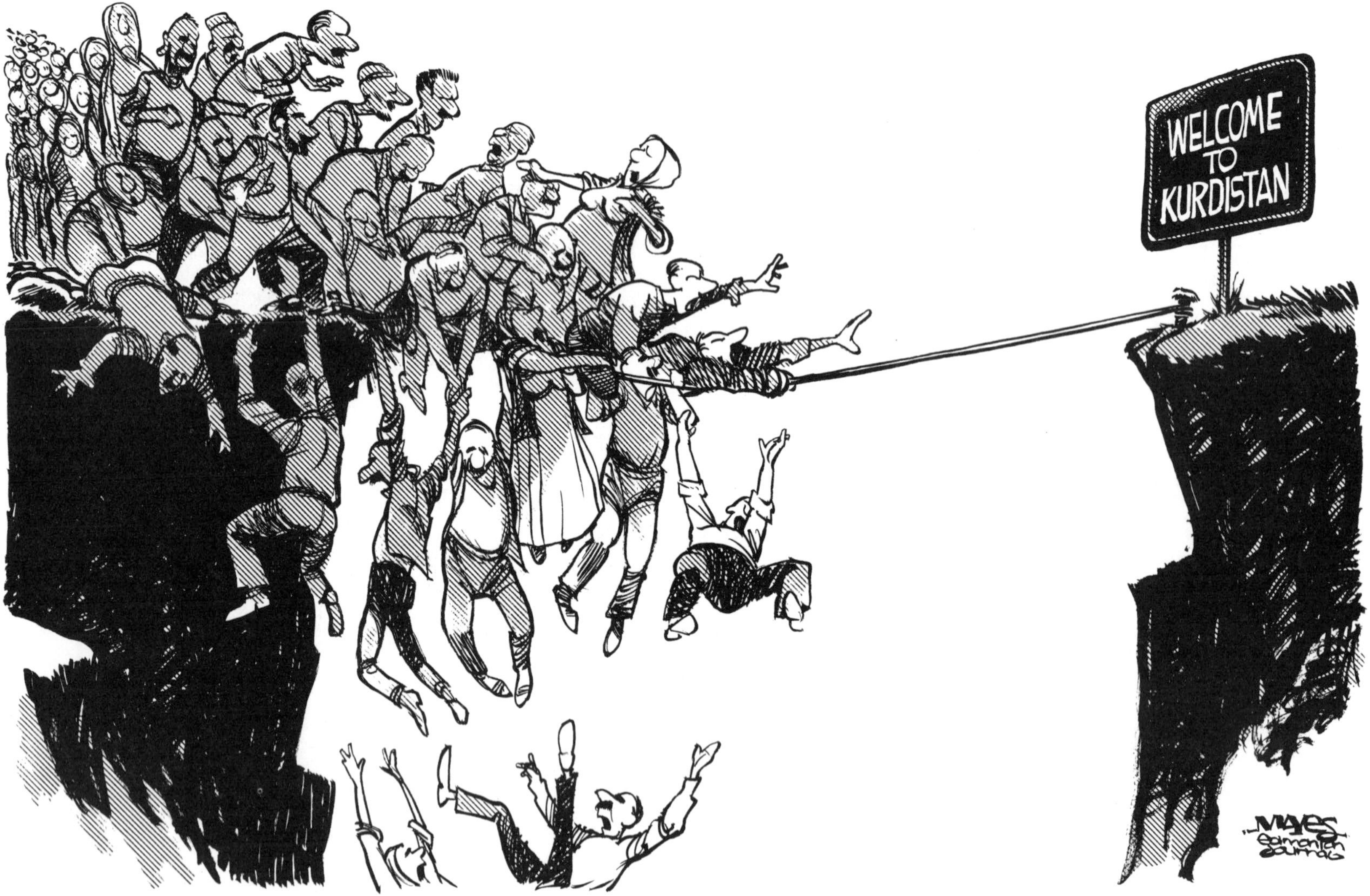
WELCOME
TO
KURDISTAN
MAYES
Edmonton Journal

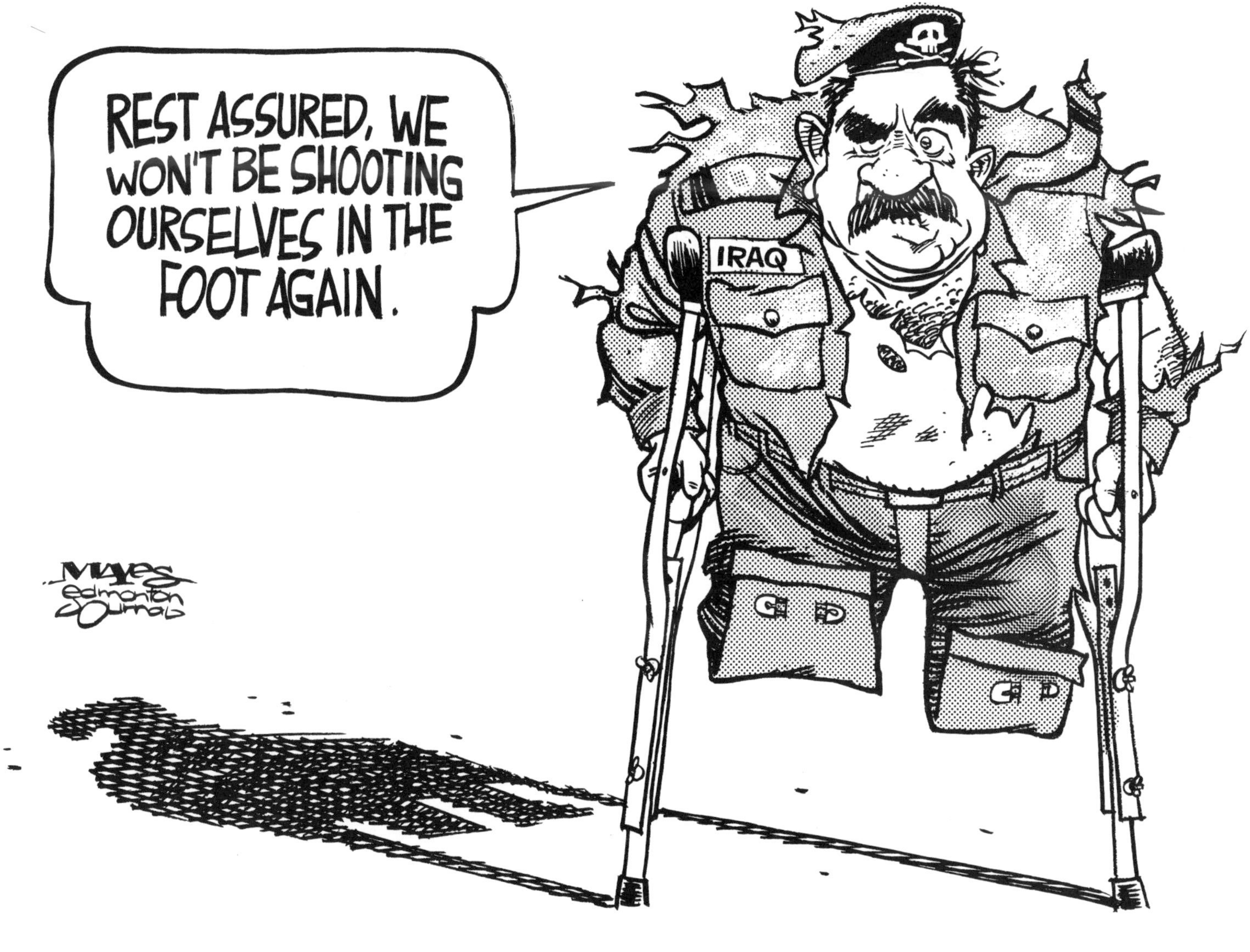
REST ASSURED, WE WON'T BE SHOOTING OURSELVES IN THE FOOT AGAIN.
IRAQ
MAYES
Edmonton Journal

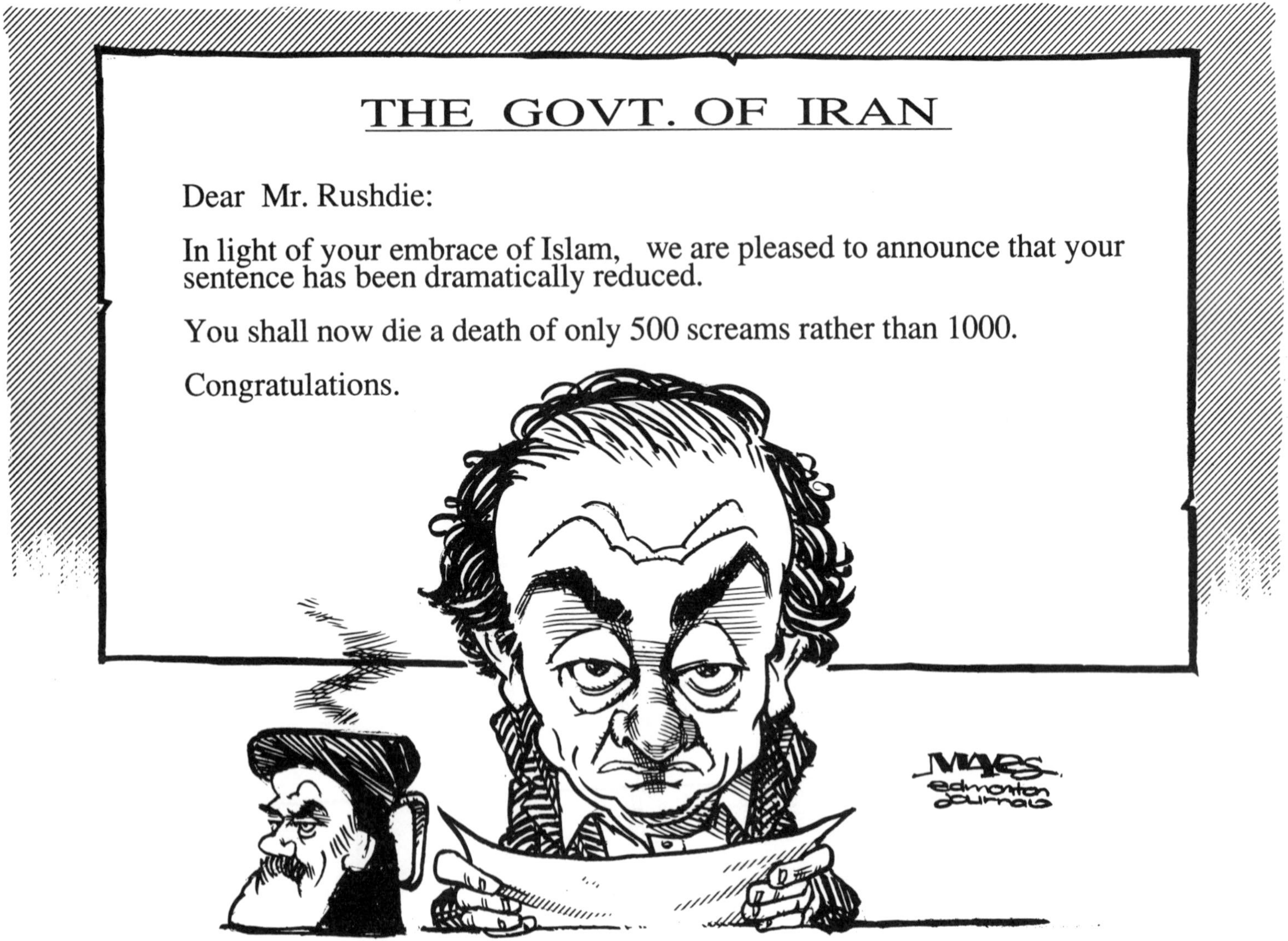

THE GOVT. OF IRAN
Dear Mr. Rushdie:
In light of your embrace of Islam, we are pleased to announce that your sentence has been dramatically reduced.
You shall now die a death of only 500 screams rather than 1000.
Congratulations.
MAYES
edmonton journal

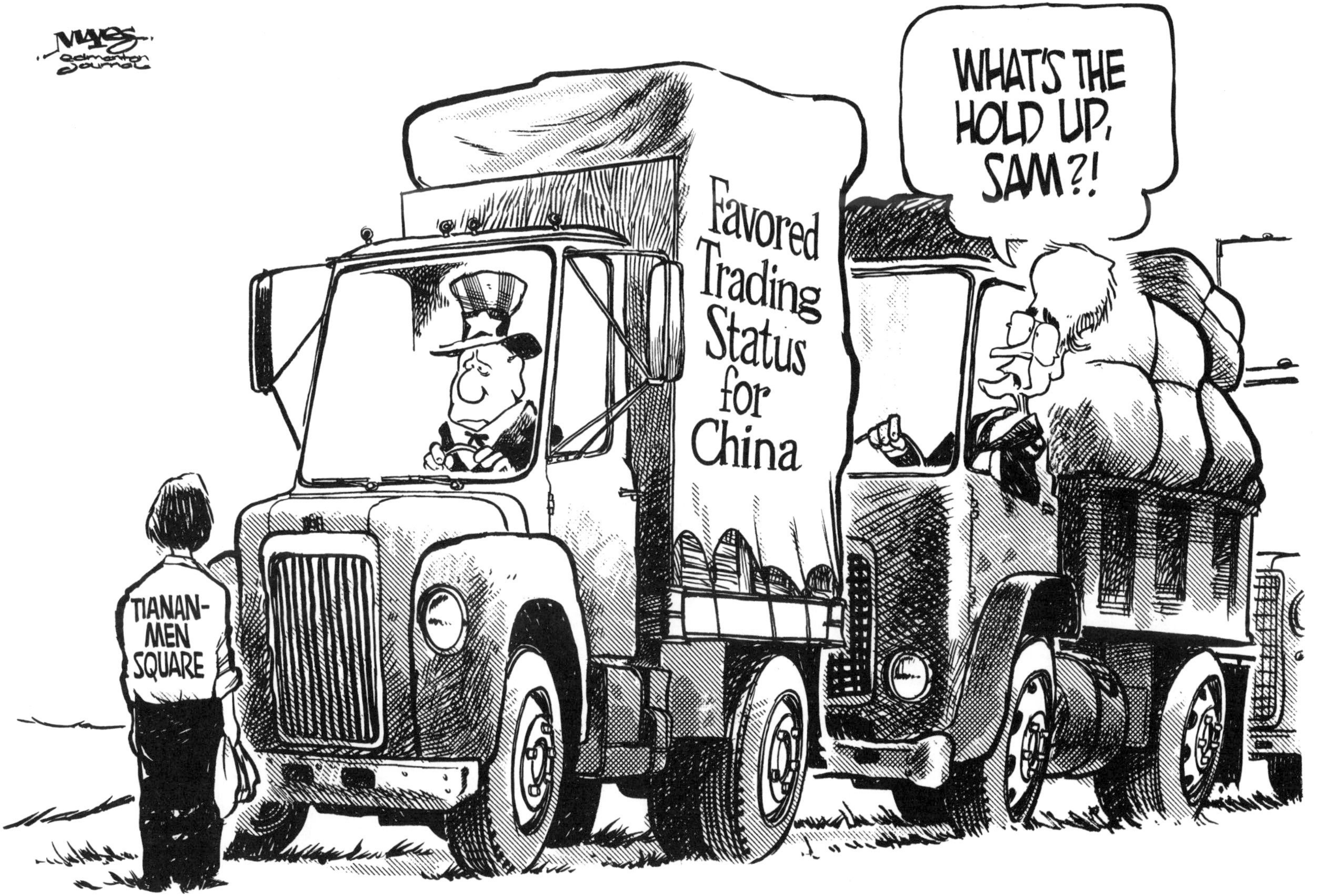
MAYES edmonton journal
WHAT'S THE HOLD UP, SAM?!
Favored Trading Status for China
TIANAN-MEN SQUARE

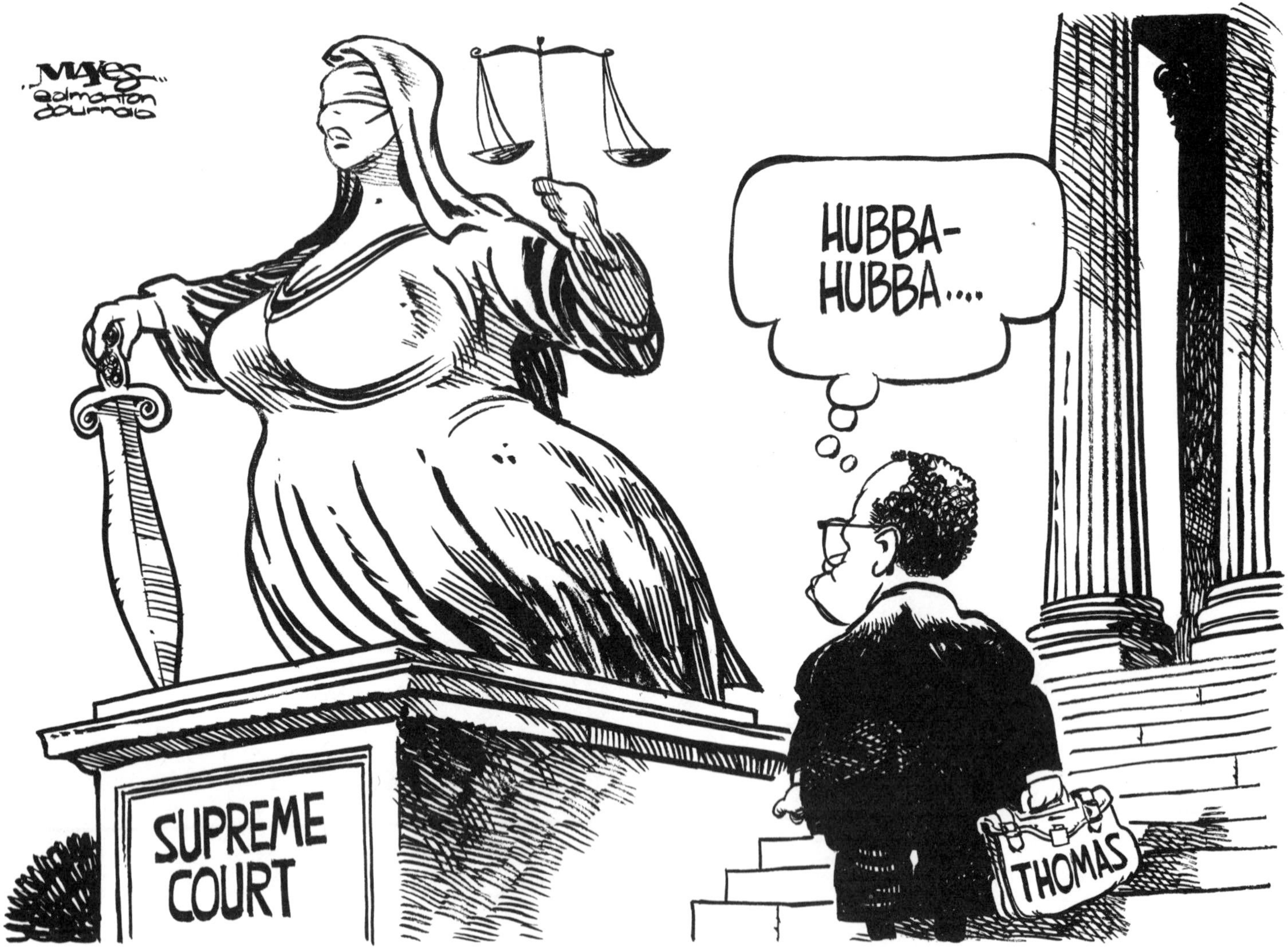
MAYES
edmonton
journal
HUBBA-
HUBBA....
SUPREME
COURT
THOMAS

U.S. Supreme Court nominee accused of sexual harassment.

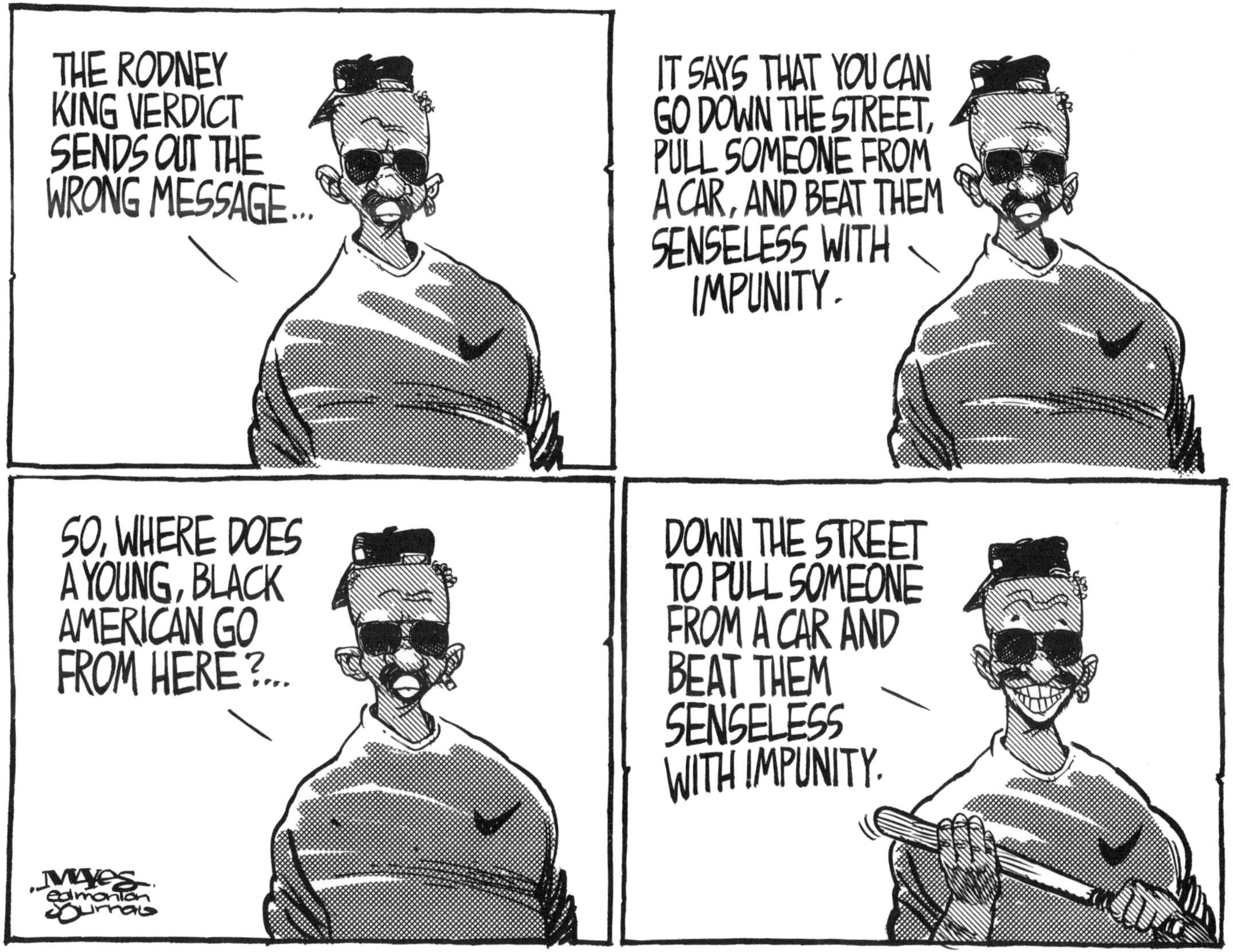
THE RODNEY KING VERDICT SENDS OUT THE WRONG MESSAGE...
IT SAYS THAT YOU CAN GO DOWN THE STREET, PULL SOMEONE FROM A CAR, AND BEAT THEM SENSELESS WITH IMPUNITY.
SO, WHERE DOES A YOUNG, BLACK AMERICAN GO FROM HERE?...
DOWN THE STREET TO PULL SOMEONE FROM A CAR AND BEAT THEM SENSELESS WITH IMPUNITY.
MAYES
edmonton journal

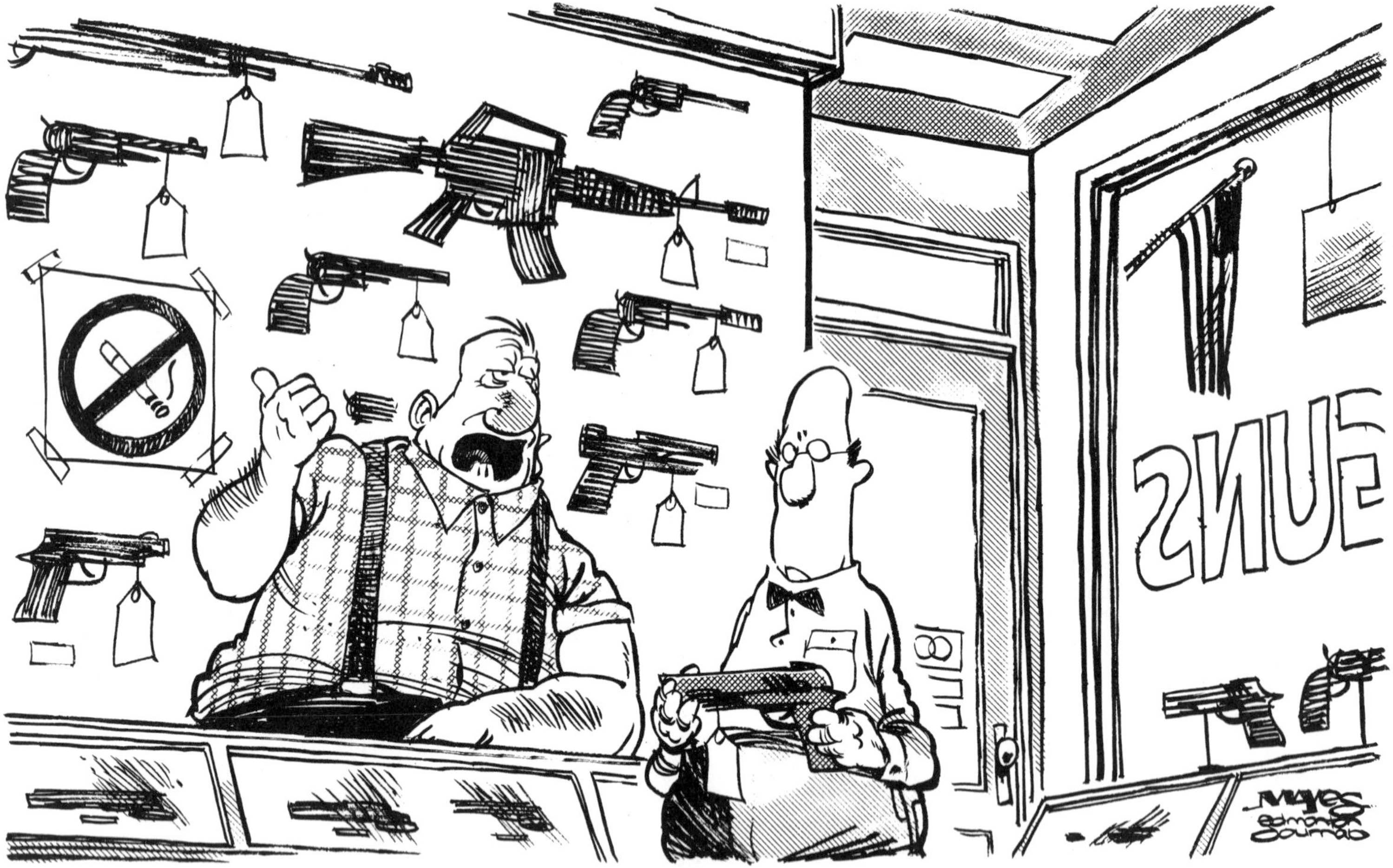
MAYES
Edmonton Journal

" I'VE BANNED CIGARETTES IN THE SHOP.... IT'S FRIGHTENING HOW MANY PEOPLE A YEAR THOSE THINGS KILL."

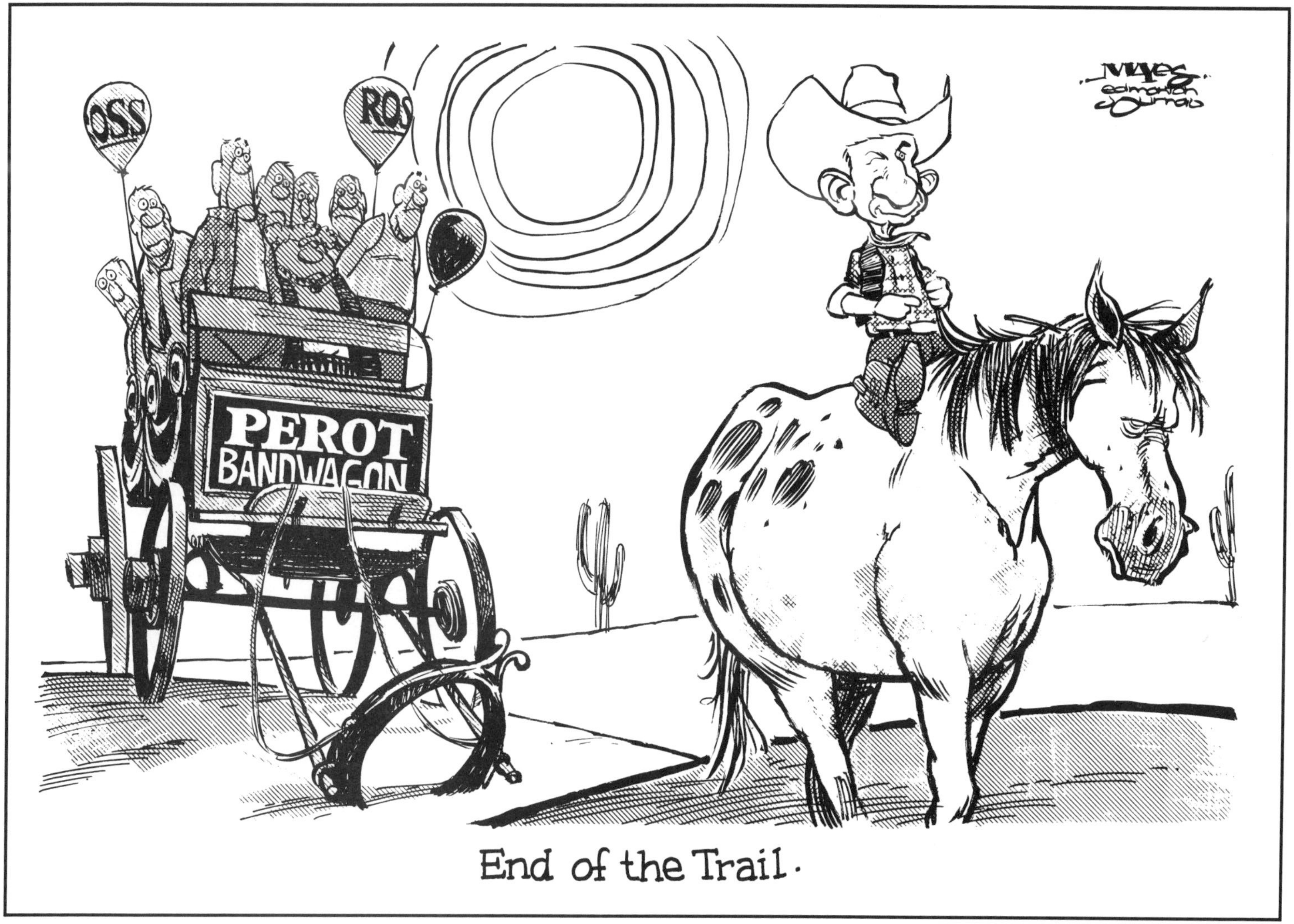

OSS
ROS
PEROT
BANDWAGON
End of the Trail.

Ross Perot quits the presidential race . . .

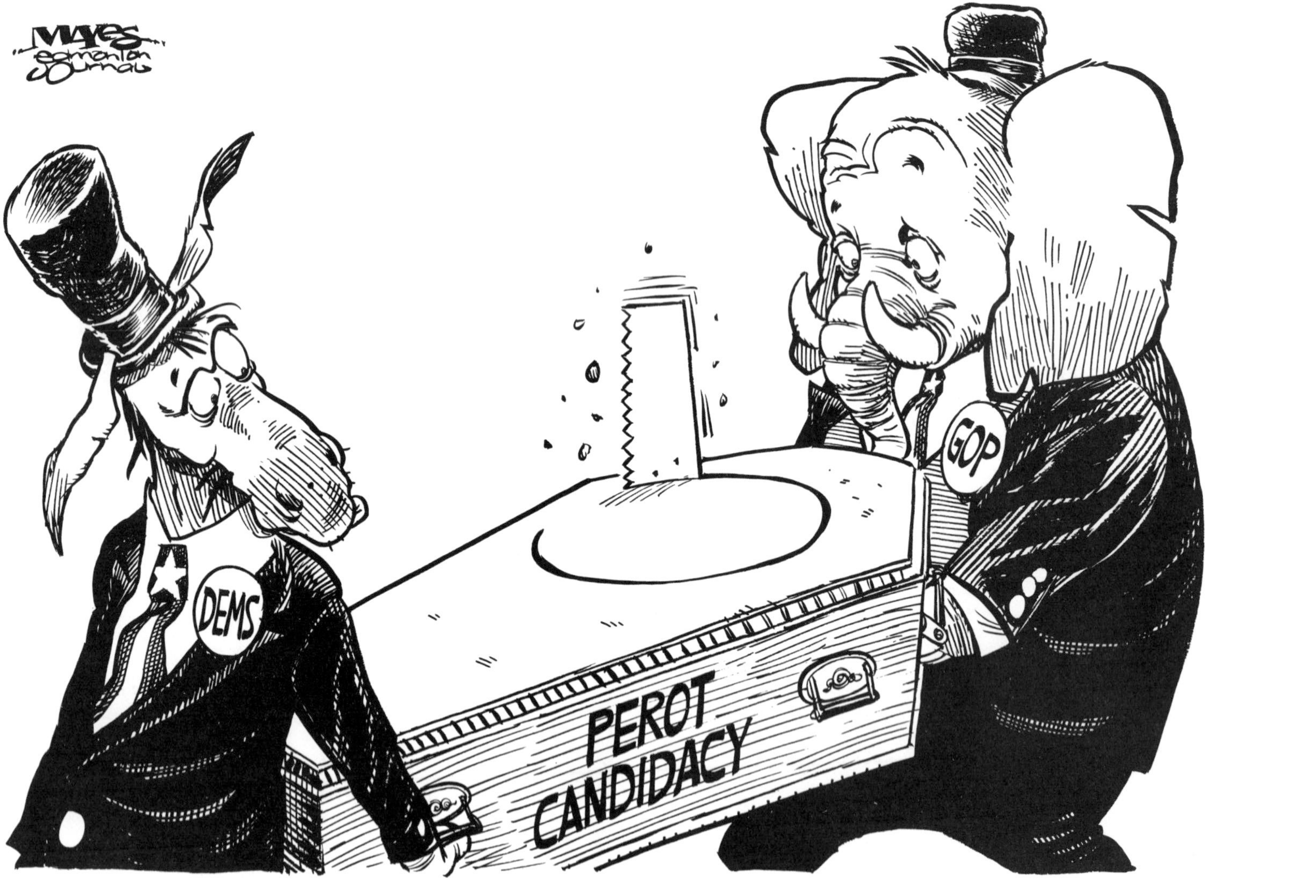
MAYES
Edmonton Journal
DEMS
GOP
PEROT CANDIDACY

. . . for a while.

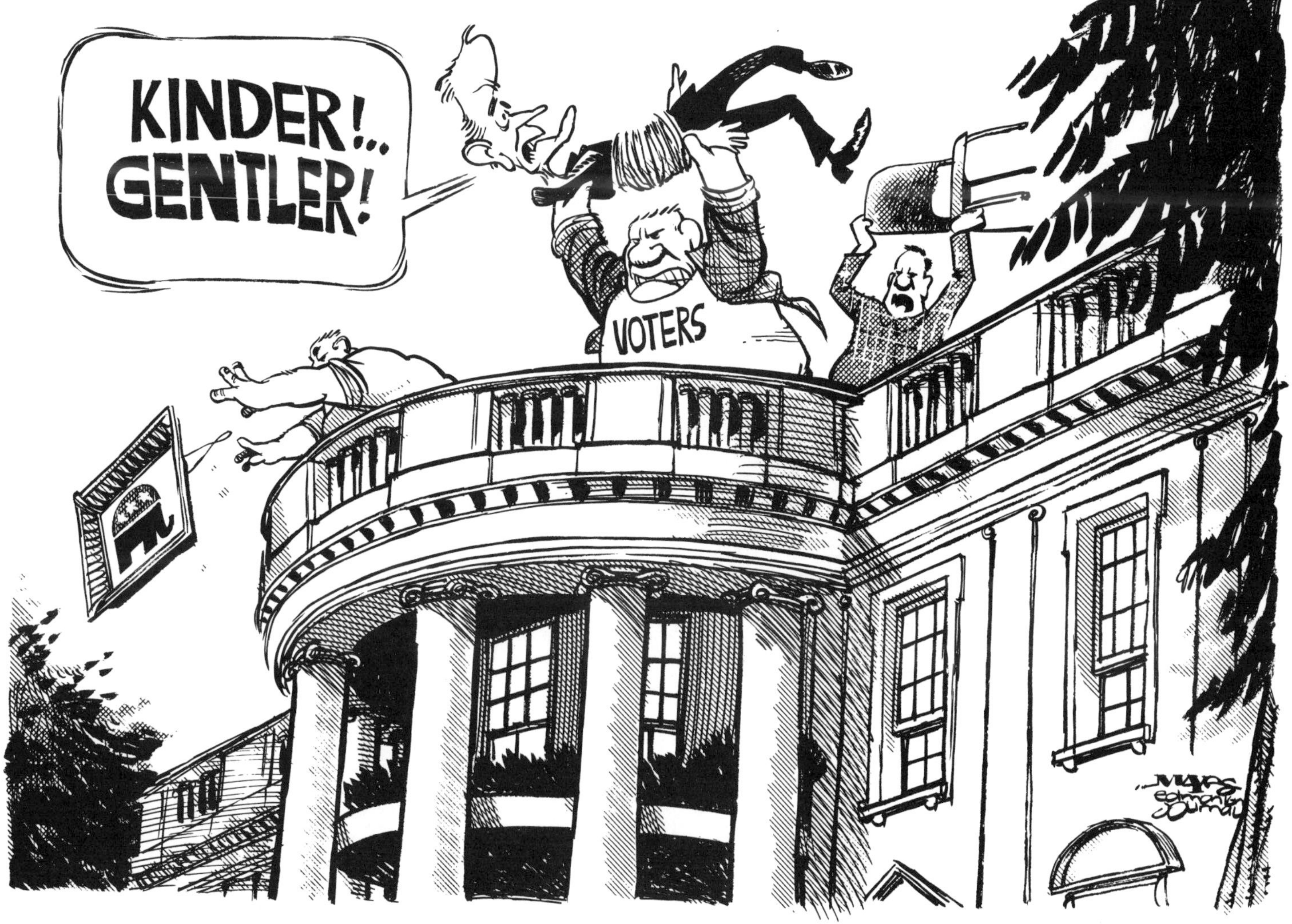
KINDER!... GENTLER!
VOTERS
MAYES
edmonton journal

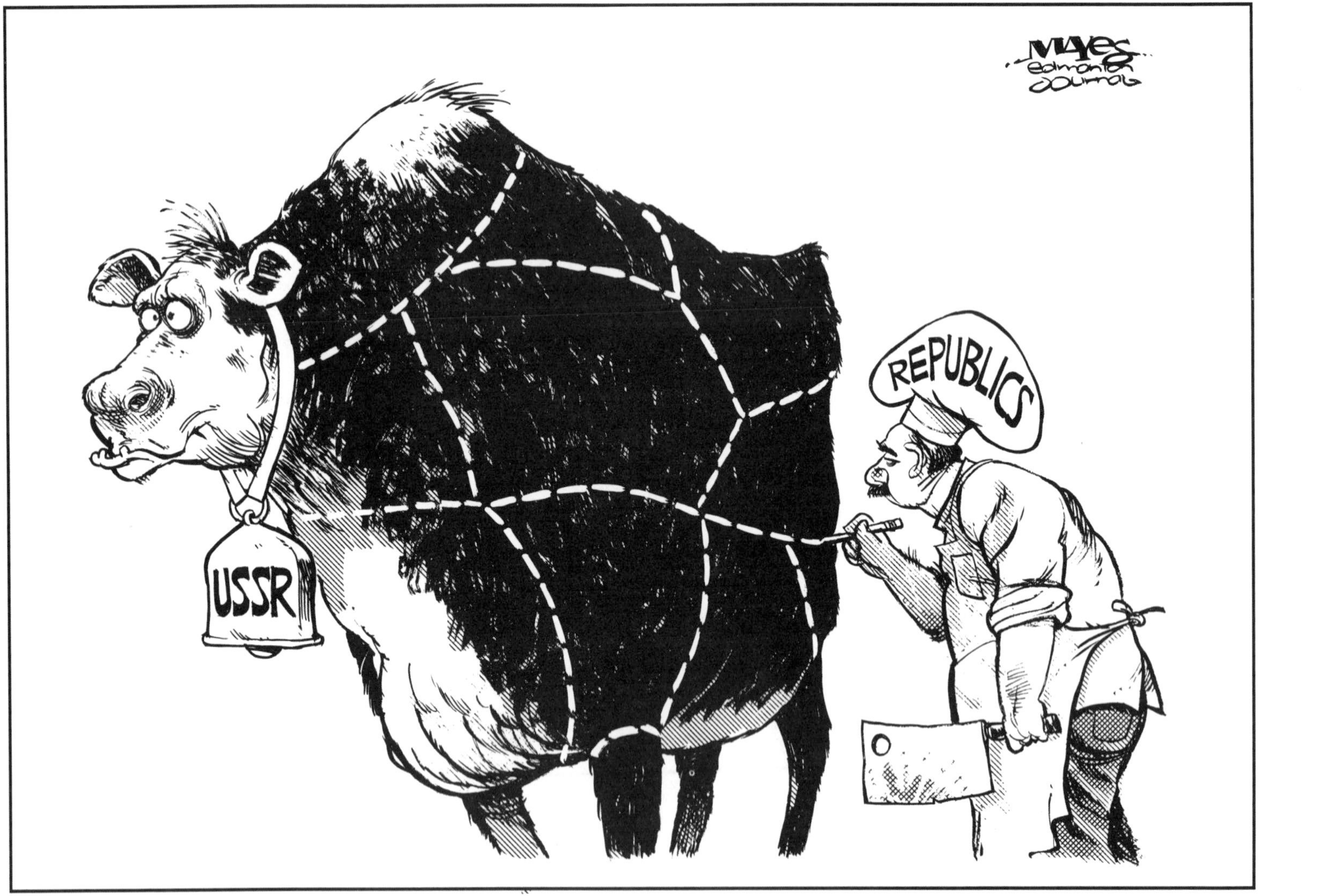
MAYES
edmonton
journal
USSR
REPUBLICS

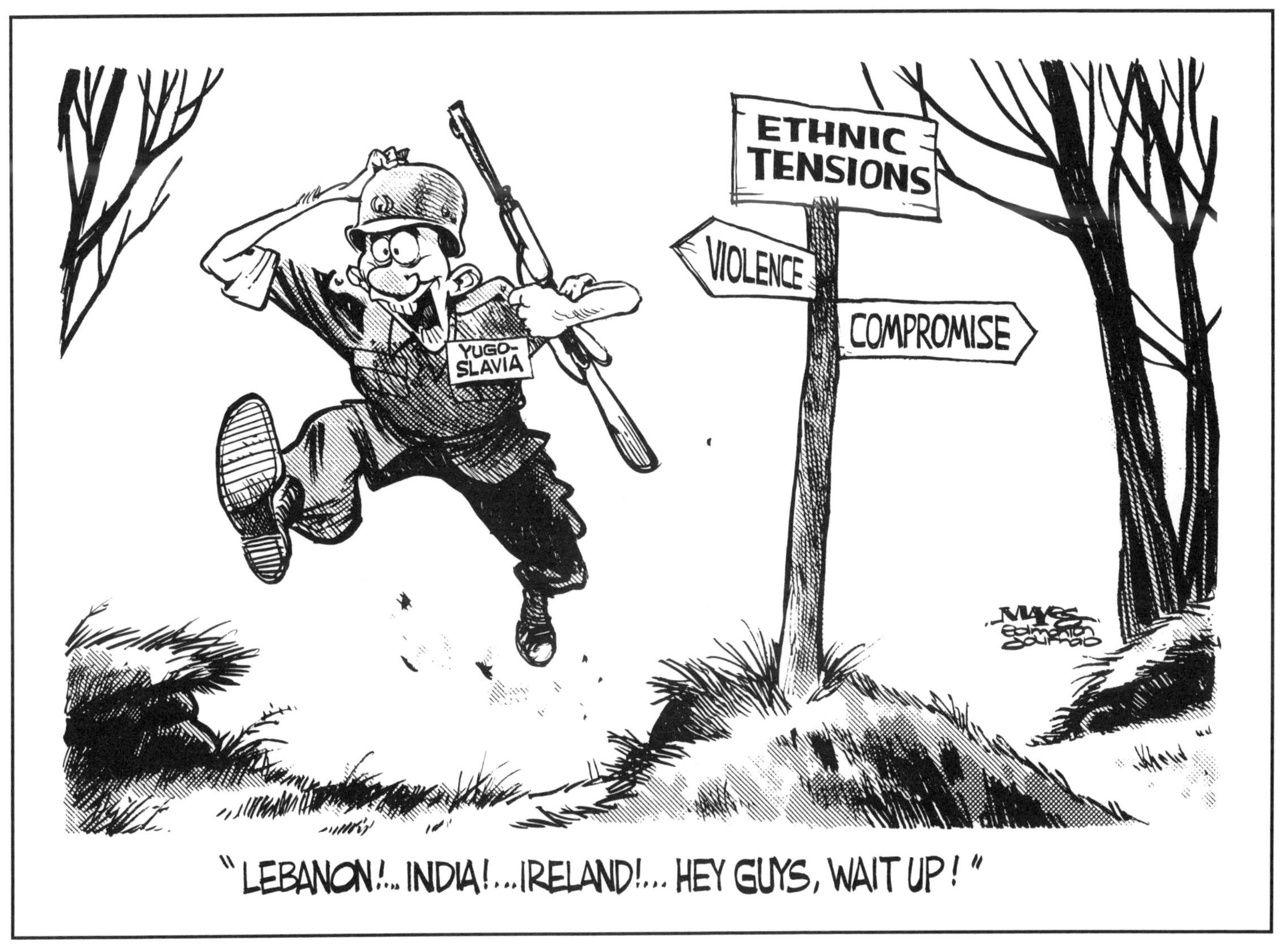
ETHNIC TENSIONS
VIOLENCE
COMPROMISE
YUGO-SLAVIA

"LEBANON!... INDIA!... IRELAND!... HEY GUYS, WAIT UP!"

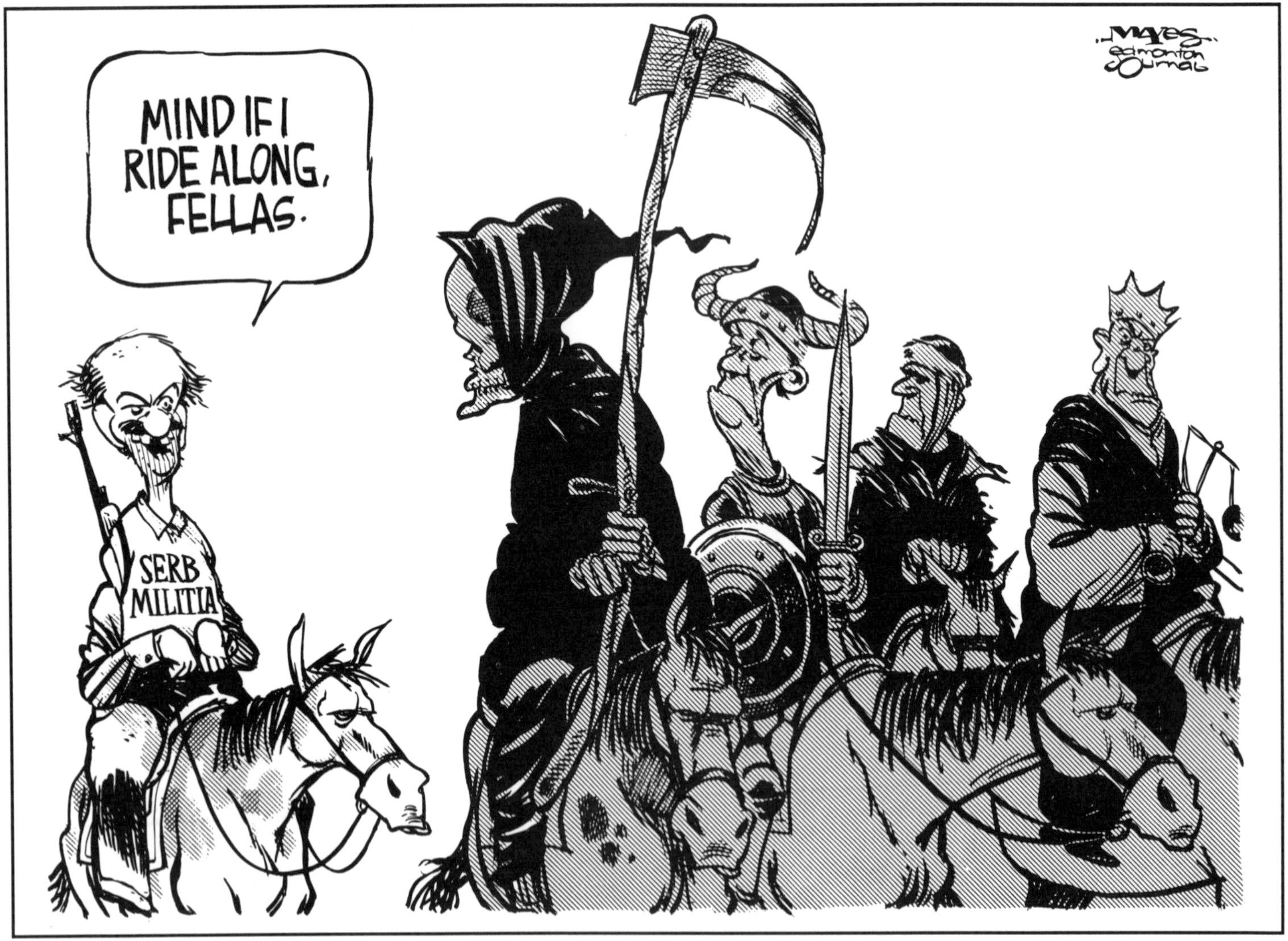
MIND IF I RIDE ALONG, FELLAS.
SERB MILITIA
MAYES edmonton journal

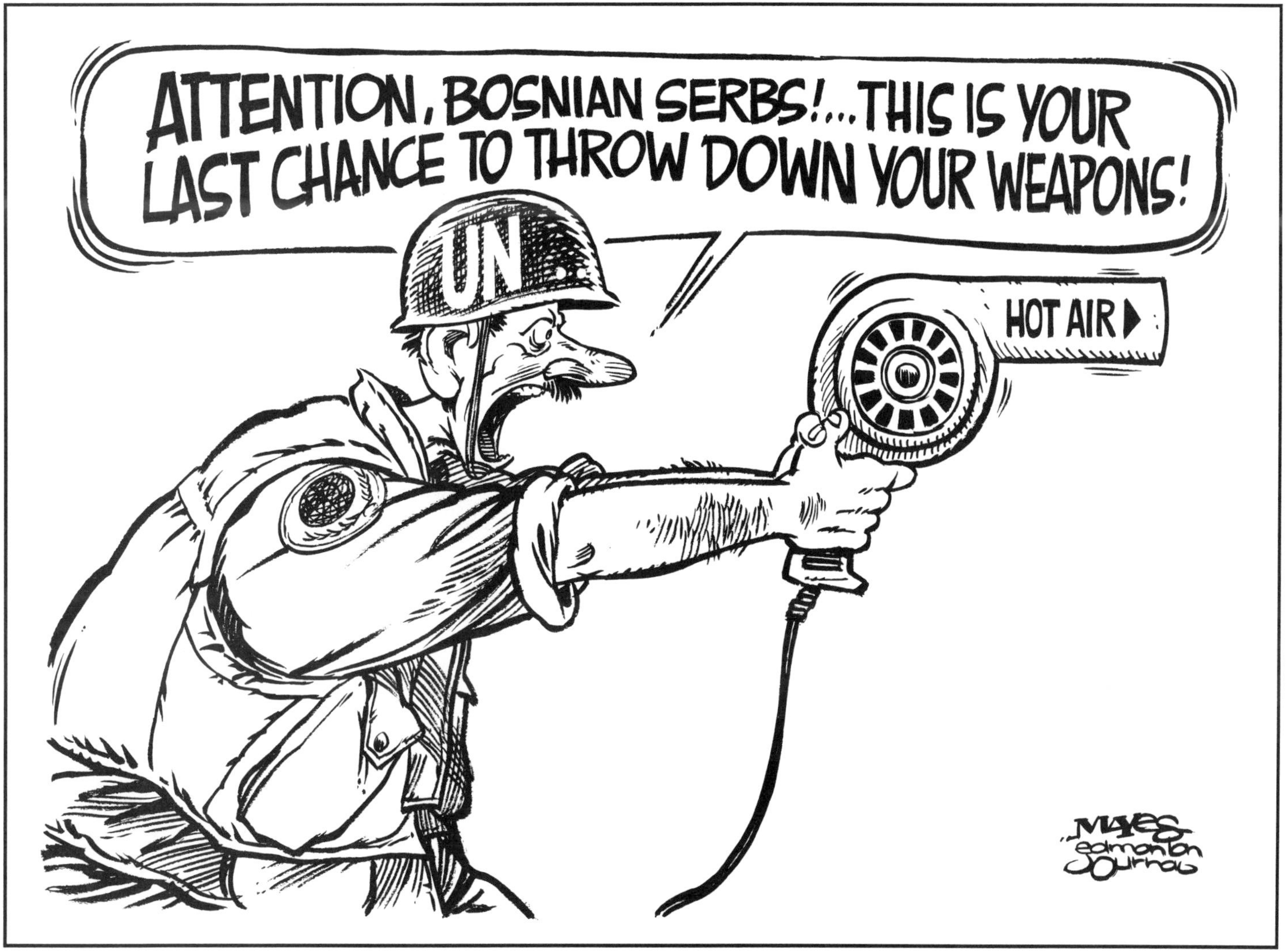
ATTENTION, BOSNIAN SERBS!...THIS IS YOUR LAST CHANCE TO THROW DOWN YOUR WEAPONS!
UN
HOT AIR ▶
MAYES
edmonton journal

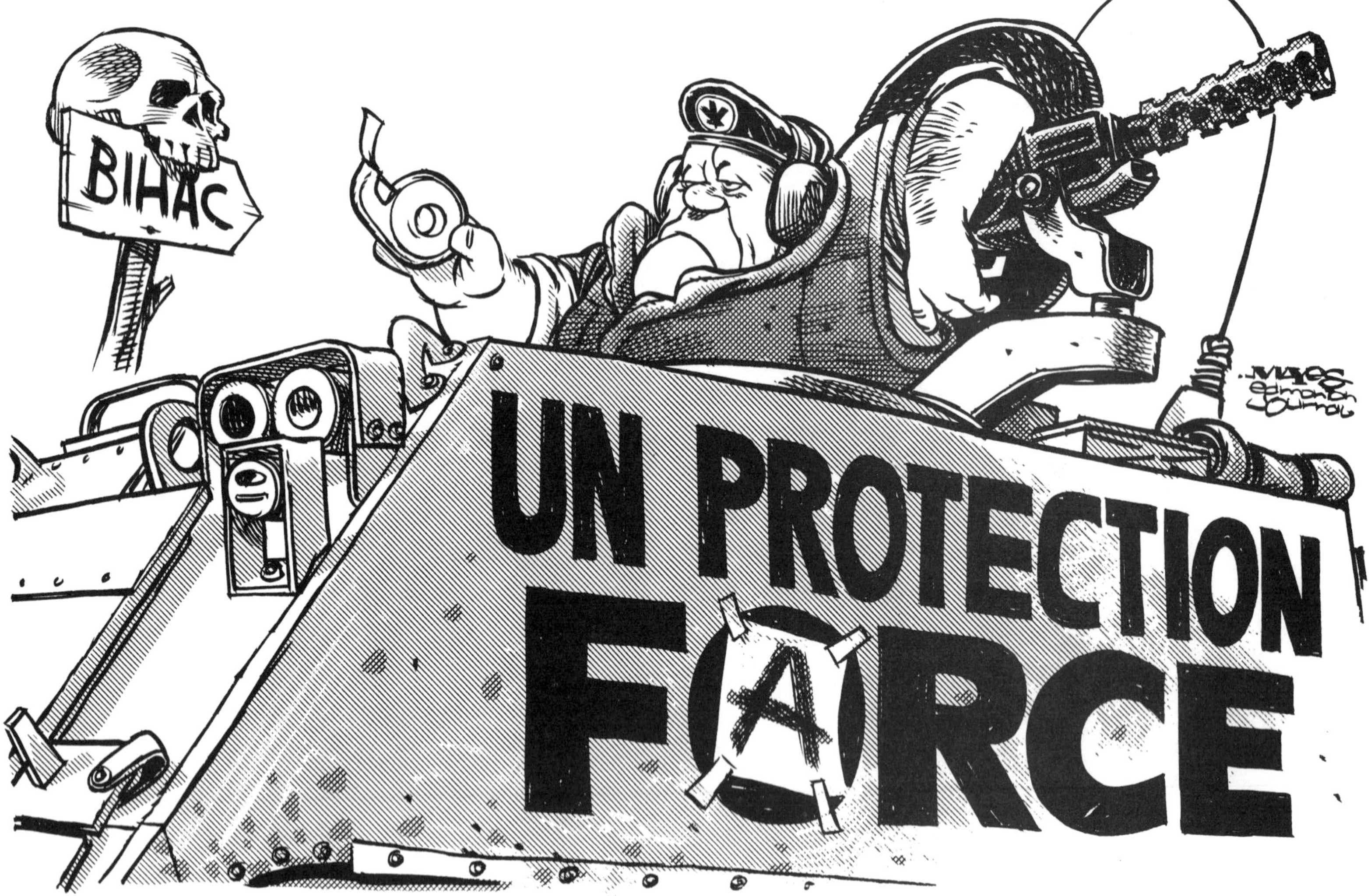
BIHAC
UN PROTECTION
FORCE
A
MAYES
Edmonton Journal

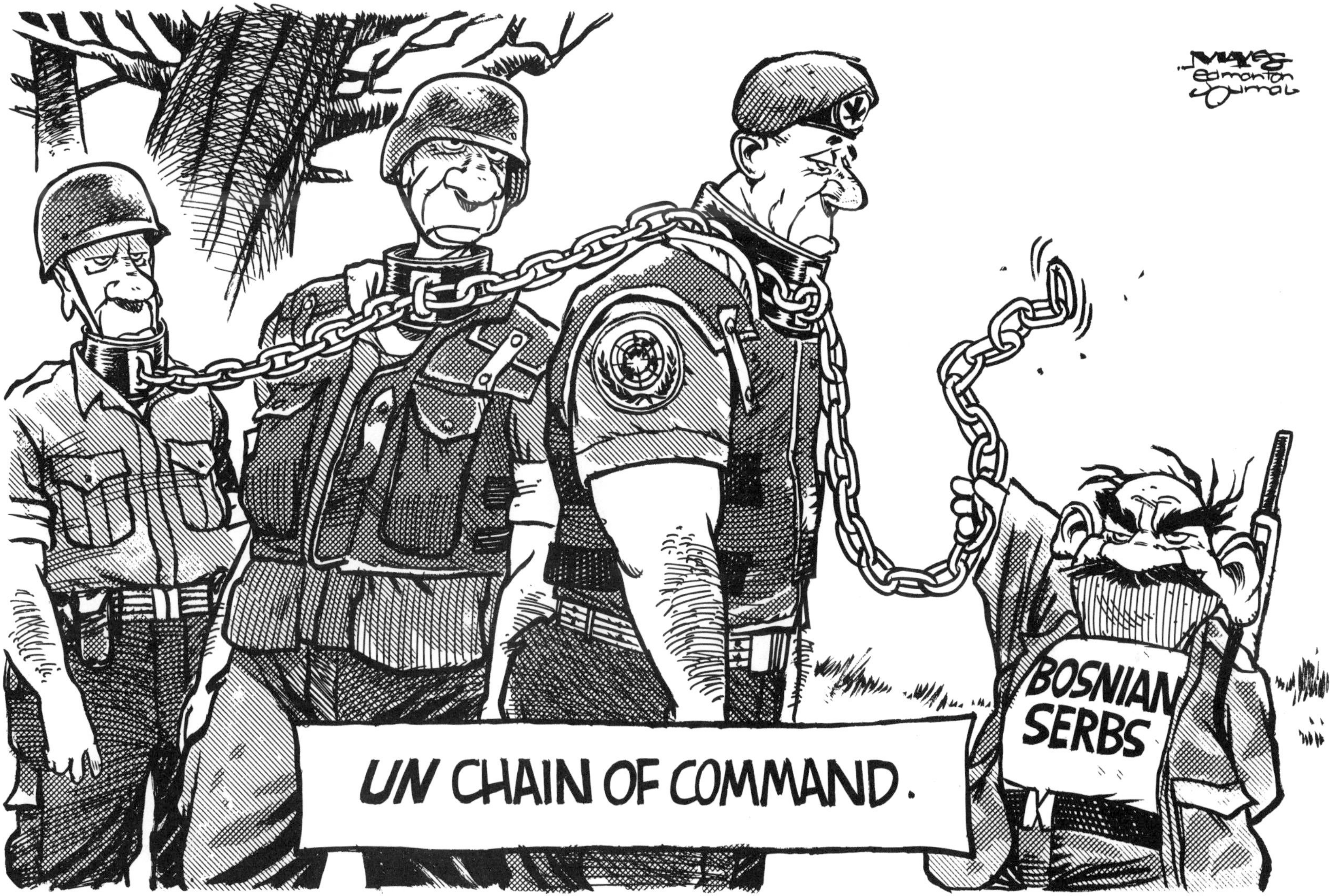
MAYES Edmonton Journal
BOSNIAN SERBS
UN CHAIN OF COMMAND.

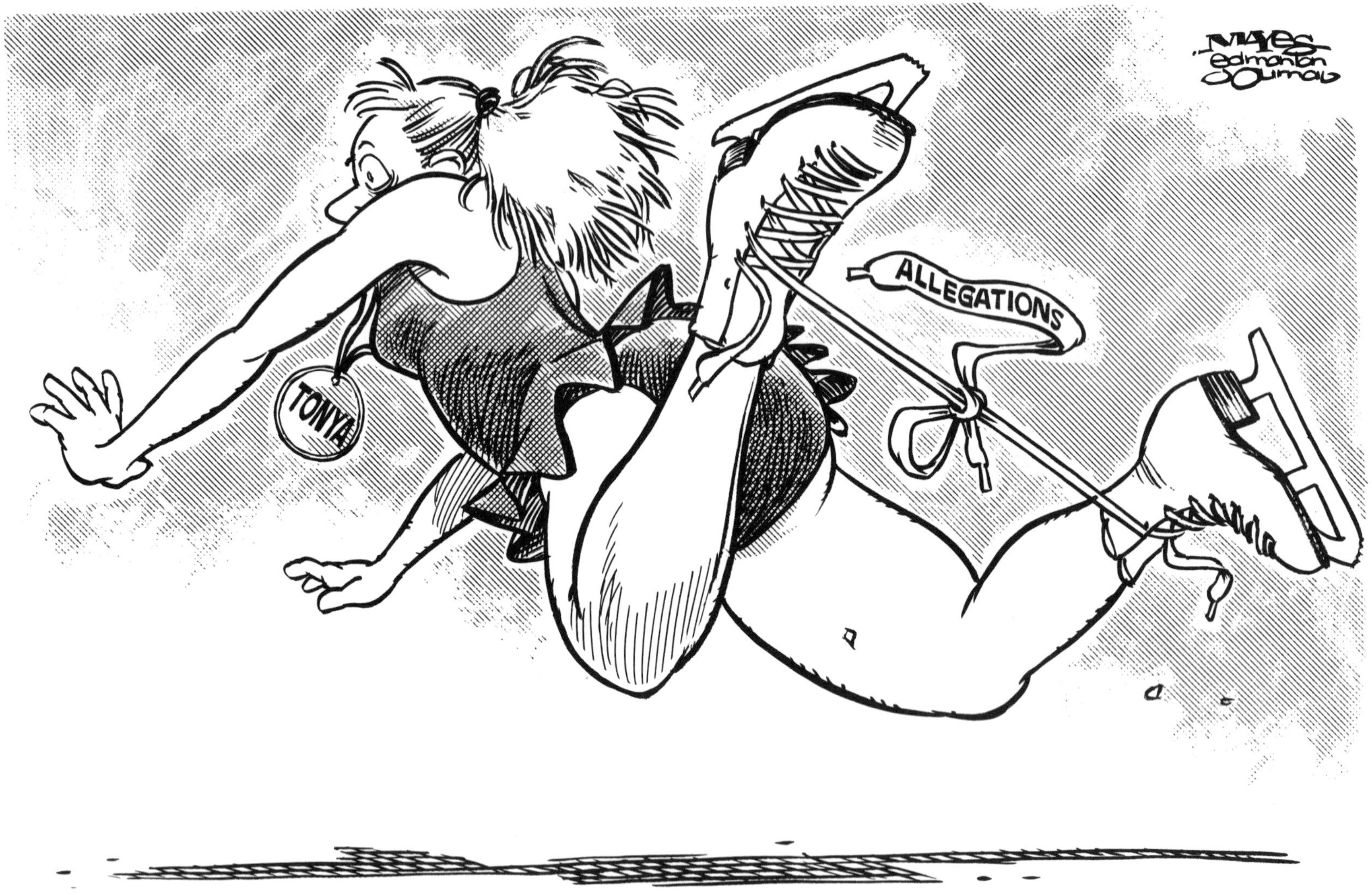
MAYES
edmonton journal
TONYA
ALLEGATIONS

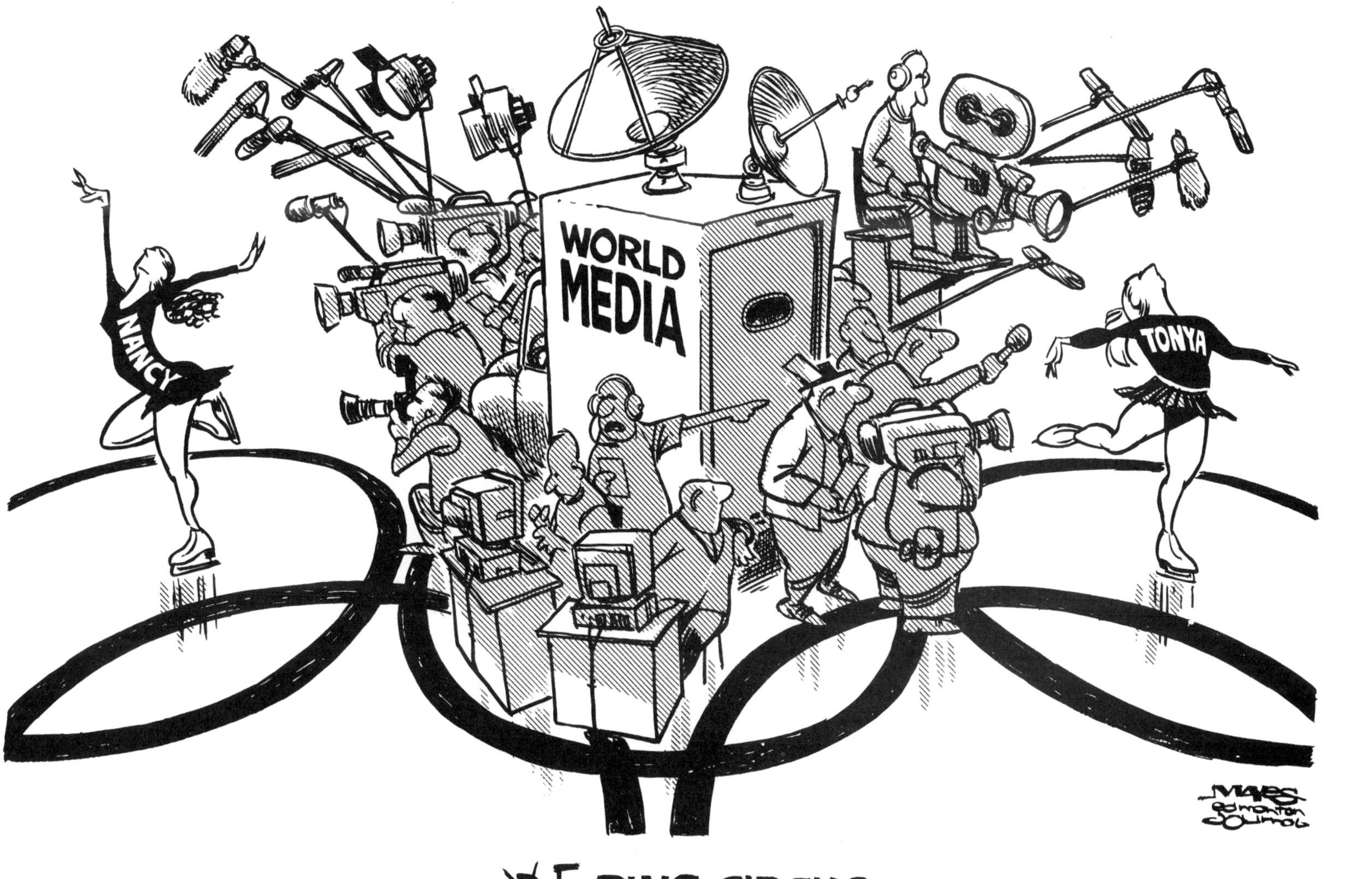
WORLD
MEDIA
NANCY
TONYA

~~3~~ 5 RING CIRCUS

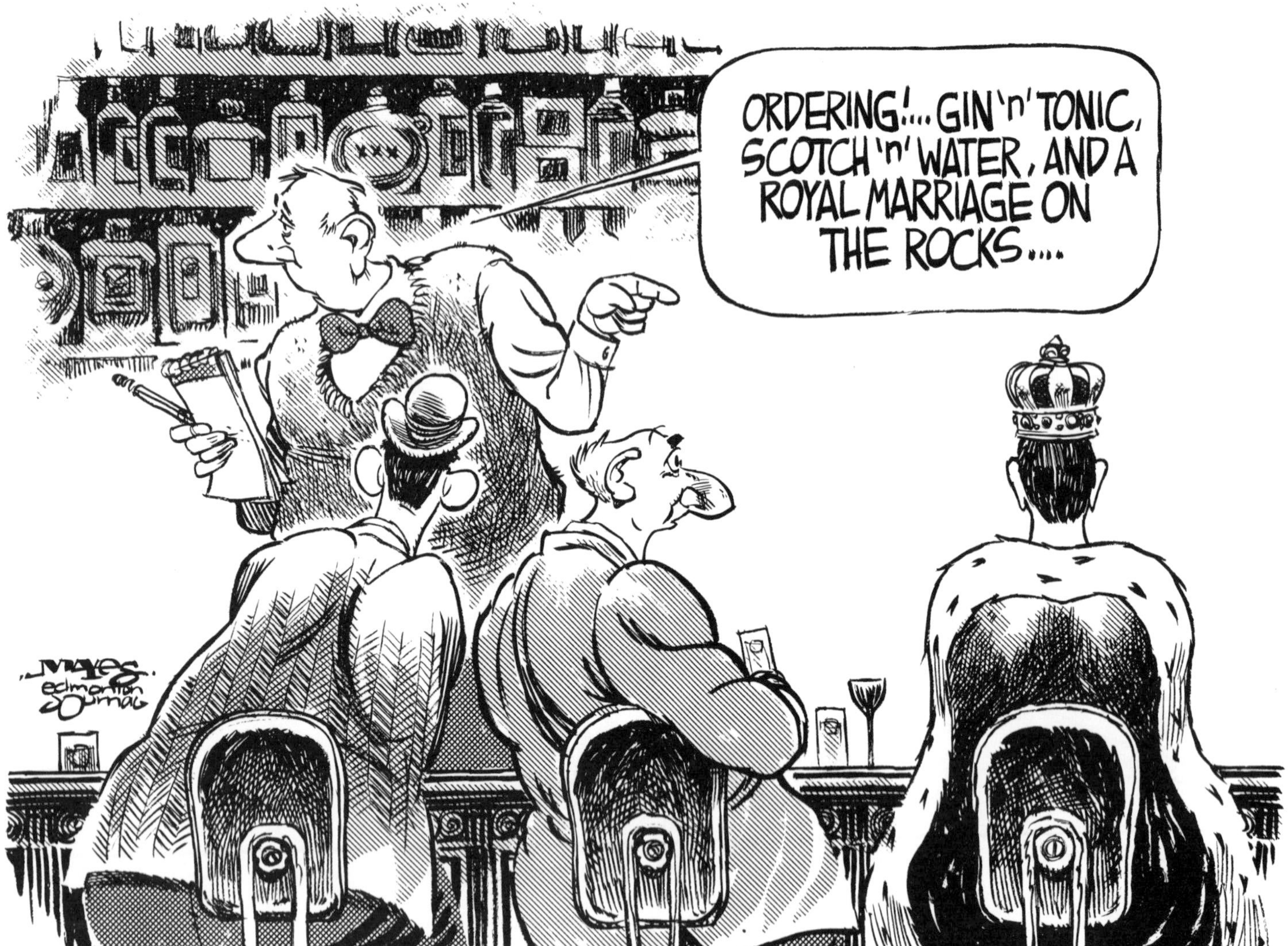
ORDERING!... GIN 'n' TONIC, SCOTCH 'n' WATER, AND A ROYAL MARRIAGE ON THE ROCKS....
MAYES
edmonton journal

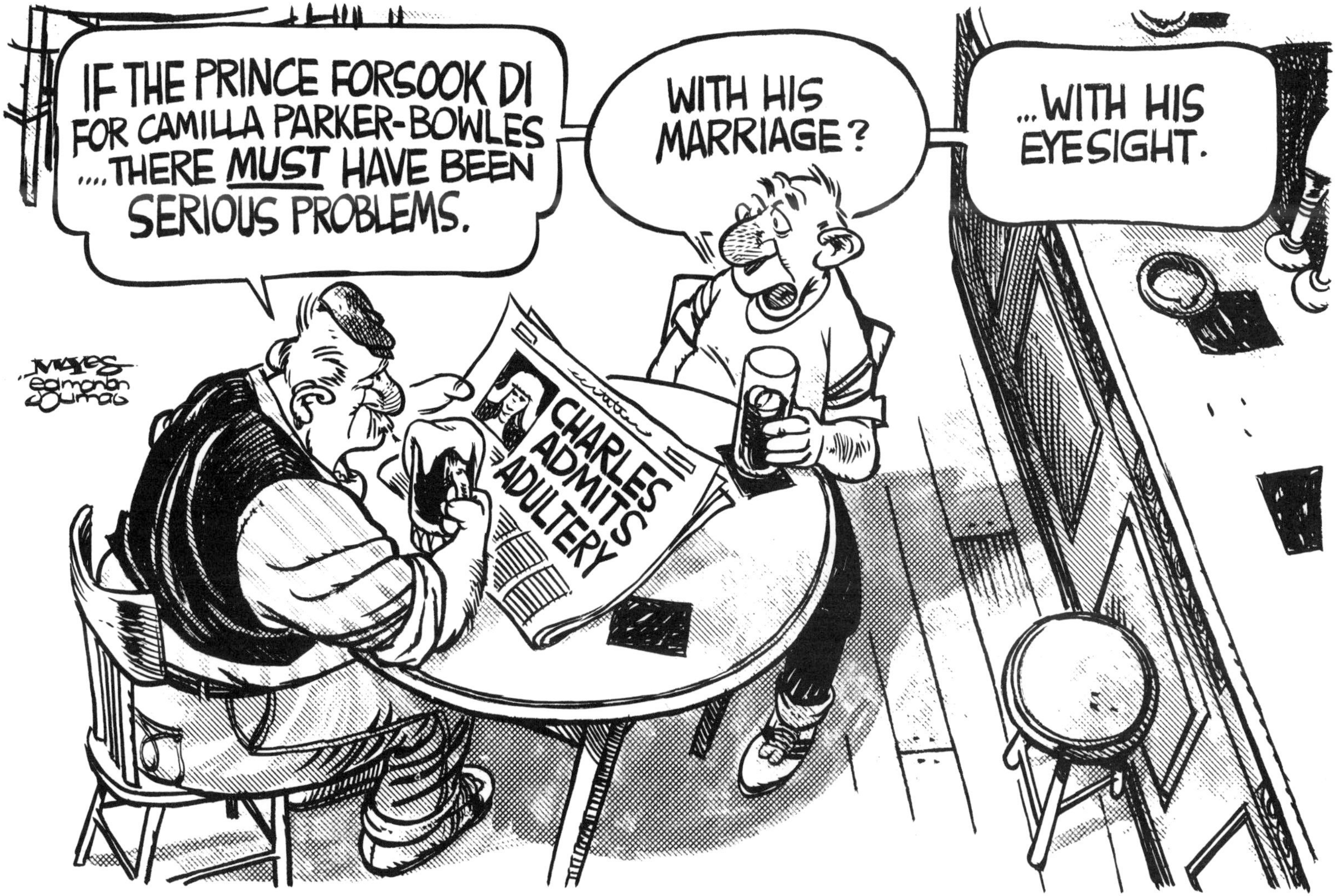
IF THE PRINCE FORSOOK DI FOR CAMILLA PARKER-BOWLES ....THERE MUST HAVE BEEN SERIOUS PROBLEMS.
WITH HIS MARRIAGE?
...WITH HIS EYESIGHT.
CHARLES ADMITS ADULTERY
MAYES
edmonton journal

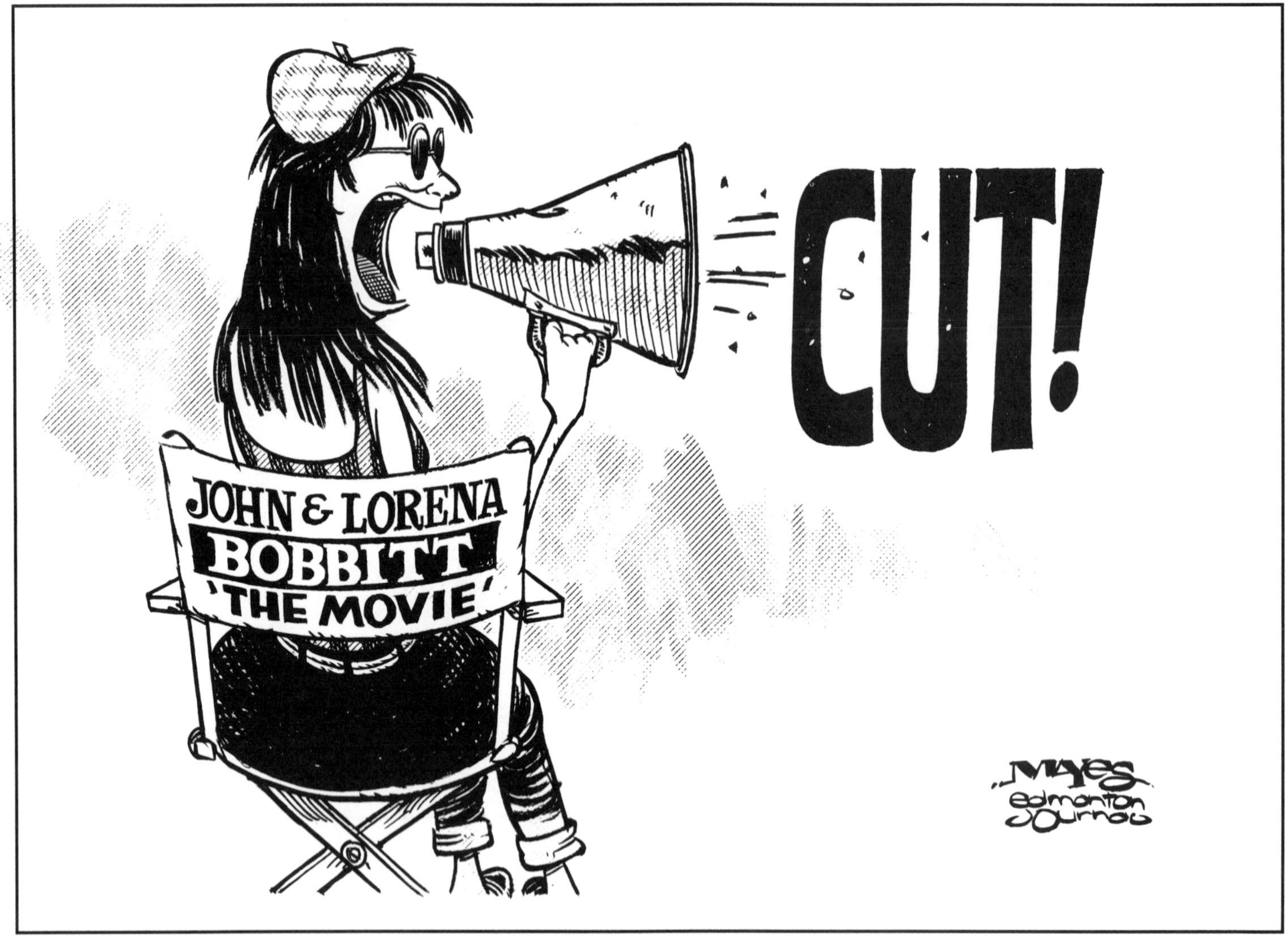
CUT!
JOHN & LORENA
BOBBITT
'THE MOVIE'
MAYES
edmonton journal

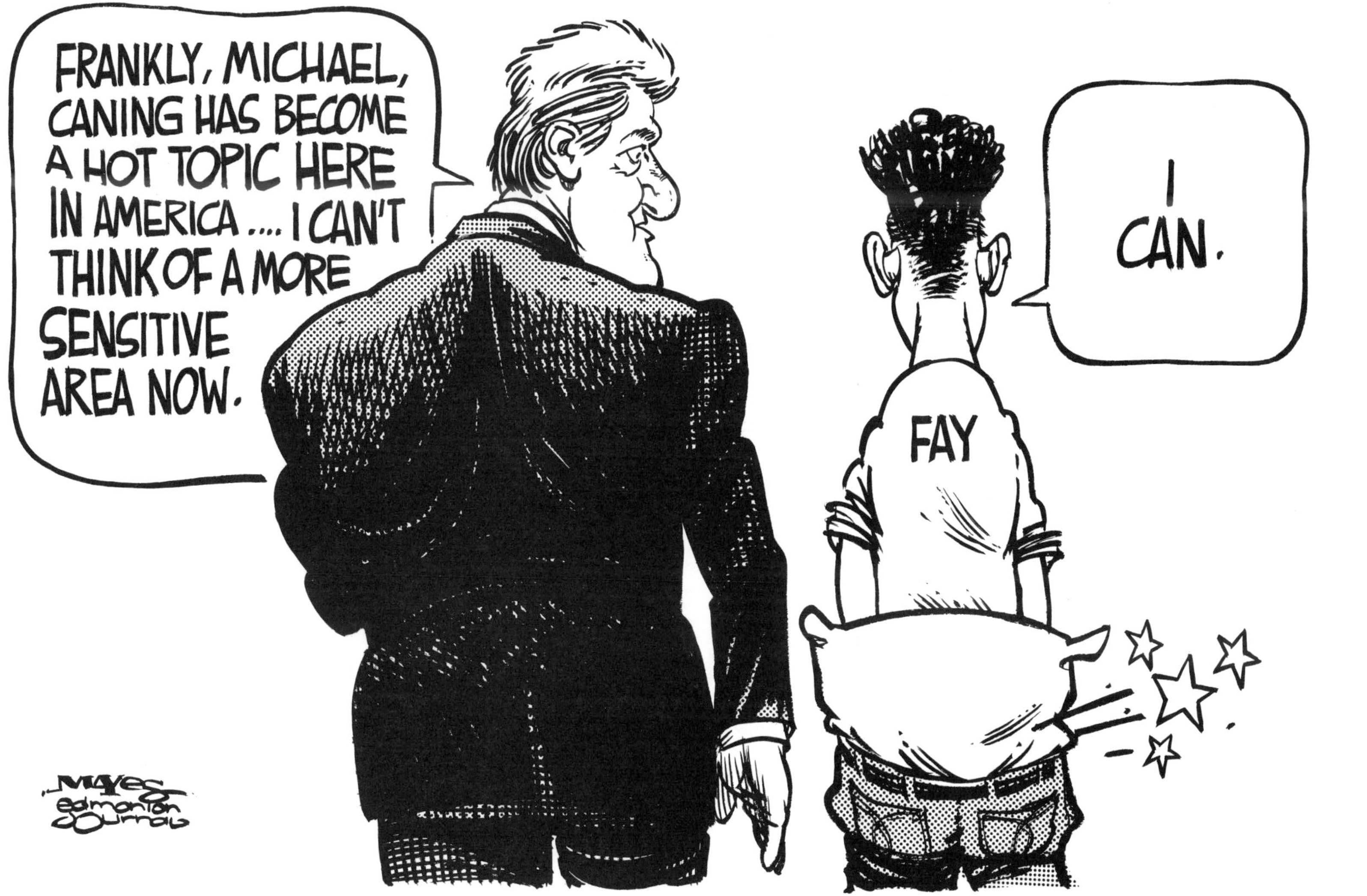
FRANKLY, MICHAEL, CANING HAS BECOME A HOT TOPIC HERE IN AMERICA .... I CAN'T THINK OF A MORE SENSITIVE AREA NOW.
I CAN.
FAY
MAYES edmonton journal

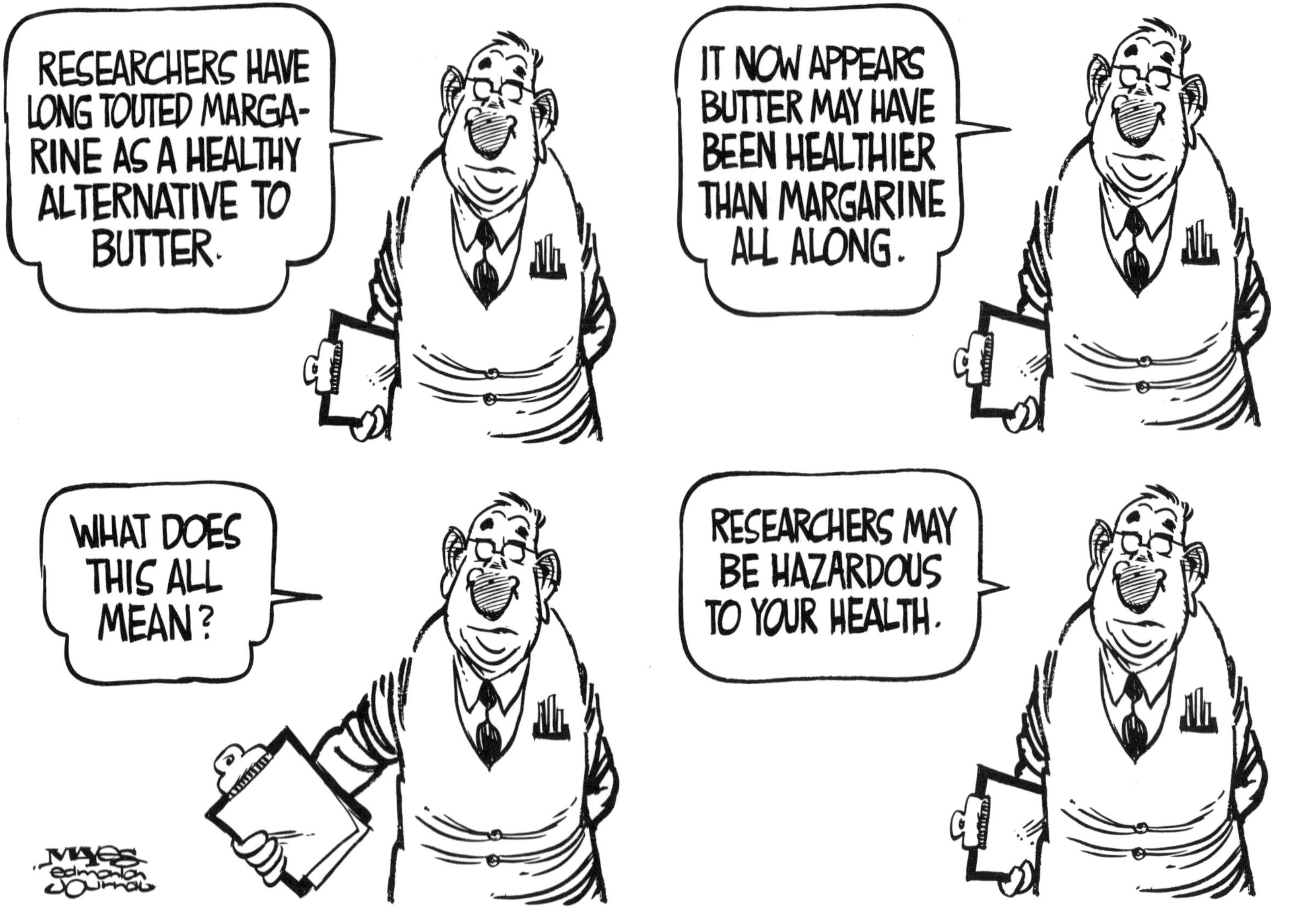
RESEARCHERS HAVE LONG TOUTED MARGARINE AS A HEALTHY ALTERNATIVE TO BUTTER.
IT NOW APPEARS BUTTER MAY HAVE BEEN HEALTHIER THAN MARGARINE ALL ALONG.
WHAT DOES THIS ALL MEAN?
RESEARCHERS MAY BE HAZARDOUS TO YOUR HEALTH.
MAYES edmonton journal

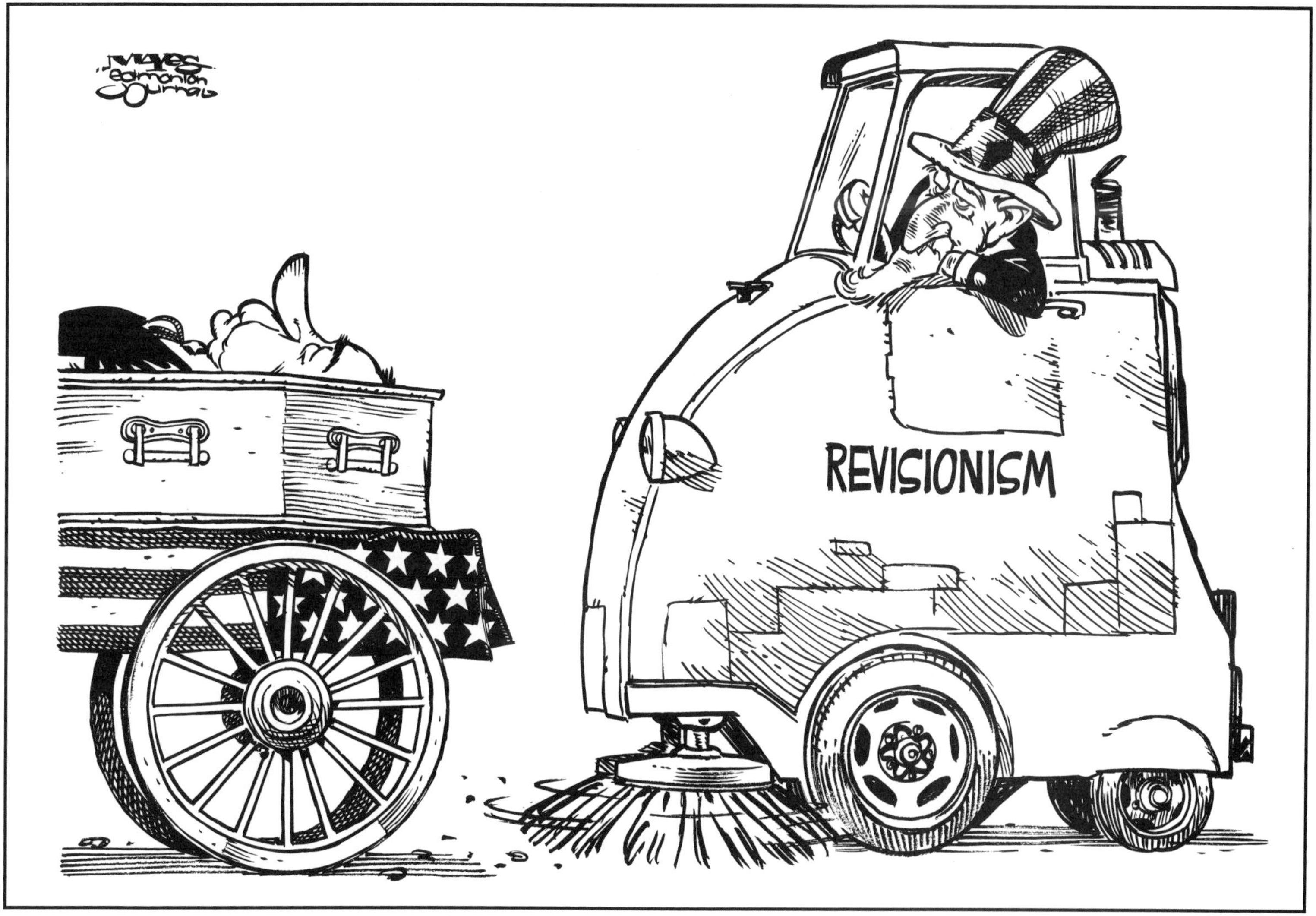
REVISIONISM

Richard Nixon, 1913 – 1994

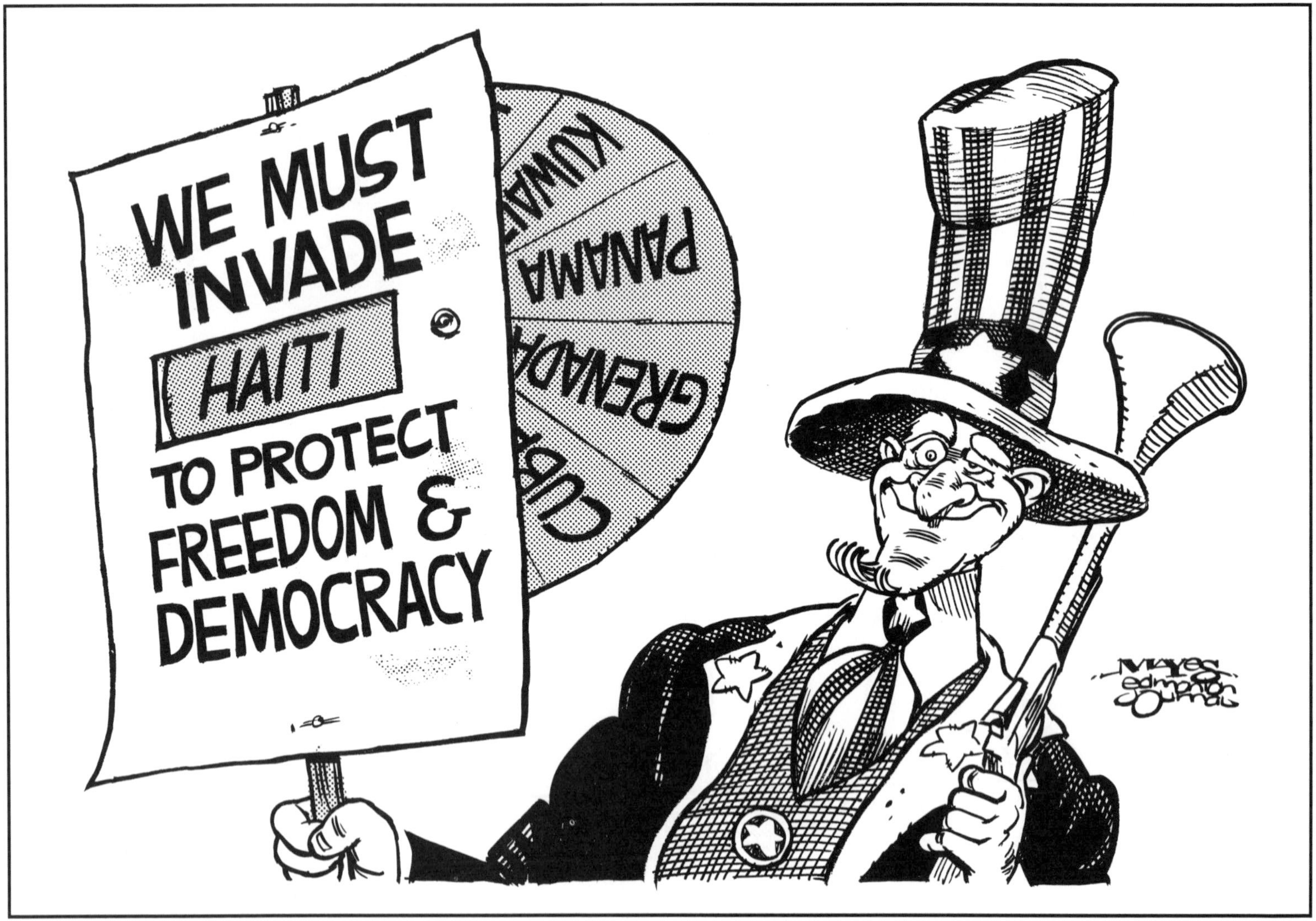
WE MUST INVADE
HAITI
TO PROTECT FREEDOM & DEMOCRACY
PANAMA
GRENADA

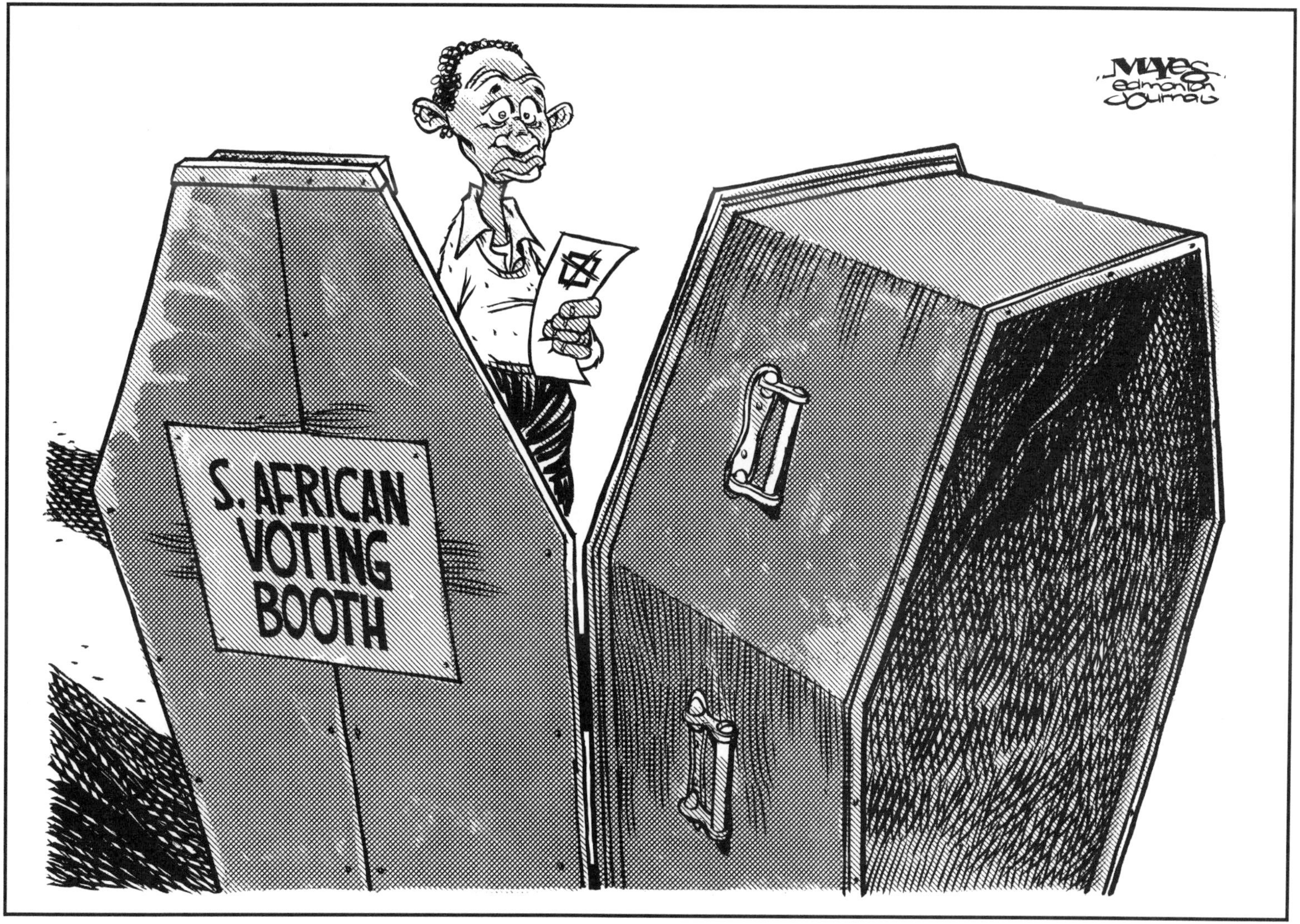
S. AFRICAN
VOTING
BOOTH
MAYES
edmonton
journal

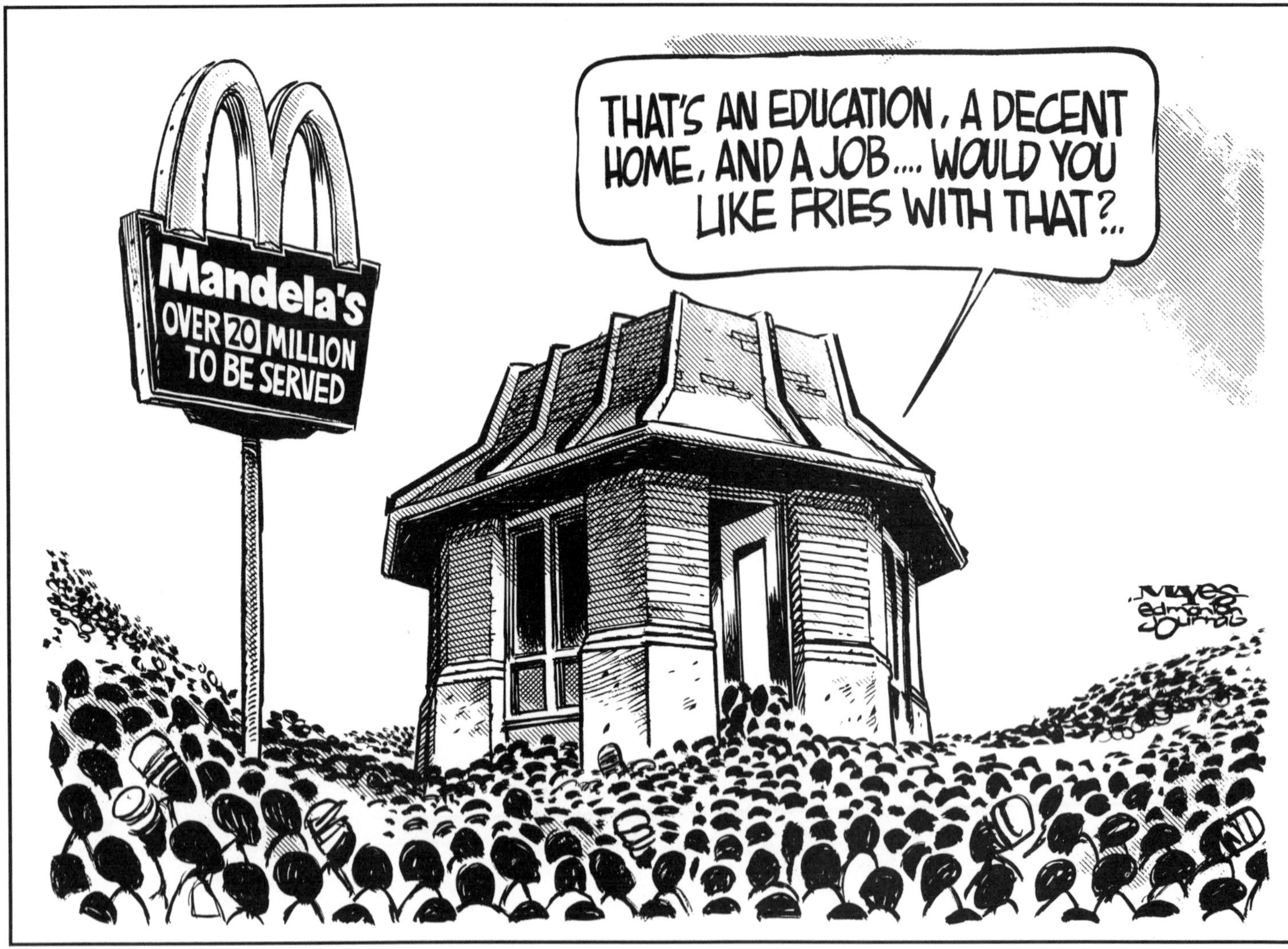
Mandela's
OVER 20 MILLION
TO BE SERVED
THAT'S AN EDUCATION, A DECENT HOME, AND A JOB.... WOULD YOU LIKE FRIES WITH THAT?..
MAYES
edmonton journal

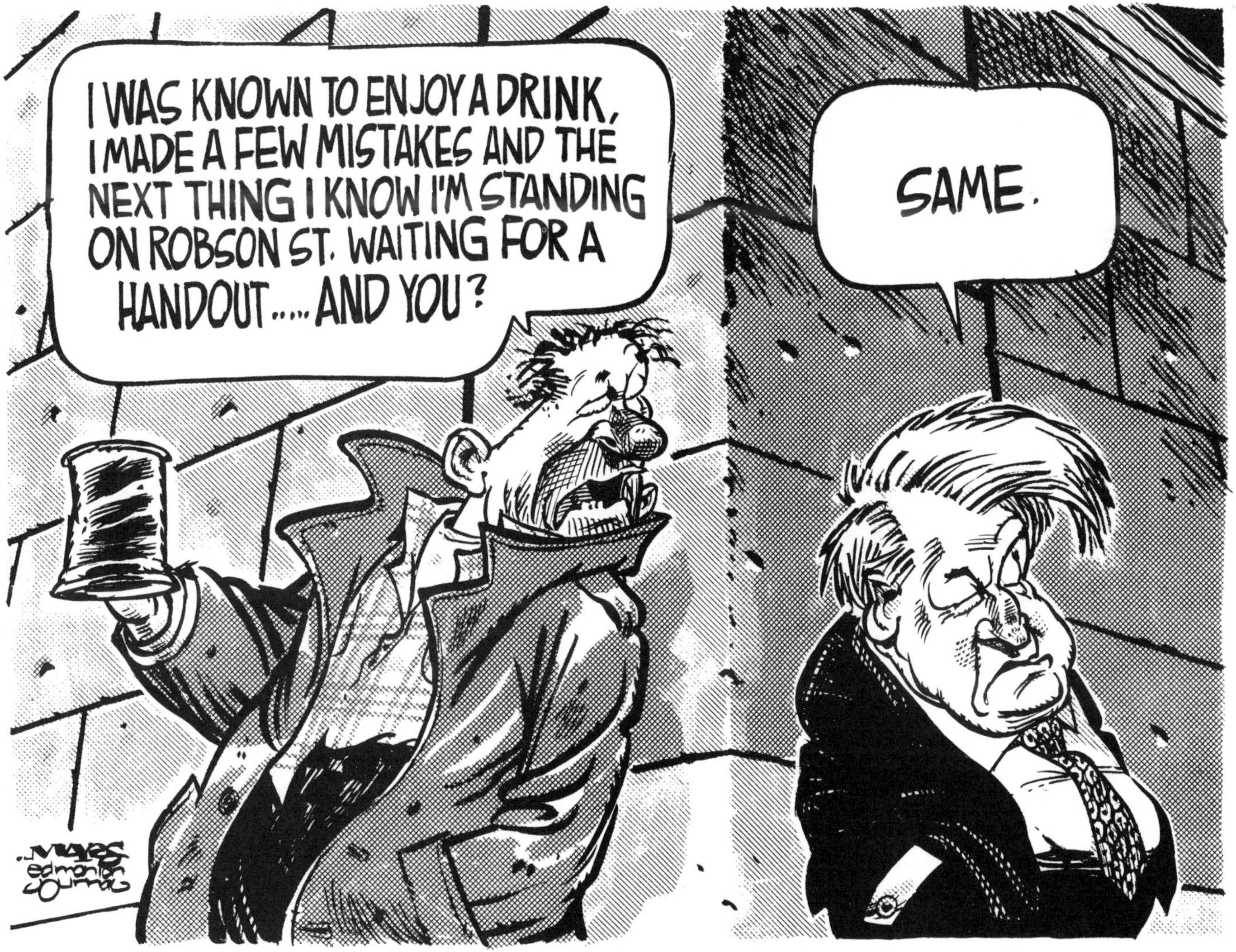
I WAS KNOWN TO ENJOY A DRINK, I MADE A FEW MISTAKES AND THE NEXT THING I KNOW I'M STANDING ON ROBSON ST. WAITING FOR A HANDOUT..... AND YOU?
SAME.

Yeltsin attends summit in Vancouver.

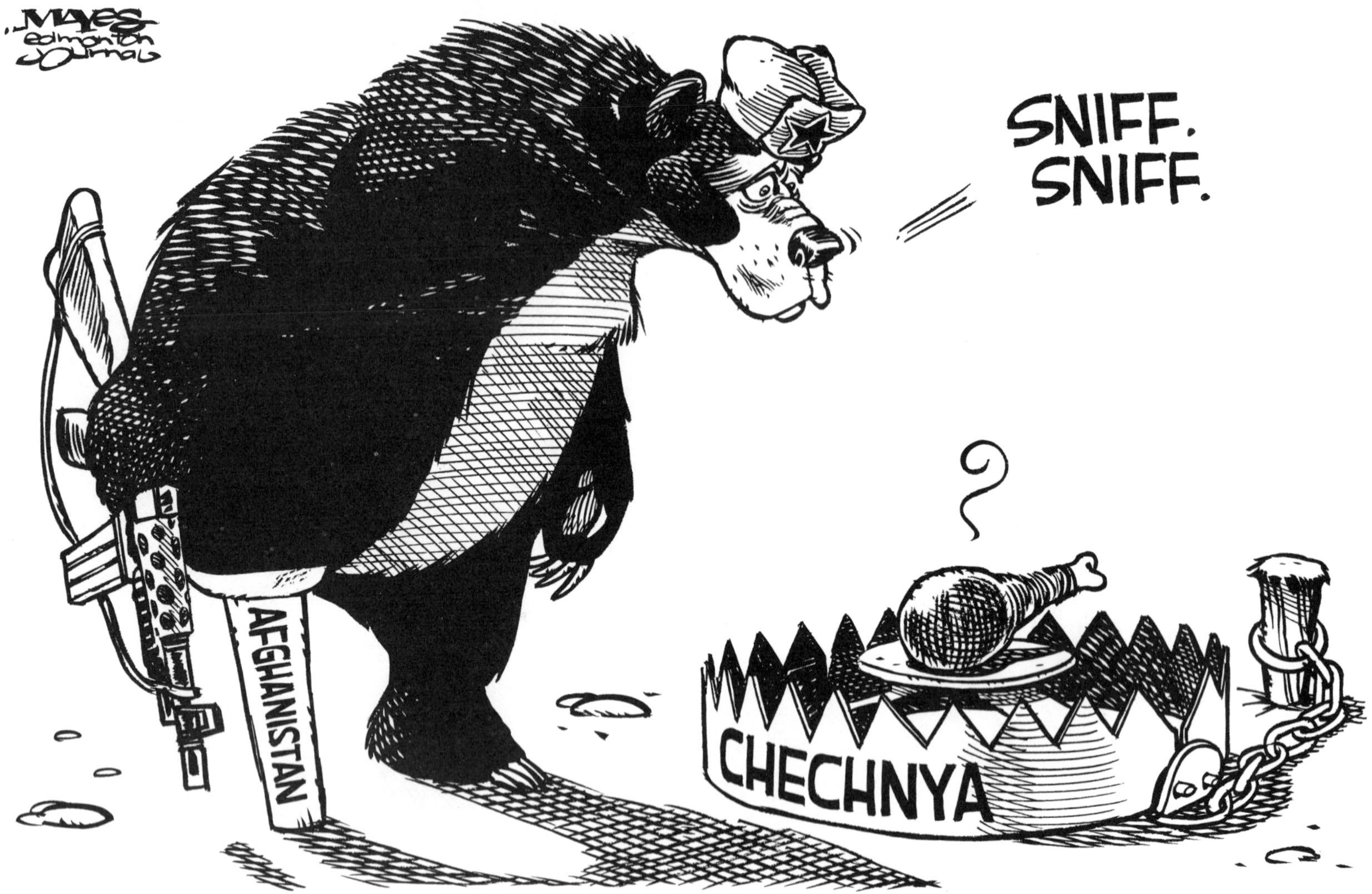
MAYES
edmonton journal
SNIFF.
SNIFF.
AFGHANISTAN
CHECHNYA

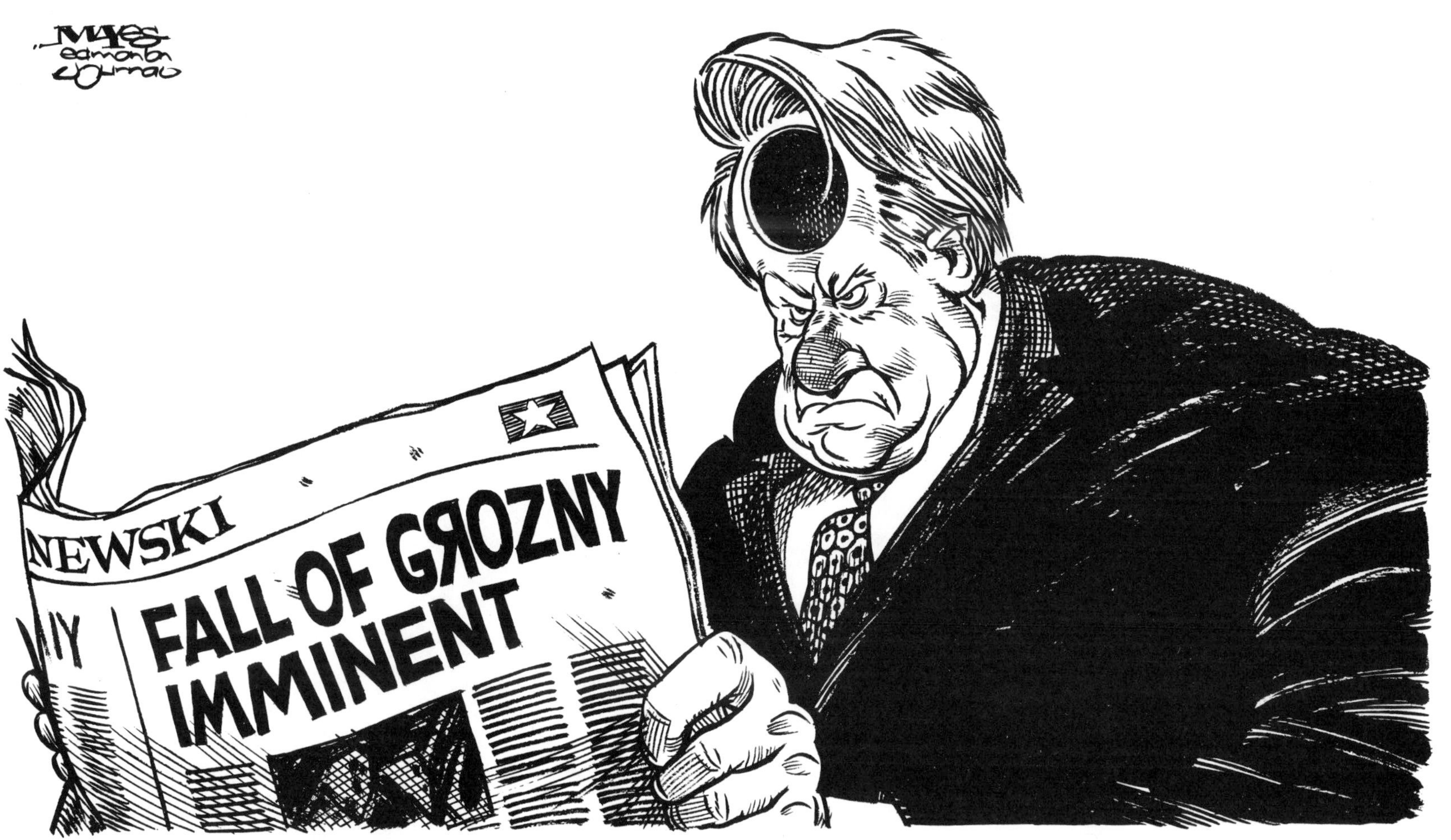
MAYES
edmonton journal
NEWSKI
FALL OF GROZNY
IMMINENT

....BUT ALAS, THERE WAS NO JOY IN MOSCOW. ANY VICTORY NOW WOULD SURELY BE SEEN AS A HOLLOW ONE.

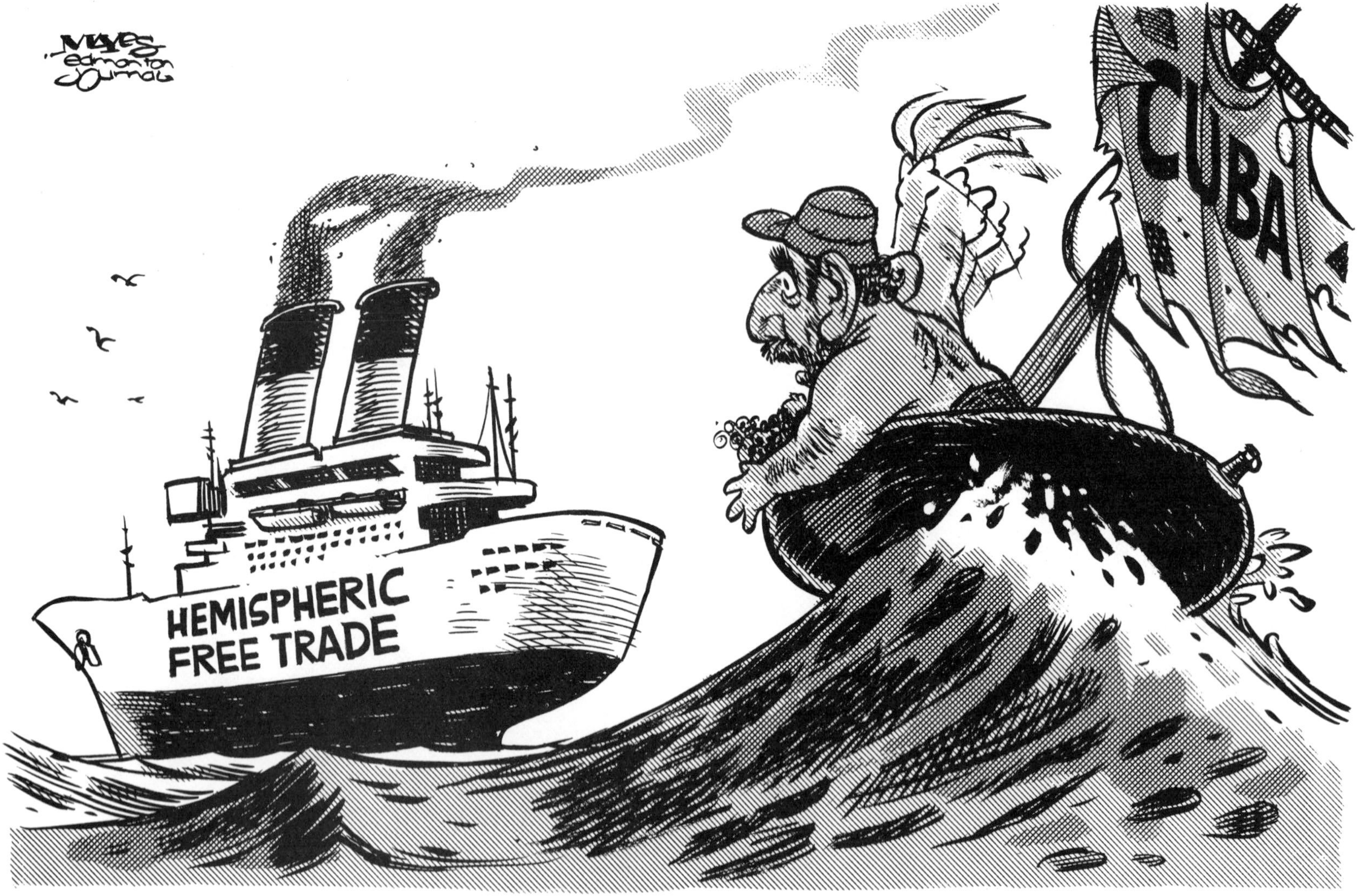
MAYES edmonton journal
HEMISPHERIC
FREE TRADE
CUBA

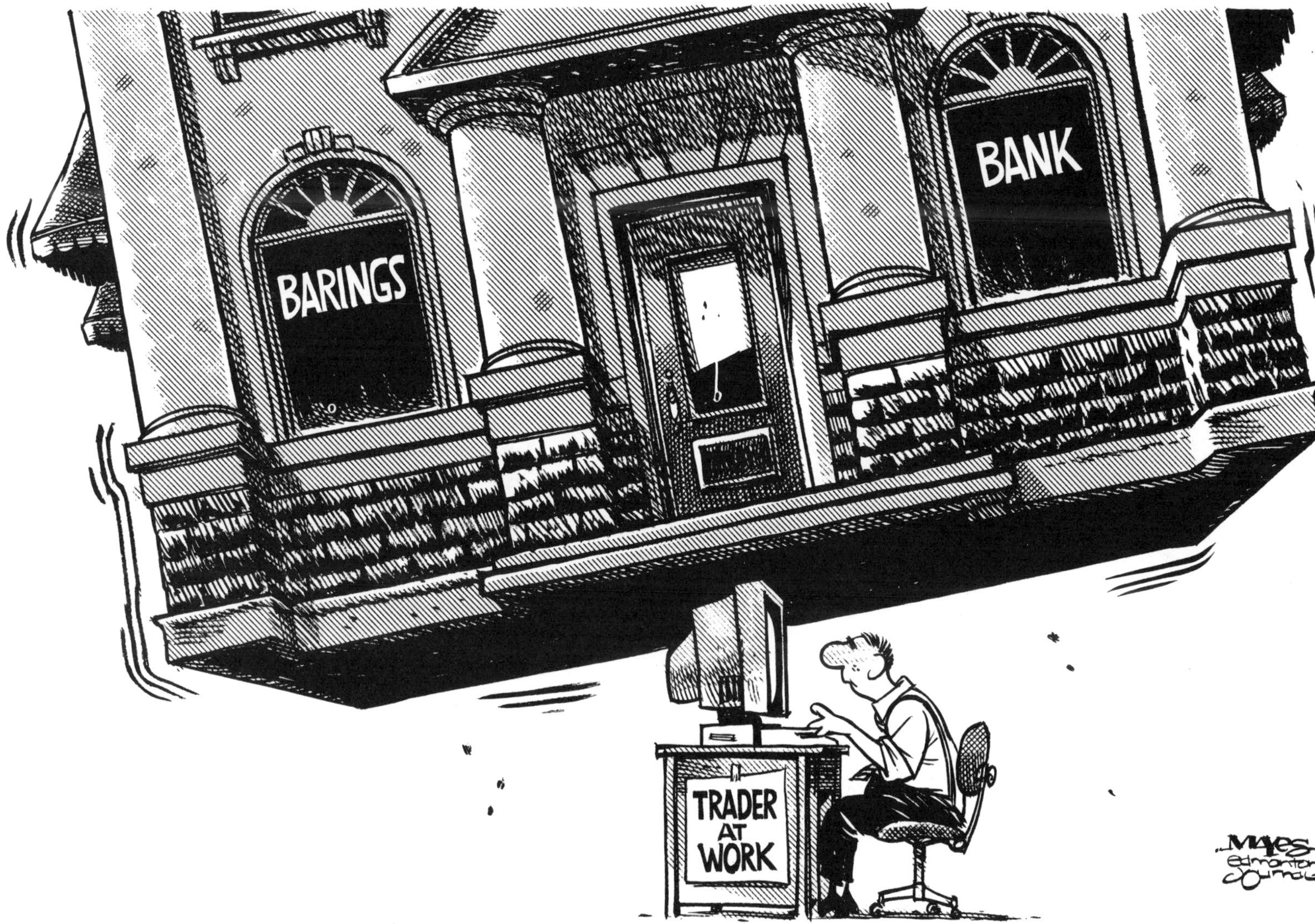
BARINGS
BANK
TRADER
AT
WORK
MAYES
Edmonton
Journal

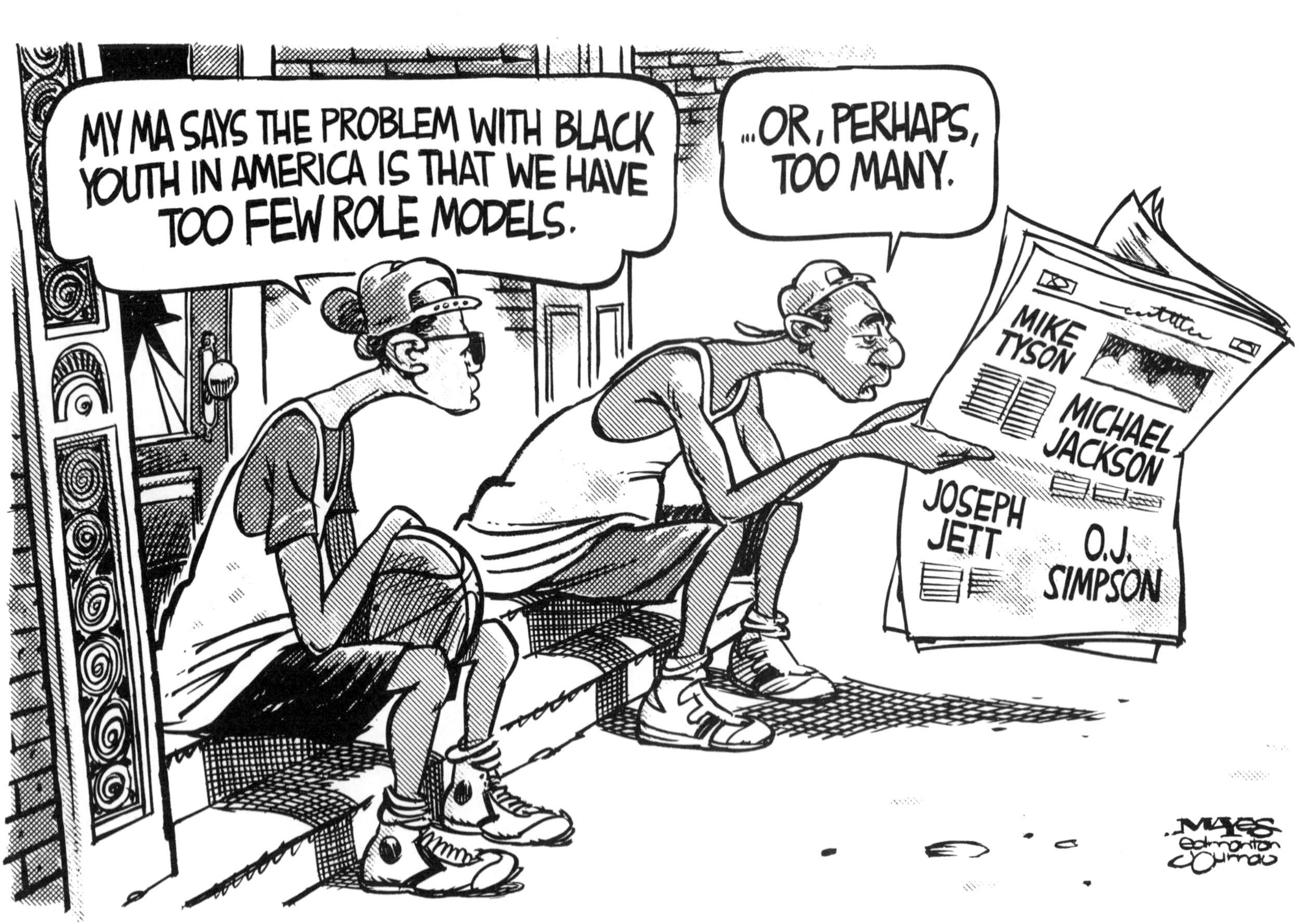
MY MA SAYS THE PROBLEM WITH BLACK YOUTH IN AMERICA IS THAT WE HAVE TOO FEW ROLE MODELS.
...OR, PERHAPS, TOO MANY.
MIKE TYSON
MICHAEL JACKSON
JOSEPH JETT
O.J. SIMPSON
MAYES
edmonton journal

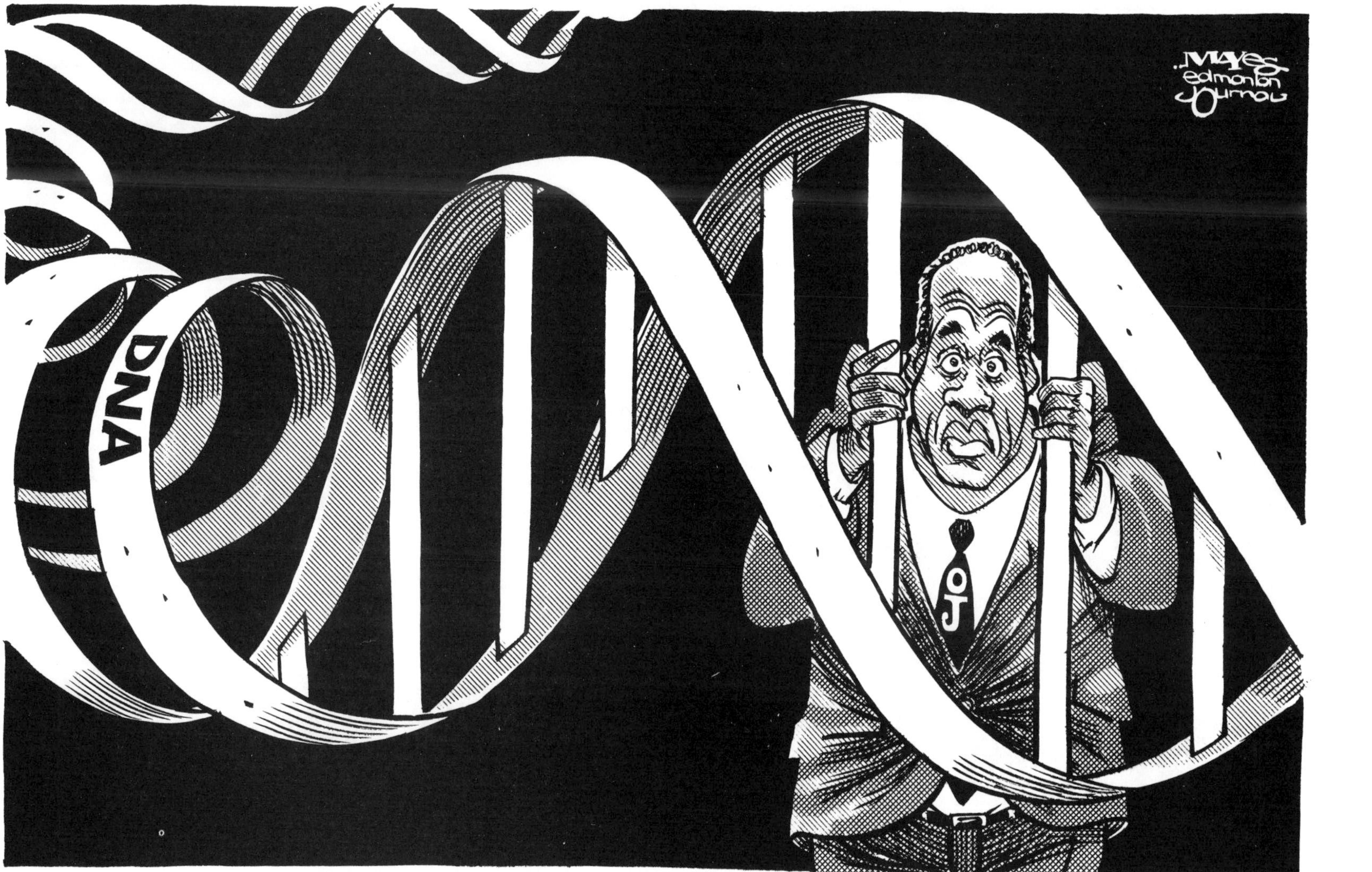
MAYES
edmonton journal
DNA
OJ

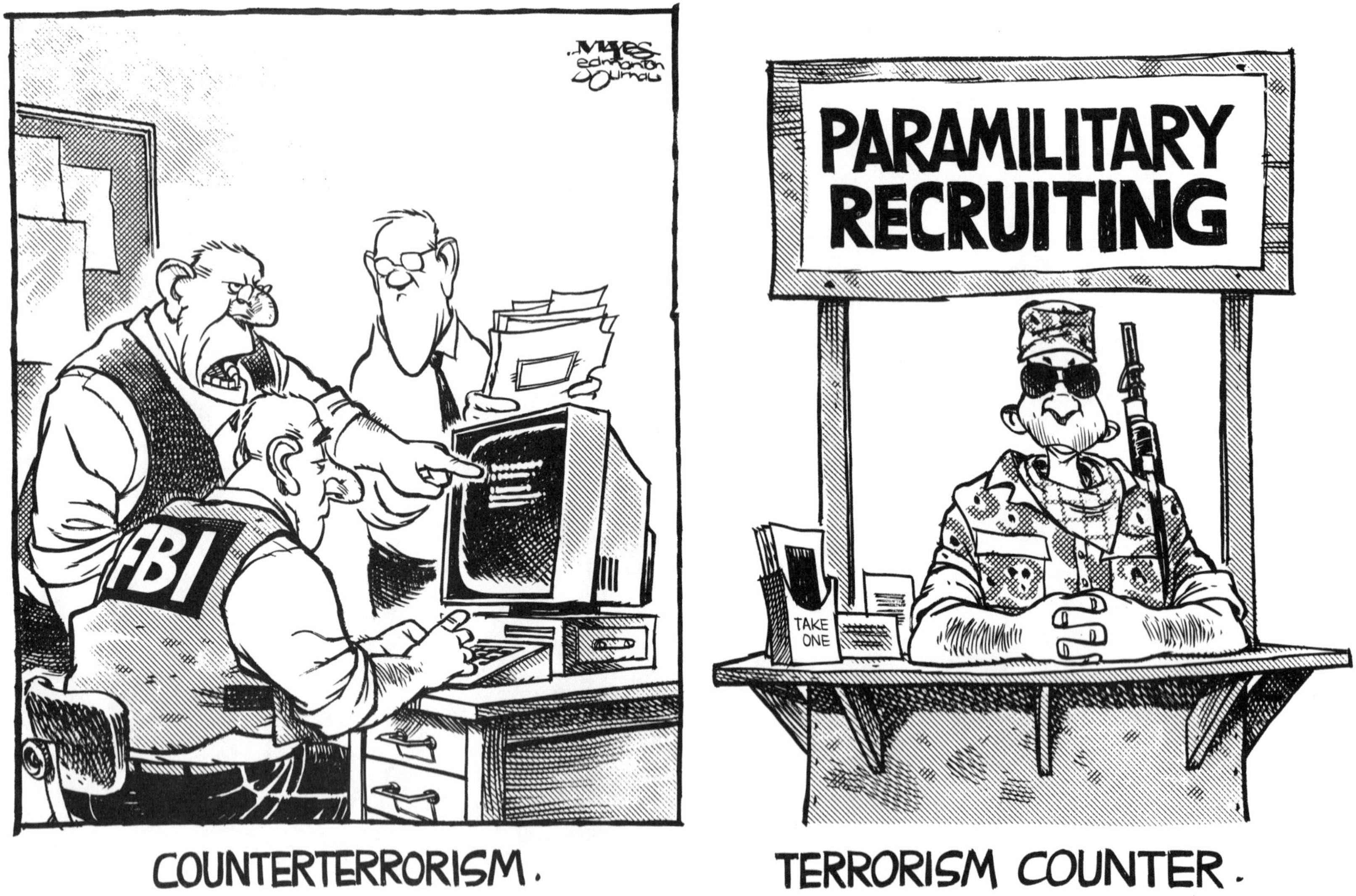
Mayes
Edmonton Journal
FBI
PARAMILITARY RECRUITING
TAKE ONE
COUNTERTERRORISM.
TERRORISM COUNTER.

Oklahoma City bombing blamed on American extremists.

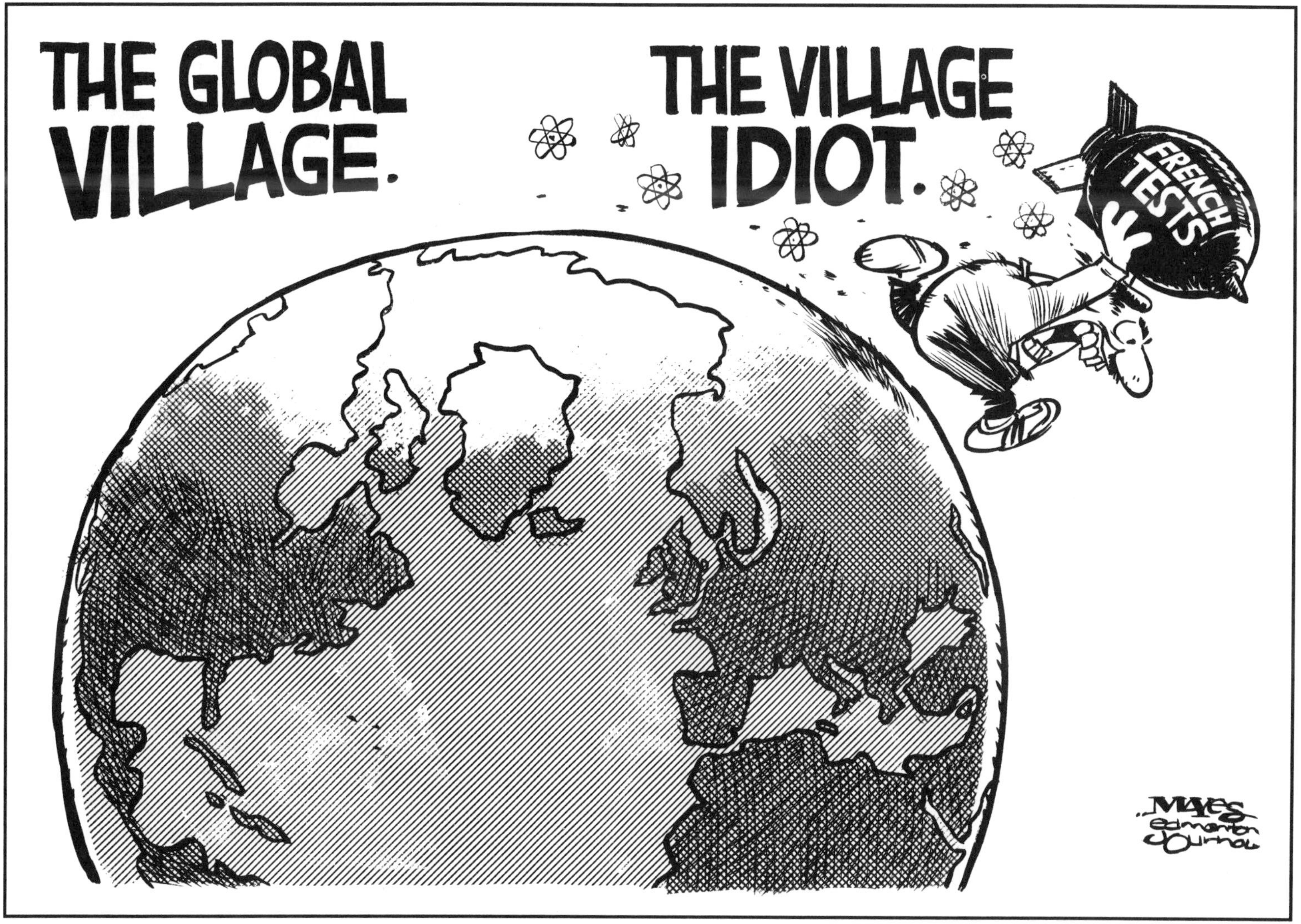
THE GLOBAL VILLAGE.
THE VILLAGE IDIOT.
FRENCH TESTS
MAYES
edmonton journal

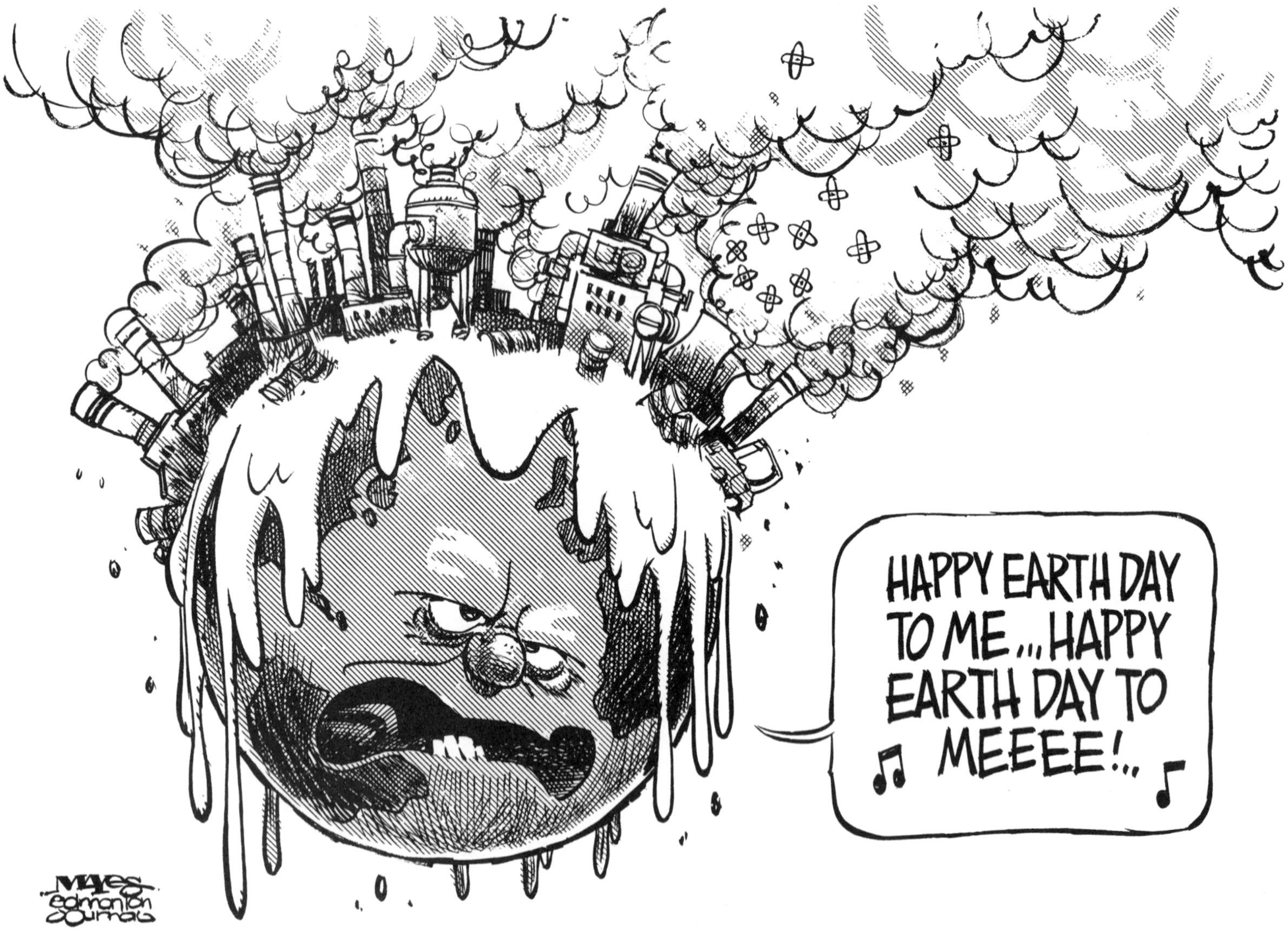
HAPPY EARTH DAY TO ME... HAPPY EARTH DAY TO MEEEE!...
MAYES Edmonton Journal